EXPORTING

THE DEFINITIVE GUIDE TO SELLING ABROAD PROFITABLY

SECOND EDITION

Laurel J. Delaney

Exporting: The Definitive Guide to Selling Abroad Profitably, Second Edition

Laurel J. Delaney
Chicago, Illinois
USA

ISBN-13 (pbk): 978-1-4842-2192-1   ISBN-13 (electronic): 978-1-4842-2193-8
DOI 10.1007/978-1-4842-2193-8

Library of Congress Control Number: 2016953347

Managing Director: Welmoed Spahr
Acquisitions Editor: Robert Hutchinson
Developmental Editor: Matt Moodie
Editorial Board: Steve Anglin, Pramila Balen, Laura Berendson, Aaron Black, Louise Corrigan, Jonathan Gennick, Robert Hutchinson, Celestin Suresh John, Nikhil Karkal, James Markham, Susan McDermott, Matthew Moodie, Natalie Pao, Gwenan Spearing
Coordinating Editor: Rita Fernando Kim
Copy Editor: Lauren Marten Parker
Compositor: SPi Global
Indexer: SPi Global
Cover Designer: eStudio Calamar S.L.

Distributed to the book trade worldwide by Springer Science+Business Media New York, 233 Spring Street, 6th Floor, New York, NY 10013. Phone 1-800-SPRINGER, fax (201) 348-4505, e-mail orders-ny@springer-sbm.com, or visit www.springeronline.com. Apress Media, LLC is a California LLC and the sole member (owner) is Springer Science + Business Media Finance Inc (SSBM Finance Inc). SSBM Finance Inc is a Delaware corporation.

For information on translations, please e-mail rights@apress.com, or visit www.apress.com.

Apress and friends of ED books may be purchased in bulk for academic, corporate, or promotional use. eBook versions and licenses are also available for most titles. For more information, reference our Special Bulk Sales–eBook Licensing web page at www.apress.com/bulk-sales.

Any source code or other supplementary materials referenced by the author in this text is available to readers at www.apress.com. For detailed information about how to locate your book's source code, go to www.apress.com/source-code/.

Printed on acid-free paper

Apress Business: The Unbiased Source of Business Information

Apress business books provide essential information and practical advice, each written for practitioners by recognized experts. Busy managers and professionals in all areas of the business world—and at all levels of technical sophistication—look to our books for the actionable ideas and tools they need to solve problems, update and enhance their professional skills, make their work lives easier, and capitalize on opportunity.

Whatever the topic on the business spectrum—entrepreneurship, finance, sales, marketing, management, regulation, information technology, among others—Apress has been praised for providing the objective information and unbiased advice you need to excel in your daily work life. Our authors have no axes to grind; they understand they have one job only—to deliver up-to-date, accurate information simply, concisely, and with deep insight that addresses the real needs of our readers.

It is increasingly hard to find information—whether in the news media, on the Internet, and now all too often in books—that is even-handed and has your best interests at heart. We therefore hope that you enjoy this book, which has been carefully crafted to meet our standards of quality and unbiased coverage.

We are always interested in your feedback or ideas for new titles. Perhaps you'd even like to write a book yourself. Whatever the case, reach out to us at editorial@apress.com and an editor will respond swiftly. Incidentally, at the back of this book, you will find a list of useful related titles. Please visit us at www.apress.com to sign up for newsletters and discounts on future purchases.

The Apress Business Team

To the center and sunshine of my life, Bob.
To my other loves, Stan, Margaret, Terry, Keith,
the Marovich family, aunts and uncles, cousins, nieces
and nephews, and precious friends. To all the other
remarkable people in my life, whether named or
unnamed in this book, all of whom I respect and
appreciate. To all entrepreneurs and small business
owners who are building enduring export enterprises
that contribute to making our world a better place.

In loving memory of Lynn Kavanagh. A sister like no other.

Contents

Author Note

Dear Readers, Friends, and Export Enthusiasts,

Welcome to the revised and expanded edition of *Exporting: The Definitive Guide to Selling Abroad Profitably*.

Exporting is the most dynamic force in producing a healthier business, and a more exciting one. It holds the promise of growth based on the individual business owner's initiation, making possibilities virtually unlimited. To become truly competitive, one must create the conditions for superior results and have a strong global presence in our interconnected world.

Whether you are already an exporter or just setting sail on an export adventure, the wealth of information, ideas, insights, and practical advice in this book will enable you to become successful in the export marketplace.

What's new and augmented in this edition?

- Data and citation updates.
- Updates on actual and prospective trade agreements (especially TPP and TTIP developments).
- New CFR and EAR rules, and export controls.
- A sample job description for an export manager.
- New contributions and updates on specialist interviewees in Chapter 30.
- Substantive enhancements adapted from articles that I have written in the past several years.
- Updated and augmented hyperlinks with new sites that have appeared since the book's initial publication.
- New export success tips in Chapter 31.

As you delve in, you will see that each chapter represents what could be a standalone book. With that in mind, use each chapter as a springboard to further research on your own to grow your business.

Keep growing, exporting, evolving, and thriving. Share what you've learned. Make the world a better place within your company and your industry, and for your employees and family.

You may be small today, but through exports, you can grow faster, grow stronger, and soar globally to be large tomorrow. Achieving export greatness requires you envision your overseas market through the lens of alternative future possibilities.

I hope this book inspires you to reach outside your comfort zone and take on the exciting world of exporting. Strive to be creative. Be fearless. And have fun.

The world awaits.

Happy exporting,

Laurel Delaney

P.S. To keep up to date on export news, trends, and resources, visit Exporting Guide (www.exportingguide.com) and join our LinkedIn Exporting Guide Group MOOD (www.linkedin.com/groups/6518842).

About the Author

Laurel J. Delaney is founder and president of Chicago-based GlobeTrade.com, a management consulting company that helps entrepreneurs and small businesses go global. The United States Small Business Administration has recognized Ms. Delaney as a world-renowned global small business expert by naming her the Illinois Exporter of the Year. She is the author of *Start and Run a Profitable Exporting Business and Exporting Essentials* as well as numerous articles that have appeared in international and scholarly publications such as *The Wall Street Journal* and *The Conference Board*. She is the creator of The Global Small Business Blog (www.globalsmallbusinessblog.com), which is ranked No. I in the world for entrepreneurs and small businesses interested in going global; President of Women Entrepreneurs GROW Global (www.WomenEntrepreneursGROWGlobal.org); director of the Global Small Business Forum (www.globalsmallbusinessforum.com); and publisher of the Exporting Guide (www.exportingguide.com). She serves as the About.com Import & Export expert (http://importexport.about.com/), is a charter member and a board member by appointment of the World Entrepreneurship Forum, and is a member of the International Council for Small Business. She also serves as the Chicago Chapter Chair for the Women Presidents' Organization. Ms. Delaney's passion for going global goes back to 1985, when she first started her business. Since then, she has devoted more than 60,000 hours of work in the area—from consulting to writing to teaching.

Ms. Delaney holds a Bachelor of Arts degree in Advertising from Columbia College Chicago and a Master's in Business Administration from Lake Forest Graduate School of Management.

Acknowledgments

Any book project involves more people than just the author, because writing and publishing a book is not a solitary effort. My list of people to acknowledge starts with the very accomplished Apress team: Robert Hutchinson, Acquisition Editor; Rita Fernando Kim, Coordinating Editor wizard; and the mighty Matthew Moodie, Senior Development Editor and copyedit king. Without Robert's encouragement and direction, there would be no *Exporting* book 2nd edition, and without the exceptional talents of Rita and Matt, it would not be nearly as great.

To Roy Paulson, Drew Greenblatt, Philip Pittsford, and Alison Larson for your insightful contributions. To Douglas Clark, Melissa Gillespie, Moji Eagan, and Becky Schilling for your special assistance.

I owe a special debt of gratitude to Brandon Reed, Special Advisor to Strategic Council, The Good to Great Project LLC, Office of Jim Collins for his patience in working with me to have Jim Collins endorse my book; and to Jim Collins, author of *Good to Great* and co-author of *Beyond Entrepreneurship*, for reading my book and endorsing it. You are both an inspiration to me.

To my family and dear friends for having to put up again with my disappearing act to update this book in my spare time in 2016. I look forward to seeing you at lunches and special occasions again. To Syd and Mellie, my precious cats, for their constant rollovers on their backs to give a flash of their bellies, which brought a smile to my face. To Bob Marovich, my husband, for his patience, support, and unconditional love throughout our life journey.

Finally, to you, dear reader: I am grateful for your desire to export. It is people like you who make the world of business far more exciting and a better place to hang out.

Rest assured that if you are not mentioned by name here and should be, the next time I connect with you online (https://www.linkedin.com/groups/6518842) or see you in person, I will thank you.

Introduction

Globalization is a reality that isn't going away. That means we're all in this together, and we're going to have to fight for what we want and need.

—Michael Froman, United States Trade Representative,
Executive Office of the President (2015)[i]

Welcome to the second edition of this book. There are more than seven billion potential customers in the world, and 3.4 billion of them are online.[ii] How many of those customers is your company reaching? In a world that is now hyperconnected by the Internet, being a successful businessperson means no longer confining your business by borders—whether those of the city, state, or country. Exporting—or sending goods and services out of a country—increases a company's sales and profits, enhances its prestige, creates jobs, and offers a valuable way to level seasonal fluctuations. Exporting is also a powerful force that contributes to economic growth, development, and prosperity in our world.

The explosion of US entrepreneurs and small businesses—more than twenty-eight million combined[iii]—engaging in the world economy in the last few years is largely attributable to the Internet. This transition has taken place as businesses have sought new ways to grow and tap into the more than 95 percent of the world's consumers and 80 percent of the world's purchasing power that lie outside the United States.[iv] Surprisingly, though, less than 1 percent of these businesses and individuals operate in the US export marketplace, even though the number of exporters has grown faster than the number of nonexporters in terms of both goods sold and employment. Converting nonexporters to exporters is what this book is all about.

Tip Start planning to sell abroad. The businesses of exporters grow faster, they employ more people, and their employees earn more than the businesses of nonexporters.

What This Book Can Do for You

Exporting: The Definitive Guide to Selling Abroad Profitably equips you with the knowledge you need to export and helps you create the enthusiasm to succeed, leading to greater revenues and profitability for your business. *Exporting* puts you in the driver's seat, so you can sell more everywhere, get on the world stage, and grow. Other benefits to exporting include:

- Improving your return on investments
- Creating jobs
- Overcoming low growth in your home market
- Outmaneuvering competitors
- Providing a competitive advantage
- Becoming more productive
- Spurring innovation
- Developing a diversification strategy
- Surviving a domestic recession
- Spreading R&D costs across larger markets
- Generating economies of scale in production
- Exploring previously untapped markets
- Making productive use of excess domestic capacity
- Extending the product life cycle
- Insulating your seasonal domestic sales by allowing you to find new foreign markets
- Broadening your personal intellectual horizons
- Enriching your country
- Traveling to new countries

The Current State of Exporting

Export-driven entrepreneurs and small businesses play a significant role in the overall economic growth and prosperity of the United States and the world at large. They have the potential to improve productivity, achieve greater efficiencies, enhance world-class competitiveness, and create jobs. This is possible because:

- *Exporting lends itself to small business.* More than 301,923 US companies exported goods in 2014 (latest available data). Small- and medium-sized enterprises (SMEs)—those with fewer than five hundred employees—accounted for 98 percent of all identified exporters in 2014.[v]

- *Exports generate revenue.* The known export revenue of small- and medium-sized enterprises in the United States rose to $479,376 billion in 2014 (latest available data), up 2.7 percent from 2013. SMEs were responsible for 34 percent of goods exports in 2014.[vi]

- *Exports are growing.* US exports of goods and services reached $2.35 trillion in 2014, hitting a record high for the fifth straight year.[vii] Service exports alone were at a record level of $710.3 billion.[viii] Goods export to the 20 economies that have trade agreements with the United States reached a record $765.1 billion—an increase of 4.3 percent from 2013.[ix]

- *Exporting helps you find new customers and develop new markets.* The International Monetary Fund (www.imf.org) forecasts that nearly 87 percent of the world economic growth during the next five years will take place outside of the United States.

- *Exporting supports jobs.* American jobs supported by total exports were 11.3 million in 2014 and contributed one-third of the United States' annual growth between 2009 and 2013.[x]

- *Exporting using the Internet offers a new sales channel.* Thanks to the Web, entrepreneurs and small business owners have a potent new way of doing business—one that leverages e-commerce, social media, and networking to find new business, no matter from where it comes. The Internet has become the ultimate platform by which businesses can innovate through personalization and export around the world.

- *Exporting is not a choice; it is an imperative.* An export-or-die mentality is required by those individuals and business owners who don't want to be beaten by their competitors—both local and global—in the world marketplace. More so, those who don't export will become obsolete in a world where global connectivity is increasingly prevalent and easy.

The Future of Exporting

Exporting intends to help US companies become more competitive internationally through exporting and to bring thousands of new businesses into the world marketplace. As already mentioned, small- and medium-sized companies account for almost 98 percent of US exporters, but they represent only about 34 percent of the total export value of US goods. With 80 percent of global demand now outside of the United States, it is expected there will be $40 to $50 billion worth of export opportunity for the United States within five years. At the Export-Import Bank in 2015, for example, nearly 90 percent of transactions—more than 2,330—directly supported American small businesses.[xi] Under new legislation, in 2016, small businesses must account for 25 percent of Ex-Im Bank's financing dollars, up from a current mandate of 20 percent.[xii] Exporting is not just an option; it's an absolute must for building and sustaining a successful future.

What will your business look like in a decade? Our world is in constant motion and growth. Whether researching, buying, or selling, can you imagine operating *anything* these days without crossing borders and riding the next wave of profitable growth? Don't be scared if your answer is "Yes." By the time you finish this book, you will be exporting successfully and be able to adapt so that you can succeed in untapped markets. Until then, don't let fear immobilize you. Keep reading.

Remember   Exporting isn't rocket science. You can do it. And your bottom line will soon show the results of your efforts.

Who This Book Is For

Exporting is for entrepreneurs and small business owners who are new to the practice and are ready to take their business to the next level of growth. It is for entrepreneurs and small business owners who currently export but are looking for new market insights and have a desire to expand into other countries. It is also for people who never expect to export, yet do, and become accidental exporters—individuals who export out of surprise rather than a business imperative.

Exporting will help you:

- Develop a clear strategy on how to export

- Find the right people for your enterprise

- Export your product or service efficiently and profitably

- Find customers, enter new markets, get paid, and ship

- Discover your best territory through statistics and market research

- Develop pricing and prepare documentation

- Take advantage of trade agreements

- Leverage the Internet—especially through tablets and mobile phones—to boost your online exports

- Learn from others who have exported successfully

How to Use This Book

Exporting has been created and structured to make it as easy as possible to export. The book's eight sections work together to achieve that goal by providing the following descriptions of the process:

Part I: Building Your Foundations for Exporting looks at whether you are ready to export; shows you how to write an export business plan that takes into consideration the positive impact of free trade agreements; explains how to prepare for exporting by describing the corporate, legal, and financial considerations; and describes how to manage the human side of your enterprise.

Part II: Creating and Using Online Platforms covers online fundamentals; shows how to create a social-networking and media presence; and demonstrates how to use e-commerce platforms (eBay, Alibaba, and Etsy) to export and sell globally.

Part III: Mapping Out Your Export Journey examines how to find a product and manufacturer for export, to draft an export-supplier agreement, to research an export market, to prepare a product or service for export, and to translate web and marketing material for a global audience.

Part IV: Developing Sales and Distribution Capabilities offers creative ways to find cross-border customers and describes several different methods of exporting.

Part V: Managing the Transaction explores transport options, pricing considerations, payment methods, cargo details, and documentation.

Part VI: Keep Building Your Business suggests ways to provide exceptional export service and analyze cross-border alliances and partnerships.

Part VII: The Export Journey delves into the importance of cross-cultural learning; suggests the rules of the export world for ethical conduct; offers a checklist of international-business travel tips; shows the impact of the operation of woman business owners in our new brave world; outlines the implications of big emerging markets for growing a small business; and lastly, describes the top ten emerging export business markets.

Part VIII: Export Mastery provides real-world experiences as told by successful export-business owners; offers sixteen essential keys to export success; and finally, introduces you to a MOOD—a massive open online dialogue—in the form of a LinkedIn Exporting Guide Group (MOOD). It will help keep you focused on exporting success.

Each chapter is written as a stand-alone topic with the intent that most people, especially busy executives, do not have time to read a book from cover to cover in one sitting. You can select a section that speaks immediately to your needs, delve into it, and find what you are looking for. Explore it at your convenience and come back to it as a reference source. A few sections in the book do warrant a reading before you get to the other chapters, such as Chapter 1, covering whether you are ready to export, but reading it is not a prerequisite for success in exporting. Learning and growing by way of exports should take place on your own terms. *Exporting* is merely a facilitator that will enable you to perform better in the world marketplace.

First things first: You need to be *ready* to take on the world, because the future of exporting lies in your hands (and, as you will read in this book, in your pocket). As you turn the page to Chapter 1, you are opening the gateway to selling globally. *Let's export!*

Notes

i.   "Remarks by Ambassador Michael Froman to the National Foreign Trade Council Upon Receiving the World Trade Award," Office of the United States trade Representative, October 15, 2015, https://ustr.gov/about-us/policy-offices/press-office/speechestranscripts/2015/october/remarks-ambassador-michael.

ii. "Internet Users in the World by Regions," Internet World Stats, June 2016, http://www.internetworldstats.com/stats.htm.

iii. "Advocacy Welcomes Its Seventh Chief Council," The Small Business Advocate, January 2016, https://www.sba.gov/sites/default/files/Jan_2016_newsletter.pdf.

iv. "The State of World Trade 2014: The Outlook for American Jobs, Economic Growth, and Global Leadership," U.S. Chamber of Commerce, May 16, 2014, https://www.uschamber.com/speech/state-world-trade-2014-outlook-american-jobs-economic-growth-and-global-leadership.

v.   U.S. Census Bureau News, http://www.census.gov/foreign-trade/Press-Release/edb/2014/2014prelimprofile.pdf.

vi. Ibid.

vii. Commerce.gov, U.S. Exports Hit Record High for the Fifth Straight Year, Department of Commerce; https://www.commerce.gov/news/blog/2015/02/us-exports-hit-record-high-fifth-straight-year.

viii. Ibid.

ix. Ibid.

x.   Ibid.

xi. The Facts About EXIM Bank, Exim.gov; http://www.exim.gov/about/facts-about-ex-im-bank.

xii. Export-Import Bank Chairman Fred Hochberg happy U.S. exporters can use agency to finance sales overseas, The Business Journals; http://www.bizjournals.com/bizjournals/washingtonbureau/2015/12/fred-hochberg-eager-to-let-world-know-export.html.

Building Your Foundations for Exporting

Are You Ready to Export?

Exports have played a critical role in America's economic comeback, and they continued to do so in 2014.

—U.S. Secretary of Commerce Penny Pritzker (2014)

Anyone who wants to export, can. The world awaits. The essential element needed to be successful exporting is readiness. The rest is mechanics and know-how. Whether you're a first-time exporter or entering a new market, selling goods and services across borders is easy and just a mouse click away. I'm here to show you how. But before I get to that, let me take you back to a little more than twenty-five years ago.

It was 1985. Even back then, I challenged conventional assumptions about how to compete and started to view markets outside the United States as the future of the business I had started: Global TradeSource, Ltd. I even put "global," "trade," and "source" in the company name, thereby shifting the buyer's possibilities from being local to those of the world and drawing upon the distinctive strengths of alternative, growing overseas markets as those that would offer the company's products and services.

That kind of vision, along with a more recent facilitator called the Internet, has broken down every imaginable barrier to growth and prosperity and has transformed not just how we conduct business but the world at large. The moment you create a Web site, blog, or Facebook account, your point of contact with consumers becomes global. The Internet is the great global leveler and gives

© Laurel J. Delaney 2016

L. J. Delaney, *Exporting*, DOI 10.1007/978-1-4842-2193-8_1

everyone a chance to make spectacular strides in exporting—by finding, acquiring, and servicing customers the world over faster than ever—which in turn drives profits and growth for businesses. The blueprint for prosperity in exports is right at your fingertips. Never has there been such attention to the Internet, interconnectedness, and exporting than now.

■ **Note** The Internet has broken down all barriers to world commerce—democratizing trade by guaranteeing that exporting's benefits are shared more widely by more of America's small exporters. It is your most potent weapon in the battle to capture more international sales.

The use of technology, especially social networks such as Facebook, LinkedIn, Snapchat, and Twitter, along with the advent of more affordable smart phones, watches, and tablets, makes finding and exporting opportunities in the world marketplace a breeze for small business owners and executives. And as a result of these incredible advancements in technology, these same empowered individuals can create opportunities on the web—not just browse for themselves—and even launch whole new enterprises in a heartbeat based on unmet needs and interests expressed by consumers.

Because social networks enable us to extend our worldwide connections rapidly, increasing our ability to identify opportunities on a more open, transparent basis, none of us operates in a vacuum as a solo entrepreneur any longer.

What does this have to do with exporting and your readiness to do so? Plenty. It defines how an export business is born and can grow, if nurtured correctly, into something absolutely amazing.

Next, let's take a look at three examples of real-world situations that could arise that will shape how you view the potential of exporting and how it gets done. After that, we'll move on to what it takes to succeed in exporting. Last, we'll make a distinction between exporting services and products, which will allow you to decide what you are going into the international market with.

You'll note that at this point I do not talk about the financial considerations of exporting. They are obviously an important aspect that you must consider before you export in order to be properly capitalized. However, I am intentionally leaving the discussion out of this section because it will be covered later, beginning with Chapter 3.

How an Export Product Business Is Born

Imagine someone named Abel Anderson who is working in the automotive industry while running a food-export business. In the evenings and on weekends, he goes to food fairs. Although he works full time in the automotive industry, his real passion is food. He's always seeking novel food items to try.

At one local trade show that Abel attends in Chicago, he falls in love with a specialty item that tastes like cheesecake, caramel, chocolate, and butter crumbs all rolled into one scrumptious cookie the size of a hockey puck. He chats with the person at the booth named Samantha and asks her if she exports the product. She tells him she does not. Abel expresses interest in working with her baking company in his spare time as an independent contractor to export its products to a select few countries. Lo and behold, she agrees.

After spending a few days with Samantha making sure the ingredients in the cookie can hold up in overseas transit and pass regulatory laws, Abel draws up a contract. He then contacts the International Trade Administration via the Internet to conduct a partner search for agents located in Dubai, Saudi Arabia, and Oman—areas of the world where he thinks there is significant demand and enough wealth to purchase gourmet food products. Within three months and with the help of ITA, he lines up importing distributors in two countries—all just by using e-mail and Skype. He sends a test shipment of cookies to each location and discovers in the process that everyone who samples the cookies loves them. He receives his first order from the Dubai agent for ten thousand packages of cookies.

Abel is now in the export product business. It won't be long before he gives up his full-time job in the automotive industry.

His story is an example of how the journey to exporting or launching an export business begins. Abel started first with his own good idea of exporting a product, and then, with the help of technology that most of us use every day, he was able to turn his idea into a new business venture. Here, then, we have a new paradigm for world competitiveness built on information and technology. So while nothing beats a good face-to-face encounter to help deepen your knowledge of a country and the customer, making the most of technology should also be a priority.

In the future, the economic transformation of countries will require businesses to rely less on selling to locals and more on selling abroad. This gets back to how exporting boosts economic productivity and also suggests its capacity to solve the problems caused by a growing world population, rapid urbanization, and even climate change.

Everything we do today is potentially relevant to consumers anywhere in the world, provided they understand what we are doing. Consider, for example, running a public relations firm. Think it has international legs? Let's find out.

■ **Tip**   Any product or service you sell no doubt has potential customers abroad. And guess what? You will need them all in order to stay relevant and thrive as the twenty-first century progresses.

How an Export Service Business Is Born

Envision offering your local marketing service, which is booming in North America, to someone in the United Kingdom. Let's imagine that someone named Katie Schroeder does just that. She runs a successful Chicago-based public relations company called Take It Viral, or TIV, representing some of the most popular big-name consumer brands in the United States. TIV has received numerous accolades for its creative social media campaigns using Twitter, Facebook, Instagram, and Google+.

As a result of media fanfare, a business owner in the United Kingdom—we'll call him Joe—has tracked Katie's work and e-mails her with a request for her company to conduct a social-media PR campaign in the United Kingdom. Joe makes luxury ties and wants to broaden his brand recognition in the United Kingdom and expand his business into the United States. Although Katie has reservations about delivering that type of specific service outside her normal selling channels, she contemplates how to go about it. All she really needs is a plan, technology, a couple of additional support people, and a few good local UK connections to make it happen.

So Katie decides to take the project. Her first step is to develop a road map. Her next step is to execute it. She deploys her existing employees to launch the program, and as the UK business grows, Katie outsources work through the online freelance employment databases Guru.com, Elance.com, and Odesk.com, specifically seeking people in the UK market who are capable of managing social media campaigns.

At the same time, Katie consults her international accountant on how best to handle the tax impact on her business for the newly generated overseas revenue stream and payments made to independent contractors located in the United Kingdom. Further, she explores all payments options—for both money received from clients and money paid to workers—with her trusted international banker. Last, she goes over the potential pitfalls on the legal front with her international attorney.

Through the advice of her banker, Katie sets up a PayPal account to pay off-site workers and receives her first UK client payment via a wire transfer to her bank account. Voila! She has gone global and achieved her first service export! She is already considering opportunities in France, Ireland, and Germany. Her new goal is to become less dependent on the ebb and flow of the North American market, build up a profitable alternative revenue stream (e.g., in the United Kingdom), and expand into additional international markets so that the world will eventually become her revenue stream.

■ **Note** Exporting requires a team of experts—accountants, lawyers, and others—who understand the markets you are selling into. Get them involved early to help you avoid missteps.

How a Business Expands into New Foreign Markets

Ever dream about branching out into new overseas markets? Meet someone we will call Alfild Nelsen. Alfild is currently running a successful specialty chemical-cleaning-product business with revenues of more than $10 million. Thanks to NAFTA, she currently exports to Canada and Mexico, but to further offset the anticipation of slowing local growth, she wants to branch out into other international markets. While thinking about that, she ventures off to Australia with her husband for a vacation. She visits a huge do-it-yourself store in Melbourne and spots a wide array of high-end cleaning products not unlike the ones she makes in her own business. She buys a couple of the products and thinks about how she could find a qualified representative for her own line of cleaning supplies to be sold in the same store. Nothing beats healthy competition!

When she returns home to the United States, Alfild places the cleaning products she bought underneath her kitchen sink and forgets about the idea of exporting to Australia. Besides, she's too busy with her efforts that go into expanding her business into the Mexican and Canadian markets! Several months go by and when she has some spare time, she suddenly revisits the idea of exporting her specialty chemical cleaning products to Australia. She pulls out her laptop, remembers a service a colleague uses for exporting to New Zealand called Gold Key Service, and finds the Web site. She e-mails the organization and within thirty days has a customized market research report, an appointment with a prospective trade partner in the chemical cleaning industry, and a trip scheduled to meet face-to-face with the partner in Australia. Alfild has made the first step in branching out into new international markets. These examples show that you can escape constraints on growth at home by way of exports and entering new markets. The potential is as vast as your imagination. Whether you are an export newbie like Abel or Katie or an experienced exporter like Alfild, at some point you must decide whether to export a product or a service, or both. As I just highlighted, most people begin with a single idea that they are comfortable with, know like the back of their hand, and have rich experience with and therefore feel that they have a competitive advantage in the global marketplace. Understanding the difference between exporting a product or a service is critical to making the right choice for your business and your personal fulfillment.

The Difference Between Product and Service Exports

Exporting a product involves transporting something you can see, hold, easily assign a monetary value to, and physically move from point A to point B. Exporting a service, such as one that is business oriented, professional, technical, financial, or based on franchising or insurance, requires a somewhat different approach. Here's a quick rundown of the differences between a product and a service as they affect the export process:

Product	Service
Tangible	Intangible
Visible	Invisible
Measurable	Immeasurable
High perceived value	Low perceived value
High freight costs	Negligible freight costs
Negligible human interaction	High human interaction
Low maintenance	High maintenance
High standardization	Negligible standardization

You cannot see or touch a service—and you often cannot assess its true value until after you have used it and discovered all the resulting benefits.

Services are in many ways a tougher sell than a product, either at home or abroad, yet once sold, they move faster thanks to technology. Each of the listed differences creates a marketing challenge for the service exporter, perhaps the most crucial being the need to convince a distant customer to buy your service sight unseen and without any real idea of how they will benefit. This is why a service business depends first and foremost on people. Of course, when you export a product, you are also relying on a whole string of people to do their jobs—banks to help you get paid, freight forwarders to move your goods, local distributors to get your product on store shelves—but exporting a service demands a special emphasis on human interaction, both at home and abroad. (I will discuss the human side of enterprise management in Chapter 4.)

U.S. exports of services are booming, topping $710 billion in 2014, according to the U.S. Department of Commerce.[i] The most competitive advantage of service exports, especially during any recession, is that they perform better than goods exports. Service exports typically don't face tariffs, as goods sold overseas often do, but some barriers still persist.

People Power Drives Your Service Exports

Selling a service requires even more people power than product sales to be successful. When you export a product, you offer it, clinch your sale, follow through, and troubleshoot as needed. Then, once the product is in your customers' hands, they oversee sales in their geographic territory and contact you to order more products when they sell out. There is little need for communication between buyer and seller once the product is in the distribution pipeline and moving—being bought, sold, and enjoyed.

By contrast, a service export requires direct interaction with your customer, not just initially but for the duration of the service contract. For some services, of course, the quality of the interaction with your customer is exactly what they're paying for. This is why people with superior communication skills, diplomacy, and—this can't be emphasized enough—acute cultural awareness are the greatest assets for delivering a quality service export.

An example of a service export is an architectural firm that designs buildings in the United States and reaches out overseas to perform its work, or it can involve providing royalties and licensing fees, including the money people pay to use American software.

I will go into greater detail on service exports in Chapter 14, but for now I reference the distinction between a product and service export because the differences have implications for the marketing and management of the export. It is important to decide at the outset what you wish to accomplish: exporting a product, service, or both. Although the process is transferable from goods to services, each type of export requires its own distinct strategic approach.

What It Takes to Export

So where do you start? As with any new business venture, you need to first take stock of both yourself and your business to see if you have the personality, mindset, and business that can benefit from exporting. Let's begin with an assessment of *you* and then we'll cover the business.

Assessment of You: The Global Mindset

What unique qualities and characteristics does it take to become a successful exporter? To crack open a new overseas market? To become a top-notch international executive at a global conglomerate? The answer is that it takes the same qualities to do any of these things. Successful exporters, international expansion artists, and global executives may vary in their temperament, personality, and experience, but in the ways that really count, they are more alike than different. What counts is their ability to venture out in the world and adapt as they go. I call it a global mindset.

■ **Note** Successful exporters have, or develop, a global mindset—the ability and courage to operate their business in an unknown environment.

I somewhat liken exporting to riding a roller coaster at an amusement park. You eagerly jump into the coaster car, fasten your seatbelt, and get ready for the exhilarating ride of your life. Exporting offers a similar experience. It's an adventure that challenges every way you run a business. So the first question I ask individuals who express interest in exporting is: Do you have the mindset and guts to ride it out? After we clarify what that means—dealing with the highs and lows of attempting to do business in far-off places that are hard to access quickly and impossible to understand culturally—we discuss what is really involved in preparing to export. It's called doing your homework.

Homework can be done on your temperament and abilities, on how to export, on researching the market, on financial considerations, and on determining whether your product or service is in demand anywhere in the world. The more preparation you undertake, the greater your chance of reducing mistakes. But before you can advance from Point A, thinking about an export idea, to Point B, launching the export idea, you must first take stock of yourself and decide if you are ready and willing to develop the dynamic outlook that will enable you to export. It starts with a determined global mindset: a mix of intellectual and behavioral qualities that enable individuals to understand and operate a business in environments unlike their own.

Examining the State of You: The Global Mindset

A global mindset starts with self-awareness, reflects an authentic openness to and engagement with the world, and employs a heightened awareness of the sensitivity of cross-cultural differences. Toss in that adventuresome spirit I mentioned early on, adaptability, a solid educational background, core business competencies, and life experiences that preferably involve international travel, and you have a recipe for the ideal global thought leader. Capitalizing on these attributes is a powerful factor in developing a global mindset and achieving success in the export world.

Here's my short list of twelve characteristics that I find work in the export marketplace. They are based on my own hands-on experiences and the observations of others who have achieved success crossing boundaries in the business world:

1. The ability to venture out in the world and adapt quickly

2. Being comfortable and confident in your own skin, along with having a heightened sensitivity to others

3. Carrying a high level of intelligence, including cultural and emotional

4. Enjoying living in different parts of the world and relishing learning a foreign language

5. Knowing how to bring out the best in people no matter where they are from

6. Getting things done with people who come from diverse backgrounds in any part of the world

7. Being curious, having a love of learning, and immersing oneself in foreign cultures

8. Being objective and open to people and the environment

9. Having enough flexibility to focus on serving and helping others

10. Possessing the ability to take something complex and simplify it

11. Confronting obstacles with optimism and a willingness to continue learning new ways of doing things

12. Being resilient—or having the ability to bounce back from even the most challenging of circumstances

You may not have all of these characteristics, and I am sure there are some I have overlooked, but if you have most of them, you will be comfortable operating anywhere in the world and well on your way to success in exporting.

Assessing Your Business: The Local Business Model

You have a successful local business; now what? You've saturated your domestic market and there's no room to grow geographically unless you look outside your own borders.

Export.gov offers a questionnaire that highlights the "state of a business" (https://new.export.gov/export-readiness-assessment/entity-type).

The following are the questions you should answer:

1. Does your company have a product or service that has been successfully sold in the domestic market?

   Yes   No

2. Does your company have or is your company preparing an international marketing plan with defined goals and strategies?

   Yes   No

3. Does your company have sufficient production capacity that can be committed to the export market?

   Yes   No

4. Does your company have the financial resources to actively support the marketing of your products in the targeted overseas markets?

   Yes   No

5. Is your company's management committed to developing export markets and willing and able to dedicate staff, time, and resources to the process?

   Yes   No

6. Is your company committed to providing the same level of service to export markets that is given to your domestic customers?

   Yes   No

7. Does your company have adequate knowledge in modifying product packaging and ingredients to meet foreign import regulations and cultural preferences?

   Yes   No

8. Does your company have adequate knowledge in shipping its product overseas, such as the ability to identify and select international freight forwarders and freight costing?

   Yes   No

9. Does your company have adequate knowledge of export payment mechanisms, such as developing and negotiating letters of credit?

   Yes   No

Once you complete the questionnaire, you will immediately receive an online score, which will help you assess your export readiness as well as identify areas that your business needs to strengthen in order to improve its export activities. Don't be daunted by the fact that you may not be able to provide an affirmative answer to all the questions. After all, that is why I am writing this book—to help you easily export in the digital age. If you don't pass the assessment, it doesn't mean you can't export; it only means you have more homework to do in preparation for the end goal: export success.

One last related question that begs to be answered: Can you use your home base—your domestic operation—as a template for exporting? The answer is: it depends. That's a tall order. You naturally want exporting to become a profitable extension of your domestic operation, but there are no guarantees.

I encourage you not to count on it. A lot will depend on your firm's orientation. For example, you might believe that because your goods and services sell well in the United States, they will sell anywhere in the world, but success will depend on your marketing approach to modifying those goods and services, if needed, to fit your selected export market. Each market is different and should be treated as such by adapting to a local country's culture.

■ **Tip** Focus on similarities in exporting across markets whenever possible to standardize your business model worldwide and to achieve economies of scale in production. We'll cover a theory related to this in Chapter 11.

Assessing an Export Start-Up: The "Born Global" Firm

There is a new class of entrepreneurs who have changed the export paradigm and show that it is possible to do business and succeed in world markets without having an established domestic base. The concept is referred to as "born global." Born-global digital companies are run by individuals of a generation that only knows of communicating and transacting business via the Internet. Virtually from inception, their digital companies compete on a global scale against large, established players in the world arena, breeding the next frontier in international trade. They are global by technology, not by strategy, and the individuals who start and run these firms tend to bypass rules and regulations to get things done.

Contrary to conventional methods, born-global individuals don't build export businesses through gradual expansion into foreign markets. Rather, they leap into the foreign market and figure things out as they go. For example, a born-global entrepreneur will review the earlier assessment questionnaire, complete it on a lark, and even if their answers are all "No," will still proceed in exporting. What they are banking on is their own tech know-how and the suitability of their product or service for the international market coupled with their own chutzpah to get them over speed bumps.

I can relate to that disruptive, adventuresome spirit. But I caution you: Rather than making progress at every step of the way during the process of exporting, you will encounter a lot of scary tunnels, twists, and sharp turns involved in figuring it out. That is because the leaders of born-global digital companies have no prior knowledge or experience in exporting—only in leveraging technology. This runs counter to the notion of using your domestic operation, one that has a history of proven success, as a template for exporting. In other words, and as mentioned earlier, don't assume what works at home will work abroad.

Big mistake. There will always be adjustments that have to be made to the changing conditions of the company, the environment, and the marketplace, rather than a deliberate strategy.

If you are a start-up or are of the born-global generation, there is nothing stopping you from plunging into exporting. So skip the assessments and just *go for it*. Sometimes the only way to learn is by doing. If that is the case, use your passion as fuel to create new market opportunities and use this book as a guide to help you master the export process.

Summary

Remember how the chapter opened? I asked boldly: Are you ready to export? Then I provided three different exporting scenarios to help you understand how export initiatives are born. Next, I defined the difference between a product and a service export. Last, I offered a simple process to assess yourself as well as your existing business or start-up as to whether you have what it takes to export.

Now it's up to you. You can choose to deal with a stagnant climate and growth constraints at home or experience the thrill of exporting to fast-growing overseas markets. It's your decision. If you have the courage and mindset to export, and you are ready, turn the page. I want you wholeheartedly on this adventure with me!

Note

i. U.S. Chamber of Commerce, The Benefits of International Trade, https://www.uschamber.com/international/international-policy/benefits-international-trade-0, accessed July 7, 2016.

Writing an Export Business Plan

A Guide During the Life of Your Export Business

"The plan is useless. But planning is essential." Former President Dwight Eisenhower said that. Planning is a process, setting concrete milestones and tracking progress, with frequent review and revisions. But you can't do planning without starting with a plan.

—Tim Berry, founder, Bplans.com

Congratulations! You have determined you are export ready. You have what it takes to export and have decided on the type of export you wish to launch: a product, a service, or both. Now it's time to map out what you intend to accomplish during the life of your export business. It's time to think about your export prosperity in a new and dynamic way. This starts with the global mindset we covered earlier and moves to crafting what's ahead for your business on the international front. The process, which many dread because it requires a deep dive into strategic thinking, becomes an operational plan for controlling the export business and serves as a guide for growth and export success. The export business plan will become a part of your overall business plan—you'll see how and why later on.

© Laurel J. Delaney 2016
L. J. Delaney, *Exporting*, DOI 10.1007/978-1-4842-2193-8_2

▓ **Note**   The Internet plays a huge part in the exporting world, and that is reflected in this book. There are lots of online tools and resources referenced throughout the book, so it will be handy to have a computer or tablet nearby.

Purpose of an Export Business Plan

There are four main purposes for the export business plan that you will write. The first is that it will serve as a guide during the initial stages of your export growth. The second is that it will give you a chance to describe your product or service offering, detail a realistic sales-and-marketing strategy (i.e., how you will reach your customers), provide a range of viable return-on-investment figures, and explain what variables will affect those numbers positively or negatively. The third purpose is that if you plan to seek out loans, whether export related or not, a business plan that includes an international expansion component is required by potential partners, lenders, and investors in order to understand your business strategy. And last, if you are looking for direction, creating a great export business plan will get you there quicker.

Putting a plan in place doesn't mean you look at it once and file it in a cabinet. It's a powerful, living document reflecting your ideas, team, and efforts. It's meant to be edited, referred to, and shared constantly throughout the growth of the business. A plan can be as simple as ideas jotted down on the back of a napkin or as thorough as a twenty-five-page report. Whether short or long, the plan should focus on what is important to you, what energizes and motivates you, and what gives you a sense of purpose and meaning—doing something bigger and beyond yourself. Start with the basics:

1. What do you like to do?
2. What are you planning to do?

Then ask yourself whether the two answers you came up with are in alignment. For example, my answers might be:

1. What do I like to do? I love to eat Italian food.
2. What am I planning to do? I plan to export hammers because I have a good supply source.

OK, you get it. I'm out of alignment on my vision for what I love to do versus what I intend to do to make that vision a reality. Let's try again:

1. What do I like to do? I love to eat pizza.
2. What am I planning to do? I plan to export frozen pizzas.

There you have it! My passion for something I love to do is in line with what I plan to do for a business—the ideal scenario for starting a business. That means my love of the product will sustain me during the sharp turns and bumps on the road to achieving exporting success. Experiment until you find your passion. Sometimes it can take several attempts before you realize what turns you on—whether it's selling pizzas or hammers, or making money!

Being purposeful is not something that just happens. You must be proactive and intentional. Did I personally start my business with an export business plan? Yes, for myself and the benefit of my team. Did we follow it? Not exactly. Our primary focus was to secure an initial overseas customer who would translate into an export sale and then push the transaction through to make a profit. We then reviewed the plan to see how we fared relative to what we were trying to accomplish, and we compared results to the realities of the market. We then decided to forge ahead on similar deals in other countries.

In getting a business or an initiative like an export transaction off the ground, customers matter the most, but you need to go further. A great plan outlines and supports the assumptions you have going into the business and serves as a guide for where you're headed.

Pitfalls of *Not* Having an Export Business Plan

Not interested in developing a plan? That's an option and it is your choice. You must be short on time and eager to get to market. Bypassing strategic thinking for short-term gain can be risky (think along the lines of driving a car to a new, distant destination without a map or GPS). Yet it can be tempting because it is a quick way to test whether a product or service will sell in the export marketplace.

In my experience working with hundreds of start-ups and business owners, those who fail to develop a plan make several mistakes along the way. Here are some of the common pitfalls. Believe me, these aren't all of them.

1. They move too soon and fast, having a knee-jerk reaction as opposed to executing on a well-thought-out and -crafted strategy.

2. They fail to take a pulse on where their business stands currently.

3. They divert attention to the overseas market to the detriment of their local business.

4. They employ too little staff to take on the overseas market.

5. They proceed to export in a complex market (e.g., where there is a lot of red tape or the natives speak a different language) or open up negotiations with the wrong party (e.g., someone who is untrustworthy or a bad fit).

6. They are too quick to execute on a sale and fail to secure a guaranteed payment.

7. They act in a too fast and aggressive manner in providing online banking information to get paid or to pay a supplier, only to find later on that they have been cyberattacked.

8. They don't state clearly on their Web site, blog, or Facebook page whether they accept international sales orders. If they don't, they should say so. If they do, then they should state specifically which countries they serve and follow through when inquiries roll in.

9. They put all their eggs in one basket and don't diversify enough to offset the ebbs and flows of the marketplace. They put too much emphasis on one product and one market that aren't working.

10. They never fully understand that they might have vulnerabilities that could impede their ability to get things done.

These so-called export sins are just the tip of the iceberg of what can potentially go wrong if you don't plan accordingly. If you are still dead set on moving ahead without a plan, do so at your own risk. I urge you, however, to at some point consider formalizing a plan so that you can fully capitalize on your idea and leverage it for luring potential partners, lenders, and investors.

Pointers for Developing an Export Business Plan

You should always measure your plan's progress against the market reality, which can be highly unpredictable. You can't go wrong with that approach. For example, you might sell designer diapers via your e-commerce site, emphasizing distribution to English-speaking countries such as Australia and New Zealand, only to find out quickly that the bulk of your inquiries are in French, the native language of the majority of your prospective customers.

Whatever plan you select, have backup Plans B, C, and D in place. For example, let's say you select Ireland to export catfish to and find out two months later that the Irish don't like catfish. Plan B might be to sell your catfish to another market, say the United Kingdom, or to sell another fish that the Irish like.

Be smart and apply the global mindset we talked about in Chapter 1, which is to stay flexible and adaptable. Just because you revert to Plan B or C doesn't mean you failed and that exporting won't work. Rather, it means the market reality is such that your original plan won't work, and thank goodness you were smart enough to develop contingency plans.

Last, free trade agreements improve foreign market access for exporters, promote economic growth, and create jobs. Study active free trade agreements (FTAs) in advance of selecting an export market and preparing your export business plan to see how they will benefit your organization. Factor that information into your decision-making process accordingly. For example, NAFTA is the FTA among Canada, the United States, and Mexico serving to remove most barriers to trade and investment in that region. The United States and 11 other Pacific region countries recently completed the Trans-Pacific Partnership (TPP), a trade deal involving countries making up almost 40 percent of the world's gross domestic product.

UNDERSTAND MARKET CONDITIONS

Once you have a good idea of what you want to export and where, you can fill out your picture of market conditions by answering questions like these (this is a list I put together for a client):

1. Who will buy your product and why?

2. What is the size of the market?

3. Is there a FTA in place between your country and the prospective market?

4. Who is your competition?

5. How new is the product to the market you have selected?

6. Are there growth opportunities in the market?

7. What do the country's demographic profile, economy, and mass culture look like right now?

8. Are there demographic, economic, or cultural trends that will shape the market in the future?

9. Does the government help or hinder the sale of imported goods? For example, are there any barriers to entry or to sales within the market?

10. Will the country's climate or geography present logistical problems for sales of your product of choice—for example, selling chocolates to hot and humid Bali?

11. Does the product have to be adapted to that market by way of a physical reconstruction, a new package, or a change in servicing practices?

12. Does the product have the same use conditions in the international market as in the home market?

13. Does the product require personal after-sales service and, if so, can you provide it in the prospective market?

14. Are you comfortable traveling to the market on an as-needed basis?

Use your own business sense and add to the list. Once you actually start research (refer to Chapter 12), more questions will arise. This is all part of the process of turning your vague ambitions into a concrete export business plan based on market realities, so the smarter your questions and more upfront your answers, the better your chances of success.

Three Types of Export Business Plans

Now you're ready to get organized and create your own plan. To keep the process manageable, let's look at three different types of sample template plans, each with distinct advantages for business people with different needs. Pick the one that works best for you, keeping in mind that you can shorten the analysis while keeping the major components of the plan intact.

- The back-of-the-napkin export business plan (suitable for born-global entrepreneurs)
- The traditional-export business plan
- The Laurel export business plan

The Back-of-the-Napkin Export Business Plan

The back-of-the-napkin export business plan is for folks who are big on ideas and pressed for time and want to get to market fast. While it's typically short and sweet, it serves a better purpose than having no export business plan at all. A back-of-the-napkin export business plan can be as simple as explaining what the business does, what you want to do next export-wise, and how you are going to get there (who is going to be on board). It might look like this:

1. "We make the absolute best purple widgets on the planet."

2. "We will export purple widgets."

3. "We will export purple widgets to France."

4. "We will consider making other type widgets, say in red, if a customer in France is large enough to justify the change."

5. "Suzy, Ted, Mike, and I will work on this initiative."

6. "We will export, at a minimum, twenty thousand purple widgets within the first year."

7. "We will not reduce efforts from our domestic business to apply them to the export business."

8. "We will figure out how much money we need and when we need it."

9. "We will finance the exports of purple widgets with profits from our domestic business."

10. "We will find our own customers directly via our Web site, blog, and Facebook."

11. "We will consult with our banker to provide payment options on all export sales."

12. "We will have fun in the export journey to success!"

Add a Web site link to show what the business does and provide an executive summary that includes the founder's bio and the key team members, and you're done.

The Traditional Export Business Plan

It's important to have a business plan, but you don't have to reinvent the wheel to create one. One place to visit and bookmark online is the Small Business Administration's "Export Business Planner" (http://www.sba.gov/export-businessplanner). It is a free, customizable tool for small-business owners who are exploring exporting. When you are using the planner, you can refer to Getting Started: Creating an Export Business Plan. It outlines the following (in Chapter 12, we guide you on market research, so don't overly challenge yourself if you can't answer all the questions at the initial planning stage):

1. Profiling Your Current Business

   a. Identify current successes.

   b. Determine competitive advantages.

   c. Evaluate companywide commitment.

2. Conducting an Industry Analysis

   a. Find export data available on your industry.

   b. Research how competitive your industry is in the global markets.

   c. Assess your industry's international growth potential.

   d. Research government market studies.

3. Identifying Products with Export Potential

   a. Select the most exportable products/services that your company will offer internationally.

   b. Evaluate the product/services(s) that your company will offer internationally.

4. Marketability: Matching Your Product/Service with a Global Trend or Need

   a. Classify your product.

   b. Find countries with the best-suited markets for your product.

   c. Determine which foreign markets will be the easiest to penetrate.

   d. Define and narrow down those export markets you intend to pursue.

   e. Talk to your US customers or other companies who are doing business internationally.

   f. Research export efforts of US competitors.

5. Determining Market Expansion Benefits/Trade-Offs

   a. Assess the benefits to exporting.

   b. Determine the trade-offs to exporting.

6. Identifying Markets to Pursue

   a. Select the top three most penetrable markets (see the sidebar at the end of this list).

7. Conducting an Export Marketing and Sales Analysis

   a. Come up with an overall marketing strategy.

   b. Figure out sales strategies.

   c. Write a detailed product or service description.

       d.   Map out the product life cycle.

       e.   Make a list of copyrights, patents, and trade secrets.

       f.   Determine research and development activities.

8.   Determining Expansion Needs

       a.   Access available export financing resources.

       b.   Determine which financing method is best suited to your exporting needs (refer to Chapter 20 for more details).

9.   Short- and Long-Term Goals

       a.   Define short-term goals.

       b.   Define long-term goals.

       c.   Develop an action plan with timelines to reach your short-term goals.

In summary, the most difficult aspect in developing an export business plan is determining the demand for a product or service offering in a foreign country. It's one thing to know a product can be sold in a market—after all, that's why you selected a particular market—but it is a totally different ball game when it comes to forecasting how much you can sell and over what time frame. Assume that the demand for a product develops in direct proportion to the economic development in each country. This might be a useful way to think about it, especially when data might be unknown. What is crucial is that you have thought through the key drivers of the export venture's success or failure—from what level of sales at which the business begin to make a profit to the impact of using various methods of distribution channels.

■ **Note** An overseas market is as mercurial as it is unpredictable. Who would have guessed that a community marketplace for people to list, discover, and book unique accommodations around the world would sell?

WHERE DO YOU WANT TO GO?

Keep your analysis of markets that you want to pursue to one page and break it into four manageable parts (use a, b, c, and d below). The purpose of this exercise is to establish a broad scope for your research-market analysis but not so broad that you overwhelm yourself. Try to begin with the end in mind: where do you want to go and how will you know that you have arrived?

A. Select the top three most penetrable overseas markets that appear to have the best potential for your product or service offering. You can conduct market research online; meet in person with an international trade expert (see the SBA's "US Export Assistance Centers": `http://www.sba.gov/content/us-export-assistance-centers`); or test your product or service by exhibiting at a local trade show. Trade shows give you access to potential customers from all over the world without you having to analyze a thing. For example, if you sell hardware tools and exhibit at a hardware show and find that you get a lot of interest from attendees from a particular foreign market, such as Australia, you would know there must be a market there, because why else would these attendees be asking for information? From there, you can address those inquiries, learn as you grow, and conduct further research.

B. Analyze the market factors and conditions in each of the selected countries. Delve into each country further by reviewing cultural attributes, geographical characteristics, political stability, demographic characteristics, market size, and growth rates. The goal here is to conduct a sound assessment of a foreign market. What might the barriers be? What makes it a good market to enter? How will the local culture influence the sales of your product or service offering? Such in-depth market research information is necessary to make sound marketing decisions, and it must be done with each new market entry.

C. Determine the pros/cons to conducting business in each market. Look at potential language barriers, legal restrictions, logistical challenges, and payment problems that might get in the way of doing business in a particular market. Include all relevant variables in your assessment. Do an analysis of your company's own strengths and weaknesses in a selected market. Will your product or service offering be at the low-, middle-, or high-end pricing level? Is there a similar product or service offering currently available in the selected market? If so, who is making it? Where are they based? Can you compete? Why would you? How would you? The more pros you have for entering a new market, the better your chance for success. If you can draw on the perspective of a native (better yet, an actual prospective customer) of the country where you are keenly interested in doing business, do so. Nothing beats an on-the-ground assessment.

D. Select one market to get started! Now you are ready to interpret your findings in light of the stated objective: where do you want to go and how will you know that you have arrived? (This gets back to the back-of-the-napkin plan.) At this juncture, you should have enough data and experience (from going to trade shows, for example) to decide which market is best for you to begin in. Hold off on the other two countries and don't start doing business with them until after you have a proven success with the first overseas market. If the first selected market doesn't work right away, say after six months or a year, move on to market No. 2, and so on. Don't muddy the waters. You don't want to do too many things at once, because it's not cost effective and you will end up not doing any of them right.

The Laurel Export Business Plan

The following plan—I'll call it the Laurel export business plan (LEBP)—has worked well for many of my clients. You can focus on each section heading and then build out accordingly based on the questions I pose and comments I make. What many clients experience as they develop an export plan is the eureka moment: "I can do this!" The trick is to craft a plan that suits you and can absorb economic shifts and shocks along the way, yet still allow for you to achieve successful results. And it can't hurt for you to use both the traditional business export and Laurel export plans to develop yours.

■ **Tip** It is important to identify where the cash will come from to support your export operation and, at the same time, access available export financing options. Conduct a complete audit of your cash situation so you are not surprised later on to learn you need more money than anticipated to reach a new overseas market. Face weak links and potential problems before you are knee deep in a fantastic opportunity.

---

1. *Introduction*: Compose an explanation of why you should export and what your company wants to gain from exporting. Your answers will serve as your guiding light and foundation for your entire export business plan.

2. *Executive Summary:* Specify your long-term financial and nonfinancial vision for developing an export business. Think three, five, and ten years out. This part shows clarity of purpose, direction, and intent. It is an understanding of the company's identity and a short, concise picture of the company in the future. Think of it as an entire business plan in miniature.

3. *Strategic Leadership*: State your leadership ability clearly. Do you have what it takes to drive results for your export operation? (Refer to Chapter 1 for a refresher on the global mindset.) The business owner must have the ability to set direction, make decisions, and provide long-term planning.

4. *Company Description*: Explain what do you do and why are you good at it.

5. *Target Export Market*: Identify your customers in _____ (pick a target export market). Think about what would motivate them to pay for your product or service and if they will be able to afford to pay for your product or service. Drill down to a more precise view of your target audience.

■ **Caution** Are you crystal clear on who your customers are and why they use your product or service? If not, go back and do a major rethink!

---

6. *The Competitive Analysis (Market and Customer):* Distinguish how your product or service is unique, and explain briefly why people in a selected export market would buy it. Do you know the strengths, weaknesses, strategies, opportunities, threats, and financial status of your top five competitors? Spell them out.

7. *Marketing and Sales Plan:* Detail and clarify how you will effectively and efficiently reach the people with whom you want to connect through your business (direct, indirect, intermediary sales, trade shows, e-commerce, mobile, etc.). Ensure existing local customers are not neglected! Are your products and services suitable for an export market, or will major modifications be required? This part should be strategic in that it outlines specific action steps to achieve future sales goals.

■ **Tip** Utilizing market and customer intelligence determines a company's ability to perceive and adapt to changes in the global marketplace. The more homework you do, the better the chance you have to achieve desired results.

---

8. *Operations Plan:* Figure out how you will support the business strategies through internal operations, systems, and organizational structures. Describe key factors to use in your business in finding solutions and in meeting the wants and needs of customers, suppliers, employees, and other key influencers. If exporting a product, how will it get made? Do you have the capacity to produce and deliver?

9. *Information Technology Plan:* State how you will leverage technology to take advantage of the export marketplace. Will your export business be heavily dependent on technology? List your business's strengths and weaknesses in the information technology area. IT will support your company's business processes and decision making and, at the same time, give it an extreme competitive advantage in the global marketplace. Plan the parts of your business you will use technology for (order taking, mailing lists, social media, finances, e-commerce sales) and how you will use it.

10. *Logistics Plan:* Outline how you will get your product or service to the chosen export market.

11. *Management Structure:* Identify the people and experts in your business who will implement your plan and exceed your goals. Compile a management team section that describes who is on your team and what expertise each person brings to the table. This section should also include an analysis of strengths and weaknesses in the team and what might be missing.

12. *Future Development:* Tailor your business plan by defining future milestones that are in line with your desired goals. Describe your vision for your business, including your exit strategy.

13. *Financials (Export Budget):* Analyze your available resources (human, material, and financial) to determine how you will support export initiatives. Get together three types of financial statements: a cash-flow statement, an income statement (also referred to as a profit/loss statement), and a balance sheet. Set budget targets and develop pricing strategies. Confront your company's finances squarely. You want your export business to be sustainable over the long term.

14. *Strategy Implementation:* How will you follow up, review, and measure results? Have you set a timeline? Home in on a detailed action plan for execution.

15. *Risk and Reward Analysis:* Provide an assessment of every-thing that can go wrong and right, and a discussion of how your export dream team (EDT—discussed in Chapter 3) can respond.

■ **Tip** Have your EDT review your plan so that they can seek external sources of advice, test it, and hold you accountable and responsible for implementing it.

As your export business grows, you will become more aware of external fac-tors that influence your business plan, which will allow you to develop ways to manage and adapt to them. These external factors might include: import regu-lations, exchange rates, availability of finance, new or unexpected competition, and disruptive technology and logistics, to name just a few. As mentioned earlier, anticipating change and adapting to it requires strategic leadership as well as Backup Plans B, C, and D.

Summary: Leaving You with Fun and Export Adventure on Your Mind

You should express and experience the passion you have for exporting in the crafting of your export business plan. If that enthusiasm is not there, recon-sider what you are attempting to do. It might not be the right time. Individuals e-mail me on a weekly basis saying, "Here's what I want to do in the export market…" Then they ask me: "Will it work?" My response: "I don't know. It depends on you." (Reread Chapter 1!) This brings us back to the goal of this chapter: creating an export business plan that meets your needs, allows room for improvement, and serves the life of your business.

Now that you know what is involved, craft your own export business plan and use it as an indispensable tool for building your export business—and don't forget to maximize profits! Look at it regularly, revise it when necessary, and pay attention to the reality of the market. It will sharpen what you are doing and why you are doing it, and help you define and achieve professional and personal goals.

Prepping For Exports

Corporate, Legal, Financial, Logistical, and Technological Considerations

> *It's stuff that is transmitted digitally, and also smaller firms packing up goods and selling them abroad. If there's going to be growth over the next decade, it's going to be in that.*
>
> —Gary Hufbauer, senior trade expert at the Peterson Institute for International Economics (2016)[1]

Now that you've set up your business plan, it's time to delve a little deeper into assembling your export company. The next step is tackling the essential details of a sound legal, fiscal, logistical, and tech operation. You'll be faced with obstacles ranging from expanding your enterprise, protecting your company, and choosing a product name and other intellectual property to opening a bank account in your home country, sourcing financing, dealing with special tax situations and setting up online platforms. Not all of these issues will come into play immediately, but you will do well to familiarize yourself with the framework in which you will be operating right from the start.

---

[1]"Recovery From Trade Swoon May Be Slow," The Wall Street Journal, last modified January 24, 2016, www.wsj.com/articles/recovery-from-trade-swoon-may-be-slow-1453229703

© Laurel J. Delaney 2016

L. J. Delaney, *Exporting*, DOI 10.1007/978-1-4842-2193-8_3

Although the expansion of any business tests us on numerous fronts—from hiring the right people to covering fixed expenses and revenue genera-tion—expanding internationally through exports performed primarily via the Internet challenges us in a whole new way that could potentially interrupt the viability of a business. When reengineering your business from local to export-ready, you must take into consideration bullet-proofing processes, additional laws governing intellectual property, hiring and firing, contracts, and marketing and financial management, as well as settling international disputes and steer-ing Internet-related activities.

Prepping for export success boils down to careful planning (refer back to Chapter 2 on crafting a business plan), being proactive in seizing opportunities, and holding transparent discussions with trusted advisors on where you are headed to ensure every move you make is done with confidence and leads to greater growth and prosperity for your business.

Note I am not an attorney, banker, logistics expert, accountant, or technology whiz. The information in this chapter is based on experience and extensive research and should not be construed as an official plan on how something is done. Before proceeding with an action plan, consult with a specialist, just as I would.

Line Up Your Export Dream Team

One of the first things you should do before officially setting up your export business, or if you are an established enterprise and haven't done so already, is to find yourself a good lawyer, a knowledgeable accountant, a savvy banker, a logistics expert, and a tech whiz, each of whom should specialize in interna-tional transactions. They are your export dream team (EDT). You may feel that you can't afford to pay for these professional services, but in truth, you can't afford to do without them.

The Fab Five: Lawyer, Accountant, Banker, Logistics Expert, Technology Master

A qualified lawyer, well versed in international trade and the Internet, will pro-tect you from those who would take advantage of your inexperience in the global marketplace, or from unknowingly perpetrating violations yourself! Any one of the big national law firms, such as Baker & McKenzie; Skadden, Arps, Slate, Meagher & Flom; Foley & Lardner; and Latham & Watkins, will be able to advise you on intellectual property issues, the Internet, mergers, acquisitions, and reorganization. The larger the law firm, the greater the overhead and the higher the hourly rates you will be expected to pay. Be aware of this starting out, and if you can't afford it, go elsewhere to make your investment more cost effective.

■ **Tip**   To find a good lawyer, ask around and research, research, research! You'd be surprised at how asking a simple question to your accountant, banker, or successful small business peer group—"Who do you use for legal representation?"—can help you home in on following up and getting a solution. Strike a balance of likeability, specialized experience, and affordability that meets your needs. You can also find additional assistance from FindLaw.com and Lawyers.com, and by consulting with a bar association, such as the American Bar Association.

A good accountant specializing in international taxation will help maximize your cash flow, limit your eventual worldwide tax exposure, and protect you from double or triple taxation scenarios. The big accounting firms such as EY and Deloitte have offices in nearly every country in the world and can offer you a broad variety of global services, but they'll cost you. A work-around is to find a smaller accounting firm that specializes in international accounting and taxation matters for small businesses.

A well-versed banker can help you finance an export sale, guide you in structuring competitive payment terms (including online options), or even advise you on risk factors before you transact business in a new overseas market. The large banks such as J.P. Morgan Chase, Bank of America, BMO Harris Bank, PNC, Citi, and MB Financial have unmistakable identities and usually have small business banking divisions, branch offices worldwide, and international banking divisions.

■ **Tip**   Even though the thought of using the *big* bank guys might intimidate you, once you are a customer—and that could be on the basis of depositing $250 to open an account—you are entitled to free consultations with the international banking experts to help you better manage your export business.

A seasoned logistics expert (refer to Chapter 18 on transport options) will help you minimize the risk, complexity, and cost of transporting products worldwide. Big logistic firms such as UPS, DHL, and FedEx transport products worldwide, prepare specialized export documentation, build shortcuts in standard export shipping processes, monitor shipments, and offer guidance on regulatory issues involving compliance and trade. Freight forwarders often serve the same purpose, but they do so on a more niche basis (by industry or geographic location). They too organize shipments to get goods from one point to a final destination. Any of these types of organizations are effective and serve as an architect for transport. Before you send your product off on a boat, get comfortable with one point person to help you navigate the choppy waters and ask her about her resources and whether she has people on the ground in the country where you desire to conduct business. And, as always, have a backup logistic provider in case something goes awry in a country where business is booming.

A technology master will positively impact your business's future, create value where you didn't know it exists (investing in e-commerce, for example), challenge your assumptions about why things are the way they are, and identify where you should disrupt in your industry to gain a new foothold or global customer base. Let's face it. Technology is the most important agent of change in the modern world right now, allowing us to make a profound upward shift in global markets. We use technology to shape our world, yet we think little about the choices we are making for our business. Few expected, for example, Apple to upend the music industry with its iPod and iTunes. A technology master is a forward thinker and reimagines what's possible through Internet technology. He or she creates new digital offerings and transforms existing ones to deliver profitable new exporting revenue streams. The investment in a technology master—one with imagination—is a necessary addition to the export dream team and can set you on a path towards a stronger global competitive advantage.

Start Small

For your legal, accounting, banking, and technology needs, I suggest you start out with a smaller firm that can attend to you on a more personal and economical basis. Many founders of small boutique law firms, for example, acquire their experience working for a number of years at a big international law firm prior to starting their own business. To keep overhead costs and client fees low for small business owners, they focus on the highly specialized practice areas that are in high demand, such as Internet law, global trademarks, and international franchising. The benefit of contracting a smaller firm to satisfy your needs is threefold: prior big corporate experience at a fraction of the cost, affordable rate structure, and specific expertise.

When a question is too tough for your small firm to handle, let them outsource it to a larger firm with a more developed international presence. That way, you can stick to your budget and your small firm will stay in charge of your legal or accounting operations. But when you reach the point where you're outsourcing more than in-sourcing, it's time to make the jump to one of the big guns! The large international firms employ individuals of many nationalities who are well versed in the laws, professional ethics, and regulations of the countries in which they operate and well positioned to serve your interests. Expect to require more extensive and sophisticated information about the countries you export to as your business grows, particularly if you do a lot of business in any one of them.

Your lawyer, accountant, banker, logistics expert, and tech master are vital to the success of your export strategy. They should be considered the charter members of your EDT. As you will see, they often work in concert to keep your new enterprise in the most advantageous legal, financial, logistical and tech position possible.

Tip I strongly encourage you to set up an export advisory board (EAB) at your company to help you tackle tough challenges, cut costs, expand rapidly, get key introductions that lead to significant business down the road, and solve problems before they fester. Unlike a board of directors, an EAB does not have authority over your business. It is purely there to offer advice that you can take or leave. If you don't know how to establish an EAB, conduct an Internet search with the keywords "How to create an advisory board." Then, follow the suggestions pertaining to exporting. The advisory board will serve in addition to your EDT because it will not charge you for consultations nor does it have any vested interest in your business other than to help you grow. Your attorney on the EDT should draw up a simple contract. What's in it for people that will encourage them to join your EAB? Perhaps a small annual fee (stipend), gift card, occasional dinner, or excellent connections to high-level people with common interests will motivate them to jump on board!

Corporate Considerations

At this juncture, I am assuming you have already chosen a form of organization. If so, skip ahead to the next section. If not, there are five basic forms of organization in which you can set up your export enterprise: the sole proprietorship, the partnership, the C corporation, subchapter S corporation, and Limited Liability Company (LLC). Each form has specific advantages and liabilities. To decide which form will serve you best, ask yourself the following questions:

1. How big do I aspire for the company to become?

2. Am I willing to risk my personal assets for the business?

3. Am I willing to grow my business alone?

4. Am I in this for the long haul?

5. Are tax savings important to me?

6. Will I sell my business someday?

Once you know your priorities and your preferred operating style, you'll be well placed to discuss your options with your attorney and accountant to determine which organizational form will best support your business objectives. If you plan to develop a Web site or blog (refer to Chapter 5), select a domain name that is preferably the same as your business name. As the U.S. Small Business Administration (SBA) says, the steps to starting an online business are the same as starting any business. However, doing business online, as we will find out in Chapter 8, comes with additional legal and financial considerations, particularly in the areas of privacy, security, copyright, and taxation.

Here's a quick course on the five forms of organizational structures and their advantages and drawbacks.

■ **Tip** Sole proprietorships, S corporations, limited liability companies (LLCs), and partnerships are also known as pass-through businesses because the profits of these firms are passed directly through the business to the owners and are taxed on the owners' individual income tax returns.[i]

The Sole Proprietorship

If you plan on keeping things small, prefer not to share ownership with anyone else, and will be dealing in relatively simple, safe products or services, then a sole proprietorship might be the way to go. Sole proprietorships are the most common form of business. This type of organization is usually taxed on income, property, and payroll. A typical sole proprietorship might be a neighborhood flower shop, hotdog stand, or shoe repair shop.

Since it is the sole proprietor's job to run the business, he is taxed for that job by way of his personal income. Since the sole proprietorship is smaller in size than a corporation, you can expect taxes to be lower. A sole proprietorship can easily be kept confidential and dissolved whenever desired, provided all of its financial obligations have been satisfied.

The downside of this unincorporated business entity is the unlimited liability you incur. Since your sole proprietorship is not legally recognized as an independent entity apart from your personal assets, it can be used to satisfy creditors if you run into serious financial difficulties in the course of your business operations. This is perhaps the best reason for limiting the size of your company, too. A sole proprietorship can hire any number of employees, but if an employee were to get hurt on the job and later sue you, there is the possibility that you would lose a significant part of your personal assets. Think through what kind of commitment you're willing to make before you choose this form of organization.

If you choose a sole proprietorship, the best way to protect yourself is to obtain adequate insurance coverage for the unexpected, such as auto or property and liability coverage. Consult with an insurance expert for additional guidance.

A sole proprietorship is usually established simply by filling out a standard business form purchased from an office supply store. Include the name of the business (you can generally skip this step if you are operating the business under your own name), have it notarized, and send the form with a check (cashier's or certified) or money order to your county clerk's office. Call the office or your local chamber of commerce to verify that this procedure agrees with its requirements and to find out the amount of the fee. While it's not mandatory to trademark your business name, my colleague Barbara Weltman, a tax and business attorney and author of such books as *J.K. Lasser's Small Business Taxes 2016,* says it is prudent to gain legal protection so that no one else can use it. This process holds true for other corporate structures as well.[ii]

Tip Independent contractors, better known as consultants, self-employed, and freelancers, are individuals who provide services to others outside of an employment situation, and receive payment only for the work being done. The providing of these services becomes a business. Be sure to consult with your accountant and attorney to determine what type of contract you need in place for independent contractor status since your agreement will serve as a legal document between you and your client and will also dictate whether you can claim any business deductions.

The Partnership

If you prefer to share liability, responsibility, and profits with another person, then a partnership is for you. As with a sole proprietorship, you will be taxed on an individual basis for your share of the partnership, but you will need to expend legal fees to have your articles of partnership (see below) drawn up. Many people prefer the security a partnership can offer, but keep in mind that a partnership is very much like a marriage: Everything that happens to one of you, good or bad, impacts both of you. Also, if your business partner walks out on you, it's as bad as or worse than being dumped by your spouse, especially if the terms of dissolution have not been negotiated at the outset of your relationship—your whole livelihood could be wiped out!

A partnership is established much like a sole proprietorship—by filling out a form establishing your business name, notarizing it, and sending it in with the appropriate fee to the county clerk or your Secretary of State—but you will also need to draw up a written contract known as the articles of partnership. This contract states the salaries of the partners, how profits and losses are to be distributed, and what happens if one of the partners wants out.

The most common type of partnership is the limited partnership, in which one or more partners gives up participation in management decisions in exchange for limited liability and at least one partner has unlimited liability. Less common is the general or regular partnership, in which all the partners have unlimited liability. In a general partnership, the personal assets of the partners can be seized when the firm defaults on its obligations. A typical partnership might be a real estate venture, law firm, or consultancy practice.

The advantages of a partnership are obvious: a larger financial base, perhaps a better credit standing (based on one or all of the partners' wealth), more brainpower, and more labor to go around. The disadvantages are that, particularly in a general partnership, you are subject to unlimited liability—not just your own, as in a sole proprietorship, but quite possibly your partner's as well if she cannot fulfill financial obligations. You also may be faced with the involuntary dissolution of the partnership if your partner dies or becomes disabled or insolvent, and difficulty in transferring or selling your interest. Your recourse in any of these eventualities will be determined by what your contract states. These disadvantages may cause you to prefer to limit the size and scope of your business operation. Discuss this option thoroughly with your accountant and attorney so you are sure you're not incurring more risks than advantages.

The C Corporation

If you want to separate your business affairs from your personal life, limit your liability, and be able to get out of the business easily if need be and you aspire to grow a huge business, then you'll want to set yourself up as a corporation. Examples of typical corporations include Apple, Intuit, Facebook, and Google. You will be taxed on a corporate basis (according to the corporation's net profit) *and* on a personal income basis (according to your salary and other compensation). Corporate and personal income are taxed at different rates and treated differently. This is a complex topic and lies outside the scope of this discussion.

It generally costs more to set up a corporation than a sole proprietorship or partnership because of the more involved procedure of incorporation and issuance of shares of stock. You can establish your own entity fairly quickly online by purchasing a how-to kit (go to LegalZoom.com, where incorporations start as low as $149 plus the state filing fee, or Nolo.com). I don't recommend this route. It is better to let your attorney handle it. If you do, ask first how much it is going to cost you to incorporate. Boutique law firms sometimes offer small businesses a flat rate for incorporating a firm, usually anywhere between $700 and $1,000 plus state filing fees and other related expenses, but you need to be careful about how that rate can rise based on where you are located, special documentation, and shareholder work.

The major parties in a corporation are the stockholders, the board of directors, and the officers. In the beginning, one person can hold all of these offices and then pass them along as the business expands. You can lay the foundation yourself and then build as big a company as you want upon it. That's the beauty of incorporating.

Some of the most interesting advantages of the corporation, though, arise from the fact that it's both a human and impersonal entity. If you set it up by yourself, you're all there is to it—but you can walk away from it and, legally, it's still a continuing enterprise. It is a self-contained entity governed by its own laws. It can sue or be sued and it can receive customer complaints or charitable donations. Best of all, no matter what happens with the business, your personal assets will be protected insofar as you will not lose more than your investment in the business thus far—provided, of course, that you did not incorporate to cover up your own misconduct (such as intentionally selling a harmful product)!

The corporation is a powerful form of business and is usually set up with the intention to operate on a much grander scale, to diversify, and to maximize profits. You can raise capital for your corporation by selling shares of stock or by pledging the stock as collateral to a person or entity that is willing to loan you money. However, the biggest drawback to a corporation is its greater tax liability. It is generally taxed higher than sole proprietorships and partnerships, which, as mentioned earlier, are taxed only on the owners' personal income. In addition, a corporation must pay assorted franchise and state taxes. Plus, there's a whole array of corporate documents that must be kept: articles of incorporation, bylaws, minutes of shareholders' meetings, and records of issuance of stock certificates, for example. Furthermore, your shareholders are the ultimate owners of your company, and that ownership gives them the right to receive dividends, review corporate books and records, and hold or sell their stock. The larger you become, the more likely you are to consider the best way to maximize everyone's investment.

The Subchapter S Corporation

The subchapter S corporation is like a regular corporation in all but a few respects. In addition to a regular corporation's advantages of limited liability and protection of personal assets, this type of corporation enables you to avoid the double taxation normally associated with the distribution of corporate earnings to the firm's shareholders. This is possible because corporate income is taxed as the direct income of the shareholders whether it is distributed to them or not. It costs about the same to set up as a regular corporation. A typical subchapter S corporation might be a small private-label food company or export consulting business.

A subchapter S corporation has a limited number of shareholders, which may be individuals, estates, or trusts, but not other corporations. The obvious disadvantage here is that the limitation on the number of shareholders accordingly limits your ability to raise capital. If that poses a problem, a corporation may qualify as a C corporation, which does not have any limit on the number of shareholders, foreign or domestic. There are also special circumstances in which a subchapter S corporation is taxed more stringently than a regular corporation.

Limited Liability Company

An LLC is a blended type of legal structure that provides the limited liability features of a corporation and the tax efficiencies and operational flexibility of a partnership. It is often more flexible than a corporation, and it is well suited for companies with a single owner.

The owners of an LLC are referred to as members. Depending on the state, the members can consist of a single individual (one owner) or two or more individuals, corporations, or other LLCs. There are no restrictions on hiring employees but you must make sure you are compliant with key federal and state regulations.

To the federal government, an LLC is not considered a separate tax entity, so the business itself is not taxed as a separate business entity. Instead, all federal income taxes are "passed through" to the LLC's members and are paid through their personal income tax. While the federal government does not tax the income of an LLC, some states do, so check with your state's income tax agency.

There are some rules and regulations for choosing the name of a business for an LLC. Be sure to inquire with your secretary of state and consult with your attorney to ensure you comply. It is also prudent at the outset to develop an operating agreement outlining all details pertaining to the members' roles, rights, responsibilities, allocation of profits and losses, percentage of interests, special provisions, and so forth.

The advantages of an LLC are limited liability, fewer formalities, fewer record-keeping responsibilities, and fewer restrictions on profit sharing. Members are allowed to contribute different levels of financial and intellectual capital.

The disadvantage of an LLC is limited life, meaning if a member leaves the company, the business dissolves and the members must fulfill all remaining legal and business obligations to close the business. However, there is a work-around: to prolong the life of the business you can elect to include a provision in the operating agreement, as mentioned earlier, that indicates what happens if someone leaves the business. In some instances, it may be more difficult to raise financial capital for an LLC, so be sure to inquire with your attorney should you be interested in eventually doing an IPO, for instance.

An LLC can elect to be taxed as a sole proprietor, partnership, S corporation, or C corporation, providing greater flexibility. Further, there is always the possibility of requesting S-corp status for your LLC. You don't have to hire a lawyer to set up an LLC, but it's a good idea to have one to advise you on the pros and cons of the legal structure and to read over documentation, including your operating agreement, to make sure your interests are protected over the short and long term.

Check with your experts to see which type of entity will give you the most advantages.

Tip To access legal document forms and additional assistance without paying top dollar, visit LegalZoom.com (which allows you to speak to an attorney) and Nolo.com (which allows you to find an attorney in your area). The sites can be used alone or together with your attorney.

Legal Considerations

Protecting a trademark in the United States—whether it's your own company name, a product, or your supplier's product name—is a very complicated procedure best handled by a very competent attorney.

Protect Your Intellectual Property

When you are considering adopting a trademark, you or your attorney must perform a search to see if anyone is using that mark on a similar product or service. If you discover that someone has beaten you to it, you then have to find out when the other party began using the mark and if it is currently in use. If it is not, you have to determine if you can have the rights to it. You may find out that another firm is using the same mark but on a totally different product or service. For example, you might have trademarked the name Violetta for your line of purple bird feeders, only to find out that another firm has trademarked Violetta for their line of candles. In either case, you'll need legal advice as to your right to use the mark.

Most trademark and patent registrations are made through the commissioner of patents and trademarks in Washington, DC. After you have taken the necessary steps to protect your design or mark on the domestic front, you will have to start the process all over again in the country in which you are about to do business. Particularly if you are registering marks in multiple countries, it will be crucial to have an attorney who specializes in international intellectual property management. Always discuss fees in advance because this process can be very costly.

Patents and copyrights need the same attention. You never want to see anyone, anywhere in the world, take what you have created and put their name on it.

Legal Protection in the Online Environment

International domain name protection requires specific skills, experience, and legal governance, so it is best to find a lawyer who is familiar with Internet Corporation for Assigned Names and Numbers (ICANN). With the help of your tech expert, you should manage domain names as carefully as any other intellectual property within the firm.

Domain Name Protection: Part of Your IP Protection

You can secure a domain name on your own in minutes (try NetworkSolutions.com or GoDaddy.com), but the international use and scope of it may not apply worldwide. Furthermore, registering a domain name does not necessarily create rights to a trademark. For example, let's say I register laurelpizzas.com as a domain name in the United States. After securing the domain name, I cannot assume that I also own it as a trademark and that the same domain is available in China (laurelpizzas.com.cn). That is where an international lawyer becomes invaluable for protection, maintenance, and enforcement of the domain name as it relates to your international business brand.

Well before deploying an attorney, a good exercise to go through when you start up or launch a new product or service via an established enterprise is to ask yourself two questions: How important is the domain name or mark to me? Is it a part of my core business? You'll be surprised at how those two questions force you to home in on what really matters to you on legal protection (think along the lines of Twitter, Facebook, and Apple—they all started out small). If something is central to your organization's growth, you'd better protect it, patrol it, and keep it updated and scalable.

A lot of online legal-environment protection will come into play based on where you are headed with your business and how the Internet factors into your overall business strategy (all the more reason to deep dive into Chapter 2). Budget accordingly and allocate resources to get the appropriate legal protection you need. To avoid the "I never saw it coming" experience, discuss with your international attorney at great length about protecting your products and services, including online properties and Internet strategy, and all aspects of trade dress— which refers to the *look and feel* of a product—before exporting them overseas. You'll be glad you did.

Tip *The Guide to Law Online*, published by the Library of Congress, is a portal of Internet sources of interest to legal researchers. It also serves as an annotated compendium of Internet links. It's an excellent source for laypeople who don't have a legal background but want to develop an understanding of a country's legal system before entering into it and contacting their own attorney for advice. Every direct source listed in the guide was successfully vetted before being added to the list. To access it, head to `http://www.loc.gov/law/help/guide/nations.php`.

Other Legal Considerations: Labor Laws, Contracts, and Agreements

Labor laws can vary overseas. You may find your export business growing by leaps and bounds, which is the goal of this book—to allow you to hire more American employees to support your exports and possibly even hire more people where your customers are: overseas. If that is the case, consult with your attorney and accountant to determine the best course of action based on the labor laws of the country you are contemplating entering and to fully understand the legal and tax consequences.

I would be remiss if I didn't highlight the fact that it is nearly impossible to run an export business without creating some form of contract or agreement covering the following: exclusive distribution and supplier agreements (refer to Chapter 11), a joint venture, partnership, or licensing agreement, to name just a few. Think of it this way: every time you are about to enter into a relationship overseas that requires a long-term commitment and your company is on the line (i.e., could help you grow or take you down), consult with an attorney to compose one of these items to protect your interests.

Opening Your Bank Account

Opening up your company's first business bank account is as simple as 1-2-3—just don't forget to mention that you plan to export. If you are an established enterprise, skip this section unless you want to be sure you've got everything covered. You'll want to set up and maintain your account in an organized fashion, because once you begin to receive money and pay bills, your statements will become the foundation of your accounting system.

Find a bank in your home country that has an international department (preferably one with extensive expertise on letters of credit), has a strong worldwide presence, and can provide strong personal service, because you will need it. Further, look for a bank that offers twenty-four-hour online access from your desk or from a secured Internet line anywhere in the world and a mobile-payment feature with industry-leading security, including proven state-of-the-art encryption software. Online banking allows you to quickly view account balances, monitor transactions, identify current foreign exchange rates, and send and receive payments—all specifically designed to increase efficiency and cost effectiveness at your business. Before you visit your bank, call or e-mail the branch and ask what you need to bring with you to open an account. Here are some of the documents you will typically be required to bring: personal identification, such as a driver's license or passport; business papers showing your type of organization, such as a copy of your business license, certificate, articles of incorporation, and corporate seal or corporate resolution; and a copy of one of your most recent utility bills (to verify your mailing address). It is also helpful to have several hundred dollars or so for the initial deposit, so that you can get your account activated right away.

Be sure you have good rapport with your banking officer. He will play a very important position on your EDT!

Banking in and with different countries can be a challenge. Choosing an international bank that is networked to branch offices worldwide and has relationships with other banks in the countries you intend to do business spares you having to open an overseas account and allows you to transact business in the currency of your choice. Further, choosing an international bank with a relationship to a bank in Japan will also allow you to save money by hedging extreme Yen-US dollar fluctuations. There will be also be times when you are unsure as to what currency you should pay in or be paid in (see Chapter 20). Other times, you might make a payment to an independent contractor as discussed earlier in one country via PayPal or Square and not know if you should withhold taxes. In some circumstances, the issue of withholding taxes may be reduced or eliminated altogether by a tax treaty between two countries. How will you know? That's where your team of export specialists, in this case your international banker, is ever so vital in keeping you informed and handling all that comes before you on a case-by-case basis.

■ **Tip**   I have known clients who have grown their exports to a point of necessitating the use of three different banks: one for domestic (local) support, one for a global reach and one for specific country assistance.

Effective Financial Planning Right from the Start

Whether you are operating as a sole proprietorship, a partnership, a corporation, a subchapter S corporation, or an LLC, you'll need to monitor your profits and operating expenses and to plan for the payment of taxes. You don't want to wait until you get to the end of your calendar year to find out where you stand in terms of profit and loss. It's best to prepare monthly financials—income statements, balance sheets, and cash flow statements—as you go. If you haven't made a sale yet, you are probably asking yourself at this point why you need to keep these detailed financial records. It's simple: Even though you may have minimal sales, or none at all, in the first few months, you are still spending money. You have expenses! And sooner or later, every business needs working capital in order to grow.

Another situation that requires monitoring expenses would be one in which, after running your company for a few months, you decide to go to a bank for a loan to help grow your business. Before the bank decides if you're a good credit prospect, it needs to see some details on your company's financial history—namely, your year-to-date sales, expenses, profit-and-loss statement, sales projections, and cash flow analysis (see Chapter 2). A financial statement, preferably prepared by your CPA or a reputable accounting organization, not only helps you to control costs but also tells you at a glance if you are making money or losing it and where adjustments need to be made. Monthly statements are best for maintaining adequate financial records. If you discipline yourself to set up and maintain these financial records right from the start, it will be a snap to produce historical data on your business for anyone who might request it.

Your financials will also serve as a basis for you and your accountant to make the determinations I will go on to discuss, each of which will affect your tax liability and, accordingly, the profitability of your worldwide business.

Maximizing Tax Benefits for Your Multinational Business

Once you've got an organization set up and an accounting system that makes sense for the way you want to run your business, you'll discover that your global growth will affect your financial planning. Depending on your form of organization, overseas business will present you with a whole new set of accounting and tax issues. Yet the name of the game will remain the same: minimize taxes, maximize profits.

At some point, ambitious as they may now seem if you're new to the export scene, scenarios like the following will become your reality:

- You generate income through a salaried employee who resides in the country in which you do business.

- You generate income from an export intermediary who conducts business in a foreign country.

- You generate income from exports worldwide.

- You generate income through the writing of an export-success article for a highly acclaimed blog in China.

- You generate income through your e-commerce site from individuals the world over.

- You generate income through a service export you are providing to a company in Bangladesh.

- You generate income from mobile payments made through PayPal, Google Wallet, and Square.

You are probably beginning to see how an accountant with international expertise becomes indispensable. You wouldn't want inappropriate accounting either to diminish the income you derive from any opportunities like these or to cause you to run afoul of tax laws. Don't think for a minute that you can apply domestic tax rules to international transactions. For each case, you and your accountant must ask the following questions: How are these business arrangements treated from a tax standpoint? Are you required to pay any domestic taxes? Are you required to pay any taxes on profits earned in a foreign country? Are you required to pay taxes online and, if so, where and to whom? If you need to transfer assets to a foreign entity, how do you do it? Will your exports involve any intercompany pricing rules or complex foreign currency provisions? Are you better off, from a profit or cash-flow standpoint, seizing a particular opportunity or passing it up? And, a very important question to ask you accountant, when you are involved in large cross-border transactions, how do you avoid double taxation? In the United States, for example, as a boost to businesses operating overseas, the government offers a reduction on national taxes based on the taxes you pay abroad, which is referred to as the US Foreign Tax Credit. Use the list as a discussion point with your international accountant. It will serve you well as you explore virgin overseas territories.

More Ways to Guard Your Bottom Line

Be aware of the several other traps (and opportunities) awaiting exporters that follow.

Trade and Customs Duties

Planning and managing customs duties plays an important role in pricing your export product so that it is profitable. First, pay attention to how your product is classified (see Chapter 19 to find out how to determine your product classification), because that classification will affect what duties are imposed and thus make or break your chances of exporting it at a profit. Be sure to get your classification in writing from transportation and logistics experts and then check with them later on to see if there is ever a time when you can reduce or defer duties or even have your products cross borders duty-free.

US customs duties vary widely based on where a product is primarily made, the valuation of the goods, and the destination country. The duties raise revenue for the federal government and protect domestic producers. There are three different types of duties: ad valorem, specific, and compound.

- *Ad valorem duties* are assessed as a percentage of the value of the goods, in the form of either a transaction value or what you would pay in the country of origin. Always try to keep your invoice value at a net sales price. Don't write up your invoice with commissions or transportation factored into your selling price or you may end up paying a much higher duty!

- *Specific duties* are assessed on a fixed-basis per-unit price, such as ten cents per kilogram or forty cents per item, regardless of the transaction cost.

- *Compound* or *mixed duties* combine the bases of ad valorem and specific duties. For example, a shipment might be assessed at 5 percent of the transaction plus ten cents per unit. This works well on very high-priced items.

Keep in mind that certain countries offer privileges on some imports. Before you export, check with US customs, your local department of commerce, or a US Export Assistance Center to find out the duties for your product and if your product is eligible for any breaks.

You should also inquire with your tax accountant about foreign trade zones (FTZs) and how they might help you reduce or eliminate customs duties. An FTZ is a domestic US site that is considered to be outside the country's customs territory and is available for use as if it were in a foreign country. A US company can accelerate the process of duty drawbacks or tax rebates in one of these zones or even have a product imported, assembled on site, and re-exported without any duties, taxes, or local ad valorem taxes being charged. In addition, there are duty drawbacks, which allow you to recover duties paid to US customs on exported merchandise, but you must perform feasibility studies to determine how this procedure might apply to and benefit your business.

For example, if a product is manufactured in the United States out of imported raw materials and then exported back out of the country, the imported materials used might be eligible for a duty drawback, less 1 percent to cover customs costs. The passages of US Free Trade Agreements enacted in more than twenty countries (e.g., the North American Free Trade Agreement [NAFTA]; the Dominican Republic-Central America-United States Free Trade Agreement

[CAFTA-DR]; and the Trans-Pacific Partnership [TPP, in negotiation; refer to Chapter 2]) along with bilateral free trade agreements (e.g., Singapore, Australia, Jordan, Israel) have brought about many favorable developments in the area of customs duties as well. Your accountant should keep you posted.

Foreign Sales Corporation

Whether you are a small, privately held, or multinational US company, setting up a foreign sales corporation (FSC; an offspring of the domestic international sales corporation [DISC]), can offer you an attractive tax incentive—exemption from a certain percentage of tax on net profits from export transactions. You need to be doing a substantial amount of exporting to make this worthwhile. Most international accountants can help you here.

For a business to establish an FSC, it must have no more than twenty-five shareholders, must maintain an office outside the United States that issues invoices and keeps financial-activity summaries, and must include at least one non-US resident on its board of directors. An FSC is usually set up for a multinational US enterprise that is in a regular tax position with no excess foreign tax credits and that is exporting products for which 50 percent or more of the manufacturing process is carried out inside the country. Profits generated or dividends issued by the FSC that go back to the company's US business are generally tax free. Check with the World Trade Organization Web site (http://www.wto. org) to ensure that FSCs are still in effect at the time that you read this and not merely of historical interest. For example, there has been much discussion on The Extraterritorial Income Exclusion Act. "The new legislation repeals the FSC rules and develops a new category of income that is excluded from gross income, absent an election to the contrary, and that does not require, but still permits, the use of a foreign corporation."[iii] Verify with an international accountant whether this new legislation can apply to your business.

Interest-Charge Domestic International Sales Corporation

An interest-charge domestic international sales corporation (IC-DISC) can increase your cash flow, provide a reduced taxable base at the export level, and even in certain instances provide a lower effective tax rate. To qualify for an IC-DISC, you must form a corporation (such as an S corp or a closely held C corp) that exports and produces or manufactures US export property (e.g., fabricated metal products and electrical machinery equipment) inside the country. It must consist of a minimum of 50 percent US content, which is sold primarily outside the country. IC-DISCs are "paper" entities and can defer commission payments of up to $10 million, a limitation that was intended to restrict IC-DISC activity to smaller businesses. According to Joseph Englert, president and founder of Export Assist, the IC-DISC acts as a commission agent on the export sales of the parent company. The commission income of the IC-DISC is calculated based on the combined taxable income and expenses related to the export sales of the US exporter and the IC-DISC.[iv] Consult with an international accountant to determine whether you should look into an IC-DISC for your business.

Summary

From the time you start out to the time you reach the mature stages of your export company, and from simple incorporation to mergers, acquisitions, and reorganizations, your EDT of international legal, accounting, banking, logistic, and tech experts can add value and help create and maximize profit opportunities for you and allow you to succeed in the dynamic worldwide marketplace. Our discussion here is only an introduction to the legal, financial, logistical, and tech issues that will affect your export business, a starting point for your long-term planning and a demonstration of the absolute urgency of getting the very best advice. Do not be bashful about consulting with your experts! As your business expands, the issues that impact it will become more complex and sophisticated. The more questions you ask, the more you will build your own expertise—and become a valuable export player in your own right.

Now that you have seen how to line up professional advisory support and build a solid management foundation from which to grow, let's turn to some practical concerns a little closer to the home front—by discussing how to put together the human side of your export enterprise.

Notes

i. Tax Foundation, "An Overview of Pass-through Businesses in the United States," last modified January 31, 2016, http://taxfoundation.org/article/overview-pass-through-businesses-united-states.

ii. Barbara Weltman, "How to Start a Sole Proprietorship," Inc. Web site, last modified October 12, 2010, http://www.inc.com/guides/2010/10/how-to-start-a-sole-proprietorship.html.

iii. Neal Block, Baker & McKenzie, Chicago, Peter Connors, Orrick, Herrington & Sutcliffe LLP, New York, "The Extraterritorial Income Exclusion Regime Increases Scope of Export Incentives," modified January 31, 2016, https://www.orrick.com/Events-and-Publications/Documents/5030.pdf.

iv. Joseph Englert, "Interest Charge Domestic International Sales Corporation," AICPA Store, last modified October 27, 2011, http://www.kluwerlawonline.com/abstract.php?id=351470.

The Human Side of an Export Enterprise

Create an Environment Where People Will Flourish

> *If you have the wrong people on [your] bus, nothing else matters. You may be headed in the right direction, but you still won't achieve greatness. Great vision with mediocre people still produces mediocre results.*

—Jim Collins, business consultant, best-selling author and lecturer (2001)[i]

Jim Collins has it right. No matter what brilliant idea or well-organized plan you have in place for exporting, the basic and most important side of your enterprise is still the human side. It starts with getting the right people on your export bus. Whether you hire employees with full benefits and perks or independent contractors, you want excellent people around you who are as passionate about your company's prospects as you are and who can

© Laurel J. Delaney 2016
L. J. Delaney, *Exporting*, DOI 10.1007/978-1-4842-2193-8_4

do something you can't do that will help transform your export business. Complementary values help, but accumulating talent with qualities unlike your own fortifies achieving a vision faster. Although the vision is yours, the talent will be ones with the skill set to get things done.

At the start of running a business, it's about you, your people, and your company's capabilities. In "Twelve Tactics for Creating Powerful Global Leadership Connections," I talk about how people are the engine of our success and every human contact is a chance for practicing great, enduring leadership—taking your organization from mediocrity to superiority.[ii] Yet, you'd be surprised at how long you can go without too much being accomplished—with all talk and no action. But as you expand internationally, you will discover that success becomes less about talk and more about execution. Executing anything requires highly motivated people. Luckily for you, due to technology, hiring globally to get the work done isn't difficult and allows you to broaden your pool of exceptional candidates.

In Chapter 1, I provided a shortlist of twelve personal characteristics that I find work in the export marketplace. These are based on my own hands-on experiences and the observations of others who have achieved success in crossing boundaries in the business world. Some of those characteristics are: the ability to adapt, to sustain a high level of cultural and emotional intelligence, and to get things done with people from diverse backgrounds. If you skipped Chapter 1, go back and read it. That's where I highlight the fundamentals of what you need as a leader to bring out the best in others. It starts with developing a global mindset. Next, it's about finding and developing your people.

■ **Tip**   To fully allow people to realize their personal goals—and thereby contribute to the goals of your organization—you must provide them clear objectives, rewards, and the freedom to use creativity and imagination.

So, how do you find great people to, as Jim would say, get on your export bus? How can you make sure they remain happy and motivated? We'll find out here. I will help you to create a functional team that thinks globally yet communicates locally with cultural sensitivity, to find the best places to outsource work, and to develop a plan to work effectively with others and nurture talent.

Creating a Functional Team

The first big characteristic to look for in people destined to do international work is their ability to be comfortable and confident in their own skin, along with a heightened sensitivity to others. After that, focus on integrity: can you trust them? Assessing a person's integrity requires frequent dealings over time. You can't rush that. There are, however, other qualities you should seek from job candidates that are easier to ascertain in a limited time, including:

- An awareness of a new breed of communication (both online and offline) that exhibits cultural sensitivity

- Persistence (competitive drive)

- Initiative

- An interest in international matters

- Bi- or multilingual language capabilities

- Cultural empathy

- Good writing and speaking abilities

- Some international experience—and not just a vacation to Disneyland in France

Last, the individual must be sensitive to the human behavior of all races, cultures, and ethnicities. They must have emotional intelligence beyond reproach. Meaning, the individual must care. If you find part or most of these characteristics in a person, hire her.

Caution   The best education in the world will not always produce the ideal hire. Initiative and international experience matter more.

Spotting a Good Global Hire

A typical hiring scenario might unfold like this: Six people diverse in ethnicity and from different parts of the world are situated in a conference room. I invite a potential hire, Steve, into the room for a preliminary interview. Steve is wearing casual clothes with sandals and no socks and immediately starts talking to everyone. He even manages to slip in a joke about his lousy plane flight. He plops down on his chair, gulps his water, and says, "I am sure you want to know how I am qualified for the job." And from there, he jumps into talking about everything he has done during the past five years without taking a breath or ever noticing if anyone in the room was paying the least bit of attention to what he is saying. He fumbles for his business cards and then tosses one out on the table to each person and asks, "Any questions?" Later, you notice that his application had numerous unanswered questions, signaling his lack of attention to detail.

We don't need to concern ourselves with whether Steve is qualified for the job. Even if he has terrific skills in certain areas, he won't cut it on manners and cultural sensitivity.

See how easy it is to spot immediately when someone falls short on manners and cultural sensitivity and etiquette?

You can see how this same scenario could play out on a Skype video call with a trade partner or client. Steve would sign in late, wearing a T-shirt and jeans, and, after fifteen minutes, abruptly leave for a moment to get a soft drink while the client wonders what just happened.

Would you want to have someone like Steve handling a critical part of your export business, like prospecting for new overseas customers? You need someone with an obsessive attention to details coupled with hypersensitivity to those around them. That's what helps fuel an incredible export business.

Contrast Steve with Bob, the second candidate. Bob is invited the next day to a similar meeting. He responds politely when introduced to each person but does not say too much until called upon. You like that; you know that being a good listener only helps navigate complex issues in the global marketplace. Bob shares his experience as it relates to the job at hand but only after being asked. That conveys his discipline and decisiveness.

Another thing you notice: Out of respect and politeness, Bob sits down last to ensure each person has a seat at the table even without knowing whether there are enough seats in the room. People attending the interview witness that he is sensitive to others, even when it could put him in an uncomfortable position (left him standing up, for instance, due to the lack of chairs). Also, he doesn't prompt the exchange of business cards. He pays attention to how business cards are presented to him—with two hands and the card in English with a person's credentials facing up—similar to Japanese-business-card etiquette and that of many other cultures as well. He responds exactly the same way and waits for others to step over to him to exchange cards—and responds in kind. Exhibiting confidence, Bob asks if he can get water for everyone during a break. Only after serving another person water does he sip his. Also impressive—he wore a navy suit with a crisp white business style shirt, with a classic stripe tie and black lace-up shined shoes. It's clear that he had found out well in advance of the interview what the appropriate attire would be.

As the interview progresses, Bob answers all questions posed to him in a seemingly honest and forthright manner. At one point, he even offers to get back to the team on a matter he is unsure about. The upshot: whatever is thrown Bob's way, he keeps his cool, acts his true self, and proves effortlessly through the course of conversations that he has vast experience in export trade.

Before hiring a person to be in charge of any responsibility within your firm, besides the usual questions you ask in doing your due diligence, also ask these questions:

- "What makes you a good fit for the role we need filled and how will your international experience support it?"

- "Tell me about a time where you creatively collaborated with a diverse team or customer base worldwide. What did you do and what was the outcome?"

- "When you're not working, what brings joy to your life?"

In response to the last question, someone might answer, "I get joy from finding export opportunities in our brave new world" or "I particularly enjoy traveling internationally." Surprisingly, they may also offer answers like "Watching thriller movies is my passion" or "Drinking Jack Daniel's is my main source of enjoyment."

It's usually pretty easy to assess who will fit in and who won't. Look for the person with the "Let's go take on the world" label planted on his forehead. Then grab 'em.

When it's time to negotiate a salary, research the rates (you can use www. payscale.com or www.salary.com) that you are willing to pay for a full-time employee so you don't make an offer that's too low (cheap) or too extravagant. Find out what real people are earning in the market relative to the job you need done and vary your offer up or down by 10 percent. After settling on a reasonable figure, stick to it and nurture the relationship from there. Help your employees get everything they deserve and it will come back to you a hundred times over in the growth and success of your export business.

Hiring is one of the biggest challenges for business owners and particularly for exporters. Accept that you will never get it right all of the time. The stories in this section were included simply to help you see how a certain kind of person will help further your export goals while many other candidates will keep you from them.

My advice: Take it slow. Resist the temptation to fill a position quickly. Check references thoroughly. You can mitigate your risks by getting a second opinion on a candidate (internally or externally), and developing recruitment strategies that avoid costly hiring mistakes.

Caution If someone you hire cannot do the job, eliminate them. If they are incompetent, eliminate them. If they are inaccessible, eliminate them. If they are rude, eliminate them. The longer you wait to let someone go, the longer the organization and others suffer. There's a saying: "Hire slow and fire fast!"

Developing a World-Class Team

Now that you've seen a couple of examples of how to assess whether some-one has what you think it takes to succeed on your export bus, let's take a look at what roles need to be filled as you grow your export business.

Success in exporting is directly related to a companywide commitment. That commitment is the responsibility of you alone if you are a sole proprietor, or in the case of a larger enterprise, of the executive committee as well as the heads of finance, operations, sales and marketing, legal, logistics, research, tech-nology, and culture departments. Assuming you manage an organization that is already in place, you need to be sure each of these people is on the export bus and ready and willing to make the journey with you and happy about it. If they are not, you must get the wrong people off the bus and reassign new people to their seats.

Once you recognize the human resources available to you and what it takes to export a product or service, you'll need to prepare a list of what is required from each of the functional areas of your company. Then it's up to you to develop your world-class team, which will work in concert. Keep in mind that many if not most of these positions can be outsourced until you are ready to bring them in-house; I'll say more about this later in the chapter. The team might look like this:

- *International Finance or Accounting Manager:* This person oversees international money matters (preparation of financial statements, determining the best method of pay-ment, and handling the payroll, for example) and reports to chief finance officer (CFO).

- *Business Development Manager:* This role is responsible for prospecting new markets and new customers.

- *Export Operations Manager:* This employee provides assis-tance to key-operations personnel on business issues linked to export business; tracks compliance measures and the use of export licenses; works closely with the international logistics manager, international legal counsel, and manufacturing manager. Note: As you expand, often-times a manager of export control compliance is needed to manage day-to-day operations of a regulatory compli-ance program.

- *International Legal Counsel:* This person oversees all legal issues pertaining to exporting (in-country compliance, contracts, trademarks, disputes, patents, and licenses).

- *International Logistics or Supply Chain Manager:* This team member works closely with operations (manufacturing), marketing, and purchasing to create a seamless export transport, and handles all technical details of the export transportation, including choice of transport mode, documentation, and varying customs regulations. These can be one in the same depending on the size of the organization.

- *Marketing and Social Media Manager:* This employee creates social media platforms, joins and manages appropriate online community groups, and is responsible for marketing the company to the world via all social media channels. As the company enters more overseas markets, a PR manager might come on board to promote the company through a variety of media channels that foster the growth of exports.

- *Customer Service Manager:* This person makes sure customers are happy and satisfied and want to return. She also handles customer complaints and disputes.

- *HR Manager:* This position plans, directs, and coordinates human resource management activities (including but not limited to outsourcing, compensation and benefits policy, equal employment opportunity matters, etc.) to maximize human potential and productivity. In addition, the HR manager and her staff (again, dependent on the size of company), recruits, interviews, and selects applicants.

- *Internet Technology Manager:* This role oversees all Internet-related issues, including but not limited to the development and maintenance of online platforms, e-commerce sites, blogs, social media and cloud platforms, banner ad designs, apps, and e-mail accounts.

- *Web Designer:* The person in this position specializes in the design and development of user-centered Web sites, blogs, and platforms and manages search-engine optimization, opt-in newsletters, and globally friendly graphic designs.

- *Administrative or Office Manager:* This person makes life for everyone far more sane by paying attention to such details as office supplies; sample mailings; answering the phone; acknowledging employee anniversaries, awards, or promotions; ensuring the company kitchen is well stocked; and coordinating and setting up meetings and web-conferencing calls.

▓ **Note** Don't be put off by the presumable number of people it takes to export. A friend and colleague of mine, Barbara Roberts, once told me that you don't necessarily need a dozen people to pull off growing an international company successfully. Over a seven-year period, she grew a stock-photography business from a $7 million to a $45 million, world-renowned, and technologically state-of-the-art company—all with just a handful of people. You can do this too, provided you take it one market at a time, hire on an as-needed basis, and persevere.

As you expand, you might have to hire additional people as situations develop—for example, to support a growth market that takes off rapidly and unexpectedly in India, Brazil, or China. Or you may need someone to handle new customer inquiries coming in online from China—in Chinese. And that even begets more decisions to be made: can the person who speaks Chinese reside in China or does he need to be located in the United States? These are just a few of the issues and considerations you must address, and oftentimes you don't have the answers until you are well into it.

▓ **Caution** Don't assume the individuals who manage a function locally will have the time or the capabilities to manage that same function on the export front. Ask. And gauge as best you can their enthusiasm for the expanded job responsibilities.

In the start-up stage, my recommendation is to have someone from each department set aside one hour each day just to work on an international sales strategy. It doesn't matter if there are no sales pending; it is critical to arrange a structured amount of time for the purpose, which requires discipline, commitment, and an exchange of information. You should have meetings to give everyone the feelings of importance and team spirit that are critical for the growth and prosperity of the company.

People will also need to be trained. You must first communicate the company's vision, goals, and objectives. This can be as simple as sitting down with each individual to discuss them: What are we going after on this project? How fast do we expect to get there? How will we get it done? Who will work on the projects as they pop up? How will we get help if we don't know how to do something? How will we measure results?

You'll quickly realize that the desire to expand internationally takes a team effort and commitment, which will define and shape the export process. If you are a novice exporter, your employees and independent contractors will learn as you learn. The point is to get input as often as possible and insist that team members execute their portion of the plan. You also want to convey that you are in this endeavor together to learn, grow, and make it a success!

Best Places to Outsource Work

Technology and the Internet have made it ridiculously efficient to search out people to do the tasks you don't want to do yourself. How do you know when outsourcing is the solution? If you are seeking better-skilled workers than you currently have on your bus for less money, that's the time to outsource. Another added benefit: Outsourcing allows you to access process superiority and physical resources. But here are a couple of questions to answer to know for sure:

1. Is there a competitive advantage to doing the job in-house? If you are a web developer, you most certainly don't need to outsource IT, but perhaps HR or accounting is not your cup of tea and you are not at a point to hire a full-time person to oversee these areas.

2. Is the task at hand related to your core competency? If not, outsource it! Focus on what you are good at and let someone else do the rest.

3. Is the task at hand a one-off situation? You might have to manage an annual dinner conference with all your international distributors or put together an e-book on your company's ethics policy for distribution to suppliers and distributors, for instance. In either of those cases, outsourcing would work.

4. Would it be cheaper to have the task at hand be outsourced vs. performed internally?

5. Do you look forward to the idea of getting rid of a responsibility that can easily be done by a more experienced firm who does it all the time and at a much lower rate than you would pay internally? Payroll and HR are two examples to illustrate this point.

Jobs that are ripe for outsourcing are those of a writer, editor, and translator; of a web developer, programmer, designer, and drafter (engineer); of a call-center operator and medical professional; of administrative support and human resources (to handle hiring, firing, and payroll); of social media experts and business development experts; of export-trading intermediaries; of public relations, marketing, and computer professionals; and of consulting.

The best way to find the right people is to vet them in a way that drills down on their capabilities to determine if they are a good fit. But before you can do that, you must create job descriptions for each position you need to fill. Be specific. You are hiring someone to get something done. What is it? Spell it out. Use the description as a basis for filling out a job request and for comparing it against a job applicant's response. Here is a sample job description for an Export Manager at a consumer packaged goods (CPG) company called ABC Company. Note: This is for an Export Manager position, not an Export Operations Manager as referenced earlier.

EXPECTATIONS

- Manage business relationships across a diverse worldwide geography of distributors, sales agents, and key retailers.

- Develop the sales plan to grow existing ABC Company's export businesses and markets.

- Identify, prioritize, and implement business development plans in new, emerging markets for ABC Company's brands.

- Deliver the annual plan for key sales performance indicators, including profitable revenue, market share, and export trade as a percent of revenue.

- Collaborate with field sales agents, marketing teams, operations/supply chain, regulatory/legal, technology, and finance to create profitable, sustainable, brand-building programs across established and new customer bases.

- Manage all financials related to export customers including demand planning monthly forecasts, annual marketing and trade budgets and actuals, and post promotion analysis to identify return on investment (ROI) on key programs.

- Communication of all ABC Company's policies and procedures, pricing and trade programs, sales and marketing programs, and new products to field sales agents and distributors.

- Ensure compliance with related governmental export requirements. Maintain effective relationships with said entities. Keep senior leadership informed of key trends & opportunities within this field.

- Develop strong relationships with key ABC Company personnel including senior leadership, supply chain, customer service, marketing, manufacturing, finance, legal, and technology teams. Leverage relationships to grow smart and fast and push ABC Company to accelerate growth in current and new export markets near and long-term.

Desired Skills and Experience:

EDUCATION, EXPERIENCE, AND QUALIFICATIONS:

- Bachelor's degree required from an accredited college or university.

- Minimum of 8 to 10 years of experience in the consumer packaged goods (CPG) industry. Key account management, sales planning, and field sales experience is essential.

- Demonstrated expertise and results in directly managing export sales and logistics in CPG industry is required.

- Excellent leadership, communication, collaboration, organizational, and cross-cultural skills necessary to manage multiple responsibilities and ability to work cross-functionally in a dynamic environment.

- Proficiency required with Microsoft Office applications (i.e., Excel, Powerpoint and Word), Skype, and Citrix GoToWebinars, and working knowledge of syndicated resources (Nielsen/Information Resources/comScore).

- Full understanding of the export landscape (outside of the US and Canada), especially in emerging markets, and complete mastery of global market trends for a consumer product business, customer strategies, and competition.

- Ability to travel both domestically and internationally.

- Must be able to communicate effectively in English both written and oral. Second language beneficial.

The following sections offer a couple of places to look for good people to match the skill sets you need.

Freelancers and Independent Contractors: The New Gig Economy

To reach freelancers and independent contractors in what is considered the new gig economy, try the following resources. Be sure to inquire about fees; they are prone to change often. For example, credit card and other payment processing charges are typically in addition to a company's fee.

- *Guru*: http://www.guru.com. Guru is a highly populated job-hunting site with an easy-to-get-started process and a good payment system (it's simple and secure, for one). Guru is free to sign up for but you can upgrade to a paid membership, which gets you certain perks (Basic, Professional, Business, or Executive) and takes a project fee of anywhere from 5-12 percent of the freelancer's invoice amount, predicated on the scope of the project. Credit card and PayPal payment processing fees are in addition to Guru's charges. Guru has more than 1.5 million members worldwide.

- *Elance*: http://www.elance.com. Elance, now an Upwork Company, is free to join and set up an account and takes a standard project fee of 8.75 percent (the quote submitted by the freelancer includes your fee). When the work is completed, Elance deducts its commission and transfers the rest to the freelancer.

- *Virtual Assistants.com*: http://www.virtualassistants. com. Virtual Assistants.com is good for finding secretarial, customer service, data entry, writing, and tech support workers. You can post a job and negotiate a fair and reasonable rate based on your budget. For members who are VAs and wish to find a job, the subscription fee is $9.99 a month or $49.99 a year. Posting a VA job is free.

- *Zirtual*: http://zirtual.com. Zirtual connects busy professionals with virtual personal assistants to do everything from research to legal and accounting to staff management. Zirtual charges $398 per month for the Entrepreneur Plan, $698 per month for the Startup Plan, and $998 a month for the Small Business Plan. The fees vary based on the work performed and the number of hours of assistance you need each month. All plans include a dedicated U.S.-based college-educated VA; 9:00 a.m.-6:00 p.m. your time zone availability; and direct contact via phone, SMS and email.

- *Upwork*: http://www.upwork.com. In 2014, Elance merged with oDesk. In 2015, oDesk was relaunched as Upwork. Upwork is an online workplace for the world, connecting clients with freelance professionals from Chicago to Paris. The Upwork fee for freelancers is a sliding service fee (20%/10%/5%) and based on lifetime billings per client relationship.

- *TaskRabbit:* http://www.taskrabbit.com. TaskRabbit is an online and mobile marketplace where you can outsource everything from everyday errands (provided they are local) to skilled tasks. The pricing model is: TaskRabbit's fee is equal to your task price (which you set) plus a service fee, which is 30 percent, excluding any reimbursements made to the Tasker (they get 100% of any reimbursements). A minimum payment of one hour is required per task.

- *Freelancer:* http://www.freelancer.com. Freelancer is a large freelancing, outsourcing, and crowdsourcing marketplace for small businesses. You create milestones on your projects, and as the freelancer reaches the milestones, payment is released. The site's fees are complicated and are based on the type of project and membership plan you sign up for. Be sure to review the site thoroughly to uncover any hidden fees. It is a good place to go for one-off jobs or project-based work. You can post a project for free.

- *Fiverr:* http://www.fiverr.com. Fiverr is a marketplace for creative and professional services. Jobs can start as low as $5. Fees vary widely. Be sure to review.

Tip Another interesting global, on-demand, 24/7 online task marketplace worth checking out to see if it fits your job requirements is Amazon's Mechanical Turk (http://www.mturk.com/mturk/welcome), whose system is based on taking a job and separating it out for many different people to work on in pieces. The beauty of AMT is that the tasks are quick and very simple (you might write a product review or complete a multiple-choice survey, for example) and require only tiny payments. Try it out.

Top Job Search Web Sites

You can also tap into what I consider to be online talent pools where people worldwide get social by making professional connections. Job candidates are only a mouse click away. These are the sites to consider when you are hiring for a full-time position:

- *CareerBuilder:* http://www.careerbuilder.com. CareerBuilder is an all-around good egg—a large US-based online job site that has a presence in more than sixty markets worldwide. More than 24 million job seekers visit the site monthly and more than three hundred thousand employers work with CareerBuilder to find good people.

- *craigslist*: http://www.craigslist.org. Craigslist is a classified ad-placement service and forum. Postings are free, except in certain geographic or industry areas—be sure to check. The site works well for finding just about anything, including jobs, housing, goods, and services.

- *Dice*: http://www.dice.com. Dice, now DHI Group, Inc., is a career hub for techies and engineering professionals. The site also provides specialized websites for financial services, energy, healthcare, and security-clearance industries.

- *Experience*: http://www.experience.com. Experience, acquired by Symplicity in June 2014, is a good resource for tapping into the resource of young adults who desire to learn from the experience of others. The site works for finding people for internships.

Tip Instead of using Google, Yahoo, or Bing for a job search, try Juju.com. It's not a job board; rather, it is a job search engine that will make a job search much easier.

- *FlexJobs*: http://www.flexjobs.com. FlexJobs offers part-time, flex-time, and freelance jobs, with an emphasis on people looking to telecommute some, or all, of the time. Most jobs are US-based, with a handful going to people located in Canada, Europe, and Australia.

- *GetHired.com*: http://www.gethired.com. What's unique about GetHired.com is that once you have identified a list of applicants you want to interview, you can set aside time in your schedule and the site will invite the candidates on your behalf to meet with you in person, on the telephone, or via their embedded video-conferencing system to conduct a virtual interview.

- *Glassdoor*: http://www.glassdoor.com. Glassdoor is a free jobs and career community. What sets it apart from other job-placement sites is the vast array of information it offers on specific companies and specific jobs, from company reviews, to anonymous actual salaries, to sample interview questions. Visit the site for job descriptions (export manager or export compliance manager, for example) and to determine the going rate on salaries for positions you need to fill.

- *Indeed:* http://www.indeed.com. Indeed is fast, and that's the best part about it. It helps people get jobs and companies to advertise those jobs, so it's a good place to shop around. With more than 180 million unique visitors per month, Indeed is available in more than fifty countries and twenty-eight languages.

- *Internships.com:* http://www.internships.com. Internships. com, a Chegg service, is an internship marketplace for students, employers and higher education institutions. The site enables students, employers and educators to optimize internship opportunities.

- *LinkUp:* http://www.linkup.com. LinkUp, owned and operated by JobDig, does things differently. The site connects job seekers to jobs directly at employers' Web sites. That's the twist. Its international reach outside of the United States only goes so far as Canada and the United Kingdom as of this writing. The fees need to be checked.

- *ManpowerGroup:* http://www.manpowergroup.com. ManpowerGroup is a workforce-solution company operating in eighty countries and territories. Whether your needs are local or global, Manpower can help you find talent.

- *Monster.com:* http://www.monster.com. Monster is a global online employment resource for people seeking jobs and companies needing great people.

- *SimplyHired:* http://www.simplyhired.com. SimplyHired is an online marketplace serving 30 million people a month and thousands of companies across twenty-four countries. Its unique value proposition is this: it operates job-search engines in twenty-four countries and twelve languages, reaching job seekers on the web, social networks, mobile devices, e-mail, and other partner sites such as Mashable, Bloomberg Businessweek, and LinkedIn.

- *StartUpHire*: http://www.startuphire.com. StartUpHire is a job search engine that recruits talent for promising emerging growth companies. Its focus is on start-up companies because they are the most difficult to identify for job seekers. If you are in this boat, give the site a look.

- *The Ladders*: http://www.theladders.com. The Ladders focuses on career-driven professionals with salaries of $40K and up. Basic membership is free for job seekers previewing job titles only, with premium membership running $25 per month for access to everything on the job search site.

- *USAjobs*: http://www.usajobs.org. USAjobs is a not-for-profit public service organization that matches job candidates with employers. It's a free web-based job board enabling federal job seekers access to thousands of opportunities across hundreds of federal agencies and organizations.

- *Vault*: http://www.vault.com. Vault is a high-potential online job marketplace. The site is particularly good for insider information on what it's really like to work in a company, industry, or profession.

Schools and Universities

Many universities make it easy for US employers to hire students. Some schools even seek out companies that are more amenable to sponsoring overseas hires. Stanford's Graduate School of Business, for instance, has an international advisor to guide US employers on hiring international students (see http://www.gsb.stanford.edu/cmc/global). The school itself helps facilitate employment authorization. In certain circumstances, an immigration attorney might be required.

It can be very beneficial to hire a student from an overseas market where you are considering exporting to. International students are eager to learn, relish the notion of working with an American firm, and are on the local ground, reporting firsthand to you on what market conditions are like. So if you are about to export to China, for example, look for Chinese students studying in your country (knowing they will return home after they complete their studies) with a worldly mind, fluency in both Chinese and English, and an understanding of the Chinese culture.

Tip   There are many other places to find good people. Check with peer-to-peer organizations (i.e., the Entrepreneurs' Organization, Vistage, and the Women Presidents' Organization); associations (i.e., The International Trade Association of Greater Chicago, the Small Business Exporter's Association (SBEA), and the American Association of Exporters and Importers [AAEI]); universities (you can stay connected as an alum); and online community forums (banks, small businesses, and start-ups).

When to Hire; When to Outsource

How do you decide when to hire employees and when to hire contractors? Positions formerly reserved for in-house employees, such as those of a web developer, a designer, or a HR specialist, can often be done faster and more effectively with qualified remote contractors. If the following conditions don't apply, it might be good to use a contract worker to fill a position:

1. Do you need a person to do the work every day?

2. Do you have funding to support what needs to be done every day over a long period of time?

3. Are you willing to pay the benefits (paid vacation, sick time, training and healthcare, for example) that come with hiring a full-time employee? Payroll and social security taxes also represent a significant expense. Watch out for hidden costs that can impact a business in a negative way.

4. Do you need the person to be physically in the office to get the work done?

5. Do you need to control the work being done?

If you answered "no" to all of the above questions, hiring contractors is your short-term solution. One of the single biggest advantages for utilizing contract help is that your company is not responsible for paying benefits to the contractor. Second to that is the added flexibility of having to hire staff only when you need them. Third is that you are changing the rules of competition. Big caution: Never treat a contractor like an employee. Misclassification of an individual as an independent contractor may have a number of costly legal consequences. Consult with your HR manager and international attorney for guidance. You don't want to mess with the law.

▧ **Caution** Be sure to thoroughly review the key provisions in the Patient Protection and Affordable Care Act designed to ensure that Americans have access to quality, affordable health insurance. "Depending on whether you are self-employed, an employer with fewer than 25 employees, an employer with fewer than 50 employees, or an employer with 50 or more employees, different provisions of the Affordable Care Act may apply to you."[iii] Depending on the size of your organization, you may find out it is more advantageous to hire contractors vs. more employees. ObamaCare Small Business Facts can be helpful to review as well.[iv]

In hiring independent contractors, set expectations right at the beginning of the project. You don't want anyone wondering if the work they are performing is adequate or not. In addition to an initial e-mail contact, consider setting up a phone appointment to further discuss your needs. This is the best way to build trust and negotiate fair compensation. If the contractor is located in another country, consider using Skype (`http://www.skype.com`) or Google+ (`http://www.plus.google.com`) to keep the costs down while you communicate.

Check in periodically with the contractor to make sure the work gets done and that it meets your expectations and is performed on time and within budget. You might set up daily, weekly, or monthly check-in points to ensure things are on track. Global projects can be coordinated on the move with your digital device, with everything stored in one place through such trusted online repositories as: Google Drive (`http://www.drive.google.com`), DropBox (`http://www.dropbox.com`), SugarSync (`http://www.sugarsync.com`), Box (`http://www.box.com`), and OneDrive (`http://www.onedrive.live.com`).

The Hiring Plan

What's the purpose of a good hiring plan? It makes the hiring and training process much easier and less stressful for all concerned. First thing's first: decide on who will be responsible for hiring and then consider these issues:

1. What kind of people do you want to hire? Tie that in to your company's value, vision, and goals—the equivalent of company culture.

2. What can you afford?

3. What is your timeline?

4. Where will you find the candidates?

5. How will you vet, choose, and notify candidates?

6. How will you make the hiring of the person official (by contract, for example)?

7. How will you measure results?

8. Who will be responsible for getting employees on board, training, and professional development (this applies more to full-time employees)?

Be specific about the skills and expertise you need from people when you interview them, and fill out a profile of the work you want done when you hire someone. Your goal is to enhance personal growth and development for each and every person you bring on board and to make each new hire feel like a stakeholder in the business. That can be accomplished by giving new hires your time, treating them with respect and care, and making sure they are an integral part of the decision-making processes that affect their job. That's the best-kept secret to keeping employees and contractors motivated and happy and moving toward reaching unprecedented success with your export business.

Tip Delegate as much work as possible to others who can do it better than you. This will make your business life easier and your employees and independent contractors happy because you put trust and faith in their abilities. Just don't overburden them. If you stay in constant contact, you will learn more quickly about little bumps in the road, and together you can fix them as they arise. Give employees the tools and resources to get a job done and then get out of the way so they can do it.

Outsourcing HR: Focus on Your Core Competencies

Is your export company growing so fast that the notion of handling your own HR initiatives is overwhelming to you? You'll have to devote a large portion of your resources for the purpose of maintaining records, nurturing employees, improving employee performance, HR management (hiring and firing), administering employee benefits, training new staff, and so forth. Or will you? You could consider outsourcing the entire HR process to an independent firm. There are several online; you just need to conduct a search to find a firm that is a good match for your organization. The reason to outsource HR is to alleviate the burden associated with the administrative cost and enable you to focus on your core competencies.

I don't recommend this route for business owners who are just starting to export because it's good to have direct involvement in the nitty-gritty detail of hiring the right human capital for your business. This gets back to getting the right people on the export bus. If you are a $10 million-plus business and are currently generating a portion of your revenue from overseas exports and expanding rapidly, perhaps now might be a good time to consider outsourcing the global HR process to better enable you to think more strategically. Use your own best case study for hiring to gauge whether the outsourcer is a good fit for your needs and the best model for going forward.

Summary

While it takes a strong global leader and enthusiastic teamwork to achieve export success, true business victory cannot be obtained without an online social presence. After all, you want the world to find you, because without customers, there is no business. We're on the export bus, so now we need to position ourselves for online success. Are you with me? If so, then turn the page!

Notes

i. "Good to Great," Jim Collins, Jim Collins Web site, published in *Fast Company*, last modified October 2001, http://www.jimcollins.com/article_topics/articles/good-to-great.html.

ii. "Twelve Tactics for Creating Powerful Global Leadership Connections," ImportExport.About.com, accessed February 7, 2016, http://importexport.about.com/od/GlobalResourceCenter/fl/Twelve-Tactics-for-Creating-Powerful-Global-Leadership-Connections.htm.

iii. ."Health Care: Key Provisions of the Affordable Care Act," SBA.gov, accessed October 23, 2013, http://www.sba.gov/healthcare.

iv. "ObamaCare Small Business Facts, accessed February 7, 2016, http://obamacarefacts.com/obamacare-small-business/.

Creating and Using Online Marketing Platforms

Online Fundamentals

Building a Web Site and Blog

Branding demands commitment; commitment to continual re-invention; striking chords with people to stir their emotions; and commitment to imagination. It is easy to be cynical about such things, much harder to be successful.

—Sir Richard Branson, CEO of Virgin

If you are good at it, people are going to read it.

—Seth Godin, best-selling author

The best damn marketing tool by an order of magnitude I've ever had.

—Tom Peters, the Red Bull of management thinkers[i]

Many people believe that the best way to find customers is to look for them. That's a mistake. In the digital age, customers from around the world should find *you*. And they can, provided you create a sustainable positive online presence. The secret to billions of customers finding you is to build a world stage comprising of a Web site and a blog. These tools define who you are as a brand and shape what is yet to come for your export business. I will discuss how to

© Laurel J. Delaney 2016
L. J. Delaney, *Exporting*, DOI 10.1007/978-1-4842-2193-8_5

market your business later on, in Chapter 10, but understand this: not having a Web site and a companion blog is like keeping your door shuttered to the world. Think I'm wrong? Take a look.

In Pursuit of Global Power: Snatching and Grabbing Curious Online Customers

Due to the explosive growth of the Internet, a Web site alone is not sufficient to promote a business, at least not if you want the entire planet to find you. That planet includes more than 7 billion potential customers—and 3.4 billion of them are online.[ii] Who wouldn't want to sell to more than 3.4 billion people or even a tiny fraction of that? Whether you are a first-timer or an experienced pro, leveraging the web is a must to become globally competitive. To achieve a powerful web presence, you must use a combination of social tools such as blogs, Facebook, LinkedIn, Twitter, and Instagram, as well as cultivate a brand presence on mobile apps and other online databases. Already, your online presence can live on your wrist like a smartwatch and quite possibly replace everything (brick-and-mortar stores, paper resumes, photo albums, and in-person meetings, to name a few), so you'd better aim to get it right the first time around.

Plan a Web Site

While a Web site is but a part of your efforts online, it is still the most important one for e-commerce. First and foremost, your Web site should be inviting and reader friendly. When developing your Web site with exporting in mind, here are fifteen pointers that should make the build-out process a lot easier:

1. *Keep content current, accurate, and relevant.* There is nothing worse than visiting a site and seeing out-of-date content or links that don't work. It's a surefire way to lose a visitor. And not just for the moment but perhaps forever. First impressions count. Don't make the information you present overly complicated or go wild with the graphics.

2. *Go mobile right out of the gate.* According to network experts at Ericsson, smartphones are only going to get more popular over the next five years. "Its estimates show an enormous jump from the 2.6 billion smartphone users recorded in 2014 to 6.1 billion by 2020."[iii] That is the equivalent of 90 percent of the world population.[iv] Make sure your Web site is configured and optimized for mobile use. If you find that most people visit your site from mobile devices, consider developing an app for your business to better serve customers. Messaging apps, for example, have become the center of online activity—don't ignore. I will go into more detail on this in Chapter 9.

3. *Express yourself but don't give your life story on your Web site.* Your message should be concise—clear, consistent, and with an on-brand conversational voice—and interesting enough for visitors to stay with you and eventually take action. Add enough value so everyone can see that something vital would be missing if you left. Keep the content focused on your business and related to the action you'd like your visitors to take.

4. *Maintain your Web site so it not only looks beautiful but works beautifully, too.* Speed matters. Customers seek fast, simple solutions to their challenges. Put yourself in their shoes. When you visit your Web site, are you impressed? Compelled to take action? Motivated to return? If not, go back to the drawing board and improve it until it turns even *you* on. All Web sites should contain a good layout, information about your company, a company logo, targeted image placement, and other strategies that boost your brand. You want your site to be attractive *and* useful. If need be, hire a professional designer to take your site to the next level.

Tip   Web hosts provide the tools you need to easily build your own Web site, or, if you want something unique and special, you can hire a web designer to create a professional site.

---

5. *Review sites you like, bookmark them, and try to incorporate the best elements of each on your site.* I've done this many times for ideas on my own company Web site. I see something I like at another Web site and send the link to my designer to see if she can do something similar but distinct enough that it does not look like we are stealing or copying information from the other company. If you sell jewelry, what are the most popular jewelry sites and why? Use these ideas as a basis or model for developing your own Web site.

6. *Make sure that every page of your Web site has a unique keyword message.* To drive traffic to your site, you must achieve high rankings in search engines. To do that, you must establish keywords that match your firm's capabilities. Short primer: Keywords are what we type in when we search for products, services, and answers to our questions on search engines like Google, Bing, or Yahoo. Matching the words or phrases with the keywords we embed in our sites is called search engine optimization (SEO). It is a means of getting people to click onto your Web site. Search engines like Google have an algorithm that decides which Web sites come up first in a search result. In order to be listed first in a Google search, you need to have the right keywords where Google's algorithm can find them. For example, if you were writing about the late Steve Jobs and how he helped change the world with the invention of the iPhone, it would be good to identify the post with the tag words *Steve Jobs, Apple, change the world,* and *iPhone.* When people search, "Steve Jobs, change the world," for example, using those keywords would greatly increase the chances of your post being listed first in a Google search. SEO is not easy. If done right, however, you have a global web green light blinking 24/7 for your business. If no SEO work is performed, you are operating in the dark—the equivalent of being offline—and this will explain why customers can't find you. Consider hiring an expert to ensure you get the most visibility out of your Web site. Once visitors arrive, your goal is to make it easy for them to find what they are looking for and purchase it easily.

SEO CASE STUDY

GlobeTrade, a company I own and manage, is a leading management-consulting and marketing-solutions company dedicated to helping entrepreneurs and small businesses go global. Our keywords for SEO purposes are: *global small business, going global, Laurel Delaney, small businesses go global, entrepreneurs go global,* and *global trade.* These keywords and phrases all relate to the content present on the respective Web pages. Every time an individual conducts a search using any of these keyword phrases, they find us. As a result, customers are rolling in, our page-rank position has skyrocketed to at or near the top of people's search results, and our business keeps growing.

Identify the products or services you sell. Now select keywords that are in alignment.

7. *Create a culturally customized Web site when you know that what you have will appeal to people in a certain country or region.* In other words, build a Web site that is adapted to local cultures. Nitish Singh and Arun Pereira, co-authors of The Culturally Customized Web Site, say, "Companies targeting global customers have little choice but to culturally customize their websites if they are to successfully draw customers, build trust and loyalty and make themselves invulnerable to competitive marketing actions."[v] If you are interested in selling primarily in the United States with the hope that you export to customers in Morocco, then study up on the country to find out about its culture—what colors do Moroccans like, what symbols do they prefer, which Web sites are the most popular and why? David Ciccarelli, founder and CEO of Voices.com, says: "You can start locally and eventually build a marketplace that serves the needs of your users globally."[vi]

8. *Make it easy for visitors to buy.* When choosing a company to host your Web site, it is important to consider all available standard and supplemental features that will make your visitor's entire experience enjoyable. If you plan to sell products and services online, select a web host that can make that happen, especially the payment part, in an effortless way and without costing you an arm and a leg. (Later in the chapter, you'll find links to potential providers).

9. *Create a newsletter and send it out regularly.* Target customers who are not only loyal in attitude and action but also profitable. This can be done during the building of the Web site by adding a newsletter sign-up area. As visitors stop in, they can sign up for the newsletter, or alternately, provided you get permission up front (after a presentation, you might ask people you meet if they are interested in receiving your newsletter), you can add people yourself. They will include prospective customers, existing customers, suppliers, employees, colleagues, and independent contractors. When you send out the newsletter, you might ask people on your list for help on the development of a new product or ask them their opinion on what key topics should be covered in a presentation you will give at an industry conference. For example, I recently sent out a newsletter to recipients with a call to action for suggestions on speakers for a Global Small Business Forum my company hosts annually. Within ten minutes, I received five different emails from subscribers recommending quality speakers for our program. Listen carefully to the answers. The end result will appeal to customers because they were involved in the process.

10. *Care about your customer in a way that is evident on your site!* Best-selling author Gary Vaynerchuk says it best: "In the end, no matter what obstacles a company faces in the *Thank You Economy,* the solution will always be the same. Competitors are bigger? Outcare them. They're cheaper? Outcare them. They've got celebrity status and you don't? Outcare them."[vii] Thank your customers for stopping by. Don't try to control an exchange; rather, facilitate the exchange by showing you are putting them in charge. Create pop-up windows that offer live support if a customer is on a page for a set amount of time without asking a question or purchasing something. Make your offerings clear and totally transparent so customers can easily compare your offer with those of competitors. Ask customers to fill out a short survey that helps you better serve them. The objective is to pinpoint specific or preferred customers who might require tailor-made products or services. The message you are sending is this: We care and you are important to us.

Tip Many web-hosting companies offer packages that include ongoing submissions of keywords to top search engines including Google, Yahoo!, and Bing. Be sure to check when you sign up for a package. These packages can be worthwhile because they help customers find you when they conduct a search, provided you properly conveyed your firm's capabilities in your keywords. Another helpful SEO keyword research tool that matches ads to relevant web pages is Google's Contextual Targeting Tool (`https://www.google.com/ads/displaynetwork/manage-your-ads/targeting-tools.html`).

11. *Cater to a global audience.* Ninety-five percent of the world's population, and **80** percent of its purchasing power, are outside the United States.[viii] It's hard to have a two-way communication if visitors don't understand you. Plan accordingly, but don't fret. Take it one step at a time so you don't get overwhelmed. Start with writing your Web site in one language and then expand based on interest and demand for your product and services. (I will cover web translation considerations in Chapter 15.) My colleague John Yunker, a leading expert on web and content globalization, says as more of the world's population goes online, web teams will need to build sites that catch as many of these users as possible. While a global gateway alone won't make a Web site global, it's an important step in making that site more globally usable. He goes on to say, "Successful global gateways cast wide nets so that most people find where they want to go."[ix] Casting a wide net means embracing languages. The more languages you offer, the greater your chance at capturing a bigger piece of the world pie.

Tip Don't panic at the thought of having to translate your Web site into several different languages right at the start. You don't have to. You can take it one language at a time and base it purely on customer interest. But beware: Yunker says, "Most websites were built under the assumption that mobile users have access to 4G networks, which many do not. Most of the world still relies on 3G (or slower) mobile networks."[x]

12. *Think about country-code-specific domains at launch, but don't get caught up on them to the degree that you don't move forward locally.* A country code serves as a local Web site in a specific country. McDonald's, for example, has `http://www.mcdonalds.com` for the United States and `http://www.mcdonaldsindia.com/` for India. If you live in India and visit the main site, you can still access the India site by clicking on "McDonald's Web sites" then going to "International Web sites" and scrolling down to India, which takes you directly to the Indian site. IBM has `http://www.ibm.com` for the United States, and from there you can go to `http://www.ibm.com/planet-wide/cn/` for China. Apple has http://www.apple.com in the United States, and from there you can go to `http://www.Apple.com/br/` for Brazil. No two companies are alike on how they approach securing country domain names. The only rule of thumb is to try to plot out where you think you want to go. Consult with your export dream team, especially your lawyer, to see what it will take to get you there and to determine if it requires you secure domain names with country codes.

13. *Make the "Contact Us" area on your Web site so big that it hits visitors on the head like a hammer.* If it's two-way communication you're interested in having, allow visitors to reach out to you on numerous fronts—from sending an e-mail, to speaking with an actual human being, to filling out a form, to providing a Skype ID—and make sure responsiveness from your company is front and center. The Contact Us space on your Web site is an area sanctioned as the ultimate visitor conversation starter, so make it easy for them to communicate with you! Include your company's address and phone number, too. The telephone still matters, even in a soon-to-come web 4.0 world.

14. *Breed visitor participation.* Give visitors a reason to engage in a conversation with you and other like-minded folks. Entice them to share their thoughts, concerns, opinions, and experiences. To accomplish this, set up an online community forum, Facebook social plug-in (such as the Like button), or Twitter feed within your Web site or as an independent resource that is linked to your site. This will foster an even greater exchange of communications. You're building a relationship that you hope will last a lifetime.

15. *Prepare for growth.* In addition to dedicated hosting of a site, many hosting companies offer hosting for e-mail and apps, blog incorporation, mobile-friendly adaptation, and cloud computing, where you sign up for free and only pay for what you use. Cloud computing allows you to collaborate, edit, and share files, applications, and business processes over the Internet whenever or wherever you need to. It's helpful to use for peak-season fluctuations. For example, if 75 percent of your business is generated in the fourth quarter of a year, you need to prepare in advance for the heavy traffic time to ensure that visitor transactions run seamlessly. Cloud computing allows you to ramp up and pay for the service as you go and then remove it when you don't need it, which is ideal for small businesses that don't have the deep pockets to invest in sophisticated Internet technology to grow their companies.

By using your web presence to facilitate two-way communication with anyone in the world, you can build relationships with your customers, enhance your company image, fine-tune your products or services, and pinpoint your preferred profitable and loyal customers. Best of all, it doesn't have to cost a lot of money.

Reserving a Domain Name and Building a Web Site

Here are places to get started in securing a domain name and creating a Web site. Some platforms allow you to build your own site. Network Solutions is one of those platforms, and it has simple tools that are already built into the site. If you want a highly professional and sophisticated look, I suggest you hire a good web designer, especially one who knows the importance of how colors and symbols translate to a cross-cultural audience. As stated in point number one, first impressions count. Excluding Google+, all hosting platforms are scalable and have e-commerce capabilities. Here are the most popular along with some new entrants:

- *Network Solutions*: http://www.networksolutions.com

- *GoDaddy*: http://www.godaddy.com

- *Register.com*: http://www.register.com

- *Verio*: http://www.verio.com

- *Intuit*: http://www.intuit.com/website-building-software/

- *Rackspace*: http://www.rackspace.com

- *Google+ Page:* `http://www.google.com/services/`
- *Weebly Website Builder:* `http://www.weebly.com`
- *Wix:* `http://www.wix.com`
- *Jimdo:* `http://www.jimdo.com`

Blog Exuberance: Brand Yourself Everywhere

Anyone can create a blog. Building a successful blog, on the other hand, requires hard work. Yet it's worth every ounce of effort because, when used correctly, this low or no-cost communication vehicle can do many powerful things including: positioning you as an expert or thought leader in your industry; helping you market your products or services globally; allowing you to test your ideas to see if they have wings; bringing your web presence to life; helping potential clients worldwide find you; and helping you engage in a conversation with your customers.

A blog, short for "web log," is an instant online publishing tool that allows anyone to add fresh content to a web page, share knowledge, and reflect their personality. A few of the top blogs are: *Seth Godin* (`http://sethgodin.typepad.com`), *Anita Campbell's Small Business Trends* (`http://www.smallbiztrends.com`), *Chris Brogan* (`http://www.chrisbrogan.com/`), *Mark Cuban* (`http://blogmaverick.com/`), and *Duct Tape Marketing*, by John Jantsch (`http://www.ducttapemarketing.com/blog/`).

The sole purpose of a blog is to share information. You use it to let your audience know you are good at something, but at the same time they learn and grow on topics ranging from making jewelry to global trade consulting or flower arrangements. You rarely use a blog to sell a product directly, unless the product is directly derived from your own work, as in the case of a release of a new book, a webinar, a podcast or tweet chat you participated in, or a presentation that your readers might like to attend.

Fact   If you have five thousand followers on one platform and two thousand on another, and all of those followers pass along your posts to their constituent base, and they, in turn, pass it along to theirs, you have the potential to reach more than a million people in a very short period of time.

You can create a blog from scratch and independent of your Web site or build it as part of your site if your web host has that capability. The advantage of adding it to your site is fivefold: It brings more life to your site, increases traffic, permits visitors to comment (which is an additional way to engage and grow your customer base), allows you to listen and join the conversation, and increases your search engine rankings. The disadvantage of adding it to your

Web site is that if your blog takes off in popularity and is dependent on your core business and you want to sell it (the *Pittsburgh Mom* blog, for example, was purchased by the *Pittsburgh Post-Gazette*), you might run into an issue if you don't also want to sell your business, which, by way of your Web site, your blog is dependent upon.

All blogs must contain the following:

- A descriptive name
- An informative tagline, a small amount of text that clarifies and supports the name
- A focused theme to ensure the right visitors keep coming back
- Catchy subject lines (headlines)
- Short, informative posts (skimmable by busy people)
- Compelling photos that tie into the content
- Attractive visuals
- Writing style that has a professional tone and pleasant personality
- SEO that allows readers to find you (refer back to number six of the "Plan a Web site" section)

THE POWER OF A GOOD BLOG

I created *The Global Small Business Blog* (http://www.globalsmallbusinessblog. com), which is considered the number one blog in the world for entrepreneurs and small businesses interested in going global. I established the blog in 2004 for the sole purpose of providing a meaningful way to share our global trade expertise and engage with our target audience. The blog now has a world following of more than fifty thousand monthly readers, with most of our new business opportunities coming to us as a direct result of our blog.

You too can achieve this same level of blog success.

The following sections outline my suggestions for creating a blog that will help your export business succeed.

Pick a Main Stage and Understand Your Audience

It may seem simple, and obvious, but if you want your blog to be a go-to source for useful information, you need to understand your audience. In our case with *The Global Small Business Blog*, our whole focus is on entrepreneurs and small business owners who are interested in going global. That can involve anything from taking a business global, to understanding globalization, to employing people who want to start a global career. *Global*, *entrepreneurs*, and *small businesses* are the three keywords and phrases that drive our posts. It's our main stage and we never lose sight of that, nor do we vary from our focus. What will your world main stage be?

Post Frequently, Consistently, and with the Reader Always in Mind

If you don't provide new, useful, engaging, and relevant content on a regular basis, your readers will stop visiting your site. Web readers are busy and have short attention spans. Consistency is far better than any one-time act of greatness, especially when it comes to blogging. Posting new content every day is great, but providing actionable takeaways is what will keep people coming back day after day. Whatever your style and format, stick to it. One other point: Don't self-promote and talk about how great you are. You can post information you create relating to your world stage, but never lose sight of the fact that it has been created to add value to your reader's knowledge pool.

■ **Tip** You can create a blog on a free blog platform and separately reserve a domain name through one of the web-hosting companies mentioned earlier. It is important to host the blog using your own domain name, as in "http://www.mycompany.com/blog."

Inspire Your Readers

Use different methods to tell your story. Shake things up to keep your blog interesting for your readers. One day you might feature a guest blog post by a thought leader in your industry or post a YouTube video. The next, you might post your own how-to content that relates to your core theme. Ideas may be plentiful, but your time might be scarce. On some days, you might report everything a reader wants to know about a particular topic. On other days, you might do a short intro and go right to an outside link. Vary your posts in line with how readers process information. Sometimes they are in a hurry; other times they slow down and want to read every last word. Once in a while, they post a comment that requires feedback (see the next point). Vary the nature and scope of information and adjust it according to the times and what's relevant to your readers.

Make Thoughtful Comments When Warranted

A blog's commenting function is a great way to engage with your readers. You don't, however, need to reply to every single comment. In our case, with *The Global Small Business Blog (GSBB)*, we do our best to comment when readers comment, but if it doesn't seem necessary, we won't. When traffic really grows, the level of commenting can too, so you might find you are spending more and more time managing comments, and begin to question whether it is worth it. Right now, we want to keep the conversation going at the GSBB. But you may find down the road that you'd rather chat elsewhere with your readers—Facebook, Twitter and Google+, for example. Just remember, if you do, to keep your trackbacks, a way to notify another of an update, enabled.

Tip Don't let your readers think that you parachute into your blog and say what they want to hear or jump all over them when they are wrong. Strive to be thoughtful with your responses, lifting the subject matter to a higher level so everyone learns in the process.

Provide Links to Better Inform Readers

You don't have to create all the content for your blog on your own. Use the web to find valuable content from outside sources and link to those resources constantly. Say we post an article about the Trans-Pacific Partnership Agreement (http://importexport.about.com/od/TradePoliciesAndAgreements/fl/Trade-Agreements-are-Not-Just-about-Lower-Tariffs.htm) but our reader doesn't know what TPP is. We can link to a video about New Zealand's signing ceremony regarding the TPP (https://www.youtube.com/watch?v=xsqoh9e5utA) to ensure that our site keeps our readers informed and constantly learning.

Feature Stunning Graphics

A blog with lots of words and no cool graphics, charts, illustrations, or photos isn't an inviting page for visitors. Whether it's your own photography, taken from the public domain, or purchased as stock photography, graphics should power blog posts. A strong graphic can tell the story, elicit emotion (e.g., a video of a starving baby being fed a nutritional product), or be used to entertain (e.g., a photo of an elephant-sized shamrock on St. Patrick's Day). Can you imagine reading and enjoying content on a popular Web site that doesn't have an accompanying picture or chart? Make it a point to do the same on your blog.

Connect with Your Readers Intellectually and Emotionally

Sure, you can provide lots of great content on your blog, but if you don't connect with your readers on some sort of emotional level, they might not come back. Colors, imagery, and symbols all affect the mood, feelings, and emotions provoked by a blog. If you want to achieve a global reach, be aware of the color preferences of different cultural audiences and then use colors accurately and effectively. The Chinese flag, for example, is mostly red. Red also represents good fortune and happiness in China. India, on the other hand, is known as a country of saturated colors, with red and green used as standard color choices for clothing and yellow and red for traditional weddings. In the United States blue is known for trust and stability and in New Zealand red is considered a sacred color. Color symbolism can be very powerful and can make or break the success of a blog. Understand the meaning of color and you will see greater success in blogging by reaching a far wider audience worldwide.

Check Your Facts

Blogging is a little like reporting: One mistake and it can be fatal in terms of tarnishing your online reputation. Check sources and resources not once, but twice, to make sure information is reliable and accurate. If it's hearsay, don't blog about it.

Market the Blog

I do not believe in the theory "If you build it, they will come." Rather, I believe in doing hard work to market your blog everywhere you and your team go. That means if you write a guest-post column for a major newspaper, your signature or byline should include a link to your blog. If you write an article for a hot online property, a link to your blog should be included. If you conduct a webinar, mention your blog at the beginning and at the end of your talk. You should also take the media outlets in which your work appears and promote them through whichever social media and networking platforms you use, such as Facebook, LinkedIn, Twitter, Google+, Instagram, or Pinterest.

Label Your Posts

Another thing you shouldn't overlook is attaching labels to your blog posts to help identify your content to search engines (look back at number six in the "Plan a Web Site" section). Just because you create a blog with relevant content doesn't mean it will be easy for readers to find. To gain insights into how to get to the top of the heap in search engines and to inspect traffic reports about your Web site and blog, visit Alexa (http://www.alexa.com), Google Analytics (http://www.google.com/analytics/), Quantcast (http://www.quantcast.com), or Compete (http://www.compete.com).

Blog Services

Here are my top five platforms for creating a blog. Most of them are either free or charge a nominal fee (around $30 a year per blog). That fee is based on whether you elect to go with a custom design upgrade (referred to as CSS, or cascading style sheets) to make major changes to the blog's layout or point your existing domain name to a new IP address, which can be provided by the web-hosting provider.

1. *Wordpress:* http://www.wordpress.com

2. *Blogger:* http://blogger.com

3. *Typepad: http://www.typepad.com*

4. *SquareSpace: http://www.squarespace.com*

5. *Wix: http://www.wix.com*

Summary

Don't let your Web site or blog be doomed to mediocrity. Make it sing. Preferably, make it sing a song the world relates to. Impart your knowledge and share your passion with the world. Next, I will coach you on how to create a social media and social networking presence where the whole world will find you.

Notes

i. "The Importance of Blogging by Seth Godin and Tom Peters," Personal Content Creation, October 23, 2013. http://professionalcontentcreation.com/importance-blogging-seth-godin-tom-peters.

ii. Internet World Stats: http://www.internetworld-stats.com/.

iii. Digital Trends: http://www.digitaltrends.com/mobile/smartphone-users-number-6-1-billion-by-2020/.

iv. Ibid.

v. Nitish Singh and Arun Pereira, *The Culturally Customized Web Site: Customizing Web Sites for the Global Marketplace* (Oxford, UK: Elsevier, 2011): p. 3.

vi. "When Creating an Online Marketplace, Start Local and Think Global," The Wall Street Journal, March 3, 2015, accessed February 14, 2016, `http://blogs.wsj.com/accelerators/2015/03/03/david-ciccarelli-when-creating-an-online-marketplace-start-local-and-think-global/`.

vii. Gary Vaynerchuk, *The Thank You Economy* (New York, New York; HarperCollins Publishers; 2011): p. 84.

viii. Trade Benefits America, accessed February 14, 2016: `http://www.tradebenefitsamerica.org/resources/benefits-trade-and-importance-tpp-resource-kit`.

ix. "Select Country; Select Country: Developing a User Friendly Global Gateway," John Yunker, UX Magazine, last modified December 30, 2010, `http://uxmag.com/articles/select-country-select-language`.

x. The 2016 Web Globalization Report card: `http://byte-level.com/reportcard2016/`.

Creating a Social Media and Networking Presence

I just made my album. I did my best. And I uploaded the video just to YouTube. That was all.

—Park Jae-sang, better known by his stage name PSY[i]

… it's that anyone with a web connection can start a global conversation. Yes, it helps to be famous in real life. But the rise of social networks has leveled the playing field, allowing unknowns to command audiences rivaling those of real-world leaders, even if by accident.

—The 30 Most Influential People on the Internet, TIME[ii]

What impact have social media and networking tools had on exporting? They are redefining the way we connect with people and how we innovate and conduct business across the world. Anyone with an Internet connection can start a global conversation. Social should be a business enabler. Using blogs,

© Laurel J. Delaney 2016

L. J. Delaney, *Exporting*, DOI 10.1007/978-1-4842-2193-8_6

LinkedIn, Facebook, YouTube, Twitter, Instagram, Pinterest, and Google+ to globally establish and build your brand on the Internet is a great way for customers to find you online—so that it doesn't have to work the other way around. Once that happens, you can open the online door to export your goods to a worldwide customer base. You'll see how here.

The Big Shift

Only a decade ago, brick-and-mortar retail operations, such as specialty bakeries, dry cleaners, and businesses displaying their newest fashions in store windows, hummed along nicely based on a local community of loyal customers. When the customers fell short, the business owner ramped up his marketing efforts by way of telephone solicitations, direct-mail pieces, cross-promoted coupons, a big display ad in a telephone book, billboards, or in-store banners to get the word out to the neighborhood that the shop was not only *still* open for business but also had some very cool things that they had just gotten in for sale. That marketing effort, considered a staple back then, always involved the same customer base: a local one. The business owner had a single-minded view of the possibilities of where his customers *could come from*, and he didn't have the means to go beyond those places to reach them. He also didn't have the time nor the means to make a change that might lead to a brighter future.

Fast forward to now, when companies and individuals are making the big shift away from the old, entrenched way of doing things by offering goods and services to a new export market-driven way of creating growth by developing a digital presence. This digital presence has the potential to reach more than three billion people and save—across all businesses that export—thousands of dollars in the costs of printing, real estate, education, distribution, human capital, and customer acquisitions. Further, when Alphabet Inc. launches its much anticipated balloons, referred to as Project Loon, into the stratosphere in such parts of the world as Indonesia and Sri Lanka, an additional four billion people, who had little or no Internet access, will have it.[iii]

The need for all businesses to have a digital presence is here to stay and will only continue to evolve and grow in new ways. Individuals and businesses who fail to adapt and make the big shift will fall to the wayside and become irrelevant. Those who embrace the shift, leverage it, and discipline themselves to stay one step ahead of technology will allow every aspect of their business to prosper. The digital world represents one of the greatest challenges and opportunities facing individuals and companies today.

■ **Note** Think of the last time you were at a formal business gathering and a discussion came up about Facebook or LinkedIn. Did everyone jump in to talk about it? Those who don't are either shy or probably won't be part of tomorrow's workforce. *Will that be you?*

Thanks to digital tools and resources, anything—from a book, to a watch, to a political campaign—can be launched, produced, or exported worldwide fairly cheaply. More and more companies are therefore using the Internet, particularly social media platforms, to enhance the way their business is established, discovered, and operated outside their physical boundaries and, as a result, many are growing by leaps and bounds. After all, more than 43 percent of the world's population is online.[iv] The same folks who have a big online voice are redesigning how their teams work, reassessing how to best serve their customers—no matter where they come from—and changing the very nature of their business.

What will your customers want tomorrow? Where will they be located? Provided you are curious and have the drive, the Internet allows you to find new customers, create the products they want, and export to them.

The Art of Getting Online Attention: Finding Digital Export Success

How do you make a digital dent in the online universe? Not everyone is as lucky as PSY, who had a music video in 2012 that exceeded one billion views on YouTube. Or, take Katy Perry, who has the largest Twitter following in the world with more than 82 million followers.[v] Perry outpaces any pop star or person (including the president of the United States) on the social network. Getting online attention (usually) requires not only one single act of greatness but rather thousands of attempts at greatness spread across many online platforms over a protracted period of time—that's how you capture attention and develop a following. There is not a one-size-fits-all digital strategy. Succeeding in the digital world requires hard work, discipline, organizational skills, something remarkable to talk about, and a long-term view.

What's digital-export success? It's people worldwide finding you and opening their wallets to buy something from you, and you fulfilling their requests profitably. To be found, you must participate and be active on as many of the top online platforms as possible. To have customers open their wallets requires developing a relationship with them, garnering their trust, and offering products they want. That causes people to take action. Don't think for a minute you can foster online success with a single stunning Instagram platform. It's a start but must be supported with a Twitter, Facebook, LinkedIn, Pinterest, and Google+ presence. Putting all these social platforms to work in concert creates a winning online strategy, provided you stick to one topic or theme you are knowledgeable about. Think TOMS, Dell, and Eli Lilly—all good examples of companies utilizing social platforms with a unified marketing message, and oftentimes associating their brands with a noble cause.[vi]

The goal is to have a holistic or big-picture view of what you are trying to accomplish with your export business and make sure the right messages get in front of the right people at the right time. The beauty with this approach to online marketing is that any person at any age now has the capacity to create content, be consistent, control messaging, engage people's hearts and minds to build a brand, integrate multiple platforms, and measure results—all things that are central to online success.

■ **Tip** If you sell kiwifruit, for example, your goal is to get as many people who need kiwifruit to buy kiwifruit. And the biggest challenge is to reach people who don't yet know they need kiwifruit. That's where online platforms can serve as a door-opener to the world, offering you the most potential for global growth.

PSY, of course, is a rarity. He came out of nowhere with his YouTube video sensation. After being propelled to global stardom, he must now harness the attention and energy of Internet users worldwide, sustain the momentum—even raise the bar—and turn his stunning one-hit wonder into a profitable enterprise that supports his goals and values in life. It took Madonna decades to reach her pinnacle of global superstar success. Had she had the luxury of the web at hand when she started out, she could have shortened the discovery of her talent to that of PSY's or Perry's. When it comes to stardom, the Internet gives equal access to everyone—of all ages, backgrounds, and ethnic nationalities—and can make success happen overnight, provided all the social platforms are put to good use.

■ **Caution** Don't underestimate the power of the unexpected. Clayton Christensen, one of the most influential business theorists of the last fifty years, coined the expression "disruptive innovation."[vii] An example of disruptive innovation is Coursera, which offers high-quality courses online for anyone to take for free, which is beginning to impact the education industry and could demolish the status quo. Other examples are: Veristride (http://www.veristride.com), Kolibree (http://www.kolibree.com), and Oculus (https://www.oculus.com/en-us/)— each having the potential to dramatically disrupt existing businesses and industries. Disruptive innovation can blindside your business and tear down whole industries. Be on alert for every new online tool that comes your way, keep an open mind to it, and master it to strengthen your export business.

The Internet: The Social Capital of the Universe

Which social media platforms are best for getting your message across and motivating your audience? All of them. However, if one platform is more widely used in a foreign market, such as WeChat in China (http://www.wechat.com/en/) or Russia-based VK (originally VKontakte), the largest European online social networking service (http://vk.com/club200), that's where you should take your messaging. Tell your remarkable story across multiple social media channels so that you can gain followers, retain those followers, and move a social media conversation to e-mail, the telephone, or direct conversation for further business development. Your first step, if you haven't done so already, is to establish accounts on several different social media platforms.

When you set up accounts on different social media platforms, ensure that each reflects your brand (whether it's you or a company) and be consistent when you complete your profile on each platform. Use a real name when possible to ensure transparency; add a nice photo of yourself (or logo of your company if that's your brand); select a gorgeous background design that's in line with your profile; include a URL link to your most popular online location (Web site, blog, or LinkedIn); and declare yourself the go-to person on a particular subject matter.

In my case, each of my accounts—on LinkedIn, Facebook, Twitter—shows a photo of me, says that I am the president of GlobeTrade.com, features a background design image that reflects my experience doing business around the world, includes a link to my Web site, and indicates my passion for helping entrepreneurs and small businesses go global. That way, people clearly understand what I do, expect me to stay focused in that area of expertise, and, thus, know who to turn to when they need a resource or help on going global. This clarity of purpose also helps for SEO purposes.

For example, if you run a bakery that makes exotic cakes, you should state on your Twitter account, for example, that you're the CEO and include your photo or your company's logo, have a beautiful background design of one of your most popular cakes, include a short description explaining what your bakery does, include a link to your Web site, and share that same information across all your social platforms. If you are a mechanical engineer who designs, develops, builds, and tests airplane engines, insert your photo, show a cool engine you built as a background design, write a nifty bio about your talent, include a link to your Web site or blog, and start sharing success stories about your engineering capabilities. How else will Boeing, Airbus, or Commercial Aircraft Corporation of China find you? This same practice holds true for building working relationships with journalists and pitching stories.

Become a Digital-Export Rock Star

As you establish your online-platform accounts, stick with using the same profile information about yourself, as mentioned earlier. Consistency matters. Focus on this question: where do you want to go with your export business? Take your messaging to where social platforms are used the most in overseas markets.

Let's take a look at the top social platforms on the web—which I'll call the magnificent seven—and see how each is vital to setting the world stage for becoming a digital-export rock star.

LinkedIn

Considered the world's largest professional network, LinkedIn (http://www.linkedin.com), recently acquired by Microsoft, is a social Web site service used for professional networking and showcasing business talent. As of 2016, LinkedIn had more than four hundred million networked business-oriented members in more than two hundred countries and territories and in twenty-four languages around the world. The membership grows by approximately two new members every second.

As of 2016, the countries with the most LinkedIn users were:

- *United States*: one-hundred twenty-four million members

- *India*: thirty-four million members

- *Brazil*: twenty-three million members

- *United Kingdom*: twenty million members

- *China*: sixteen million members

- *Canada*: twelve million members

- *France*: eleven million members

- *Spain*: eight million members

- *Mexico*: eight million members

- *Italy*: seven million members

■ **Tip** Map out where the LinkedIn users are in your export strategy. If you plan to export to Norway and find there are hardly any LinkedIn members there, that will indicate a piece of your online export pie might not work! Go elsewhere with your online social strategy—try China, for example, which is one of the fastest-growing countries using LinkedIn.

LinkedIn makes it easy to connect and stay connected with everybody all over the world—old friends, colleagues, suppliers, vendors, employees, independent contractors, classmates, people you meet during international travels—in order to spread the word that you are looking for a serious business opportunity. Their main app has gone through a complete overhaul, with new features such as: Home, Me, Messaging, My Network and Search—all aimed at making communication faster, more casual and expressive. It also offers multiple ways to keep in touch with your global base—from your own LinkedIn feed, to posts and comments of groups that you join, to direct messaging and group conversations. It enables powerful introductions to valuable new contacts and even allows you to give and receive endorsements. If you use it in a meaningful way, you can channel the activity to benefit your export business.

LinkedIn allows you to set up a company page that is static until you change it. Visitors can click on tabs to access the sections of your company page they are most interested in. Think of it as another mini Web site—furthering building your brand. It helps others learn more about your company's job opportunities and products and services.

LinkedIn also supports the formation of special interest groups. The largest groups are related to finding employment; however, all sorts of professional and career issues are central to LinkedIn's focus. Joining a group is a great way to make connections peer to peer, share tips and experiences, ask and answer questions, and be on the lookout for customers and potential partnerships worldwide. Choose a group that is active and is central to your export business. A couple of groups that I belong to:

- China Trade Group
- Exporting Guide Group (MOOD)
- Global Intellectual Property & Business Lawyers
- Global Sourcing
- Global Trade Central
- Go Global—Internationalization Forum
- Import/Export Global Trading Group
- International Business
- International Entrepreneur Club
- International Trade Network
- Trade Professional.Net
- WAIB: Women of Academy of International Business

- Web Globalization
- Women Entrepreneurs GROW Global
- World Entrepreneurship Forum

■ **Tip**   If you can't find a group that interests you, start your own! It's a great way to declare your authority and develop a following. Whether through your own individual LinkedIn account, a company page, or a group membership, maintain a daily and consistent presence.

Facebook

Facebook (http://www.facebook.com) is known to be one of the fastest-growing and most popular web activities in the world. As such, it has been able to reach over half the U.S. population in 2016.[viii] Facebook was founded in 2004 with the mission "to make the world more open and connected." People use Facebook to connect with friends and family, to comment on and like activities, to discover new things in the world, to stay relevant, to pass time, and to share and express what matters to them. With Facebook's Messenger, a mobile instant messaging app, and its acquisition of the largest chat-based service in the world, WhatsApp, our ability to control the way we interact with people and businesses globally just got better.

As of December 2015, Facebook had more than 1.59 billion active monthly users, of which approximately 83.6 percent resided outside the United States and Canada.[ix] As a whole, 21 percent of the entire Internet world was using Facebook as of November 2015.[x] So, Facebook alone offers more than billion and a half users a month that your export business can reach. CEO Mark Zuckerberg has noted that "the next billion users will come from regions outside North America.[xi]

■ **Tip**   Facebook is the force to reckon with in North America, but there are other social networks that play in the same space, including Xing (http://www.xing.com/en) in Germany; Renren (http://www.renren-inc.com/en/) in China; Twoo (http://www.twoo.com) in Belgium; and MyMFB (http://www.mymfb.com) in Pakistan, a Muslim alternative to Facebook that is becoming popular in other parts of the world. It can't hurt to look into these and, when you are ready, become a part of them through an intermediary who knows the lay of the land and the language.

YouTube

YouTube (http://www.youtube.com) was founded in 2005 with the sole intent of helping people broadcast themselves or their business. YouTube is an online place to share videos with friends, family, colleagues, and the world. By subscribing to a channel, you can connect with an individual or a company you are interested in and keep up to date on their activities.

YouTube Viewership

Now owned by Google, YouTube has more than one billion users, with 80 percent of its traffic coming from outside the United States. YouTube is localized in more than 70 countries and across seventy-six different languages.

Thousands of channels earn money from their YouTube videos by becoming a YouTube partner. When you become a YouTube partner, you can display ads on your videos, and when people click on those ads, you earn a percentage of revenue.

There is a bit of competition to YouTube. French company Dailymotion (http://www.dailymotion.com/fr, or in the United States, http://www.dailymotion.com/us) also lets users share videos. It competes against YouTube. Dailymotion is owned by Vivendi. Other newcomers are: Vessel (http://www.vessel.com) and Amazon Video Shorts (http://www.amazon.com/b?ie=UTF8&node=9013971011).

Tip To earn money on your videos, you must set up an AdSense account (http://www.google.com/adsense).

Twitter

Twitter (http://www.twitter.com), established in 2006, is an online social networking and microblogging service comprising a global community of friends and strangers answering one simple question: What's important to you? You can answer that question via your phone or right on the web with an instant text-based message of no more than 140 characters.

░ **Tip**   Link your Twitter profile to your other social media accounts and apply the use of hashtags to better organize and cement brand loyalty. A hashtag is a # symbol used before a relevant keyword or phrase with no spaces to make up a Tweet. It's used to categorize Tweets and help them show up more easily in a Twitter search. For example, "#globalsmallbiz" is one I use often in my Tweets; it relates to expanding globally. If people do a search on "#globalsmallbiz," my Tweets will show up.

Twitter Users

Twitter has 320 million monthly active users with 79 percent of the accounts located outside the United States.[xii] The service is available in thirty-five languages.[xiii]

To see who's tweeting right now, visit A World of Tweets (`http://aworldoft-weets.frogdesign.com/`). Twitter is a great way to quickly share information and make strong global connections. Its new tab called Moments will allow you to discover the best of what's happening on Twitter in an instant.

Instagram

Instagram (`http://www.instagram.com`), established in 2010 and subsequently sold to Facebook in 2012, is a free, fast, and easy way to share your photos with friends, family, suppliers, colleagues, and prospective customers. You can snap a picture and then post to Instagram, where you can filter it several different ways to transform its look. You can easily share posts to Facebook and Twitter, too.

Instagram has more than 400 million monthly active users, with more than 75 percent living outside of the US and more than half living in Europe and Asia.[xiv] The fastest growing countries for Instagram use are Brazil, Japan, and Indonesia.[xv] Its new video app, Boomerang, lets you turn everyday moments into something fun and unexpected.

Pinterest

Launched in March 2010, Pinterest (`http://www.pinterest.com`) is a content-sharing service that allows members to "pin" images, videos, and other objects that interest them to their virtual pinboard. It is a tool for collecting, organizing, and sharing things you are passionate about.

Although Pinterest's global reach is not as strong as Instagram's, it is still a popular Web site in the United States. Pinterest has more than 100 million monthly active users.[xvi]

With Pinterest, you can browse other pinboards for inspiration, re-pin images to your own pinboards, and find a new and a more passionate audience to build your brand.

Google+

Established in 2011, Google+ (https://plus.google.com) is a social networking and identity service owned and operated by Google that gives you yet another unique way to build a social network, share information, and connect with people all over the world.

According to Business Insider, there are about 2.2 billion Google+ profiles and of these, 9 percent have any publicly posted content.[xvii] Your Google profile is what people find when they search your name (mine is: https://plus.google.com/+LaurelDelaney). You can include a brief bio, picture, links to other online platforms, and so forth. It becomes your online calling card to the world.

The concept of Google+ Circles is a major benefit to using Google+. This is where you choose who you want in your contacts. Circles lets you compartmentalize and keep the silos of your life separate. You can have a friends circle, a family circle, a colleagues in Japan circle, a suppliers in Korea circle, a customers in Germany circle, and so forth. Google+ allows you to share what you want with whom you want, making the control issue a major boon to this social platform.

Another great feature of Google+ is Hangouts. As the name suggests, Hangouts provides a virtual place for you and a group of up to 150 people to hang out. Through your computer or mobile app, the group can talk and see each other. This works great for impromptu gatherings or scheduled meetings to discuss status updates from around the world.

All of these Google+ tools and resources—from the Circle, to Hangouts, to hosting virtual meetings—allow you to reach a global audience and better manage your business relationships as you grow your export business.

Digital Road Map to the World

Remember the export business plans we covered in Chapter 2? My Laurel export business plan included a section on information technology and asked you what technology you will use (order taking, mailing lists, social media, finances, or e-commerce sales) and how you will use it. Let's take a moment to map out your social media and networking strategy. It might look like the following list, using the airplane engineer we talked about earlier as an example. Don't forget to assign someone to champion the cause—that champion can be you.

1. *"Facebook—post once a day"*: You might post a daily photo you've taken of one of your most successful projects, such as a shot of the latest airplane engine you built, and include a short paragraph on why it's unique from any others on the market.

2. *"YouTube—feature one video every month"*: An informative video that you could come up with in a month would be one that shows a complete installation of an airplane engine, where you talk about what could have gone wrong technically but didn't because you conducted five thousand hours of research beforehand.

3. *"Twitter—post three times a day"*: In order to get three Tweets up a day, you might first tweet about your upcoming presentation on how airplane engines are developed nowadays to optimize and reduce fuel usage. Then you can tweet about a dramatic improvement on your airplane engine. Your last tweet can be about a survey that was conducted on airplane engines manufactured in China and should include a link to the survey results. Be sure to track the most talked-about stories in your industry via Moments.

4. *"Instagram—post once a day"*: A daily Instagram photo might feature an airplane engine you spotted in an open lot that was ready for the trash bin.

5. *"Pinterest—post once a day"*: A post for Pinterest might be an infographic on how a clean airplane engine performs more efficiently than a dirty one.

6. *"Google+—post twice a day"*: Post a couple of related arti-
    cles each day. The first could be about airplane engines,
    describing the maintenance and offering the contact
    information for your supplier in Korea; the second could
    be an article about airplane engine efficiency, which you
    send to all of your Circles.

7. *"Blog—post three times a week"*: You might make blog
    entries on Monday, Wednesday, and Friday sharing your
    own original content on designing, developing, building,
    and testing airplane engines. Your blog will allow you to
    intersperse your posts with other articles from outside
    sources that support your message.

You can understand why it's important to be passionate about what you do—
because you must sustain the communications across all the social platforms
for a very long time and never tire.

■ **Tip** Posting on a blog, whether once a day or once a week, counts toward your digital road
map. I've always felt that blogging is the real meat and potatoes of your digital marketing strategy.

Emerging Social Media Networks That Will Shake Up the World

Emerging social media networks allow you to connect with new user groups
beyond the magnificent seven. Here are a few to watch. These can be good
places to broaden your brand reach, test new campaigns, and develop a following before your competitors do. Add these networks to your digital road
map once you get comfortable using them. Think along the lines of: What do
people need to know more about your business? What would they like to
know more about? How can I be helpful to them?

Snapchat

Established in 2011, SnapChat (http://www.snapchat.com), a video messaging application, allows its users to send self-destructing images to each
other, which is unlike other social networks where what you post online stays
there forever. Millennials describe Snapchat as awesome.[xviii] There are three
key ways to communicate via Snapchat: through photos or videos, a story, and
one-to-one text chatting.

Blab

Blab (http://www.blab.com), founded in 2012, is a world news aggregator that lets users add news from any news website and share and comment on news stories. Blab enables brands to target specific audiences. With its predictive visualization tool that highlights up-and-coming topics at any given moment, it can help companies decide which conversations they should join and which topics they should focus on.

Slack

Founded in 2009, Slack (http://www.slack.com), is a team-based cloud collaboration tool that provides services such as real-time messaging, archiving, and search for 21st-century teams. It offers one-on-one messaging, private groups, chat rooms, and direct messaging as well as group chats organized by topic. Everyone has a transparent view of all that's going on.

Periscope

Periscope (**http://www.periscope.tv**), established in 2014 and bought by Twitter the following year, is a mobile app that allows users to livestream whatever is happening around them for anyone who wants to watch. Unlike YouTube where a viewing experience is passive, Periscope is active. Viewers can comment, ask questions, and heart broadcasts in real time. Even The White House is on Periscope: **https://www.periscope.tv/WhiteHouse**.

Wanelo

Wanelo (http://www.wanelo.com), launched in 2012, is a social shopping app that allows you to peruse millions of different products offered by major brands, online retailers (more than 550 thousand stores) and even independent artists. Think of it as mall-browsing, with a click. You can create wishlists, make connections, and discover what your friends are interested in.

Summary

Your social media and networking presence will allow you to broaden and deepen existing relationships, attract new prospects around the globe, build thought leadership within your industry, create strong brand awareness, and grow your business. Be open to new experiences. Once you've mastered the basics, you are ready to use eBay, Amazon, Etsy, CafePress, and Zazzle—and even the popular Chinese site Alibaba—as stepping stones to exporting.

Notes

i. Jae-sang is a South Korean singer, songwriter, rapper, dancer, and record producer who is often considered the most famous Korean in the world. Jae-sang's hit single "Gangnam Style," which went live on December 21, 2012, exceeded one billion views on YouTube, becoming the first—and only—video to do so. As a result of his popularity, Jae-sang was invited to perform at the White House's Christmas concert in 2012 and at South Korean President Park Geun-hye's inauguration ceremony in 2013. http://en.wikipedia.org/wiki/Psy.

ii. "If we've learned anything from the Dress That Broke the Internet, first posted to Tumblr by a 21-year-old singer from Scotland, it's that anyone with a web connection can start a global conversation. Yes, it helps to be famous in real life. But the rise of social networks has leveled the playing field, allowing unknowns to command audiences rivaling those of real-world leaders, even if by accident." ß This quote appears in the body text. –LP http://time.com/3732203/the-30-most-influential-people-on-the-internet/.

iii. "'Project Loon' Is Aloft in Sri Lanka," accessed February 21, 2016, http://www.wsj.com/articles/project-loon-is-aloft-in-sri-lanka-1455661492.

iv. "Here's How Many Internet Users There Are," accessed February 21, 2016, http://time.com/money/3896219/internet-users-worldwide/.

v. Twitaholic: http://twitaholic.com/top100/followers.

vi. "10 ways brands are using social media marketing for good," accessed February 21, 2016, https://www.clickz.com/2016/01/27/10-ways-brands-are-using-social-media-marketing-for-good.

vii. Disruptive Innovation, Clayton Christensen: http://www.claytonchristensen.com/key-concepts/, accessed February 21, 2016.

viii. "Facebook to reach over half the U.S. population this year," VatorNews, accessed February 21, 2016, http://vator.tv/news/2016-02-08-facebook-to-reach-over-half-the-us-population-this-year.

ix. Company Info | Facebook Newsroom, `http://newsroom.fb.com/company-info/`.

x. Internet User Stats For All the Americas on November 30, 2015, World Total, `http://www.internetworldstats.com/stats2.htm`.

xi. "Facebook 'internationalizes' awards with global bracket system," Campaign US, accessed February 21, 2016, `http://www.campaignlive.com/article/facebook-internationalizes-awards-global-bracket-system/1378099`.

xii. Company About, accessed February 21, 2016, Twitter: `https://about.twitter.com/company`.

xiii. Ibid.

xiv. Celebrating a Community of 400 Million, accessed February 21, 2016, `http://blog.instagram.com/post/129662501137/150922-400million`.

xv. Ibid.

xvi. "Pinterest finally shares its size: 100M monthly active users and counting," VentureBeat, accessed February 21, 2016, `http://venturebeat.com/2015/09/16/pinterest-finally-shares-its-size-100m-monthly-active-users-and-counting/`.

xvii. "Google+ Active Users," Business Insider, accessed February 21, 2016, `http://www.businessinsider.com/google-active-users-2015-1?r=UK&IR=T`.

xviii. "How to Use Snapchat," The Wall Street Journal, accessed February 21, 2016, `http://www.wsj.com/articles/snapchat-101-learn-to-love-the-worlds-most-confusing-social-network-1452628322`.

Using e-Commerce and Social Media Sites as Stepping Stones to Export Success

Right now there is a prime opportunity for all of us to change the rules of the game through e-commerce and shift the balance in favor of entrepreneurs like you. The Internet levels the playing field and gives everyone—be they big or small—a chance.

—Jack Ma, founder of Alibaba[i]

© Laurel J. Delaney 2016
L. J. Delaney, *Exporting*, DOI 10.1007/978-1-4842-2193-8_7

If you do build a great experience, customers tell each other about that. Word of mouth is very powerful.

—Jeff Bezos, American technology entrepreneur and investor; founder and CEO of Amazon.com[ii]

Artist Gina Ayers Signore has been interested in art her whole life. She remembers drawing and painting when she was five years old. Today, she sells her artwork on her own Web site, Dahlia House Art Studio (http://www.dahliahousestudios.com), as well as on Etsy, Zazzle, and Art.com. Is it a bad idea for Gina to sell her artwork on another company's e-commerce platform that takes a small slice of her profits? Not at all.

Selling Goods, Services, and Unique Creations Online

Whether you are like Gina and sell art or you sell hamburger buns or steam engines, using a proven e-commerce platform is beneficial, provided its visitors are in line with your ideal target market, it is easy to use, it has a global reach, and it can help you sell more goods worldwide at a profit. It also allows you to test the salability of your product on someone else's proven successful infrastructure before making a substantial investment to set up an e-commerce site from scratch. Not all buy-sell platforms will work to your advantage, but with a little effort, you can try out the top ones with minimal risk by creating multiple store fronts simultaneously.

■ **Caution** Not all the popular e-commerce channels have the international part down pat. Some marketplaces charge a monthly fee; some don't. Some claim they ship worldwide, yet at the same time, they state restrictions may apply based on if the company has a physical international presence in your location. When it gets confusing is at the point where a shopping-cart feature does not properly reflect customs duties for internationally bound packages. Don't be intimidated or overwhelmed. Just as you are learning the export ropes, so are these e-commerce platforms learning them on the international front. Read the fine print on each site, and when in doubt, contact the company for additional assistance.

In getting started, you might want to set up a PayPal account to receive payments if you don't already have one (http://www.paypal.com). Your customers, on the other hand, can pay you without creating a PayPal account. Most online stores process payments through credit cards, verified bank accounts, and PayPal.[iii] (Refer to Chapter 20 for more on methods of payment.)

Let's take a look at the most common e-commerce marketplaces that can serve as a stepping stone to exporting and allow you to get your products in front of the largest number of potential customers worldwide. I include Facebook, because you can set up a store on your Facebook page to sell products. I also include it because of its tremendous connectivity power and global reach.

Note Test the digital-storefront waters for a short period of time—say six months to a year—and then decide whether the work you put into it is commensurate with the additional business you receive. If you find you are selling products like hotcakes on one site and in one specific overseas market, that is a sign there is customer demand for your products! At that point, it's probably time to make a decision to set up your own e-commerce system so that you can pocket all the profits vs. just a portion. Like any new venture, you must market the heck out of each e-marketplace through your own social channels. How else will you be discovered?

Online Storefronts: Cash in at World Marketplaces

The following online storefronts—all US based except for Alibaba.com—are considered the most popular. Most are used primarily for selling products, not services (except for Amazon, where you can sell intellectual work in the form of a white papers, books, or e-books).

Don't get discouraged by the lack of e-service representation. If you are exporting services, revisit Chapter 4, because many of the freelancer and independent-contractor Web sites that I talked about—such as Guru, Elance, and oDesk—can be useful not just for finding freelancers and independent contractors but also for marketing and exporting your own services. Review all applicable fees, because they will vary on each project and on the type of membership you choose. You can also set up your e-services similarly to how an online store might set up a physical product, but check to see if you can disable shipping since you won't mail anything out. Another option to bring attention to your services is to run paid ads on Facebook[iv] or on Google (using AdWords,[v] for example) based on keywords related to your business (refer to Chapters 6 and 10).

■ **Tip** Begin with the end in mind. At the same time that you are eagerly opening a store, find out how to close a store or cancel your subscription. Find out if there are any penalties or additional fees associated with the termination of your account. Can you do a redirect to a new site location (such as your own Web site or blog) when people attempt to reach you at your old location?

Amazon

When it opened in 1995, Amazon (http://www.amazon.com) was the world's biggest online bookseller, and that alone. Since then, Amazon has transformed itself into "the Earth's most customer-centric company, where customers can find and discover anything they might want to buy online, and endeavors to offer its customers the lowest possible prices."[vi]

Amazon has gone from being a simple Web site to an e-commerce and publishing partner to a sophisticated development platform. Some of the properties it owns include Audible (http://www.audible.com/mt/anon-home; offers downloadable audio books); AfterSchool.com (http://www.after-school.com/; sells kids' sports equipment, footwear, dance, and crafts); Woot (http://www.woot.com/; features new deals every day); CASA.com (http://www.casa.com/; selling kitchen and storage items and everything for the home); Zappos (http://www.zappos.com/; sells shoes and clothing); Alexa.com (http://www.alexa.com; provides commercial web traffic data and analytics), and CreateSpace (http://www.createspace.com; indie print publishing made easy), to name just a few.

Amazon helps sellers reach customers in thirteen marketplaces spanning across Europe, North America, and Asia. In addition to the United States, Amazon has Web sites for doing business in Brazil (http://www.amazon.com.br); Canada (http://www.amazon.ca); China (http://www.amazon.cn); France (http://www.amazon.fr); Germany (http://www.amazon.de); India (http://www.amazon.in); Italy (http://www.amazon.it); Japan (http://www.amazon.co.jp); Mexico (https://www.amazon.com.mx); Spain (http://www.amazon.es); The Netherlands (http://www.amazon.nl); and the United Kingdom (http://www.amazon.co.uk). And the company continues to add countries to help sellers expand internationally.[vii] When you set up your account, each overseas marketplace requires a different account, except for the EU!

■ **Tip** In deciding whether to go with one of Amazon's local sites, determine if your products are in demand in that overseas market. Do you have the staff to support these areas—particularly that speaks the native language of the country you wish to conduct business in? Is this country selection in line with your export business plan developed earlier?

People from all over the world can shop at Amazon using a credit card or a verified bank account for payment. That means that if you sell on Amazon, your product can be purchased with ease. Amazon makes it user friendly for the buyer, by placing prices in the home currency of each site.

Setting up Your Own Amazon Marketplace

When you set up your own marketplace on Amazon, you have the potential to get in front of a huge volume of traffic—tens of millions of customers. Selling on Amazon requires you to do a simple five-step process:

1. List your items
2. Get orders
3. Ship
4. Get paid
5. Process refunds and returns

Amazon offers a training guide, "Getting Started Guide: How to Get Set Up Selling on Amazon,"[viii] where you can check off tasks as you complete them.

Caution Amazon does not offer a language translation service. That is your responsibility. If you only have an English-speaking staff and want to sell to China through Amazon's China site (http://www.amazon.cn), for instance, you'd better get a Chinese-speaking person on staff to handle that part of your business, including writing the listings to sell your products! Another option is to look into a professional translation service online (e.g., One Hour Translation[1]), which can streamline the process.

Amazon Global Shipping

Amazon.com ships orders worldwide with Amazon Global. Items can be shipped to a long list of countries, but bear in mind that this does not necessarily mean Amazon has fulfillment capabilities in each of these countries. Fulfillment by Amazon (FBA) picks, packs, and ships inventory on your behalf.

Amazon only has fulfillment centers located in: China, France, Germany, India, Italy, Japan, Spain, the United Kingdom, and the United States. They, however, ship to more than 75 countries.[ix]

---

[1]https://www.onehourtranslation.com/translation/press-releases/one-hour-translation-becomes-official-amazon-web-services-technology-partner

To see if the items you are interested in selling on Amazon are included for global shipping, do a search for "items eligible for international shipping" at the Amazon site. Product lines, shipping rates, and fees vary depending on the delivery address, so be mindful of that when you conduct your search.

For certain eligible countries, Amazon Global offers customers estimations on customs duties and clearance, taxes, and import fees applicable during checkout. These expenses vary greatly from country to country and region to region. Amazon Marketplace sellers should check the site's policies to ensure their product is covered, determine what fees will be levied on their shipment, and find out who will be responsible for these additional expenses. (Typically, it is up to the recipient of the product to pay these costs.)

■ **Tip** Consult your tax accountant and attorney on Amazon Global to find out the tax consequences, if any, to your business of using their services. It also can't hurt to also consult with your entire export dream team to get its wise counsel.

Amazon Marketplace: The Full Monty

You can sell to the world in two ways on the Amazon Marketplace—professionally (as a business) or individually.[x] If you are looking to sell only a few products (fewer than forty items a month) or a one-off item as a test, sign up for an individual account because there is no monthly fee. You pay only when the item sells. The marketplace approach helps you avoid the time and costs of developing a stand-alone Web site on your own.

When you sell on Amazon, you also have the ability to use one of Amazon's fulfillment centers (serving the nine countries mentioned earlier) and shipping capabilities, which give you the tools you need to grow your business but without ever letting you know who is buying your product (yes, you read that right). You very rarely know who your customers are and thus lose the opportunity to tailor your offerings to their evolving needs. By putting your products in someone else's hands, you are a step removed from the actual sales transaction. Hence, it will be hard to redirect your efforts accordingly should you decide to take back control and sell directly. The fulfillment part is also tricky. For example, if you have inventory that is located in a different country than one of Amazon's fulfillment centers, you will need to export your products from the source country and import them into the destination country. You should consult with Amazon on the best way to do this, as the company has strict procedures for how shipments must be received. These include the size of pallets you use and the type of carrier you use. There are monthly costs and other selling fees associated when you sign up.[xi]

Before you do anything, check to see whether your product is permitted for sale on Amazon within its selling categories. Then, calculate all costs—the wholesale price of your product, shipping costs, handling fees, taxes, duties, payment service fees, and Amazon's fees and other related selling costs—to determine if you will make a profit on each item you sell overseas. After you look at your profit, ask yourself: is it worth it? To save money, you can opt out of the shipping option and do it on your own through a private carrier. This ensures that you have greater control over all aspects of the transaction, including knowing who your customers are. You also know who to contact if something isn't working. It's your choice.

Amazon Webstore: E-Commerce Store and Shopping Cart Solution No Longer Exists

The Amazon Webstore (http://services.amazon.com/content/webstore-by-amazon.htm?ld=SCWBAStriplogin) used to be a one-stop e-commerce shop that enabled you to build and operate a profitable online store within Amazon to sell to the world but it is no longer available to new merchants.[2] Amazon now offers Shopify, the preferred Webstore migration, as a solution provider. Once complete, you can leverage Amazon's infrastructure to build your online store on a solid and secure platform (it may require help from a designer to make it look visually attractive), utilize Amazon's fulfillment, and tap into its expertise on an as-needed basis. Monthly subscription and per-transaction fees apply and vary greatly. Be sure to read the fine print.

Caution   The biggest obvious downside to partnering with Amazon is that you will essentially compete against it on everything related to your product. If you sell jewelry and Amazon does too (which it does), you compete against the company for customer attention and acquisition. And, if Amazon raises your rates or decides to offer a product similar to yours at a lower price, guess whose ads will be next to yours? Go into this with your eyes wide open!

---

eBay

Founded in 1995, eBay (http://www.ebay.com) is a leading e-commerce company and helps individuals and small businesses sell their products world-wide. The company's global portfolio of businesses enables hundreds of millions of diverse and passionate people to buy, sell, and pay online.

---

[2]http://webstore.amazon.com/?ld=SCWBAStriplogin

You can buy or sell individual or multiple items on eBay. If you are selling multiple items on an ongoing basis, you'll probably want to start your own storefront, where buyers can learn about you and the products you sell. When you list an item on eBay (known as a business-to-consumer—B2C—sale), you're charged a listing (or insertion) fee. Insertion fees are charged per listing, per category regardless of the quantity of items. If the item sells, you're charged a "Final value fee." Final value fees are calculated based on the total amount of the sale. The total amount of the sale is the final price of the item, shipping charges, and any other amounts you may charge the buyer. Sales tax is not included.

Every item gets its own unique listing. You may need to pay extra for an upgrade or supplemental service, such as international site visibility, which attracts buyers from other countries by showing your item in search results on other eBay Web sites. These supplemental features, including global shipping charges, will be included on your seller invoice as fees.

The site currently ships to about sixty-four countries,[3] requiring you to ship your items domestically to one of eBay's US shipping centers. Some items are restricted (e.g., antiques, vintage collectibles, and real estate) due to export limitations and restrictions identified by designated global shipping providers. Other items have general restrictions, like child pornography, tobacco, and perishable items, for example. To give yourself the best chance of success selling through eBay, review its "Taking It to the Next Level" (`http://pages.ebay.com/sellerinformation/ship-smart/global-shipping-program/next-level.html`) on how to attract more international buyers to your listings. One best-practice tip from eBay is adding more countries to your selling program.[xii]

■ **Note**   The devil is in the details. In your listing, the buyer sees an estimate of the international shipping charges and the import charge. At checkout, she is presented with the final charges, which include the cost of the item, the international shipping charges, and the import charge. The international shipping charges include any US shipping costs as well as program fees, third-party international shipping charges, fuel surcharges, and processing and handling fees. The import charge includes applicable customs duties, taxes, and third-party brokerage.

---

eBay Store

When you sell more than fifty listings a month on eBay, it's time to consider opening an eBay store—an e-commerce solution that helps you leverage the eBay marketplace and tap the millions of buyers worldwide who shop on eBay.

---

[3]`http://pages.ebay.com/sellerinformation/ship-smart/global-shipping-program/index.html`

You can classify your account as a business or an individual, should you want to test the waters discreetly on a solo basis. The site allows you to enter your current selling activity into what is called the Fee Illustrator to determine which eBay store subscription best fits your needs. If you meet the requirements to open a store, eBay makes it easy to get started. Any items you currently sell individually on eBay automatically become a part of your eBay store.

With your store comes exclusive marketing and merchandising tools from eBay plus customization features to build a strong brand. By staging all of your products in one central location, an eBay store creates a one-stop shop where buyers can learn more about you and your products. The site also provides demarcation by way of placing a red store tag next to your user ID to indicate you have an eBay store.

When you open an eBay store, you pay a monthly store subscription fee, which becomes effective immediately. Your next seller invoice will include a prorated fee for the number of days between your subscription date and the end of that month as well as subscription fees for the following month. Fees range anywhere from $15.95 to $199.95 per month based on your needs and the benefits of each subscription.[4] Store fees can change by way of company directives and other related fees may apply, such as PayPal (now a separate company from eBay) and seller tool fees.[xiii] Always read the fine print on eBay when it comes to your costs. And it can't hurt to e-mail or call customer support to confirm your understanding.

The benefit to using eBay is the opportunity to brand your store, receive payment through PayPal, and sell internationally, where eBay has a far greater reach than other sites in general.

Etsy

Conceived in early 2005, Etsy (http://www.etsy.com) is a vibrant marketplace spanning nearly every country in the world.[xiv] Users on Etsy sell everything from handmade goods to vintage items and art supplies, with many professional artists using the site to make a living.

With Etsy, you can enhance and grow your brand by acquiring new customers, using built-in promotional tools, and becoming a part of a vibrant online community to help form relationships and gain mentors. There are no membership fees with Etsy. It costs twenty cents to list an item until it sells. Once you sell your item, Etsy collects a 3.5-percent fee on the sale price.

---

[4]http://pages.ebay.com/sellerinformation/stores/Subscriptions.html

When you create an account, you can sign up using Facebook, Google+, or your full name. Before you list a product for sale, Etsy highlights the fees you will be charged in order to inform you of what your net profit will be. As a shop owner, you are sent a bill at the end of every month containing the fees you owe. You have until the middle of the following month to pay it. Buyers can purchase products with Visa, MasterCard, American Express, Discover Card, PayPal, or the Etsy Credit Card Reader. If you use the Reader, be sure to first download the Etsy App.[5]

Etsy has rolled out a direct checkout method, which allows you to pay with and accept payment by credit card, debit card, Etsy gift card, some bank transfer services, PayPal, Apple Pay, Google Wallet, and the Sell on Etsy Reader—all in their local currencies. This solves the problem of how to efficiently get paid after you sell your wares online.

Like a lot of e-commerce platforms, perfecting the global end of transactions for Etsy continues to be a challenge and work in progress. If your desire is to easily cross boundaries on someone else's e-commerce platform, it is better to find out in advance if it is feasible before you invest your time and energy using Etsy.

CafePress

Dubbed the world's customization engine, CafePress (http://www.CafePress.com) began in 1999 as a nifty little idea—to apply printing and technology innovation to make it easier for people to express themselves on T-shirts. This expression has led to people quickly becoming e-commerce entrepreneurs with no risk and no overhead. Some of the brands CafePress currently manages are: CafePress.com, Great Big Canvas, Imagekind, InvitationBox.com, and Canvas On Demand.

CafePress makes it easy enough to open a shop on the Web site—it's free. There are no up-front fees, but, as is the case with all the online marketplaces, the site takes a piece of your selling price as profit. You create the idea for the product or choose one of the company's, choose what type of product you are selling, and pick your retail price, and CafePress prints your product on demand when customers order it. CafePress also handles the fulfillment on the transaction.

---

[5]https://www.etsy.com/reader?ref=ftr

■ **Note**   If you have funds to invest and are serious about becoming an international e-commerce entrepreneur, get your personalized products printed by a third party, carry inventory, and start selling them in your own online store. That way, you pocket all the profits. If you don't want to fuss with the production side of the business and don't have a dime to throw into your creative endeavor, stick with CafePress provided they show signs of global growth!

Zazzle

Zazzle (`http://www.zazzle.com`), established in 1999, is considered the world's leading quality custom-products platform. You can upload images and create your own merchandise (see my store, the Global Small Business Depot, at `http://www.zazzle.com/laureldelaney`) or buy merchandise created by others. It does not cost you anything to open a Zazzle store, and you can customize your store to meet your design standards. Pricing is determined by you and includes an option to select your royalty rate, ranging from 5 percent to 99 percent. For Zazzle to pay you the royalty you select, it must increase the product price by a commensurate amount. On royalties of 20 percent or greater, a 5 percent transaction fee applies. Be careful not to raise the royalty so high that you price a product right out of the ballpark. For example, you wouldn't want to try to get a 99 percent royalty by selling a T-shirt at $50! Keep the customer in mind: what are they willing to spend on a product like yours? A good royalty range is generally 12 percent.

Zazzle International (`http://www.zazzle.com/international`) spans four continents and includes seventeen countries, allowing users to shop in their native language and pay in their local currency.

Zazzle ships worldwide and takes anywhere from two to seven days when you use express shipping or four to twenty-one days for standard shipping. If you choose United States Postal Service for your international shipments, do not expect to receive any tracking method. It's only when you use Zazzle's primary couriers (UPS or FedEx) that you can track the status of your shipments. The site indicates that international packages can be delayed for reasons ranging from customs inspections to the standard delivery times of local mail services.

As with Amazon, there are some big distinctions between what Zazzle ships worldwide free and clear of taxes and customs fees and what it doesn't. For example, if you are based in the UK and order from the Zazzle.co.uk website, Zazzle will pay the import duties and local taxes for you. However, this may not be the case when that same order is placed through Zazzle.com.

You will be paid by check on the products you sell and in the primary currency denomination (Zazzle.com, for example, in US dollars). If you prefer, Zazzle will transfer your earnings to a PayPal account. You can also use your earnings to buy other items but that defeats the purpose of building of revenue stream, which generates sustainable profits over the long term.

Check all tools that are available on the site to help sell your products, including store link, email to a friend link, international banners, and an RSS feed where you can send any store, product or search term to any RSS reader or website. All of these work to enhance your brand. Leave no stone unturned in finding out Zazzle's true global reach.

Facebook

Launched in 2004, Facebook (http://www.facebook.com) is the world's largest social network. It connects people with friends and others who work, study, or live around them. People use the site to keep up with friends and to promote their businesses globally.

With Facebook, individuals can build a page and businesses can create ads that will help promote any page you select, and reach your current as well as potential customers worldwide. The goal for the pages is twofold—to get more page likes and to promote page posts. If you have an idea of the ideal customer you want to target, you can choose the audience for your ad.

For example, if you sell kitchen aprons and want to sell to people age eighteen to thirty-five who reside in Germany and are in the broad category of cooking, you can select the demographics that you want to reach. Facebook makes it clear that you will never exceed your budget, meaning there are no hidden fees and you'll never pay more than what you set for your daily budget on a specific campaign to reach those people who are most likely to purchase your products. The site also provides tools to monitor and measure results.

Shopping carts, a piece of e-commerce software that allows visitors to an Internet site to select items for purchase, adapted for social commerce— Shopify (http://www.shopify.com/facebook); Bigcommerce (http://www.bigcommerce.com/); EasySocialShop (http://www.easysocialshop.com/); ShopTab (http://www.shoptab.net/); and Ecwid (http://www.ecwid.com)—provide the infrastructure for Facebook stores. Businesses can then create a storefront with a shopping cart and promotions offering discounts and coupons.

Many entrepreneurs and small business owners use Facebook to supplement sales at their local retail shop, while others use it to augment sales from their Web sites or e-commerce stores, including eBay, Amazon, and Etsy.

▨ **Tip** Watch for up-and-coming online marketplaces such as Redbubble.com, Spreadshirt.com, and Customink.com, which allow individuals to design, buy and sell creative and personalized apparel and art.

China-Based Alibaba.com

Founded in 1999, Alibaba.com (http://www.alibaba.com) is a group of twenty-five business units that allows anyone located anywhere in the world to buy or sell online. Alibaba has come to dominate Internet retailing in China, with the goal of becoming the biggest e-commerce market in the world.

Alibaba went public in September 2014. "The initial offering price valued the company at $168 billion, making it bigger than its closest American analogue, Amazon, and one of the biggest IPOs of all time."[xv]

Below are a few of the more prominent businesses within the Alibaba Group (unless noted as being an affiliate of the company):

- *Alibaba.com*: (http://www.alibaba.com) An international e-commerce platform for small businesses

- *Alibaba.com China*: (http://www.1688.com/) A domestic e-commerce platform for Chinese small businesses

- *AliExpress*: (http://www.aliexpress.com) A global e-commerce marketplace for consumers

- *Cainiao Logistics*: (http://www2.alizila.com/tags/cainiao) Operator of a logistics information platform

- *1688.com*: (http://www.1688.com) An online wholesale marketplace in China

- *Alimama*: (http://www.alimama.com) Online marketing technology platform

- *Ant Financial Services Group* (http://www.alibabagroup.com/en/news/press) Financial services provider focused on serving small and micro enterprises and consumers

- *Taobao.com*: (http://www.taobao.com) China's C-to-C online shopping destination, which allows members of the public to sell to each other

- *TMALL.com:* (http://www.tmall.com) China's B-to-C shopping destination for brand name goods, letting companies sell directly to the public

- *Juhuasuan:* (http://ju.taobao.com) Shopping platform in China

- *eTao.com:* (http://www.etao.com) Shopping search engine in China

- *Aliyun.com:* (http://www.aliyun.com) Developer of platforms for cloud computing and data management

- *Alipay.com:* (http://www.alipay.com) China's leading third-party online payment platform and an affiliate of the Alibaba Group, not a business within it

Alibaba.com is a leading global e-commerce B-to-B platform for small businesses that desire to source material from manufacturers, suppliers, exporters, and importers. Categories to buy-sell range from electrical equipment to shoes and accessories to toys and hobby items. As of January 16, 2016, Alibaba has more than 407 million active users.[xvi]

■ **Note** Alibaba just took a 5.6 percent stake in daily-deals company Groupon. Watch for growth in coupons, discounts and online ticketing and the like soon.

Alibaba makes all the basic services it offers free to both buyers and sellers. It earns money through online advertisements and extra value-added services it offers clients, such as website design. Many sellers pay for beautifully designed storefronts and online advertisements to help them stand out from the crowd.

International brands like Tabasco, Mars, Nike, Apple, Burberry, and 3M are all on Tmall. Some use Tmall as the exclusive channel for online purchases in China; others are experimenting with having both their own site and a Tmall storefront.

In order to get the most out of Alibaba, register your company at the site. That readies you to use their TradeManager software program (http://trademanager.alibaba.com/), considered the best tool of the entire site for staying in close touch with key people, including Alibaba support personnel. If you are looking for manufacturers, suppliers, importers, exporters, business partners, market information, upcoming trade shows, and the like, Alibaba will serve you well in those areas. If you wish to sell products to consumers in China, definitely consider setting up a Tmall storefront. No matter what you decide to do, do your homework on potential suppliers or customers.

Through its Chinese language Web site Taobao, Alibaba offers a C-to-C online shopping experience similar to that of eBay and Amazon for small businesses and individual entrepreneurs operating in mainland China, Hong Kong, Macau, and Taiwan. Listings are free as of the time of this writing.

If you want to sell products through any of Alibaba's Chinese sites, it is best to find a Chinese partner to interpret and assist you because you will have to deal with supply-chain issues, import duties, regulations, packaging adjustments, shipping considerations, returns, refunds, and marketing your products to stand out from the crowd, all conducted in Chinese.

Tip If you like what you see through Alibaba.com, pay a visit to Tencent (`http://www.tencent.com/en-us/index.shtml`), which has set up a stand-alone e-commerce platform called Paipai (`http://www.paipai.com/`) to compete directly with Taobao. The company recently bought 51buy.com (known as Yixun in China: `http://www.yixun.com/`), to compete with Tmall. Also, strictly for manufacturers and suppliers, look into Global Sources (`http://www.globalsources.com`).

Summary

Each e-commerce marketplace has its own strengths, weaknesses, opportunities, and infrastructure—those come into play based on what you are selling, the intensity of competition in your category, the marketplace restrictions, shipping fees, fulfillment capabilities, payment mechanisms, and the extent of your global reach. Exporting can be as straightforward as testing your products in new online marketplaces where you can enjoy significant revenue returns or delving further into expansion by developing an e-commerce site within your own Web site. The opportunity for export success is everywhere.

Now that you've sampled what's involved in selling your products through an intermediary online marketplace channel, it's time to advance and create your own e-commerce platform to sell to the world and pocket all the profits. Let's move on to Chapter 8, where we'll look at the e-commerce craze!

Notes

i. Excerpt from the "Official Alibaba.com Success Guide: Jack Ma's Foreword Part 2," Alibaba Team, AliBlog, accessed October 21, 2013, http://aliblog.alibaba.com/2009/12/02/excerpt-from-the-official-alibaba-com-success-guide-jack-mas-foreword-part-2/.

ii. "What Is Customer Experience?," Huffpost Business, accessed February 28, 2016, http://www.huffingtonpost.com/don-dodds/what-is-customer-experience_b_8936286.html.

iii. You can find a description of PayPal's fees on its site:"PayPal Fees for International Payments," accessed February 28, 2016, https://www.paypal.com/us/cgi-bin/marketingweb?cmd=_display-xborder-fees-outside.

iv. See "Advertising on Facebook," accessed February 28, 2016, https://www.facebook.com/business/products/ads.

v. See "Google AdWords | Google (PPC) Pay-Per-Click Online Advertising," accessed February 28, 2016, https://www.google.com/adwords/.

vi. Amazon Fulfillment – History & Culture, accessed February 28, 2016, http://www.amazonfulfillment-careers.com/about-amazon/history-and-culture/.

vii. Amazon sites from around the world can be found at: "Amazon International Around the World," accessed February 28, 2016, http://www.amazon.com/gp/feature.html?ie=UTF8&docId=487250.

viii. "Selling on Amazon; Getting Started Guide: How to Get Set Up Selling on Amazon," Amazon Services, last modified July 1, 2008, http://g-ecx.images-amazon.com/images/G/01/AmznServices/en_US/files/Getting_Started_Guide1._V181643274_.pdf.

ix. "Amazon Where We Ship," Amazon, accessed February 28, 2016, http://www.amazon.com/b?ie=UTF8&node=11533661011.

x. "Sell on Amazon and Reach Hundreds of Millions of Amazon Customers," Amazon Services, accessed February 28, 2016, http://services.amazon.com/selling/benefits.htm/ref=as_mnu_soa?ld=SCWBAStriplogin.

xi. For an overview of the procedures and costs associated with the fulfillment centers, see "Fulfillment by Amazon," accessed February 28, 2016, `http://services.amazon.com/fulfillment-by-amazon/pricing.htm?ld=SCWBAStriploginAS`.

xii. "Taking it to the next level" – Global Shipping Program | eBay Seller Center, accessed February 28, 2016, `http://pages.ebay.com/sellerinformation/shipsmart/global-shipping-program/next-level.html#faq=faq-2`.

xiii. For an overview of selling fees, see "Standard Selling Fees," accessed October 18, 2013, `http://pages.ebay.com/help/sell/fees.html`.

xiv. About Etsy, accessed February 28, 2016, `https://www.etsy.com/about/`.

xv. "Alibaba Just Went Public," NYMag, accessed February 28, 2016, `http://nymag.com/daily/intelligencer/2014/09/alibaba-just-went-public.html`.

xvi. "76 Amazing Alibaba Statistics (February 2016)," accessed February 28, 2016, `http://expandedramblings.com/index.php/alibaba-statistics/`.

The e-Commerce Connectivity Craze

Buying and Selling Globally and Managing an International Supply Chain

Communications is at the heart of e-commerce and community.

—Meg Whitman, president and chief executive officer of
Hewlett-Packard

*The sooner we drop the 'e' out of 'e-commerce' and just call it commerce,
the better.*

—Bob Willett, former President of Best Buy International
and CIO of Best Buy

© Laurel J. Delaney 2016
L. J. Delaney, *Exporting*, DOI 10.1007/978-1-4842-2193-8_8

If you want a symbol of how technology is transforming the way we conduct business worldwide, look no further than e-commerce, which refers to buying and selling on the Internet. It's easy to forget that as short as 15-18 years ago, buying books or shoes online seemed novel. Not anymore. The new digital reality is upon us. Is there anything you can't buy online almost anywhere? The driving force behind e-commerce growth is the proliferation of tablets and smart phones, technology improvements, greater convenience, competitive prices, global choices, and bountiful product information.

The Future of Selling: The E-Commerce Revolution

Welcome to the future of transcendent selling, where there will be an obliteration of lines between the traditional old-world way of commerce and e-commerce. Soon they will merge into one seamless function, as former President of Best Buy International Bob Willett suggested, be treated the same way, and simply be called digital business. In-store retail shopping will never fully go away, but in the future there will be less of it. How will you set up your business to react? Will you be prepared? More people are spending an inordinate amount of their time surfing the Internet—sometimes not even thinking about why. That's why harnessing these people and their buying power worldwide is the key to success for small business owners.

The problem is that many small business owners don't have the technical know-how or capital to set up their own e-commerce platform. This chapter prepares you for the e-commerce revolution and how—astonishingly—you don't have to go broke or be a technical wizard to become part of it! The end result is that you will easily and affordably export by selling online. In the 1990s, Dell became the e-commerce leader by hitting a milestone of $1 million in Web site sales per day. What the company didn't anticipate was that its e-commerce business would grow to be one of its largest revenue-producing sources. That could be you. All the more reason to get e-commerce right from the start.

In this chapter, I will look at the growing scope of e-commerce, discuss why it is important to your business (think of the power of China's Tmall and Taobao discussed in Chapter 7), and help you target your market.[1] In addition, I'll give some pointers on finding a manufacturer for a product you may want to export and a primer on the ten thousand-pound gorilla: your international supply chain and how best to manage it.

Then we'll review an array of e-commerce platforms for your business from which to choose, while assessing what makes e-commerce sites reliable and secure for business transactions. Last, we'll look at how to measure e-commerce success. Depending on the stage of your business's growth, some of these topics may not apply, so feel free to jump in anywhere that applies to what you are looking for. The intent here is to keep you focused on learning, growing, and pushing boundaries with your business.

The Growing Scope of E-Commerce

There are more than 7 billion potential customers in the world, and 3.4 billion of them are online. How many of those customers is your company reaching outside your own borders? Let's say your international sales last month included three products sold through Zazzle, one through Amazon, five through eBay, five at CafePress, and four on your own Web site by way of a shopping cart adapted for Facebook. Do you think you've captured enough sales? Hardly. Sure, you generated more sales and profits than you would have had you not created these accounts, but could you sell more?

Nearly 87 percent of world economic growth during the next five years will take place outside of the United States, according to the International Monetary Fund. Are you prepared to tap into it?

According to A.T. Kearney, "Sales [e-commerce] increased more than 20 percent worldwide in 2014 to almost $840 billion, as online retailers continued expanding to new geographies and physical retailers entered new markets through e-commerce."[ii]

"Total e-commerce sales for 2015 were estimated at $341.7 billion, an increase of 14.6 percent (±0.9%) from 2014. Total retail sales in 2015 increased 1.4 percent (±0.4%) from 2014. E-commerce sales in 2015 accounted for 7.3 percent of total sales. E-commerce sales in 2014 accounted for 6.4 percent of total sales, according to the U.S. Census Bureau News, U.S. Department of Commerce."[iii]

eMarketer projects (refer to Figure 8-1) that "Retail ecommerce sales, those purchased over the internet, will make up 7.4% of the total retail market worldwide, or $1.671 trillion. By 2019, that share will jump to $3.578 trillion, yet retail ecommerce will account for just 12.8% of retail purchases."[iv]

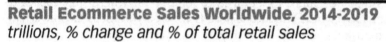
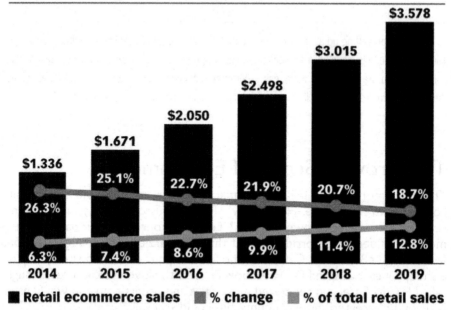

Retail Ecommerce Sales Worldwide, 2014-2019
trillions, % change and % of total retail sales

- **$1.336** (2014)
- **$1.671** (2015)
- **$2.050** (2016)
- **$2.498** (2017)
- **$3.015** (2018)
- **$3.578** (2019)

% change: 26.3%, 25.1%, 22.7%, 21.9%, 20.7%, 18.7%

% of total retail sales: 6.3%, 7.4%, 8.6%, 9.9%, 11.4%, 12.8%

■ **Retail ecommerce sales** ■ **% change** ■ **% of total retail sales**

Note: includes products or services ordered using the internet via any device, regardless of the method of payment or fulfillment; excludes travel and event tickets
Source: eMarketer, Dec 2015

201892   www.e**Marketer**.com

Figure 8-1. "Worldwide Retail Ecommerce Sales: eMarketer's Updated Estimates and Forecast Through 2019," Douglas Clark, eMarketer, March 6, 2016. Used with permission.

It is also projected by eMarketer that Asia-Pacific will be the main driver behind this growth, "accounting for over half of global retail ecommerce sales in 2015, or $877.61 billion. We [eMarketer] expect ecommerce sales in the region to climb $1.459 trillion by 2019, contributing to over three-fourths of the worldwide growth of 1.907 trillion."[v]

What's in store for future digital buying from country to country? The following chart (Figure 8-2) shows the growth in the number of people buying goods over the Internet:[vi]

Digital Buyers Worldwide, by Country, 2014-2019
millions

	2014	2015	2016	2017	2018	2019
China (1)	372.8	418.7	468.1	514.4	556.6	600.0
US (2)	164.6	171.8	179.0	185.8	191.2	195.1
India	54.1	82.3	112.7	153.2	192.6	239.7
Japan	75.0	77.0	78.3	79.5	80.3	81.1
Germany	45.6	47.1	47.9	48.5	49.1	49.5
UK (3)	39.5	40.6	41.6	42.4	43.0	43.5
Brazil	33.2	37.3	41.1	44.3	47.3	49.7
Russia	30.6	32.9	34.5	35.5	36.6	37.6
France	28.7	29.9	30.7	31.3	31.9	32.4
South Korea	23.1	25.0	26.6	28.3	29.8	31.2
Indonesia	14.6	22.5	30.8	40.4	50.5	61.7
Canada	17.4	18.1	18.6	19.2	19.7	20.2
Spain	16.2	17.5	18.5	19.4	20.2	20.9
Italy	15.1	16.2	17.4	18.3	19.0	19.5
Mexico	14.3	16.2	18.2	20.0	21.9	23.6
Australia	11.8	12.1	12.4	12.6	12.9	13.1
Argentina	10.2	11.2	11.7	12.2	12.5	12.9
Netherlands	9.6	9.9	10.2	10.3	10.4	10.5
Sweden	5.4	5.5	5.6	5.7	5.8	5.8
Denmark	3.4	3.4	3.5	3.6	3.6	3.7
Norway	2.9	3.0	3.1	3.2	3.3	3.4
Finland	2.7	2.8	2.9	2.9	3.0	3.1
Worldwide (4)	1,317.8	1,462.4	1,610.1	1,765.2	1,914.1	2,068.7

Note: ages 14+; internet users who have made at least one purchase via any digital channel during the calendar year, including online, mobile and tablet purchases; (1) excludes Hong Kong; (2) forecast from Aug 2015; (3) forecast from Sep 2015; (4) includes countries not listed
Source: eMarketer, Dec 2015

Figure 8-2. "Worldwide Retail Ecommerce Sales: eMarketer's Updated Estimates and Forecast Through 2019," Douglas Clark, eMarketer, March 6, 2016. Used with permission.

Why Do I Need a Stand-Alone E-Commerce Site?

Having a stand-alone e-commerce site—on which you can sell your products beyond eBay, Amazon, or Etsy—offers greater control over the sales process, larger revenue and profits for your business, more focused global brand development, new interactions with people across the world, and a 24/7 open-for-business model. A hosted stand-alone e-commerce solution will provide everything from domain name registration to the tools and resources you need to build an e-commerce Web site with minimal technical and Web site design knowledge.

Selling in a Digital World: Business-to-Business, Business-to-Consumer, Consumer-to-Consumer, or Business-to-Government Experience?

When you set up an e-commerce shop, you must decide who your primary customers are going to be: other businesses, consumers, or the government. Let's go over what each means. Please note, it is possible to focus on two at once, provided you make it clear on your Internet platform.

Business-to-business (B-to-B) describes commerce-based transactions between two businesses, such as between a manufacturer and a retailer.

Business-to-consumer (B-to-C) describes commerce-based transactions between a business and a consumer, such as a retailer selling directly to you. Target, for example, sells directly to you, the consumer. (Target's supply chain, on the other hand, would be B-to-B.)

Some companies are both B-to-B and B-to-C. Think along the lines of my business, GlobeTrade.com. My customers are primarily other businesses, so it's B-to-B, but I also have consumers who come to me directly asking for help before they start a global business. That's B-to-C. Another example of B-to-B that moves into B-to-C is Procter & Gamble, which manufactures Tide laundry detergent. The company's production supply chain involves B-to-B transactions, but once Tide is in finished form, P&G shifts its selling to B-to-C where you, as a consumer, buy Tide.[vii]

Consumer-to-consumer (C-to-C) describes commerce transactions between consumers. Think of eBay and Alibaba's Taobao. You, as an individual, as opposed to a legal business entity, would sell directly to other consumers.

Business-to-government (B-to-G) describes commerce transactions between a business and the government, including ones that are local, federal, and state-based. Think along the lines of a business bidding on governmental opportunities in the form of a request for proposal (RFP) and offering those bids through an online marketplace.

An easy way to figure out which type of customer is best for your business is to ask yourself: where will I get the biggest bang for my buck? If you sell hammers, will you sell more hammers directly to consumers (B-to-C) or through a business that buys twenty-four hammers in a box at once and resells them individually to consumers (B-to-B)? Either way, you must fulfill the orders or have the vendor do it.

In the case of selling directly to consumers, can you handle shipping individually to every consumer who buys your product? That's where most business owners stop dead in their tracks. They either don't want to do it or aren't set up to do it at the outset. It's too labor intensive. If that is the case with you, go with B-to-B to minimize additional handling and labor costs. You can always change course or do two different selling avenues at once, provided you make it clear on each of your sites who your target audience is.

Now let's really change courses. A challenge you could be faced with involves the sourcing of a product domestically or overseas. You may want to familiarize yourself with these pointers on how to go about it.

Finding a Manufacturer for the Product You May Want to Export

To find manufacturers—which can be located in different countries in different continents—for the product you may want to export, you'll need to consult some specialized sources. Sourcing a product globally for a particular brand offers many benefits for the exporter, including lower costs, faster go-to-market time, and a broader resource pool. You can identify an existing product you think might sell in other countries and make a deal with the producer (more on this in Chapter 11). But you can also contract manufacture (also known as outsourcing), where your company arranges with a manufacturer to make a product to your specification (or those of the manufacturer you represent). Here are a few places to get started (some are more United States centric):

Tip A five-point strategy for making your first global sourcing foray successful should include sourcing from a country with low labor costs and good quality (look for ISO certification) where you can take a plane ride with comfort and ease; where you can understand the language; where you can respect and abide by the laws; and where you can trust the people you do business with. Oh, and did I mention the importance of access to a huge and growing market?

- *ThomasNet:* http://www.thomasnet.com/. The ThomasNet is a free platform designed for sourcing components, equipment, MRO (maintenance, repair, and operations) products, raw materials, and custom manufacturing services.

- *The Gale Book of Associations:* http://www.gale.cengage.com/DirectoryLibrary/. Gale lists associations related to your product type; e.g., if you look under "Consumer Household Products" you will find "National Housewares Association." If you contact the National Housewares Association, you may find that it offers a membership, manufacturer lists, exhibition dates, and industry mailing pieces. These references will be invaluable to your exporting efforts.

- *Global Sources:* http://www.globalsources.com. Global Sources is a B2B marketplace that connects global buyers and suppliers.

- *Alibaba:* http://www.alibaba.com. Find products, suppliers, manufacturers, and exporters by categories.

- *United States Manufacturer Directory:* http://www.manufacturerusa.com/. Find links to manufacturer websites, browse for wholesalers, business, and manufacturing services in the United States.

- *National Association of Manufacturers (NAM):* http://www.nam.org/. NAM is a top manufacturing association in the United States.

- *Alliance for American Manufacturing:* http://www.americanmanufacturing.org/. The Alliance for American Manufacturing explores common solutions to public policy topics such as job creation, infrastructure investment, international trade, and global competitiveness.

- *Kompass:* http://www.kompass.com. Search and find suppliers across the world by industry, products, or services.

- *Maker's Row:* http://www.makersrow.com. Access industry-specific factories and suppliers across the United States.

- *IndiaMART:* http://www.indiamart.com. IndiaMART is India's largest online marketplace, connecting buyers with suppliers.

- *MFG.com*: http://www.mfg.com. Source suppliers and get pricing at the same time. After you post a request for quotation, complete with engineering drawings, MFG. com matches your requirements with suppliers around the world (or anywhere you choose).

Once you find a contract manufacturer to your liking, here are your next steps. Let's say you are looking for a manufacturer that can produce an all-around tote bag for cleaning products. Think of it as swag—a branded tote bag with your company information embroidered on—that provides value to your customers and enhances the brand for your family of products. You plan to offer this tote for free when consumers show proof of purchase on six or more of your products within ninety days. Historically, consumers buy one of your products within the same time period. Here's how you get started with a potential manufacturer.

1. Send your idea sketches and screenshots to him for review. Indicate you are interested in importing a test production run of 1,000 all-around tote bags (or whatever number of totes you can afford to buy on the initial trial run) and state, according to your market analysis, that you need a price point of U.S. $5 a tote to go to market competitively.

2. See whether the supplier can produce what you need within your specific timeframe, manufacture a minimum production run quantity without a glitch, and maintain your price point.

3. Anticipating future success, ask for volume pricing, too. For example, let's say your swag campaign works so well that you need to order 20,000 totes as opposed to 1,000 at a time! You might find that your pricing drops from $5 a tote on 1,000-tote orders to $1 a tote on 20,000-tote orders. Talk about a customer response and profit boost. You may end up selling six times more product within the ninety days!

4. Confirm that pricing is FOB (also known as Free on Board or Freight on Board) from the factory, meaning all charges (taxes, duties, transport and insurance) are your responsibility once the product leaves the door. You can always get a logistics expert to help you on the import.

5. How will you pay the manufacturer and will there be any chance to receive extended terms—thirty, sixty, or ninety days—as opposed to an immediate wire transfer?

6. Lastly, ask for three to five complimentary samples made to your specs and find out when they can be delivered. Then sit tight. While you wait, draw up a plan for your online swag campaign party.

As for suppliers, not all are equal. Some can be timely and send requested samples in a heartbeat. Others can take forever but can meet your pricing. The worst case is when a supplier provides poor-quality samples of products. Even asking at the very beginning for ISO 9000 certification proof from a supplier[viii] does not guarantee that product samples will meet your quality standards and be to your liking.

What if you receive shoddy product samples from a potential new supplier? Although the answer seems like a no-brainer, you'd be surprised at how many companies expend an inordinate amount of time trying to work things out. Let's take a look at how the scenario plays out when the first round of product samples is not up to par.

Within forty-five days, suppliers send you samples made to your specification for review and within the price range you desire. Even the minimum order requirement meets your budget! But four out of the five all-around totes are crappy quality. What should you do?

Go with the supplier with the best quality and start thinking about how you will visit the supplier in person at some point to evaluate operations. For now, reject the other four and tell them why. No ifs, ands, or buts. If you start out with poor product samples, do you really think product quality will improve over time? Don't be fooled. First impressions count. Quality matters.

Now that you've covered selling in a digital world, who your customers are, and where your products are originating, it's time to manage your global supply chain.

Managing a Global Supply Chain

After deciding who your customers are going to be and setting up an e-commerce site designed to attract them comes the responsibility of managing an effective and efficient supply chain. This process focuses on the flow of goods from the origin source; through the distribution channels; to the end consumer; and, finally, to disposal and recycling. Supply chains that were once purely local are now global in nature and more complex and interconnected as goods, services, and information flow across borders easily.

When entering new markets, as often is the case with exports done via e-commerce, the goal is to service the customers efficiently and in a fast manner, at the lowest possible cost, and with minimal inventories to keep your profits soaring.

A plan of action for a supply chain might look like this:

1. Source components or products (if required)

2. Produce products (at your own manufacturing facility)

3. Manage the handling and storage of raw materials and finished products (from your own manufacturing facility)

4. Combat cyber crime activities by developing a framework for evaluating and responding to risks

5. Develop transportation and logistics strategies, including customs processing and border crossing

6. Integrate transportation strategies with production and marketing plans

7. Analyze, plan, and monitor the global supply chain process

8. Check profits

9. Measure customer satisfaction

10. Develop a process to convert returns or defects into recyclable materials for subsequent use

11. Design a way to dispose of and recycle products on an as-needed-basis

We'll touch on some of these elements in subsequent chapters, but for now it is essential to be aware of them in the understanding of maximizing customer value and achieving sustainable profitable growth for your business.

Tip Most companies start out manufacturing a product domestically and then exporting it. When they achieve success in a single export market, they consider setting up a contract to manufacture the product in the overseas market where the product is in demand—all with the intent to lower costs, increase profits, and expeditiously fulfill customer demand.

Tips for Managing a Global Supply Chain

Your global supply chain should be short, simple, and manageable. Whether sourcing a component part used in the production of a product or finished goods, treat the chain as a strategic asset—one that, handled deftly, can provide a competitive advantage.

It is worth mentioning that many large companies use software programs for managing the export supply chain process, for purposes including item classification, order taking, compliance with export regulations, and generation of export documentation. The use of export software enables companies to manage the supply chain with greater ease and efficiency. Conducting an Internet search for third-party vendors using "export supply chain management software" or similar search terms will generate a number of specialized companies who offer sourcing, transportation, and fulfillment services. Due to the complex nature and the costs associated with export software management, most small businesses tend to manage their supply chain by working closely with logistics experts that offer you approved vendors who integrate their technology into your business applications and software solutions. These companies include UPS, FedEx, and DHL; UPS will custom fit a solution based on your supply chain needs.

Here are ten tips to assist you in managing a global supply chain:

1. Source products from countries where regulations and restrictions are minimal. You want the ability to transport materials in and out of a country fast.

2. Focus on minimizing costs but not to the detriment of sacrificing quality.

3. Make sure that in performance-based contracts the supplier has a stake in where the product is sold. That way, you share risks and rewards.

4. Establish a secondary source of supply to ensure that your primary source can be replaced easily. The performance of a primary supplier can quickly go south. Perhaps the company runs into financial problems, produces shoddy products, or falls short on delivery times. Should this occur, you will need a backup supplier.

5. Tailor the locations of the supply chain directly to those of your customers, wherever they are.

6. Test the reliability of the supplier. When you order, how long does it take for the company to respond and deliver? Does it invoice you accurately?

7. Address cultural differences at the outset of the relationship, because if not treated skillfully, it can create barriers that impede or completely stymie the global supply chain process.

8. Know where all your materials are coming in and out of and what the costs are to move them to any point.

9. Retain as much control as you can over the entire supply chain process.

10. Conduct regular assessments of every supplier contracted to manufacture your products in order to ensure they are meeting labor, health, safety, and environmental requirements.

Efficient global supply chains can be a weapon of widespread competitiveness. And keep an eye out on how you might use drones—unmanned aerial vehicles—as part of your supply chain strategy. It's not too far out in the future, because drones are finding a niche, especially in remote areas of the world.

Get to Know the Suppliers in Your Supply Chain

Today, most supply chains are built on a sourcing strategy that emphasizes value creation. What that means is that instead of looking for the lowest possible price of a product, you should first determine what value you are trying to achieve for your business. You could determine that what is most important to you is exercising control, minimizing risks, balancing costs, or gaining speed-to-market.

Caution What's the likelihood of having a critical supply shortage and how would it impact your business? Always have a contingency plan in place for the most catastrophic event ever.

A working global supply chain must be responsive and flexible on a local level as well as overseas. It will morph several times during the course of a product's lifetime. Whatever it takes to fulfill the needs of your customers worldwide, that should be your goal.

Finding the Best E-Commerce Store for Your Business

Before you do anything, draw up a list of what you need to do to establish the features you need for your e-shop based on what you are selling. Factor in the supply-chain process we just covered. For example, if you are selling knit caps for babies, your list might look like this:

1. Integrate e-shop that accommodates all major social media platforms;

2. Have a program with the ability to serve customers worldwide when collecting payments;

3. Calculate the cost of shipping on demand, where an all-inclusive shipping rate can be quoted to customers (including taxes, currency conversion, duties, insurance, and payment fee, if any) through UPS, FedEx, DHL, TNT, or USPS; and

4. Organize 24/7 customer support.

Run the list by your potential e-commerce-platform vendor to make sure the company can accommodate your needs. The type of product you are selling affects the features you want for your e-shop.

Factors to Consider

What follows is a list of fourteen factors to consider when researching your e-commerce storefront platform. This is the list I use in working with clients; however, there are likely more factors than what's included here. Not all of them will apply to your current business needs, but it's better to be aware of them in advance than be blindsided by a lack of needed support later on. Let's take a look at the features a platform should offer:

1. *It should be simple to set up, have the ability to use your own domain name, and be affordable and easy to run.* Most e-commerce stores are free to set up, but they cost anywhere from $29 a month for 100 products or fewer to $179 a month for unlimited bandwidth. Some platforms allow you to use your own domain and others don't, so if using your own domain name is important to you and a company can't do it, go elsewhere with your business.

■ **Tip** Many popular web-hosting companies (e.g., Network Solutions, Go Daddy, Bluehost, and Verio) offer e-commerce solutions such as tools, resources, and storefronts. And some blogging platforms allow you to transform your Web site into an e-commerce store for free. (Check out WooCommerce [http://www.woothemes.com/woocommerce/] and Jigoshop [http://jigoshop.com/].) Before making a move, investigate your existing host's complete e-shop capabilities, including order fulfillment.

---

2. *It should have a good selection of design templates and excellent shopping-cart functionality.* Look for an e-commerce platform that offers hundreds of beautiful design templates along with the ability to preview and customize the design with the help of your own technology designer. Make sure photos can be easily uploaded so that they will look fantastic on your site. Having a smooth shopping cart and checkout experience will create an exceptional buying event for your customers.

Tip A bad e-commerce design with ineffective functions can damage your whole online business before you know it. You can minimize shopping cart abandonment—whereby a customer gets almost to the finish line at checkout and leaves the site for whatever unknown reason—by making the checkout process one step. Some e-commerce platforms offer a special add-on feature at a minimal cost to treat shopping-cart abandonment issues.

---

3. *It should have unlimited e-commerce hosting.* Whether you are selling two products or two thousand, ask your vendor if there are any hosting restrictions. For example, you don't want an additional charge for increased traffic to your site. Success shouldn't bring you lower profits—it should bring you more! It's always best to look through the lens of the best-case scenario and seek vendors that offer scalability and the opportunity to quickly add more capacity.

4. *It should offer real-time carrier shipping that includes complete international coverage and calculates real-time rates.* Real-time carrier shipping connects your storefront with a UPS, USPS, or FedEx account that your customers can use to calculate shipping costs. This means you don't need to manage your shipping rates manually. Pushing that concept further, inquire as to whether the e-commerce platform provider can quote international shipping costs in real time, quote customers without including shipping costs, and build the shipping into the customer's cost.

5. *It should accept currency from all over the world.* Be sure the e-commerce stores you set up will be able to accept payment from all around the world, whether dealing in your own currency or another country's. When operating beyond U.S. borders, adopt a local payment platform and you will see your revenue skyrocket.

6. *It should be able to serve as your host platform if you don't already have a domain name.* Shopify is a good example of a platform that provides this. You will then add content, design, products, payment methods, taxes, shipping, and a domain name. Then you are ready to sell to the world.

7. *It should offer a web host if you don't have one already.* All Shopify plans, for example, include secure, unlimited e-commerce hosting for your online store. On the other hand, Network Solutions requires you to have a domain name registration and web-hosting package before you can use its e-commerce Web site.

8. *It should have mobile-friendly add-ons.* Shoot for responsive web design (RWD), which allows web visitors to access the same site and content no matter what kind of device they are using—whether it is a PC, tablet, or mobile device. Snowboard retailer Burton (http://www. burton.com/) and Houzz (http://www.houzz.com) are both good examples of companies that have designed their Web sites for their customers to use from their phones and tablets.

9. *It should not require you to have IT experience to build and maintain your site.* Choose a platform that offers a plug, play, and sell e-shop. You should be able to plug in all the information about your company and products, play with it to get it looking good and working right, and then start selling. It should take only a couple of hours to get things up and running.

10. *It should offer 24/7 service and tech support.* Inquire as to how the vendor would handle a situation where your e-commerce platform crashes. It should have a cloud backup, offer support after hours and on weekends, and operate in several different time zones. For every minute you are down online, you lose existing and potential business.

11. *It should have social media support.* Ensure that it has buttons to connect to Pinterest, Instagram, Twitter, and so forth. Strategic use of social media will increase your customer base and your bottom line.

12. *It should have app support.* Some e-commerce sites, like Magento, offer what are called white-label e-commerce apps. These apps essentially translate an existing e-commerce site into a mobile app that fits each device, complete with a full catalog, a product-search mechanism, a shopping cart, and the ability to offer ratings and reviews. A few sites now also offer an app for order fulfillment. Inquire.

13. It should have built-in search engine optimization (SEO) and conversion tools to scale your business globally.

14. *It should offer strong protection against potential fraud, viruses, and scams while not getting in the way of e-commerce.* Security—or the lack of it—is at the top of the list concerning e-commerce, so cover this issue extensively with your vendor until you are convinced that the company can protect your business interests and your customer's business interests. Some e-commerce platforms provide a badge that you can install on your design to show your customers that your checkout is safe and secure. Despite the absolute importance of security, the bottom line is that security measures must be implemented so that they do not inhibit or dissuade the use of e-commerce.

Note Educating the consumer on security issues is still in the infancy stage but will prove to be the most critical element of the e-commerce security architecture in the future.

Creating Your Own E-Commerce Platform

As discussed, setting up an e-commerce platform is a fast way to expand your market base, exercise greater control, and increase sales and profitability. Starting an e-commerce platform on your own rather than contracting with a hosting vendor comes with additional legal and financial considerations. The most significant of these are in the areas of online business protection, including security (making it payment card security compliant, known as payment card industry [PCI] compliant—both keep your customers' credit card data safe); reliability; and intellectual property issues.

Also be aware that you must adapt to an international market's import regulations (tariffs and taxes, for example). This includes but is not limited to shipping prohibited and restricted items, which vary by country. Further, it is your responsibility to comply with export laws, as some governments do not permit companies to legally ship to specific countries. Here are a select few stand-alone e-commerce platforms to get started with that can be integrated into your existing Web site (they all offer robust e-commerce solutions with greatly varying monthly price points):

- *Bigcommerce:* (http://www.bigcommerce.com). This site gives you everything you need to sell online.

- *GoEcart* : (http://www.goecart.com). GoECart is a fully integrated web-based ecommerce suite that offers ecommerce storefront technology with inventory management, fulfillment, and warehouse management and customer relationship management (CRM).

- *Intuit:* (http://www.intuit.com/websites/ecommerce-how-to/). This site, which is now powered by Homestead, gives you a free thirty-day trial period. You can build a store with up to a hundred products, integrate it into your Web site design, and give customers an easy-to-use checkout experience.

- *Magento:* (http://www.magentocommerce.com). The Magento platform is a leading platform for open commerce innovation with over $50B in gross merchandise volume transacted on the platform annually. Magento is built on open-source technology, enabling businesses of all sizes to control and customize the look and feel, content, and functionality of their online stores.

- *NetSuite SuiteCommerce:* http://www.netsuite.com/portal/products/netsuite/ecommerce/products.shtml). NetSuite SuiteCommerce offers a great shopping experience on any device, in any language, and through any business model.

- *Pitney Bowes:* (http://www.pb.com/ecommerce/).

  Pitney Bowes provides an interesting feature—fully guaranteed landed (door-to-door) cost quotes along with everything else you need to facilitate the global e-commerce experience.

- *Shopify:* (http://www.shopify.com). Shopify does a good job with plug-ins (special functions) and also offers you pay-as-you-grow usage. They also give you a free 14-day trial. When you add features or services to your e-shop, you will be charged extra.

- *Volusion:* (http://www.volusion.com). Volusion is worth a look purely from the standpoint that the company currently has more than forty thousand online stores, fostering more than $21 billion in online merchant sales worldwide to date. You can try it free for 14 days. Volusion also owns Mozo (http://www.mozo.com), another commerce platform for the global marketplace.

Here's a sampling of a few foreign-based e-commerce platforms:

- *base.com* (Japan): http://www.base.com

- *Rakuten* (Japan): http://global.rakuten.com/en/

- *Ozon.ru* (Russia): http://www.ozon.ru/

- *E-bit* (Brazil): http://www.ebit.com.br/

- *Flipkart* (India): http://www.flipkart.com

- *SnapDeal* (India): http://www.snapdeal.com

- *Rocket Internet* (Germany): http://www.rocket-internet.com

- *Souq.com* (Dubai): http://www.uae.souq.com/ae-en/

Tip   See if your e-commerce vendor allows for customers to pin a specific product or anything that you're selling to a Pinterest pinboard. This helps get the word out on your product offerings to increase purchases. Some platforms have built-in apps for this, and others provide a step-by-step guide on how to get it done. The goal, in this instance, is to have every pin become a "buyable pin" on Pinterest.

The Ultimate E-Commerce Must-Have: Trustworthiness

You can have all the bells and whistles operating perfectly on your new e-commerce site, but the key ingredient to customers enjoying their visit and actually buying products or services online is trustworthiness. If you lack trustworthiness, customers won't stick around, and those who give your shop a chance better be treated right or else they will never return. Convince your customers that you can be trusted. How can that be done? Here are some tips based on what has worked for many of my clients on their Web sites:

1. *Showcase a reputable security badge such as Verisign, TRUSTe, PayPal, or McAfee.* Feature more than one to make customers feel secure and confident with their purchase. Other things that reinforce trust are large corporations that praise you (but get permission from individuals at the companies to use testimonials), awards you received, a mention in the press—all these should be promoted on your e-commerce site with links to the source if still active.

2. *Show a phone number, e-mail address, and real physical address—not a P.O. Box.* Or have a live chat button that is easy to find. If people plan to purchase a product from your e-commerce site, they want to know how to get ahold of you to ask questions. Or let them know how they will get help if a purchased product arrives damaged.

3. *Respond to every customer's question.* The question can be about the size of a product, the material used in the making of it—"Do your earrings contain lead? Because I am allergic to lead"—or if its color is sky blue or turquoise blue. The more you offer candid and direct communications with customers and address their needs, the more likely you are to produce sales and repeat customers. From their perspective, you showed you are responsive and care.

4. *Use psychology to your advantage with your customers.* There are a variety of meanings, interpretations, and perceptions between cultures and contexts. Use color wisely. If trust is critical to your brand, think along the lines of using lots of blue on your site, because it reflects honesty, trust, and reliability. Red, on the other hand, emits excitement, attention, and love. Certain colors appeal to certain cultures and markets.

5. *Test it in a real-world scenario.* Monitor the system to see what can go wrong—especially from the customer's perspective. Test it yourself, have an employee do a dry run, ask a family member to go through it step by step, or select someone from your Facebook fan base to give it a try (then offer him something in return for his effort, such as a free sample product, a helpful how-to book, or a gift card). One bad impression from a customer not only costs you that customer but also hundreds and thousands, if not millions, more customers largely due to the power of social media where people can say what they want when they don't like an experience.

■ **Caution**   Capturing low-hanging fruit or tiny export deals by offering a "Buy Now" or "Buy With" button on your site to be used with PayPal, Google Wallet, Apple Pay, or Amazon Checkout won't power up your export business. Yes, these functions are reliable and trusted to sell to anyone with an email address and funds in their bank account, but do you want to sell one product a day or millions of products a month? That's the difference between selling via a Buy Now button versus a secure, reliable and easy-to-use platform that addresses the full range of e-commerce needs.

Measuring E-Commerce Success

Now that we've looked at everything involved in setting up an e-commerce shop, how can we measure results? That's a challenge, because you cannot predict customer behavior nor can you forecast sales and profits accurately at the start, but you will be able to after a couple of months. However, if you address these five questions concerning your site, you are more than likely to discover quickly if your e-commerce program is working or not:

1. What is the dollar value (revenue) of the activities completed through e-commerce?

2. What is the number of visits—site traffic?

3. What is the number of new customers gained through e-commerce?

4. What is the site's profitability?

5. What is the cost factor involved in running the e-commerce platform?

The goal of an e-commerce initiative is to increase the revenue and growth of profit for your business while decreasing costs, thus contributing to the long-term success of the corporation.

Summary

Building a powerful, cost-effective, and complete e-commerce site prepares you for takeoff in the export world. As more and more consumers adapt to Internet technologies in the coming years, there will be a huge demand for mobile functionality and apps that power user engagement. After all, the world works better when it's connected in every way imaginable, including making an export sale. One final thought: Who does not get excited over the notion of taking the world by surprise? That's what happens when you build a great e-commerce site that tells people in a compelling way what your business brings to the world.

In the next chapter, we'll look at mobile commerce and computing, apps, and cloud computing. All of these enable you to continue to build your brand, find and service new customers, engage and deepen your user base relationships, and grow revenues and profitability through exports.

Notes

i. The markets include business to business (B-to-B), business to consumer (B-to-C), consumer to consumer (C-to-C), and business to government (B-to-G).

ii. "Global Retail E-Commerce Keeps On Clicking," accessed March 6, 2016, https://www.atkearney.com/consumer-products-retail/e-commerce-index/full-report/-/asset_publisher/87xbENNHPZ3D/content/global-retail-e-commerce-keeps-on-clicking/10192.

iii. "Quarterly Retail E-Commerce Sales, 4ᵗʰ Quarter 2015," U.S. Census Bureau News, U.S. Department of Commerce, accessed March 6, 2016, http://www.census.gov/retail/mrts/www/data/pdf/ec_current.pdf.

iv. "Worldwide Retail Ecommerce Sales: eMarketer's Updated Estimates and Forecast Through 2019," eMarketer, accessed March 6, 2016, http://www.emarketer.com/public_media/docs/eMarketer_eTailWest2016_Worldwide_ECommerce_Report.pdf.

v. Ibid.

vi. Ibid.

vii. For Tide's B-to-C Web site, see "All Products," accessed March 6, 2016, http://www.tide.com/en-US/product-Landing.jspx.

viii. ISO 9000 is a certification of the production process only and does not guarantee a manufacturer produces a quality product.

The Mobile World at Work

A Great Challenge and Opportunity for Businesses Today

If you look out, maybe five or 10 years, when all 5 billion people who have feature phones are going to have smartphones, we're soon going to be living in a world where the majority of people who have a smartphone—a modern computing device—will have never seen in their lives what you and I call a "computer."

—Facebook Founder and CEO Mark Zuckerberg (2013)[i]

A Facebook page is an instant mobile marketing strategy, and a way for you to have a mobile presence really easily and free of cost.

—Bess Yount, who heads up Facebook's efforts to engage with smaller businesses in North America (2016)[ii]

My morning starts with coffee and a check of the news on my tablet. I'll also check out my social media sites, starting with accepting LinkedIn invitations before heading to Facebook to see what others are up to. As I start making breakfast, I switch from tablet to smart phone to see if anyone has sent an

© Laurel J. Delaney 2016
L. J. Delaney, *Exporting*, DOI 10.1007/978-1-4842-2193-8_9

important text message. I scan my e-mail, open a few apps to skim more news, and receive a prompt that my phone has not been backed up on the cloud for several weeks. I turn back to my tablet for the TuneIn radio app, which streams music that I can listen to as I make breakfast.

That is a glimpse of my typical Sunday morning, and it's quite possibly the same for you and for many others who have access to web-enabled devices. Why mobile Internet? In 2015, networking giant Cisco estimated that mobile data traffic grew 74 percent in 2015.[iii] More than half a billion (563 million) mobile devices and connections were added in 2015. Smartphones accounted for most of that growth. Global mobile devices and connections in 2015 grew to 7.9 billion, up from 7.3 billion in 2014.[iv] According to Cisco, "'smart devices' refers to mobile connections that have advanced multimedia/computing capabilities with a minimum of 3G connectivity."

Over and above that, three-fourths (75 percent) of the world's mobile data traffic will be video by 2020 and global mobile data traffic will increase nearly eightfold between 2015 and 2020.[v]

No matter how you view the mobile world, get this straight: mobile devices will soon be used by everyone on the planet and will become the center of online activity for researching, connecting, sharing, collaborating, buying, exporting, and producing local content worldwide, revolutionizing all methods of communication. And it is no secret that millennials and Generation C (the connected consumer) are key drivers of this usage through a strong attachment to their mobile devices.

The potential of mobile Internet is huge and has already started by opening our lives to the world with a swipe, tap, click or zoom on a digital device that's right in your pocket or sitting next to your bedside table. Each of us has the capability to become a roving global merchant with a digital device in hand and a connection to the Internet, capturing customers for life.

And that leads us to where your next export might come from. In this section, I'll cover mobile and what I call MAC (mobile, apps, and cloud computing), and I'll show you plenty of profit potential. What I can't do here is cover the topic as thoroughly as I would like because that would entail a separate book and mobile technology is rapidly changing and evolving. So consider this a start—a primer of sorts—in understanding the power of mobile, what it means to you and your export business, and how to create and harness the mobile Internet experience to build a better future for your business. In addition to reading this book, you should connect in chat rooms and online forums to further the conversation and get up to speed with new technology and developments.

Case Example: Low-Cost Internet Device Taking India by Storm

Aakash (http://www.akashtablet.com), an Android-based, low-cost, seven-inch-screen tablet computer, officially launched in New Delhi in October 2011. Distributed by British company Datawind, Aakash was manufactured by the India-based company Quad Electronics and was procured by the Indian government to help enhance the quality of education. The government's goal is to equip the country's 220 million students with Aakash tablets and other similar products in the next few years.

Originally projected as a $35 laptop, the device was sold to India's government and has been distributed to university students—initially at US$50. When there is more demand, the price will drop until it reaches the target goal of the $35 selling price. The tablet price continues to change regularly.

Datawind's CEO Suneet Singh Tuli has said: "DataWind is open to driving the pricing down even further as it scales up. The company's roadmap charts a path to sub-$20 tablet in less than two years."[vi]

Datawind has risen to become one of the top three tablet suppliers in India, alongside Apple and Samsung.[vii]

Another India-based company poised for growth is Ringing Bells Freedom 251 with its Android smartphone for just Rs 251, which is less than USD 4 (actually $3.65 at present rates).[viii]

Expect more of these affordable Internet devices to be manufactured and sold, because they level the playing field and allow everyone a chance not just to connect, but to sell or buy things with anyone in the world. All the more reason to get your business tuned up for global mobile.

Harnessing Mobile Business Opportunities

For many people, checking the Internet has quickly become a habit, like brushing your teeth, making your bed, or combing your hair. As the world is revolutionized by the availability of more low-cost tablets and smart phones, the Internet will serve as the CCV—chief communication vehicle—for billions of people.

How will mobile technology affect small businesses? For any company offering information, e-commerce, tools, or deals, apps and mobile-friendly Web sites or blogs will be the ultimate way to communicate and interact quickly with consumers worldwide. Because mobile technology has conditioned people to expect instant gratification, the information you offer must hit the mark right away, be digestible by anyone, and be in sync across all devices. What will come out of this warp-speed activity? A new breed of global mobile business leaders attempting to predict not only what customers buy, but also precisely where, when, and how they are most likely to buy it. There will be an increasing use of mobile to drive revenue and profit margin growth—not to mention a further complete analysis on how and why consumers shop on their mobile devices. The future effect of mobile technology on exports and global trade in general will be huge. It will help erase distances and allow you to quickly share information and buy and sell cost-effectively from any corner of the world.

Consider these findings about smart phone owners and Internet usage by a recently released Pew Research Center report:[ix]

- Smartphone ownership rates have skyrocketed in many countries since 2013. This includes increases of over 25 percentage points among the total population in large emerging economies such as Turkey (+42 points), Malaysia (+34), Chile (+26) and Brazil (+26).

- South Korea stands out as the country with the highest smartphone ownership rate, with **88%** of respondents saying they own one. The countries with the least smartphone ownership rates are also among the poorest: Tanzania (11%), Uganda (4%) and Ethiopia (4%).

- In a number of emerging and developing countries, more people have access to the internet and are also using it more frequently. In 12 emerging nations surveyed in 2014 and 2015, there were significant increases in the share of adult internet users who say they access the internet several times a day, including in Nigeria (+20 points), Ghana (+19) and China (+13).

- There are gender gaps in many aspects of technology use. For example, in 20 nations, men are more likely than women to use the internet. These differences are especially stark in African nations. Elsewhere, equal shares of men and women use the internet. But large gender gaps also appear in reported smartphone ownership (men are more likely to own a smartphone) in many countries, including Mexico (+16), Nigeria (+13), Kenya (+12), and Ghana (+12).

Take a good look at the following graph (Figure 9-1) from eMarketer[x] to see what the top content activities were among mobile phone users in February 2015. What is striking about the data is how buying and selling goods and services on mobile Internet devices (referred to as m-commerce), is not highlighted in the chart. Yet, eMarketer indicates this: "The ecommerce audience on mobile is also growing robustly. This year, eMarketer forecasts, 121.8 million US consumers ages 14 and up will make at least one purchase via a mobile browser or app this year, whether on a tablet, smartphone or other device. That represents 70.9% of the total US digital buying audience this year. While nearly 100 million people will make a purchase via tablet this year, fewer than 80 million will do so on a smartphone—but that's up from 67.2 million in 2014, and is expected to reach 105.6 million by 2019, when nearly half of all smartphone users will make a mobile purchase."[xi]

All the more reason to ready your business for mobile now, before everyone else gets to your customers before you do!

US Mobile Phone Content Usage Metrics, 2013-2019

	2013	2014	2015	2016	2017	2018	2019
Mobile phone video viewers (millions)	**76.7**	**94.1**	**107.1**	**117.2**	**123.9**	**131.4**	**136.9**
—% change	20.0%	22.6%	13.8%	9.5%	5.7%	6.0%	4.2%
—% of mobile phone users	31.0%	37.2%	41.5%	44.7%	46.6%	48.6%	50.0%
—% of population	24.2%	29.5%	33.3%	36.2%	37.9%	39.9%	41.3%
Mobile phone music listeners (millions)	**71.6**	**87.2**	**100.1**	**112.3**	**121.3**	**128.5**	**134.5**
—% change	31.9%	21.7%	14.8%	12.2%	8.0%	5.9%	4.7%
—% of mobile phone users	29.0%	34.5%	38.8%	42.8%	45.6%	47.5%	49.1%
—% of population	22.6%	27.4%	31.2%	34.7%	37.1%	39.0%	40.5%
Mobile phone gamers (millions)	**129.3**	**147.6**	**164.9**	**180.4**	**192.2**	**202.8**	**209.5**
—% change	21.1%	14.2%	11.7%	9.4%	6.6%	5.5%	3.3%
—% of mobile phone users	52.3%	58.4%	63.9%	68.8%	72.3%	75.0%	76.5%
—% of population	40.9%	46.3%	51.3%	55.7%	58.9%	61.6%	63.1%
Mobile phone search users (millions)	**109.6**	**133.6**	**157.3**	**177.8**	**196.5**	**207.6**	**215.8**
—% change	32.7%	21.9%	17.8%	13.0%	10.5%	5.6%	4.0%
—% of mobile phone users	44.3%	52.8%	61.0%	67.8%	73.9%	76.8%	78.8%
—% of population	34.6%	41.9%	49.0%	54.9%	60.2%	63.1%	65.0%
Mobile phone social network users (millions)	**118.6**	**136.4**	**151.2**	**162.6**	**170.7**	**178.4**	**183.5**
—% change	23.0%	15.0%	10.9%	7.5%	5.0%	4.5%	2.8%
—% of mobile	48.0%	53.9%	58.6%	62.0%	64.2%	66.0%	67.0%

Figure 9-1. From "Mobile Content and Activities Roundup," eMarketer, April 2015. Used with permission.

The MAC Attack

MAC is an abbreviation I coined. It stands for mobile, apps, and the cloud. These are really three modes in which a mobile user can experience the Web. The more you understand the experiences of users (think of users as potential customers), the better your chance of succeeding with your mobile efforts, especially on an international scale. Let's examine what each type of experience involves and how to go about creating ones that are compelling, engaging, and useful for your customers—wherever they might be located.

Mobile

Mobile consists of all the devices designed to provide on-the-go widespread communications and computer power via the Internet. Mobile acts as the glue that connects various elements together to ensure a seamless user experience. A quick response (QR) code, for example, is a matrix bar code that is readable by smart phones. I only reference this now because you'll see more QR being used in the future to engage people. It's a way to integrate mobile and traditional media across various mediums, including product packaging, print publications, and billboards.

Applications

Applications (apps) facilitate efficient use of mobile power. The top US smartphone apps are Alphabet's Google Play, Maps, Search, and Gmail and Facebook's Instagram and Messenger.[xii] An app is a compressed software program that runs on a mobile device without the use of a software license, as explained by author and respected colleague and friend Anita Campbell, who runs Small Business Trends.[xiii] Apps are relatively cheap to make, easy to distribute, and effective for small business owners, and they connect people with information and business processes wherever they may be at the moment. Apps are especially good technology for remote workers, allowing them to manage workflow and communicate user status to colleagues, suppliers, and customers.

Cloud Computing and Storage

Using cloud computing and storage involves sharing and transmitting files and applications over the Internet through a remote digital-storage system that offers unlimited capacity. Some cloud-storage providers offer free trials to get started and then charge you on a pay-as-you-go model, so you pay only for what you use. All of these technological advancements—from cloud computing, to storage, to apps—force old-line industries and businesses to rethink how they conduct business. As an exporter, you must leverage all these mobile mediums to best communicate, interact, and conduct business with everyone across the planet.

In Pursuit of Global Power: Mobile Will Overtake Desktop Access

Mobile Internet is making it easier for business owners to export by allowing them to find customers when they are outside the confines of the office and turn those export sales into working capital. Instead of issuing regular invoices with thirty-sixty-ninety-day terms, business owners can ask for payment via a mobile-payment service such as Square, Google Wallet, Apple Pay, PaySimple, Intuit GoPayments, or PayPal Here and get cash on the spot (refer to Chapter 20 for more on mobile-payment vehicles). Many of these payment applications come with credit and debit card readers for mobile devices. The benefit of these mobile-payment technologies is speedier cash flows, which helps business owners focus more on what counts: growing a business one export at a time as opposed to worrying about how to meet payroll, paying vendors, buying supplies, and funding a new product launch.

■ **Caution** There is a lot of talk about the increased likelihood of fraud on mobile payments. Provided you use a name-brand payment service, mobile payments can be as safe as using a credit card over the telephone or making an in-person charge at a restaurant. Of course, there's a risk with a stranger accessing your credit card information, just as there is an inherent risk in making payments online. Don't be intimidated. Be vigilant.

Getting Started: Create and Design a Great Mobile Web Site

Just because you've created a Web site doesn't mean it's mobile friendly. Web sites that haven't been designed for a mobile platform often show up wrong on mobile devices or are hard to use when accessed. Start by checking with your hosting company to see if it provides a mobile-ready site based on your existing regular site. Some don't. Blog-hosting platforms such as Blogger and WordPress (see Chapter 5) allow you to choose a mobile setup in addition to your regular blog platform. If your Web site runs on WordPress, you can install a free plug-in such as WPtouch, which will automatically transform your WordPress Web site for mobile devices. It even includes an option for visitors to switch between WPtouch view and your site's regular theme.

Social platforms like Facebook, Twitter, and LinkedIn have what is called responsive themes, which automatically adjust to fit your viewer's mobile browsers, so no worries or concerns there.

To find out if your Web site is mobile friendly and how to convert it, go to Internet domain registry Afilias (`http://afilias.info/mobile`). Its MobiReady affiliate (`http://ready.mobi`), also provides a free analysis and testing tool to evaluate your site's mobile readiness and to see how well your site performs on mobile devices. It's that simple. Conduct your check on all important stand-alone platforms, including but not limited to your Web site, e-commerce platform, and blog. What happens if they don't easily convert over to a mobile platform? You can inquire with Afilias or your current host provider to see what tools it has available to convert your platform so that it is mobile ready. You can also talk with a web developer who specializes in converting platforms to become mobile friendly.

Valuable Business Tools: Using Apps and Cloud Storage

Apps and cloud computing have taken the world by storm in a positive way, but only for those who know how to use them. In that spirit, I'll highlight some of the most important aspects to these types of technology and show you how to use them to grow your export business.

Apps

The killer app isn't a program, game, or map, but access to computing power itself. For some individuals, as Facebook's Zuckerman points out, having access to the Internet via a smart phone in maybe ten years will be their first experience with what we all call a computer.[xiv] Small businesses are still at the early stages of discovering how best to build and use apps, but the primary reason for using an app is to save time, increase productivity, and reduce costs. Some business owners desire to build their own app so they can tap into a new revenue stream or marketing channel. The challenge with that notion lies in taking an app from conception to high-tech reality. With that comes a series of questions that need to be addressed:

1. What is the purpose of building the app?

2. Who is your customer and what do they value (refer back to Chapter 2)?

3. Should you build or farm out the coding for the app?

4. How will users interact with the app?

5. How will you promote the app and be there for moments that matter for your customers?

6. How will you find new ways to be useful to your customers as they try to find or buy on their smartphone?

7. How will you monetize the app (to charge or not to charge)?

Once you answer all the questions, it's a matter of turning to an outside developer to build your app, which could be either a large firm that specializes in this type of coding work or an individual freelancer (refer to Chapter 4). The cost can be anywhere from $1,000 to $1 million depending on what you are trying to accomplish and how many bells and whistles you want on your app.

■ **Tip** To attract global customers, gain loyalty, and deliver value with an app, you might read "Principles of Mobile App Design: Engage Users and Drive Conversions" – Think with Google, `https://www.thinkwithgoogle.com/collections/principles-of-mobile-app-design-engage-users-and-drive-conversions.html`.

Many companies are now launched entirely on the premise of an app, connecting buyers and sellers of a particular unique item such as designer clothing, jewelry, or refurbished computer equipment. The use of apps without any additional technology relies on the theory that many individuals will bypass computers altogether and go directly to mobile for accessing everything they need and want in life.

Benefits of an App

Apps provide useful information, make us more efficient, give customers an alternative way to shop, fill a void in how to get tasks done if you have to cut positions, and might even help you grow without adding staff.

What follows are a few examples of messaging apps where people from all over the world can speak to each other by sending text messages, photo applications, and voice notes: WhatsApp (http://www.whatsapp.com/, owned by Facebook); Kakao Talk (http://www.kakaotalk.com.ph/, South Korea); Line (http://line.naver.jp/en/, Japan); WeChat (http://www.wechat.com/en/, China); Kik Messenger (http:// kik.com, Canada); and Facebook Messenger (https://www.facebook.com/mobile/messenger,; United States). Why are these apps important? Because they give you another outlet to find, service, and sell to customers.

Best Apps in Town

Here's a roundup of the apps that enhance my business and help me focus on achieving results faster. Many of them are free. Some have fees or carry a monthly subscription, so be sure to check before installing. All are available for iPhone, Android, and Blackberry devices (except where noted).

Tip If you would like to learn more about why apps have become such a powerful force in our daily lives, download the white paper published by comScore, Inc., "The 2015 U.S. Mobile App Report:" http://www.comscore.com/Insights/Presentations-and-Whitepapers/2015/The-2015-US-Mobile-App-Report

---

- *Desk.com:* (http://www.desk.com; a Salesforce.com company). This is a customer support app for small businesses that allows you to see your customers in one place and engage them across all your support channels and social media (Twitter, Facebook, phone, chat, email, discussion boards, and so forth), enabling users to quickly address requests or assign them to others in a team.

- *Evernote Business:* (https://evernote.com/business/). Evernote Business includes all the features of Evernote and Evernote Premium—easily taking notes and snapshots or recording audio and sharing it between as many digital devices as you need, anywhere at any time—plus special business-only tools and capabilities. The cost is $12 per user per month.

⬛ **Note**   There are thousands of small business apps not listed here that can help you better manage your business. They cost anywhere from $100 to thousands of dollars apiece. Among them are Adobe Acrobat, KoolSpan, TrustCall, and Parallels Desktop. Do an Internet search using the keywords "Best small business apps" to find the most popular apps that fit your specific needs. Start budgeting now.

- *Google Translate:*(`www.google.com/mobile/translate/`). This app lets you translate languages from around the world while on the run. It is used for quick translation solutions (communicating with a taxi driver or asking a hotel concierge for directions in a foreign country where you don't speak the language, for example), not for a seamless mobile-translation experience.

- *Perka*: (`https://perka.com`). This app lets small businesses set up customer loyalty programs over their mobile phones and track shoppers' purchases automatically. The cost is free for consumers to get the app, made by First Data Corp. For businesses, inquire with FDC on costs involved in creating multiple offers and accessing additional features.

- *Polaris*: (`https://www.polarisoffice.com`). This app allows users to manage Microsoft Office files from the road. Polaris Office 5 version, considered the best edition, is $12.99, whereas the Android version is free.

- *QuickBooks*: (`http://quickbooks.intuit.com`). This app, run by Intuit, allows you to organize your business all in one place and to handle a variety of financial tasks that can be accessed at home or on the go. Prices start at $10.36 a month based on your needs for the first 12 months; $12.95 and up after. For all QuickBooks apps, visit: `https://apps.intuit.com`.

- *Skype*: (`http://www.skype.com/en/`). This app allows you to talk for free with anyone, anywhere in the world! Who can resist? If you can't use Skype Mobile, Skype to Go numbers are also available without an Internet connection. These numbers offer discounted international calls as well as access to Skype's services without downloading or installing software.

- *Slack:* (http://slack.com). This app lets users set up instant group or private chats and direct messages, and drop in videos, images or files. The cost is free for limited use; up to $15 per user a month for additional features.

- *Square:* (http://www.squareup.com). This app collects credit card payments from anyone anywhere in the world via the Square Card Reader, which plugs directly into your smart phone and allows you to accept credit and debit card transactions at a fee of 2.75 percent per swipe. I'll never forget the first time my technology expert used the Square reader at my office after he had taken care of some Wi-Fi issues. He finished his work, invoiced me while standing there, and asked if I wanted an e-mail or text receipt for accounting purposes. Done. The funds were available to him the next day.

- *Webex:* (http://www.webex.com). A Cisco product, WebEx allows you to schedule, attend, and host meetings with anyone, anywhere. You can get a free account, or full-featured account for an affordable monthly fee. Separately, you might also check out Google+ Hangouts to start a video chat with up to ten people.

- *Yaldi:* (http://yaldiapp.com). This app enables users to track key performance indicators for their business, such as revenue, profitability, cash flow, and customer-acquisition costs. It also integrates QuickBooks accounting software. The cost is $9.99 a month; $99 a year. Note: Not available for Android.

- *When I Work:* (http://wheniwork.com). This app tracks everyone's schedule in one place to see who's available, when, and where. The cost ranges from $29 to $99 per month depending on the number of users.

Caution Whether for a site, blog, or mobile platform, translation is not a simple matter (see Chapter 15 for a discussion of web translation). It involves keeping your fingers on the pulse of who's buying your products from what part of the world, finding out what language your customers speak, and then planning accordingly by choosing a translation platform that fits your business and your budget. A good mobile translation solution can increase your user base and improve customer engagement worldwide.

Apps for Global Shipping

Here are a few apps that can help you make and track your shipments:

- *UPS Mobile*: (http://www.ups.com/content/us/en/bussol/browse/iphone.html). With this app, you can access shipment information anytime and anywhere.

- *FedEx*: (http://www.fedex.com/us/mobile/). This app helps you find the FedEx drop box, office, or authorized shipping center location nearest you "without leaving the app." You can also manage and track your shipment status. FedEx indicates its app for Android is coming soon.

- *DHL Activetracing*: (https://activetracing.dhl.com/DatPublic/smartphoneApps.do). This app allows you to order, track, and trace your DHL shipments while on the go.

- *TNT Express Mobile*: (http://expressmobile.tnt.com). Using this app, you can track, trace, and get real-time updates on the progress of your shipment.

Apps Specific to International Trade

There are also some apps out there designed for international trade:

- *Incoterms:* (http://m.darkpsytrancer.store.aptoide.com/app/market/com.icc.incoterms/1/3747697/Incoterms). The Incoterms rules are an internationally recognized standard developed by the International Chamber of Commerce (ICC) and are used worldwide in international and domestic contracts for the sale of goods. For Android use only.

- *HS Code Handbook*: (http://www.appster.org/app/hs-code-handbook-418821351). HS stands for Harmonized System and is administered by the World Customs Organization. The app features a search engine for the full list of six-digit international export codes that serve as the foundation for the import and export classification systems used in the United States. You can search by product, keyword, or number. Available for iPad and iPhone only.

Tip Many banks catering to small businesses are just beginning to develop apps for international trade. In most instances, you must be a client to use them. Wells Fargo, for example, offers the TradeXchange product under the CEO Mobile App. Citigroup rolled out its Trade Advisor product (not necessarily an app, but close), which provides online updates on letters of credit, trade finance loans, and documentary collection. Check with your bank to see if it has an app available for imports, exports, and other B-to-B transactions.

We are only at the tip of the iceberg when it comes to creating apps and leveraging them to grow a business. Watch for more to come in the future, and definitely stay in front of the trend. Meanwhile, connect in chat rooms and forums online to further the conversation and get up to speed with new technology and developments.

Cloud Storage and Computing

Cloud storage and computing make web-scale computing easier for developers and enable small business owners to back up critical computer files online. They give you the flexibility of accessing all your files anytime (24/7) from anywhere in the world, securely, and in sync with all your devices. Don't get confused. The apps that enable them generally offer a set amount of information you can store plus some ability to sync files to your devices, along with other features. But there are surprisingly subtle and not-so-subtle differences between what the cloud service providers offer businesses—businesses that require a more advanced, customizable file-storage tool should look beyond a single free app (Dropbox, for example) and consider a pay-as-you-go cloud spot.

Benefits of Cloud Storage

Cloud storage simplifies document sharing and collaboration, reduces risk, saves money, increases business capacity when you need it, enlarges access, and strengthens mobility—all of which is a huge boon for productivity. It also makes for a perfect backup system for the on-the-go export warrior.

Best Cloud Storage Spots in Town

The top US cloud storage spots are as follows (fees range from $.99 a month to more than $55.00 a month depending on the number of users and storage capacity):

- *iCloud*: (http://www.apple.com/icloud). This cloud storage spot, run by Apple, allows you to store data such as photos, music, apps, calendars, and documents for download to multiple devices. The service also allows you to wirelessly back up all your devices.

- *Google Cloud Platform*: (https://cloud.google.com/). This platform lets you build applications and Web sites and store data as well as analyze data on Google's infrastructure.

- *Cloud Drive*: (https://www.amazon.com/clouddrive/home). The storage tool, run by Amazon, allows you to store your photos, videos, documents, and other digital files in the cloud.

- *OneDrive*: (https://onedrive.live.com/about/en-us/). Microsoft's cloud storage allows you to store photos, documents, and other important files to your phone, tablet, PC, or Mac. If you're on Windows 10 and signed into a Microsoft account, information is baked right into the operating system, so that your background, your display, and your settings also roam with you.

- *Dropbox*: (https://www.dropbox.com/mobile). This app lets you store your photos, documents, and videos anywhere and share them easily with anyone.

- *SugarSync*: (http://www.sugarsync.com/free/). This storage site offers online backup, file synching, and file sharing. Prices range from $7.49 a month to $55.00 a month depending on storage and user capacity.

- *Box*: (https://www.box.com/apps/). This app offers online sharing, storing, accessing, and content management from anywhere. Prices range from $5.00 a month per user starter plan to $15.00 a month per user for a business plan.

Cloud computing is positively impacting the way businesses work globally. Yet, the market is still very young. Even Microsoft recently opened up Office so that businesses can access all their Box files, for example, from Office on an iPhone. Watch for more similar dramatic changes in the future where companies recognize how important it is to maintain an open work environment for managing, sharing, storing and collaborating worldwide from any device.

Summary

If there is one key takeaway from this chapter, it's this: get your business global by going mobile. Prepare to sell to anyone on the planet who has a digital device and an open e-wallet. The mobile movement is about fulfilling potential customers' needs instantaneously and capturing business profits in the process. Now that we can see how MAC allows the Internet to flow into every hand, everywhere, and in every circumstance, you're ready to market your business. Turn the page to learn how to boost your online visibility and get those exports rolling!

Notes

i. "Mark Zuckerberg Lays Out His Vision for the Future and How the Next 5 Billion People Will Use Computers," Nicholas Carlson, Business Insider, last modified April 5, 2013, http://www.businessinsider.com/mark-zuckerberg-lays-out-his-vision-for-the-future-and-how-the-next-5-billion-people-will-use-computers-2013-4#ixzz2R8rHMjSC.

ii. "Mom-And-Pop Shops Get Facebook's E-Commerce Message," Wendy Lee, SFGate, accessed March 13, 2016, http://www.sfgate.com/business/article/Mom-and-pop-shops-get-Facebook-s-e-commerce-6885585.php.

iii. "Cisco Visual Networking Index: Global Mobile Data Traffic Forecast Update, 2015-2020 White Paper," accessed March 13, 2016, http://www.cisco.com/c/en/us/solutions/collateral/service-provider/visual-networking-index-vni/mobile-white-paper-c11-520862.html.

iv. Ibid.

v. Ibid.

vi.   "Datawind's $38 Tablet Is Turning the World Upside Down," Josh Ong, accessed March 13, 2016, http://thenextweb.com/insider/2014/01/17/datawinds-38-tablet-turning-world-upside-better/#gref.

vii.   Ibid.

viii. "Ringing Bells Freedom 251: Cheapest Android Smartphone for Just Rs 251 ($3.65)," Raju PP, accessed March 13, 2016, http://techpp.com/2016/02/17/freedom-251-specs-price-features/.

ix.   "Smartphone Ownership and Internet Usage Continues to Climb in Emerging Economies," Pew Research Center, accessed March 13, 2016, http://www.pewglobal.org/2016/02/22/smartphone-ownership-and-internet-usage-continues-to-climb-in-emerging-economies/.

x.   "Mobile Content and Activities Roundup," eMarketer, accessed March 13,2016,https://www.emarketer.com/public_media/docs/eMarketer_Mobile_Content_Activities_Roundup.pdf.

xi.   Ibid.

xii.   Facebook, Alphabet Dominate U.S. Smartphone App Field, Brian Deagon, accessed March 13, 2016, http://www.investors.com/news/technology/facebook-alphabet-dominate-u-s-smartphone-app-field/.

xiii. "What the Heck is an 'App?,'" Anita Campbell, Small Business Trends, last modified March 7, 2011, http://smallbiztrends.com/2011/03/what-is-an-app.html.

xiv.   "Mark Zuckerberg Lays Out His Vision for the Future and How the Next 5 Billion People Will Use Computers," Nicholas Carlson, Business Insider, last modified April 5, 2013, http://www.businessinsider.com/mark-zuckerberg-lays-out-his-vision-for-the-future-and-how-the-next-5-billion-people-will-use-computers-2013-4#ixzz2R8rHMjSC.

Marketing Your Business Worldwide

You can buy attention (advertising). You can beg for attention from the media (PR). You can bug people one at a time to get attention (sales). Or you can earn attention by creating something interesting and valuable and then publishing it online for free.

> —David Meerman Scott, marketing and leadership speaker[i]

When we care, we share.

> —Jonah Berger, Wharton School of the University of Pennsylvania professor; expert on word of mouth, viral marketing, social influence, social contagion, and trends; author, *Contagious: Why Things Catch On*[ii]

You need loyal and passionate advocates, ambassadors, and supporters, who, in their own potent words, will share with the world just how great you are, and how important and helpful it is for others to collaborate with you as well.

> — Kathy Caprino, international career success consultant, writer, speaker and trainer dedicated to the advancement of women in business[iii]

© Laurel J. Delaney 2016
L. J. Delaney, *Exporting*, DOI 10.1007/978-1-4842-2193-8_10

The twenty-first century will belong to the Internet consumer. So it follows that if content is the soul of an online enterprise, marketing is the heart. Put the two together and you can assemble the next wave of Internet consumers who have unlimited options and freedom of choice. Our digital experience is now about engaging consumers with information, new products, new brands, new movements, and new individuals that they care about. To that extent, you don't want to just market a product or service to Internet consumers; you want to own or dominate the space you operate in. You want to become, for lack of a better descriptor, an export rebel with a cause. What is critical is to watch and learn as you go, seize the opportunity when you can, exploit it, and inspire others to get involved.

In this chapter, we look at how marketing has changed over the years due to technology and how to create an international marketing plan that hits the mark every time, serves customers the way they want to be served, and helps promote your brand worldwide. I will also provide a few additional resources that take us back to the good old days of cold calling—all with the intent of getting your online business found around the world.

The Four Ps of Classical Marketing

Traditional marketing, through newspapers, radio, television, and print advertising, for example, has its place and value. Remember the four Ps of classical marketing—product (or service), price, promotion, and place? This is better viewed as the marketing mix and the foundation for satisfying customers' needs. You can also use the four Ps to anticipate and create the future needs of customers in order to profit from them. However, thanks to the Internet, traditional methods of marketing have changed and improved. Online marketing, as you will learn later on, is not a replacement for marketing basics. Rather, it's a new, more cost-effective way of interacting with customers and other stakeholders. Consider it to be another tool in your toolbox to use for marketing purposes.

Promoting products, brands, and businesses on a new and different stage— the Internet—calls for a different mindset from the one used in the old days, where you could simply tell or push consumers over and over to "Buy this!" Now, it's about pulling users in as needed, rather than pushing them, developing a relationship, having a conversation, and engaging consumers in a way that creates trust, loyalty, and dedication. If you do these things, they will be customers for life. That's why organizations are now facilitating two-way communications via social channels.

Take Procter & Gamble (P&G), one of the world's largest consumer products companies. Its brands include Tide detergent, Ivory soap, and Crest toothpaste. P&G used to spend gazillions of dollars on direct-mail coupons and television and print ads to reach its target market. The company still spends a good deal on similar activities, but a large portion of its marketing dollars are now apportioned to where most people spend their time: on the Internet. This includes P&G's Web site; blo;, Facebook page; Twitter handle; and Google+, Instagram, and Pinterest accounts.

■ **Tip** Procter & Gamble's classic marketing rules, such as emphasizing a solution and not a problem or showing a package in the first eight seconds of a television ad, will never go out of vogue. If anything, these principles become the foundation for online social conversations now and well into the future.[iv]

Internet marketing is about creating a solid marketing plan, increasing visibility, staying the course, monitoring results, and making appropriate changes along the way on an as-needed basis. Instead of focusing primarily on the four Ps, we need to look at the four Cs of social media: content, conversation, community, and connections. The ultimate goal with Internet marketing is immediacy and to make your online platforms the go-to resource when people want information on your type of product or service.

Making the Most of the Internet: The New Rules of Marketing Your Business to the World

Online marketing should rely on strategies that leverage the Internet and mobile devices. The goal is to manage your brand and increase revenue and profits for your business by targeting potential customers using different online channels. Let's take a look at a few key tactics of online marketing that get you from here to there—how to get to excellence in online marketing. Many of them should be used when drafting your international marketing plan.

Search Engine Marketing

Search engine marketing (SEM) is about procuring a favorable position on search engine results pages. SEM is done by building links and writing strong content for your site and submitting data to search sites. People trust search engines because of the perceived objectivity of the results. Studies have shown that online visitors are likely to click on an organic, or nonpaid, result vs. a paid result—all the more reason to get to that top rank organically.

Display Ads

Display ads are a type of graphical advertising that is positioned next to related content on a web page. They usually contain a company's logo; a text description of what is being sold; images, illustrations, or photographs; contact information, such as the company's web address, phone number, or e-mail address; and rich media (a video or animation link).

Affiliate Marketing

Affiliate marketing is a way to make money online whereby you as a site's publisher are paid a commission for helping a business by promoting its product, service, or site on your platform. As the publisher, you earn a commission, referred to as a conversion rate, when someone follows a link on your blog to another site where he then buys something. Commissions are often a percentage of a sale but can also be a fixed amount per action (a click-through rate or pay-per-sale conversion rate, for example).

Conversions can be tracked when the publisher uses a link with a code (exclusive to that entity) embedded into it, enabling the advertiser to track where conversions come from. Other times an advertiser might give a publisher a coupon code for her readers to use that helps to track conversions.

Another variation on this is when you earn something for referring a visitor to another site through an online campaign who then takes some kind of action—for example, signing up for a newsletter, taking a survey, or providing an e-mail address. Affiliate marketing works best when there's a relationship of trust among an advertiser, a publisher, and its readers; you advertise relevant products; and you have a huge following. It's all about generating extra revenue, and that becomes easy when you know your customers' needs.

E-Mail Marketing

An e-mail marketing campaign, such as a weekly newsletter, is about reaching consumers where they tend to go most: their e-mail inbox.

■ **Tip** Constant Contact and MailChimp are good e-mail marketing platforms should your own Web site host not have this capability.

E-mail marketing—considered the ultimate marketing asset—involves directly marketing a commercial message to a target group of people that has given you permission to contact them via e-mail. It's a cost-effective solution that allows you to keep in constant touch with your existing or soon-to-be customers. Using e-mail marketing, you can provide a free white paper, PDF file, e-book about your company, or anything else your customers might consider to be of value, when they visit your site. You should also put a sign-up form on your Web site (review Chapter 5) and a link to sign up in your e-mail signature. You can also invite people to sign up via your social media circles. Remember to use the same logos, colors, and slogans in your newsletter as you do everywhere else.

Inbound Marketing

Rather than conducting outbound marketing to the masses of people—many of whom are trying to block you out—inbound marketing can be used to help people who are already interested in your industry find you. In order to do this, you need to set your Web site and blog up like a watering hole for your industry and attract visitors naturally through search engines, the blogosphere, and social media. Most global marketers spend about 90 percent of their efforts on outbound marketing and 10 percent on inbound marketing. Once marketers understand the power of inbound marketing, you'll see those percentages shift dramatically.

Referral Marketing

Word-of-mouth marketing (also known as referral marketing) leverages your existing customers to advocate for your business. It costs little to implement and can be as simple as asking people to refer business to you with an incentive tied to it. Testimonials further help validate your work as long as they are given by well-known and respected individuals in your industry.

■ **Tip** Use a Referral Fee Agreement to get paid for referring potential customers, or to compensate someone else for sending a customer your way. Try: `https://www.rocketlawyer.com/document/referral-fee-agreement.rl`

Social Media Marketing

Social media marketing (SMM) can help break barriers and is designed to foster attention and traffic through conversations you have on social media sites such as Facebook, LinkedIn, Twitter, Google+, and YouTube. Keep messages consistent (in your slogans, pictures, colors, and contact information, for example) to ensure that branding on all platforms works together.

■ **Tip**   Creating a video—via YouTube or Periscope, for example—for your business, product, or service offering is a compelling way to get people to take action—like visiting your Web site and, preferably, buying something. You can create a video yourself or hire a professional to do it for you. Think about how it will be used to market your business. Make it entertaining, educational, and short. Focus on the value it will have for the visitor and not on specifically selling something.

Content Marketing

Content marketing is communicating with people in a way that makes them feel like you are not directly selling them. Instead of pitching, you're storytelling, educating, or entertaining people through blogs, Web sites, web casts, podcasts, videos, articles, and e-books.

Mobile Marketing

Mobile marketing is marketing that is conducted through a mobile device such as a smart phone or tablet. The only difference in strategy between mobile marketing and other forms of marketing is that you should keep it short, sweet, and to the point. Convenience is crucial. For example, consumers expect to take out their phone, ask for service, and get it. They don't want to wait. A key advantage to marketing to smart phones is the ability to send and receive text messages and buy on the move.

Now that you thoroughly understand the importance of online marketing and the major tactics used, you are ready to draft an international marketing plan.

Creating an International Online Marketing Plan

If you want to export to more than 3.4 billion people online who are interested in buying your product, it will most likely be accomplished through using search engines and other social media channels. You should put all the different marketing mediums previously mentioned to work simultaneously in a highly targeted yet seamless fashion. Diversification is best when you want to maximize resources and to increase online visibility. It will take time and effort, but the payoff will be worth it in terms of bringing the world to your online export business.

When drafting an international marketing plan, the simpler, the better. Begin by addressing these five key questions:

1. What do I want to accomplish with my business online?

2. How much money do I have to spend?

3. Who will work on the marketing procedure?

4. How much time will I devote?

5. How will I make it happen (which tools will work best)?

Let's take a look at a sample international marketing plan for a fictitious company we'll call Organic Berry Company, which takes into consideration all of the above.

Organic Berry Company

San Francisco–based Organic Berry Company (OBC) grows, packages, and sells certified organic blackberries, blueberries, raspberries, and strawberries throughout the United States. Established in 2014, OBC has $2 million in annual revenue and fifteen employees, and has established that each customer spends an average of $50 a year. The company's marketing plan might look like this:

1. What do we want to accomplish with our business online?

   "OBC wants to create an international marketing plan that will enable it to increase its online visibility—and sales—to Southeast Asia, specifically Taiwan, Vietnam, Singapore, Hong Kong, and Malaysia."

2. How much money do we have to spend?

   "OBC has set aside $50,000 for the first year of online marketing. Once it generates enough new business to offset that initial expenditure, the company will allocate 7 percent of after-tax profits to future marketing efforts on a worldwide basis."

3. Who will work on the marketing procedure?

   "The company will ask one employee, who is excellent with communications, to work on the online marketing activities. The company will make sure to get her buy-in first and confirm that she is passionate about taking on this new initiative."

4. How much time will we devote?

   "The one key employee will devote herself full-time to online marketing activities until such time that the company needs more people to come on board to assist her."

5. How will we make it happen (which tools will work best)?

    That gets us to the plan! The first step of creating that plan is to figure out where our customers are most likely to look for us.

    "OBC will devote time and energy to all online platforms, with heavy emphasis on search engine optimization, since that is where consumers worldwide search and find information. OBC will support the SEM efforts with quality blog posts, podcasts, Tweet chats, Skypecasts, webinars, videos, published articles, and e-books that will help to further promote our business to the world as well as transact business in every corner of the planet."

Building Brand Recognition through the International Marketing Plan

The international marketing plan should be strategic in nature and executed in a consistent manner. The goal is to get more customers from around the world to export to and to increase your business's profits. (I am assuming at this juncture that you have already read Chapter 6 and set the world stage for becoming a digital export rock star; if not, go back and read it.) Here's how a plan might look. Keep in mind how the four Cs of social media (content, conversation, community, and connections) might play into each point:

1. *Define a keyword strategy (set objectives).* As we discussed in Chapter 5, you need to come up with a string of keywords that best describes your business. Think of it this way: If you were to call a bunch of folks together at an online water cooler every week to talk about something related to your keywords, what would they be? Mine is, for example, "Global small business."

2. *Optimize your Web site to get found.* In Chapter 5, we discussed how to optimize your Web site. That effort is critical for getting found by the billions of consumers you are interested in selling to. While keywords are not the only search engine ranking factor, they do support the relevancy of your page and they're within your control when creating new page content. Consider controlling keywords by optimizing content across all of your pages, including those in different languages. Feature your blog on your homepage and provide clear ways that people can connect with you on their favorite social media platforms. All of these efforts in combination will determine how well you rank in a Google, Bing, or Yahoo! search result.

▓ **Tip** There's a lot of talk that you don't need a Web site. That's bunk. A Web site serves as your single biggest business calling card on the Internet and a lead nurturer of sales. It's where you post your best content and carefully craft what you are about and how you serve customers. More important, you own this online real estate by way of a great domain name hosted by a company you pay to take care of that real estate. If customers get lost about what you do when looking at Facebook, LinkedIn, Twitter, or Google+, they can always go to your Web site for reassurance of your capabilities. Keep it current, vibrant, and inviting.

3. *Create a blog and other related marketing content.* Your online success is directly proportional to the quality of your web design and the information you provide. Consider creating podcasts, Tweet chats, Skypecasts, YouTube and Periscope live streaming Q&A session videos, and webinars to further promote your business to the world, better connect with existing and potential customers using these platforms, and transact business around the world. Write articles, white papers, and e-books in your area of expertise. Internet consumers visit and return to those sites that consistently provide a high-quality, informative, and engaging online experience.

4. *Promote content and participate in social media.* Set up a schedule, start promoting, and stick to it on a regular basis. Here's what you might be dealing with: a Web site, blog, and Facebook page; LinkedIn, Google+, Twitter, Pinterest, Instagram, and Periscope accounts; and an app and mobile site. Whether you start with a daily blog post, an affiliate marketing program, a display ad, or an e-mail campaign, keep the conversation going until you generate new business.

5. *Convert site traffic into leads.* Getting lots of visitors to your Web site and social media channels is terrific, but how do you turn those visitors into leads and then into customers? Here's a simple four-step solution that I encourage you to implement:

   • Step 1: Decide on your offer (give 'em something they can't refuse!).

   • Step 2: Create a call to action (can be an image, video, text question, or survey, for example).

- Step 3: Create landing pages (these are where your visitors end up after they click on your call to action).

- Step 4: Test what worked best—in the form of a text question, poll, or survey, for instance—in terms of converting visitors to quality leads and to new customers.

6. *Nurture leads with targeted messages.* One of the best ways to build a relationship with your leads and convert them into sales is to find out more about the people who are visiting your site. They might e-mail questions, view newsletters, comment at the end of blog posts, fill out opt-in forms, or take a brief poll. It's a courting process. You want to reach engagement (serious interest) and then marriage (a purchase). The objective is to start the conversation, be sensitive to moods and needs, and respect privacy by not pushing too deeply, instead inquiring about things such as what your visitors want to see more or less of on social platforms as it relates to your business and their interest. Stay in the picture—keep the conversation going—until the lead is ready to buy. It's that simple.

   Whether you're dealing with positive conversations or complaints over social media, avoid negativity at all costs. Be polite and appropriate. In other words, don't ridicule or defame, be unresponsive, or waver during complaints or adversity. It's the test of your strength and resolve during the courting process. Take the high road and have the attitude that the customer is king and can do no wrong. Serve everyone politely and with respect and you will encourage a great fan base and returning customers.

7. *Optimize your marketing for mobile.* Mobile users want quick, actionable access to relevant and useful information on the move, wherever they might be, and at any given time. So put the users in control. Test out your social platforms to make sure they are mobile ready (see Chapter 9). Enabling consumers to have an active hand in choosing how, when, where, and why they wish to be marketed to results in a highly targeted, highly engaged audience. It gets back to the basics of starting a conversation with customers, listening to them, and understanding what they want. Then you need to deliver on it.

8. *Develop a mobile campaign that leverages your existing, highly visible marketing assets and also invests in creativity.* These might include in-app ads, app games, mobile banners, and blogs and social media channels (i.e., Twitter, LinkedIn, Facebook, and Google+), and allow users to engage with your business in the unique ways that mobile devices allow.

Tip Keep the messages in your mobile marketing efforts short, sweet, and easy to understand. Stick only to helpful tips. That's what consumers on the go can handle. Always keep the line of communication open with consumers.

---

9. *Evaluate, refine, and improve strategies.* Now that you've had a chance to test and power up your marketing efforts via your international marketing plan, evaluate how it's working for you. Do you have more followers and fans, especially from overseas (refer to *Google Analytics Dashboards: A Step-By-Step Guide*[v])? Have you converted any of them into customers? If not, how could you improve on what you are doing? Your return on investment can be calculated by dividing the excesses in benefits (new customers) within a year by the costs of the Internet marketing investment. In the case of OBC mentioned earlier, the fictional company determined that its average customer spent $50 a year, so it would take one thousand customers to bring in sales of $50,000. In other words, to cover the additional marketing investment, it would need to gain one thousand new customers based on its Internet strategy.

10. *Get the leadership right.* People must be digitally minded, highly motivated, and collaborative. Develop appropriate performance-based metrics for the business and its leaders to ensure global growth.

Tip Are you noticing that many of the communications you receive online are in a language other than your own? Is there an abundance of messages coming from one country? You are on to something that should be addressed. Perhaps that's a market you should consider entering. Consider hiring a translator so you can turn those conversations into legitimate export business.

---

11. *Recommend action.* Based on your activities, ask yourself what you should continue doing because it is working and what you can do differently to generate more revenue and profits for your business. Take time to recommend a new course of action that will benefit the company, key stakeholders, and consumers. Remember, the best marketing is marketing that doesn't feel like marketing.

Tip Aside from a brief mention of display ads, I am intentionally leaving out advertising here because this chapter's emphasis is on marketing that you can do yourself. However, that is not to say you should not consider advertising if your marketing efforts fall short of your desired results. Starting online is fast, affordable, and easy to track (refer to Chapter 6). Look at Facebook ads, LinkedIn ads, Google Adwords, and StumbleUpon ads to further boost your Internet marketing initiative. Sometimes the best place to get your company seen online is to pay for it, but you need an interesting image, headline and body text.

Other Marketing Tactics and Promotional Elements

In addition to online marketing tactics, the following sections describe offline measures that also can be an effective way to connect with readers and export more stuff.

Public Speaking Events

A good way for potential clients to find out about you and your company is through a seminar series, conference, convention, festival, or any other public speaking events that they can attend. These can be done through community organizations, professional groups, and trade associations whose events take place in overseas markets, provided they have an international membership in markets you want to enter. It is a chance for individuals to hear information directly from you and oftentimes before formally connecting online. Speaking to groups is nothing more than having a big conversation with a lot of people. Make sure you leave sufficient time to take questions from the audience at the end. Since you are the best spokesperson for your business, holding seminars and speaking engagements offers a powerful and efficient marketing tool that can quickly establish your credibility and expertise with an audience. Speaking to a group is marketing, not selling. With that in mind, always focus on providing value. This will bring customers later.

Networking

Nothing tops good old-fashioned networking, provided you target like-minded folks in your sphere of influence. Networking can take place at peer-to-peer organizations, professional affiliations, international conferences, industry trade shows, and so forth. For example, once I received an invitation from the Chicago Council on Global Affairs to hear Eric Schmidt, CEO of Google, speak. Although you may not be able to secure new business at the event, you can collect important business cards, have critical discussions on international business, and envision ways to someday speak at the same event to share expertise and sell products and services. Make a list of fifty people you know who are at the top of their industry. Ask if you can speak at their next event. And don't forget to add them all as contacts in your social media circles.

E-Mail Blasts to Purchased Lists

Some companies allow you to buy an e-mail blast list of targeted customers. This is a carryover from sending snail-mail postcards and hard-copy letters, and is still practiced by some today (mostly B-to-B). I don't have any experience with this marketing tactic, especially as it relates to prospecting internationally. You will have to be careful that your audience, if they have never heard from you before, doesn't consider your e-mail to be spam. That said, you might be better off developing your own opt-in means for international customer acquisition. Once you connect, you will still have to develop a trusting relationship, and that will take time. What you don't want to do is alienate customers who could have become very profitable had you taken the time to cultivate a genuine relationship but were turned off by your e-mail blast tactic.

Tip Don't be surprised if at some point Facebook, Twitter, and LinkedIn all have packages in place that allow you to buy global Likes, Fans, and other related connections (referred to as "click farms"). It's only a matter of time.

Tip In 2015, we hosted our first ever Global Small Business Forum (http://www. globalsmallbusinessforum.com) in Chicago. After the event, we created a list, which included names and email addresses of all the attendees. We uploaded it to our MailChimp newsletter account. This works so much better than purchasing a list because now we met each of the attendees in person and can continue to cultivate the relationship through our newsletter outreach campaign.

Opt-In Lists

Whether in person or over the phone, cold calling is an icebreaker and can be an effective way to snag customers—and not necessarily overseas ones. Many people still believe in the old ways of training salespeople and cold calling. They figure if someone makes one hundred cold calls, one will develop into a sale. However, if you want the biggest bang for your marketing buck, go the e-mail route! When you have an opt-in list, people have already given you permission to communicate with them. Those hundred calls leading to one sale could instead be done as a hundred e-mails leading to twenty sales in a shorter period of time and with less human effort. And you can always send someone in person to service those twenty customers.

Outsourced Telemarketing

Some businesses do well by outsourcing telemarketers (refer to Chapter 4) to help pitch their business capabilities to potential customers. Don't rule out the use of the telephone. It works for businesses that need a personal, local touch. Hire individuals whose speech you can clearly understand and who know something about the product or service you are selling. If you want to open doors in the United Kingdom, for example, hire someone in that market who knows the key players you are trying to reach and speaks in a similar manner as the people in those regions. Nothing is worse than the sound of a robotic voice or a voice that has such a strong accent that it is impossible to understand.

Advertising/PR

This should be one of the last parts of a marketing strategy, not the first. If your marketing efforts don't pan out, that's when it's time to turn to advertising or public relations efforts. But be careful here, because you don't want to overspend. If you do go this route, make sure you have a clear call to action where you can track results. If your campaign doesn't generate new leads or business, get rid of it.

Personal Selling

Sometimes, what is required is to get out there and sell something face to face. Or you might hire a whole force of people who sell on your behalf. Or maybe it's just providing information . . . whatever the tactic, the goal is to convince customers to purchase a product. It's more expensive to do it in this fashion, but the contacts you will generate make it worth the effort.

Referral Marketing

This method involves promoting products or services to new customers through referrals, usually word-of-mouth, with an incentive tied to it. It's considered a networking technique and one that, if done well, can bring you new business. The silver lining in referral marketing is that typically every referral you receive has either an intro or story tied to it by the individual making the referral, making your job of selling that much easier.

Media Outreach Campaign

Media coverage—the amount and quality of attention you get from other influential people—can play a huge role in getting consumers and businesses alike to visit your Web site or other related online platforms. Create a media list and reach out to those on it. Bloggers are well known in the industry for getting information out to the masses (my company, for example, personally gets pitched daily on the Global Small Business Blog by companies who want to reach our audience). Craft several different ways you might present your company and its offerings so that it will appeal to a variety of media outlets. But you don't want to appear that you are pitching per se, so focus on providing superior and exclusive content instead of pushing to get coverage. Plus, you don't want to give the same pitch twice to the same person—you'll lose that key person forever, so be sure to diversify your audience. Keep track of your outreach efforts in an organized fashion, because later you will want to measure results. (Side note: I wish more people would adhere to the don't-pitch-twice model! It would make my inbox a lot less cluttered.)

Making the Most of Traditional Marketing Channels

As you wrap your arms around marketing your business through online channels, you will find there is no single right way to win export customers. It's a combination of many factors that all contribute to success. But remember, always focus on your target audience. Here are a couple of other traditional marketing channels you won't want to miss.

Exhibiting at Trade Shows: A Powerful, Hands-on Approach

Exhibiting at or attending a trade show in your industry is a uniquely effective way to contact cross-border customers, especially if you have a difficult product to sell or if it is a type that a customer needs to actually see. The Department of Commerce's Foreign Buyer Program certifies a specific number of US trade shows each year. As of this writing, the DOC supported about eighty international fairs and exhibitions held in markets worldwide.

Exhibiting is an especially powerful form of marketing because it allows you to get your company name out there and have potential buyers come to you. The only drawbacks to exhibiting are the cost and future commitment involved. It's expensive, especially for a new exporter. It can cost anywhere from $5,000 on up for a ten- by ten-foot booth. Even if the government subsidizes your exhibit, it can still cost you at least half of that. And once you exhibit, others in your industry will expect to see you there every year as long as you're in business. If you exhibit once and then disappear, they'll think you gave up on the market or went out of business.

But if you can find a way to manage the cost, the following advantages of exhibiting should convince you to keep it up:

- It will provide high visibility for your company and products.

- It will provide instant industry credibility.

- You can do your own preshow promotion. High booth traffic is no accident!

- It will give you a chance to meet potential buyers face-to-face. Whether customers visit your booth intentionally or discover you accidentally, it's good prospecting. Even if you don't end up doing business, these visitors can give you trouble-saving "insider" recommendations for capable and reliable distribution channels.

- It will allow you to meet important intermediaries, such as sales agents, brokers, importing wholesalers, trading companies, distributors, independent sales reps, and international business consultants.

- You will be provided a listing in the show directory. These directories are given to both participants and visitors, who usually then take them back home for a more leisurely look. Some copies will be passed on to friends and business associates. Your exposure can triple by the time the directory has made its rounds.

Don't forget that when you're participating in an international road show, you still need to manage your booth as if you were operating out of your office. Be prepared. Here are some things to keep in mind:

- The staff managing the booth should be polite, enthusiastic, and knowledgeable about your company, or the company or companies that you are representing, and the products on display. At least one person with the authority to make final decisions should be present in case an opportunity to do business on the spot should arise.

- A person with the potential to interpret other languages should be brought in, if possible, to ease potential communication problems.

- The booth itself should be attractive and comfortable. Have a table and several comfortable chairs at hand for on-the-spot meetings and to accommodate weary guests. Also, offer nonalcoholic beverages and snacks to make your booth a more inviting place to stop by.

- Business cards are your passport to trade networks, and you should bring an ample supply, written in your own language on one side and in the language of the host country on the other. Don't forget to have a personal cardholder for when potential customers give you their cards.

- Your sales literature must be attractive and easy to read and should be written in a multilingual format to meet the needs of local audiences.

- You should have plenty of product samples on hand for display, demonstration, and handout purposes.

- You should have special export-pricing schedules prepared. Show free on board (FOB) factory prices and cost, insurance and freight (CIF) prices (refer to Chapter 19), referencing the host country's international port of entry. (See Chapter 19 for other important data that should be included on your export price schedule.) If you do not have time to prepare special export pricing, you can just use your domestic schedules and offer enough of a discount (about 25 percent) to serve as an incentive for your international customers.

- You should have an extra camera available at your booth in addition to a digital device that has a built-in camera, to add an enjoyable personal touch to the proceedings. When you return home and write follow-up notes to the contacts you made, this will allow you to include photos of them standing at your booth. Alternatively, if you are in the moment, you can design and send postcards on the fly via MyPostcard.com and Touchnote.com.

- There are a variety of little supplies and amenities you need to remember to bring to the show: writing utensils, notepads, electrical converter, technology adaptors and power devices, a bilingual dictionary, a garbage bin, a staple gun, tape, aspirin, and even a small sewing kit from your hotel! Look out for useful shops like a pharmacy, an office supplier, and a variety or convenience store near the exhibition center for emergencies. Keep a list of things to remember for next time.

■ **Tip** Take a look at the "U.S. Department of Commerce International Buyer Program 2016 Trade Show Schedule," which will help you plan accordingly about trade show activity: `http://www.export.gov/build/groups/public/@eg_main/@ibp/documents/webcontent/eg_main_088750.pdf`.[vi]

What Do Local Buyers Expect When Visiting Your Booth?

When visitors stop by your booth, they want answers to their questions immediately, not months later after you have returned home and sorted through your inquiries. If you don't have an answer to a particular question, promise to get one within a day. You can always text, e-mail, or phone your home office for help. Don't forget to ask for your prospect's business card so you can get back to her. Deliver on your promise, and do it on time.

Cross-border buyers will typically spend several hours right there at your booth to discuss all the details of future business. The more you and your sales staff know about the prospective customer's company, the products it handles, and its position in the marketplace, the better you look to the buyers. Make extraordinary efforts to please. If you fail to convey credibility, your chances of success in the international marketplace are slim. Don't think these buyers can't spot a novice or a lightweight. Most of them attend the international shows quite routinely, often because their own national economy cannot support the business growth they are trying to achieve. They are experienced traders.

Do not expect to write orders during the show. If you do, great, but remember, this is the time to get long-term associations off to a good start, not to rack up sales. Take it easy and allow the customer to drive the transaction. His needs come first.

Attending a Trade Show

Attending a trade show rather than exhibiting at one allows you to eliminate the cost of a booth (keep in mind you'll still have airfare, lodging, and meals). It also gives you a first-hand opportunity to discover:

- who the major local manufacturers (and competitors!) are;

- what products they make;

- what products they import from the United States in order to expand their product offerings and broaden distribution channels; and

- industry trends and cutting-edge developments and breakthroughs.

Attending a trade show gives you a panoramic overview of your entire industry for minimal expense. But to take full advantage of it, you've got to work it for all it's worth. Don't be shy! Introduce yourself to every likely contact, tell them about your business, and offer them a company brochure or at least a business card. The show directory alone will give you invaluable contact information. Every exhibitor will be listed by name and address with an indication of the types of products handled. Some directories also list the brands and the other companies that also market them. Also, keep your eyes open for a directory of attendees, which can be another important pool of contacts. Add whomever will allow you onto your newsletter distribution list and online social media platforms, such as LinkedIn, Facebook, Twitter, and Google+.

For beginning exporters, attending a show rather than exhibiting is also a practical strategy for finding cross-border contacts because it allows you to move about freely, meet with whomever you choose, and determine if the show is worth the investment to exhibit your wares the next time around. The only disadvantage is that you don't make as powerful and professional an impression as you would if you were to exhibit because the people you meet do not have a tangible sense of an organization that bears your corporate name. You might explain to your contacts that you are sounding the market to decide whether you should have your own booth next year and ask for their input. Local businesspeople will enjoy giving out information about their homeland and industry, and they will be flattered that you value their opinion.

Whether you're exhibiting or not, you've spent a lot of money to get to the show. Use the opportunity wisely.

Government Programs, Trade Missions, and Industry-Sponsored Programs

Government- and trade industry-sponsored programs are designed to match you up with the various types of trading intermediaries that are looking to buy exactly what you are looking to sell. These programs, in some instances, cost money, but the potential returns are great. You will be making contact with the people most likely to become long-term business associates or, better yet, customers. Here are a few such programs and listings along with the organizations that sponsor them:

1. *International Partner Search*: (http://export.gov/salesandmarketing/eg_main_018197.asp). Run by the US Commercial Service, this organization finds qualified buyers, partners, or agents without traveling overseas. US Commercial Service specialists will deliver detailed company information on up to five international companies that have expressed an interest in your company's products and services.

2. *Gold Key Matching Service*: (http://export.gov/salesandmarketing/eg_main_018195.asp). Run by the US Commercial Service, the Gold Key Matching Service is great for a small company with a bigger budget. It is one of the most efficient ways for a small business operator to meet with prescreened potential cross-border business associates, whether you are seeking an agent, a distributor, or a joint-venture partner. Individual meetings are arranged in advance, most taking place at the US embassy of the host country. Many companies testify that this method is a wise investment because you pay only for the usual airfare, lodging, and entertainment, and have a series of productive meetings already arranged. The Gold Key program will also help you to participate in trade shows sponsored by state and federal agencies.

3. *Organized Trade Missions*: (http://export.gov/trademissions/). Run by the Department of Commerce, these missions are designed to help beginner exporters establish sales and set up representation abroad at a low cost. The organizer of the mission typically sets up the agenda (itinerary), which covers

travel arrangements, accommodations, appointments with prospective customers, and opportunities to sound out the market to learn about other appropriate trade intermediaries for your products.

4. *Featured US Exporters Service:* (https://emenuapps.ita.doc.gov/ePublic/finance/participation-agreements/edit-fuse-reg.do). FUSE is a directory of US products featured on the Web sites of the US Commercial Services around the world. Being listed on this directory gives your company an opportunity to target specific markets in the local language of business. Listings are available to qualified US exporters seeking trade leads or representation in more than fifty markets worldwide.

5. *Various programs through the Department of Commerce:* (http://www.commerce.gov/about-commerce/grants-contracting-trade-opportunities). Your local department of commerce (DOC), which houses the US Export Assistance Center, the International Trade Administration (ITA), and the US Commercial Service, runs a number of programs to put exporters and their customers in touch. Some are free and others require a fee. Check in advance.

6. *Various matchmaking services:* (http://www.trade.gov/cs/services.asp). Both the International Trade Administration and the DOC offer matchmaking services that introduce beginner export companies to agents, distributors, or large retailers with specific interest in the exporters' products.

7. *Export USA:* (http://www.thinkglobal.us/). Being listed in this product catalog will promote your products and services to more than a quarter of a million readers in 178 countries. It is distributed by US embassies and consulates worldwide and has a track record of high response rates and solid sales results.

8. *Search engine for trade events:* (http://export.gov/eac/trade_events.asp). This search engine, run by export.gov, offers participants one-time-only company promotions, seminars, webinars, trade shows, and missions.

9. *Catalog exhibitions*: (http://export.gov/salesand-marketing/eg_main_018199.asp). Run by the US Commercial Service, the organization offers US companies trade specialists who will display your sales literature at US embassies throughout the world as well as at appropriate trade shows. There are three types of exhibitions offered: Multi-state Catalog, American Product Literature, and U.S. Embassy/Consulate-sponsored exhibits. Your marketing material will be seen by prospective distributors, agents, and other interested buyers.

10. *Various contact-list services*: (for Singapore: http://export.gov/singapore/servicesforu.s.companies/contactlist/index.asp). Managed by the U.S. Department of Commerce's International Trade Administration, these are services that generate a mailing list of potential importers for your product from the organization's automated global network of overseas firms. The list includes company names, addresses, fax numbers, key contacts, Web sites, e-mail addresses, and specific products or service interests.

11. *Trade Leads Database*: (http://export.gov/trade-leads/index.asp). Run by the US government, the TLD contains prescreened, time-sensitive leads and government tenders gathered through US Commercial Service offices around the world. You can search leads and receive notification when new leads are posted.

12. *World Trade Centers Association*: (https://www.wtca.org). WTCs are maintained by some cities to house all the services associated with promoting and facilitating international trade under one roof. These services include trade information and communication services; trade education programs; and exhibition, conference, and office facilities. These agencies will permit you to advertise your product or service on an electronic bulletin board that is transmitted worldwide. Each local world trade center property (refer to the centers, https://www.wtca.org/locations) is supported by 15,000 WTC professionals located in more than ninety countries, so contacting any one of them provides a valuable link to global opportunities.

Summary

Unless you aspire to be a one-trick pony, using only one marketing tactic will hardly lead you to success with your export business. You should instead become that export rebel with a cause and implement a variety of marketing tactics in a consistent manner over a long period of time, and place a strong emphasis on search engine marketing. This will help the world find you a lot faster and put Internet connections to profitable use. Internet marketing is the prelude to successful exporting. See your marketing ideas to completion until you have placed the world at your online door.

Now, you're ready to export. What will that process involve? Let's find out.

Notes

i. "Leadership Speaker," David Meerman Scott: Marketing and Leadership Strategist, accessed October 23, 2013, http://www.davidmeermanscott.com/leadership-speaker/.

ii. "Jonah Berger Quotes," Goodreads, accessed March 20, 2016, https://www.goodreads.com/author/quotes/1170746.Jonah_Berger.

iii. "The 3 Top Reasons Your LinkedIn Profile Isn't Generating Positive Results," Kathy Caprino, accessed March 20, 2016, https://www.linkedin.com/pulse/3-top-reasons-your-linkedin-profile-isnt-generating-positive-caprino.

iv. Charles L. Gamble, *Winning with the P&G 99: 99 Principles and Practices of Procter & Gamble's Success* (New York: Pocket Books, 1999).

v. "Google Analytics Dashboards: A Step-By-Step Guide," Daniel Waiseberg, accessed March 20, 2016, http://online-behavior.com/analytics/dashboards.

vi. "2016 Trade Show Schedule," U.S. Department of Commerce International Buyer Program, accessed March 20, 2016, http://www.export.gov/build/groups/public/@eg_main/@ibp/documents/webcontent/eg_main_088750.pdf.

Mapping Out Your Export Journey

PART

III

Mapping Out
Your Export
Journey

Choosing a Product to Export

Exporting is a win-win for America's economy. Export sales contribute to a strong middle class by fueling economic opportunity and jobs in communities across the United States, while the countries buying our products gain access to some of the highest-quality products and services in the world.

—Karen Mills, former administrator for the US Small Business
Administration[i]

... the global economy is being transformed by a new Millennial creative class and novel new uses of technology. Governments have a special role to play in helping entrepreneurs navigate a borderless marketplace. We've all seen how advances in technology have created new possibilities for our entrepreneurs in the globalization era. The moment an SME goes live with a company website, they are effectively an international business with the potential for communication and commerce with consumers across

© Laurel J. Delaney 2016
L. J. Delaney, *Exporting*, DOI 10.1007/978-1-4842-2193-8_11

the world. Given this reality, all of us must be advocates inside of our governments for trade agreements that reduce tariffs and trade barriers that make it harder for SMEs to gain market access

— Maria Contreras-Sweet, administrator for the US Small Business Administration[ii]

Forgive the directness in the following questions, but we've come this far together and now I must test your resolve. Do you know what you will be exporting? If not, how will you decide? Will it be a product your firm already manufactures and sells or will it be someone else's product for which you serve as a middleman? Or what if you discover a product made by someone else that you think has export potential? How will you approach that firm? What do you do if something goes wrong? Will you need a legal contract to get started?

This chapter explores all those questions, offers an array of solutions, and provides a real-life example of a company slowly making its way into international territory. From there, it will be up to you to take action to get your export business underway.

Whether you manufacture products and have decided to export them or want to export the products someone else makes, you still must select something to export to get going. It's not always the case that you will be selling whatever you are selling at home. Let's take a look at how you go about making that choice.

For the Manufacturer: Finding the Best Product to Export

If you currently run a robust manufacturing company, you most likely have products in mind that you would like to export. If not, you might have to do a little research to determine what types of products are the most exportable. Either way, not knowing what to export is not a bad thing. If it were, you would not be reading this book right now.

Priority number one is to select a product you make that is successful in its present domestic operation and has the look and feel of export potential (meaning everyone—everywhere—already loves it and is likely to continue doing so). Priority number two is to go to market with what you are familiar with. Priority number three is to view the potential of the product in front of you through the eyes of consumers in your export market of choice. That said, let's say you manufacture more than twelve different chemical cleaning products. Which one should you export? Easy. The one that sells like hotcakes in your local market. The one you love the best. The one you know that customers in XYZ market will love the best. Try to choose one item that you can come close to providing an affirmative response for in regard to all of those statements!

You might have to modify your best-selling cleaning product for exportability (we'll cover that in Chapter 13) because making cultural and product changes as well as packing and labeling changes are a necessary part of preparing your business for exporting. Once you get to the point of selecting a country to export to, you need to examine it thoroughly, or you risk marketing poorly conceived products in incorrectly defined markets with an inappropriate marketing effort. Many products must be adapted to some degree, while others can be sold as is but their acceptance is greatly enhanced when tailored specifically to market needs.

■ **Tip** You can export a service, too (we will discuss that in Chapter 14). The United States is already the largest exporter of services in the world, both in overall commercial services and in most major services categories,[iii] and plays a crucial role in employment and productivity growth. Trade in goods is only part of the big international trade picture. Due to the Internet (technology), watch for stratospheric growth in service exports. *It will come!*

Choose a Product You Like—And Others Will Like It, Too

You might also start with a product you really like and know something about. How about a product you currently make that is selling like hotcakes? This will probably prove much easier than deciding where you want to sell it. For example, let's say you make amazing specialty soaps. You might ask yourself, "What if I could take some of these soaps and get them to consumers in other parts of the world who might enjoy them?" That's how you plant the seed, so to speak. Then it occurs to you that a great box of soaps won't be enough. You might start off by offering your customers something simple but later broaden your product offerings, continuing to use your own enthusiasm for soaps as a guide to what others might find useful and enjoyable. By marketing your product's advantages and continuing to expand on the features that people are most responsive to, you will allow it to obtain a competitive niche in foreign markets. Not only will you also ward off your own potential boredom this way, but you will keep customer interest alive all the way down the line. Your export customer will need your product innovation to support her sales, too, because her customers, in turn, will look to her for line expansions and novelties. People want to position themselves on the cutting edge in their fields! Now you have a vision of building an export business in specialty soaps. Start with a single product—say, your best-selling box of soaps—and look for someplace to take it.

▓ **Tip**   More often than not, product packaging must be adapted (we'll get to that in Chapter 13) to suit the needs of the intended overseas market. Other factors might need to be modified as well, such as the name of your brand, the electrical power systems your product works with, its weight and measurements, the ingredients in it, the physical environment it is suitable for, and so forth. Selling a product abroad in the same manner as it was produced for the domestic market increasingly proves to be less effective. Keep that in mind as you think through which product to select for export.

Case Example: Vosges Haut-Chocolat

Consider high-end Chicago-based chocolatier Vosges Haut-Chocolat, which was started in 1998 by Katrina Markoff. The story goes like this: Three days after her graduation from Vanderbilt University, Katrina moved to Paris to study at Le Cordon Bleu. She would continue to travel east through Southeast Asia and Australia and would later return to Spain to apprentice.[iv] Markoff's global adventures inspired the birth of her business, which began out of her kitchen when she sold truffles to specialty food stores in 1998. She opened the first Vosges Haut-Chocolat stores in the Bucktown neighborhood of Chicago in 1999. There are now eight boutiques, including two locations at O'Hare International Airport.

Vosges Haut-Chocolat's chocolates are made to "create a sensory experience that nurtures awareness of and appreciation for the world's diverse cultures," according to the company's Web site. In fact, one of the company's big draws is its mission to "invite you to travel the world through chocolate." How could anyone resist? When you visit Vosges's Web site, you don't want to leave, because there is so much enriching information offered, from how the company's chocolate is made to what social/environmental causes it belongs to—and all this occurs well before you get to the part about actually ordering the chocolate! And by then, you can't help yourself from ordering more than your budget calls for because the exquisite detailing compels you to try everything.

Markoff and her team constructed a forty-three-thousand-square-foot facility she's calling the "Chocolate Temple" to serve as an exhibition of her brands for local Chicagoans and tourists (for example, to learn about cocoa, create one's own truffles, and participate in guided chocolate meditations) and a point of differentiation from other retailers. Sales are expected to increase 15 percent in 2015, up from a projected total of $30 million in 2014. Despite the high cost of shipping, Vosges exports all over the world at a premium price!

Markoff has gone on to receive numerous accolades, including the *Bon Appétit* Food Artisan of the Year Award, a mention as "the innovator in chocolate to lead the US through the next 30 years" by *Food & Wine Magazine* (September 2008), the 2008 Woman Entrepreneur of the Year honor by OPEN American Express and *Entrepreneur* magazine, one of The Top 100 Most Creative People in Business by Fast Company (2015), and recognition as one of the ten best chocolatiers in the world by *National Geographic*.ᵛ

The key point of this example? Do exemplary work and customers will buy your products from all over the world—regardless of price. Once Vosges accomplishes everything it needs and wants to do domestically, watch for a big growth push on retail store locations internationally.

As discussed early on, picking the first overseas market you want to enter should be a logical-next-step growth move for a business, not an act of craziness or desperation. The target market you select should speak your language, have plenty of consumers who are willing to buy your product, and offer business-friendly regulations. Given Markoff's love of Europe, it is likely that the United Kingdom will be her first foray abroad for a physical store. Watch for it. Meanwhile, e-commerce in select overseas markets might be a temporary option for Vosges, as in the case of doing business in Japan: http://www.vosgeschocolate.jp.

What if You Don't Manufacture Gourmet Chocolates? Try Exporting Someone Else's Product!

So you don't currently manufacture gourmet chocolates but love the idea of exporting someone else's? Once you have a likely export product in mind—if you don't, you will get more ideas of how to do so by reading on—learn everything there is to know about it. If you were its creator, how would you improve it? Go to a domestic manufacturer, offer your export services as a middleman, and casually suggest product improvements that you know could turn a mediocre product into something ahead of its time. Then your job will be to sell the product.

Finding a Product to Export

If you don't have products you make in-house, you've got to figure out what you want to export. Ask yourself these questions to help you determine what product to export: What gives me the most pleasure as a businessperson? Is it the challenge of spotting a trend, taking advantage of it, and striking it rich? Or is it the chance to spend my time dealing with a commodity I love? Does it create satisfaction for me to meet consumer demands? You have two viable reasons for choosing a product to export—because you know it will sell or because you like it. Let's consider both alternatives.

Choosing a Product that Sells

Start with a product that you know will sell—if not everywhere, at least somewhere. And when you find a product for exporting, show it to anyone who will listen to your pitch. If every person responds positively, you are on to something big. If, on the other hand, you receive a lukewarm response from most listeners, you need to find another product. And remember, once you find the right product, you have to find the right market.

Also, you will improve your odds of picking a winner if you cultivate a knack for tracking trends, spotting potential trends, or even creating game-changing trends (as in the case of Vosges). Getting in on the ground floor and exporting a product before it becomes a super seller in its country of origin could be the business breakthrough of a lifetime! Remember the popular line of stuffed animals called Beanie Babies, or the Cabbage Patch dolls? Had you realized those products' export potential early on before they became best-selling products, you would have made yourself a millionaire four times over in a very short period of time (assuming you could arrange distribution or licensing deals). That's the kind of foresight needed to pick export winners.

■ **Tip** In addition to choosing a product that sells, there must be a competitive global advantage. Are you the only expert on earth who knows how to make safe and reliable o-rings (mechanical gaskets), produce an e-paper watch for the iPhone and Android platforms, or use light-emitting diodes (LEDs) and computer-driven imagery? If so, you have a core competency and can gain a competitive advantage in the global marketplace—most likely achieving more with less—by bringing a unique good or service to market that your competitors can't easily replicate. Consider it a strategic business function. If you don't have a competitive advantage right away, get it: research a product, study cultures, find people who know something unique, and innovate—push the envelope yourself.

What to Look for in Your Relationship with the Manufacturer

To ensure a good fit between you, in your capacity as exporter, and a domestic manufacturer with a product you want to sell globally, here are some things you should watch for:

- Good chemistry between you and your key contact (you can usually tell right away), and preferably with all of the top management as well. This helps ensure a company-wide commitment to the export program

- Trust is vital for creating and maintaining loyal customers, employees and suppliers and is the most valuable asset in a relationship

- Detailed product information

- Impressive packaging, quality, convenience and price

- A company environment that is friendly, creative, and well organized at both operational and administrative levels

- A company positioned to achieve a world-class reputation in the industry

- Responsiveness on two different levels: speed of service and sensitivity to your needs

- Prominent online social status (having a Facebook page and Twitter, LinkedIn, and Google+ business accounts)

These traits are positive indications that you will achieve success in your export sales efforts. Look for them on every level as you search for a manufacturer to supply a product for export.

Can the Manufacturer Keep Up with Demand?

After you have found companies that manufacture the product you wish to export, you must make sure they can keep up with customer demand. Here are some ways you can check:

- *Look for information about them on ThomasNet.com.* When you're narrowing your list to the most likely prospects, refer to ThomasNet.com (http://www.thomasnet.com) for information on company size, sales volume, number of employees, and so forth.

- *Order an International Company Profile.* The profile details a company's key officers and senior management, banking and other financial information, and market information, including sales and profit figures, as well as potential liabilities (refer to: http://www.export.gov/salesand-marketing/eg_main_018198.asp).

- *Survey retail stores to check product availability.* If you spot the product you are interested in exporting in a major mass-merchandising outlet, there's a good chance the manufacturer can keep up with demand. E-mail some out-of-state friends or family and see if they know about or have purchased the product. The wider the manufacturer's distribution, the greater the likelihood that the manufacturer will be able to meet the demands of your overseas customer.

- *Look for marketing/advertising by the company on billboards, print ads, and radio; coupons in newspaper inserts; and extensive use of social media.* All these forms of company exposure cost money and, usually, the more a company spends on marketing/advertising, the greater the chance that it can keep up with consumer demand.

- *Ask directly whether your prospective supplier can fulfill demand.* When you meet with the representative at your prospective supplier, ask him directly, "Will you be able to keep up with demand—potentially a thousand-case order every week?"

Can You Keep Up with the Work?

Once you've found a likely domestic manufacturer, you must understand what will be required of both of you and make up your mind that you will be able to do what it takes to carry out the proposal you're about to make. When you speak, you'll need to be prepared to inspire confidence. You'll have to have a passion for the product that equals or exceeds the manufacturer's own. You'll need to trust your own ability to export the product before manufacturers will put their trust in you. It's that simple. If you come across as having doubts about your abilities, they will have doubts, too.

So let's visualize the exporter's working life. No two days will be alike. After six months, orders may begin to come in. They might be few in number but intimidatingly large in size. The details that need your attention may seem overwhelming. You may feel that you are in over your head. Take a deep breath, look in the mirror, and announce, "I am becoming an exporter," because that's exactly what's happening. You won't have time to worry—you'll need to act and act fast. You'll keep your chin up and work until the transaction is done. Then you'll check to be sure you're really done by making sure your clients and customers are satisfied. You and the manufacturer will have to get used to the idea that you'll have to do the seemingly impossible on a regular basis. Convince yourself, and you will convince the manufacturer.

Scripting Your Call to the Manufacturer

Before you make that first call (on the telephone or over Skype) to feel out your prospective manufacturer and hopefully set up a meeting, I suggest that you create a phone script. No matter how tedious it is to prepare, it can be a powerful sales tool. You might compose something along these lines. The exporter, in this example, is based in Chicago (my hometown):

Exporter: "May I speak with your export manager?"

Receptionist: "What does that refer to?" (Her not knowing is a good sign—it means an opportunity for you!)

Exporter: "The person who is responsible for selling your products overseas."

Receptionist: "Hmm, I don't know who that would be. I'll have to check. Would you hold on a moment, please?"

Receptionist: "Thank you for waiting. Sam Smith handles such things. He's the person you need to talk with. I'll put you through."

Manufacturer: "Sam Smith speaking."

Exporter: "Hello Mr. Smith, I'm Julie Jones, the founder of Jewelry Exporting Co., an exporter of high-quality, affordable costume jewelry. I understand your company manufactures this type of product. We are seeking new sources of supply for our overseas customers. Are you interested in exploring new markets and increasing sales? Our jewelry exporting firm can give you instant access to *customers worldwide* ...."

In order to set up a meeting, the call might continue like this:

Manufacturer: "Absolutely. I'd be happy to explore the opportunity. When would you like to meet?"

Exporter: "How does next Monday morning, 10 a.m., at your office sound?"

Manufacturer: "Perfect, I'll see you then. Is there anything I should have available for our meeting?"

Exporter: "Yes, a company brochure, your current wholesale price schedule, product samples, and any other important information that you think is important to our discussion. If we have a good fit, I'll need more brochures, say, twenty, that I can use for my customers."

Manufacturer: "No problem. I'll see that we have them available."

Exporter: "One more thing. I don't think it's critical for this initial meeting, but if things go smoothly when we meet next week and you decide to use our services, you might want to ask your top management to be a part of our subsequent session to make sure we have their commitment to our export program."

Manufacturer: "I'll see if they are available when I hang up. If so, we can have them attend next time."

Exporter: "Great! I look forward to meeting you on Monday. And incidentally, Mr. Smith, if you choose us to represent you in your export transactions, our profits are earned directly out of the sales we generate for you. You cannot get any more cost-efficient than that!"

Sometimes you are too far away from being in the position to propose such a meeting. Instead, you want to elicit interest but also get some additional information and sales materials. In response to your question "Are you interested in exploring new markets and increasing sales?" your call might continue something like this:

Manufacturer: "Absolutely. I'd be happy to discuss the opportunity."

Exporter: "Would you be kind enough to send me your company brochure?"

Manufacturer: "Sure. I'll get one out by e-mail today."

Exporter: "Thank you. In the meantime, I'll also send an e-mail to you, furnishing you with my company background."

Manufacturer: "That would be great. I look forward to receiving it."

Exporter: "Good. If we have a good fit, the next step is to set up a meeting. What would be more convenient, your office or mine?"

Manufacturer: "I generally get to Chicago once a month. Perhaps on my next trip we can arrange a meeting at your office."

Exporter: "That would be fine. I'll phone you in a week or two."

■ **Tip** I urge you to also script out a list of potential objections that a manufacturer might have as to whether your company will be able to get a foot in the door (pricing, not understanding the process, no need for your service, and credibility, for example) that you can prepare to overcome well in advance of your communications. The more you know about your decision maker and the key people who influence his decisions (the latter can prove far more important than you realize), the greater your chance of achieving successful results in your outreach effort. When you're done, determine what worked, what didn't, and what your next steps are.

Setting up the script helps to keep you focused and effective on the phone. It will also help you accomplish what you set out to achieve: an appointment to sell your export service or a request for information to review. The script is there to lend structure, not to constrain you, so tailor it to fit your style—in it, you can be knowledgeable, be friendly, and be yourself. Rehearse your pitch to your friends. If it inspires a small amount of ridicule, you're on your way to developing a winning script, because you have their attention. Find out why they're poking fun and improve your script.

It's a given that there will be rejections, put-offs, and "Call-me-again-in-six months" responses, but that doesn't mean that you are ineffective in your approach. It means that the party you are calling is not interested—or is busy—at the time. Accept that and move on. Don't dwell on it or belabor the issue. But when a contact seems interested, sell yourself and your service for all you're worth and zero in on the appointment date or the request for information. After a few calls to prospective manufacturers, you will feel confident without the script. Once you reach that point, don't throw it out—pass it on to the next aspiring exporter!

From there, the next step is to make sure you are thoroughly prepared for your next contact with the manufacturer.

Meeting with the Manufacturer

Once you have gathered information on your prospective supplier's product and reviewed the product for export readiness, you must convince the manufacturer that you are capable of exporting the company's widget to a remote part of the world. How do you go about it?

It goes like this: focus, explain, emphasize, and stroke.

- Focus on the target market. Give the manufacturer an introduction to the market conditions in an unknown country. This will intrigue him.

- Explain how you do all the work and incur all the risks.

- Emphasize that he will make most of the money from the transaction.

- Stroke him by enumerating the benefits you can bring to his business by exploring export markets on his behalf.

Your goal is to get the manufacturer excited about the possibilities and to convince him that you've got the expertise to pull it off. It's best to be prepared for a range of possible responses. Your follow-up exchange might go like this:

Exporter: "Do you sell to Stockholm, Sweden?"

Manufacturer: "Never heard of the place."

Exporter: "Well, I think you're going to like it! I'm in touch with several agents and distributors over there who are looking for your type of product, and that means fast, hassle-free additional business for you!"

Manufacturer: *"Sounds great! How do we get started?"*

In this instance, you're breaking totally new ground for him, so you can offer him your strategy as to how to get started. But you might find yourself dealing with a manufacturer who already has some international operations in place.

If you want to get in on that action, you must convince the person you're dealing with that you are flexible, cooperative, and interested primarily in generating additional business for him. Here's how you might work such a situation to your advantage:

Exporter: "I have contacts in Stockholm, Sweden. May I offer your products there?

Manufacturer: "We already do business there."

Exporter: "On an exclusive basis?"

Manufacturer: "No, but we are open to expanding our business there."

Exporter: "I sell through importing distributors who service the mail-order gift business over there. Does that differ from your present customer base?"

Manufacturer: "Yes. Right now we sell only to small mom-and-pop retail outlets that are serviced by a local trading company."

Exporter: "If I generate reasonable business within a few months, will you allow me exclusivity in Stockholm on all mail-order gift business?"

Manufacturer: "If I see you generate the sales, I'll have no problem giving you exclusivity."

Exporter: "Fair enough! I am confident that I can generate the sales you'll want to see in six months. At that point, if it is acceptable to you, I would like to meet with you to work up an agreement protecting my efforts."

Manufacturer: *"Fine. In the meantime, let's get some idea of what you need to get started."*

It's a good idea to come prepared with a market analysis so you can convince the manufacturer that you have enough insight into the marketplace and competition to generate the amount of sales for his widget that you proposed. Your dialogue might go like this:

Exporter: "I'm interested in exporting your widget to Stockholm. Are you interested in having me represent you on an export basis?"

Manufacturer: "What makes you think you can export our widget to Stockholm?"

Exporter: "I have researched the market and found that there's a shortage of quality machine parts of this particular class. They will be lining up to buy your widget! I've got contacts lined up who'd jump at the chance to purchase it for distribution. I know for a fact that your competitors aren't there—you'll really be getting a jump on them!"

Manufacturer: "So what do you need from me?"

Exporter: "Color catalog sheets, your lowest possible price list, and eventually product samples for customer review."

Manufacturer: "That's it?"

Exporter: "Well, I'll also be coming up with all kinds of questions along the way, and so will my customers. If I'm going to serve them properly, I'll need you to line up someone from your firm who knows your business and products inside and out to be my key contact."

Manufacturer: "No problem. I'll assign Joe Helpful. He's been with the firm for more than twenty years and has always wanted to sell our products worldwide."

Exporter: "Sounds like an ideal export front man! I should meet him as soon as possible."

Manufacturer: "How about tomorrow?"

Exporter: "Great. At that time, we can nail down the next round of details."

In an exchange like this, you win over the manufacturer by showing him that you have a well-thought-out and workable plan. Being able to provide detailed, specific information about potential product success and the resources you'll need to launch the export effort will help you to convince the manufacturer that you have the knowledge and skills to take the company global.

Now that you have gone to the trouble of finding a product to export and proving to a manufacturer you *can* export it, it's time to consider whether you need a written agreement as to how you will do business with the company.

Export Sales Agreements

I've been asked by many an exporter whether to get a contractual agreement drawing up export sales terms and conditions between itself and the manufacturer. The answer is yes. Most international lawyers feel the export sales agreement is by far the most important single document in an export sales transaction. Yet oftentimes, I feel that the person asking the question is in danger of making what they are about to do more complicated than it has to be. You don't need to overanalyze the relationship or try to hedge yourself against every conceivable risk. It's lack of confidence that causes most people to lock up and avoid doing business outside of their comfort zone. Granted, you should inform yourself about all options available to you, but when you know what you want to do and can do it reasonably well, get on with it. The rest will fall into place.

However, if you do not trust the manufacturer, you should not enter into any kind of business relationship with that company! Sometimes, though, a customer will ask you to source a certain product, so you will find yourself doing business with people you would have preferred to avoid. If that is the case, and you are picking up bad vibes from your supplier, then absolutely, positively, get everything in writing.

Draft something simple that meets your needs and those of the manufacturer, including a complete specification of pricing, quantity of goods to be sold, commission (if applicable), geographic jurisdiction, exclusivity or nonexclusivity, duration of contract, and so forth. The more specific and clear the agreement is, the more useful it will be for enforcing everything you expect done. Before you proceed with securing the manufacturer's signature, consult with an international attorney to minimize potential risks, including but not limited to protecting a manufacturer's intellectual property rights. One last critical thing that everyone tends to overlook: you need to establish a clear understanding of how to get out of the contract should it not work.

Tip For general requirements for an export contract, go to http://www.tradeforum. org/Export-Contracts/. The International Trade Centre has produced guidelines to get you started. But remember—the best export sales agreement in the world will not protect you against a company that is a royal pain in the #@* and produces zero results.

In most cases, though, if you have a healthy exporter-supplier relationship, you will sense mutual trust. There will be no need for a contract because you will both see the relationship as a win-win situation. If you generate business overseas, your supplier will be loyal. If you do not, it will look elsewhere to find opportunities to grow the business internationally. So beware—be absolutely sure you can deliver results or else bargain for a contract that will protect you.

Summary

Select a product you make, or represent a company who makes a product that is exportable, that is successful in its present domestic operation, and that has the look and feel of export potential (meaning everybody—everywhere—absolutely loves it). Go to market with what you are familiar with. View whatever the potential in front of you is through the eyes of consumers in the export market of choice. When it comes to picking a product for export, that's a winning formula for export success.

Even if a manufacturer, as well as your own operation and top brass, gives you the go-ahead with very little discussion or needs convincing with hardcore facts and figures, at some point you'll have to face the task of finding promising markets for your chosen export product—and it's not an easy one. Luckily, there's a world of online resource help out there! In the next chapter, I'll guide you through the complicated and time-consuming job of market research and introduce you to a wide array of government-sponsored and private sources of assistance for all the phases of your export project.

Notes

i. "It's a Small (Business) World: The Benefits of Exporting," Karen Mills, *Huffington Post*, March 6, 2013, http://www.huffingtonpost.com/karen-mills/small-business-exporting_b_2814446.html.

ii. "2nd Global SME Ministerial," Maria Contreras-Sweet, March 15, 2016, https://www.sba.gov/content/2nd-global-sme-ministerial.

iii. http://trade.gov/press/press-releases/2014/export-factsheet-december2014-120514.pdf.

iv. Vosges Haut-Chocolat "The Story," accessed March 24, 2016, http://www.vosgeschocolate.com/story/.

v. Vosges Haut-Chocolat, "The Story," accessed March 24, 2016, http://www.vosgeschocolate.com/story/.

Exploring Your Territory

How to Research and Pick the Best Foreign Market

"But what I want to emphasize is that exporting is worth it," Barber continued. *"That trade is good for your business and for the U.S. And that exporting success is well within your reach."*

—President of UPS International Jim Barber[i]

"How in the world do you figure out what the next big thing is?" he *[Steve Jobs] asked. I [Noland Bushnell] replied, "You have to be aware of everything that's going on, and be open to adapting to it."*

—"Finding the Next Steve Jobs: How to Find, Keep, and Nurture Talent," Noland Bushnell, Gene Stone[ii]

Once you've decided on a product to export, you've got to find an export market where you can sell it profitably. At this point, I am assuming you know what you need to do to get export ready based on the results of the export readiness questionnaire you took in Chapter 1. As for market research, it can be a slow, painstaking, and tedious chore, but as you add to your knowledge,

© Laurel J. Delaney 2016
L. J. Delaney, *Exporting*, DOI 10.1007/978-1-4842-2193-8_12

by tracking the movement of goods and tapping into the world's networks of purchasing and distribution, you will create your own living and changing map of international trade that will serve you throughout your export business.

There are a variety of methods by which a company can locate the best—meaning the right—potential foreign markets for its product or service. This chapter outlines a range of efficient methods for researching export markets, focusing on where to get export-market data and intelligence, and how to use it.

Since you will be consulting a variety of resources, you will want to take some time to plan your approach. In this chapter, I offer you ways to nail down specifics about your product, your consumer, and the market conditions necessary to support healthy sales of your product—all of which will help you to identify a hot target market when you move on to your research.

You will be assembling information about two kinds of customers: the everyday citizen who buys goods for personal use (B-to-C) and the various high-volume traders who buy goods from you to sell to other businesses (B-to-B; refer to Chapter 8 for more on both kinds of transactions). I will provide you with numerous ways to find out about both kinds of customers, so that you can determine what modifications, if any, will be needed to prepare the product for your target markets. You'll find that there are dense networks of information and support, largely government sponsored, for every aspect of the development of your export business. Most of these sources of assistance are easily accessible online and within the reach of even a modest operating budget. Once you have a good idea of where and how to direct your marketing efforts, you can create an action plan to get your export program underway.

■ **Caution** In the words of the late Steve Jobs: "Some people say, 'Give the customers what they want.' But that's not my approach. Our job is to figure out what they're going to want before they do. I think Henry Ford once said, 'If I'd asked customers what they wanted, they would have told me, 'A faster horse!'" People don't know what they want until you show it to them. That's why I never rely on market research. Our task is to read things that are not yet on the page."[iii] Keep Jobs's remark in mind as you conduct your market research, and use gut instinct, humanity, and commonsense as you research data. But don't get analysis paralysis where you keep researching but never take action. That's the worst outcome. And never forget the end user—the customer—for that is who buys the products and services.

Market Research—a Dreaded Chore, a Powerful Tool

One of the tasks I dreaded while getting my business underway was conducting market research. I hated it because it cost both time and money. When I promised a potential supplier that I would study a foreign market to determine whether it would be receptive to the product, I would rack my brain about (a) how I would go about it and (b) how I would go about it inexpensively!

Sometimes you'll get lucky and an inquiry will land in your e-mail inbox pointing you right to an ideal market for a product. For example, you might have a friend who runs a company in Botswana and loves a certain type of sandal but can't find it there. He contacts you and asks you to source a supplier of the shoe or an equivalent product. You now have a country (Botswana) to export to, a potential buyer (your friend's company) to sell to, and a product (a sandal not available in Botswana) to offer. Furthermore, now that you know that these sandals or anything like them are not sold in Botswana, you've been alerted to an untapped market that you can develop on a larger scale. But don't take these windfalls for granted. If you want to keep the orders coming in, you're going to have to ramp up your social media conversations and go out and approach customers. Market research tells you where customers can be found.

Your first market research project is usually the toughest because it's all unfamiliar terrain. But once you have searched out the data you need in order to predict how a specific type of product will sell in a specific geographic location, you can use the information over and over again as a guideline for exports of similar products in the future. As you build your personal information database on global markets and learn to keep yourself up to date on developments in international trade, it will become less and less of a chore to determine where to take your product. You will find that market research is a powerful tool for exploring and taking control of your export territory.

Get Yourself Organized

There is no getting around the fact that market research is *not* a tidy, linear process! It involves several closely related objectives: to put together a working profile of your actual consumer or end user; to determine if the country's market conditions (its economy, demographics, level of political stability, trade barriers, distribution system, competition, transportation, and storage, etc.) will favor or hinder your product's success; and to identify the people who will buy your product from you (consumers, wholesalers, importers, etc.). Before you consult your resources, I recommend that you sit down with pen and paper or PC (it can be a tablet if you prefer), and try the following procedures to help you structure the task. The idea here is to establish a few attractive or promising directions for your investigations and to clarify exactly what kinds of information you'll be looking for.

Choosing Your Market—Pleasure, Profit, Competitive Advantage, or Challenge?

In Chapter 2, I talked about the various motivations that might guide your choice of a product to export. When deciding where to concentrate your sales efforts, the same range of motivations comes into play. You should choose a market that intrigues you, is easy to reach, presents a competitive advantage, or offers a challenge and then consider products that you might want to sell there. You will be visiting this market frequently and getting to know its people intimately, so, just as you should pick a product that will delight you for years to come, you should plan on exporting to a country that delights and fascinates you. If you are enthralled with French culture and you are excited at the prospect of cracking that market, then you want to sell to France. If you have dolls to sell, you should sell them to France. It's a place to start! But use common sense: Don't ignore other countries that offer good prospects for your dolls, and don't expend too much time and energy on your first-choice market if it turns out to be a poor prospect. The trick is to find the right market.

■ **Tip** Even though in Chapter 2 I talked about selecting a product that is wildly successful on the domestic front to export, don't overlook the possibility and opportunity of selling products that are less successful in the United States, as they could be in high demand elsewhere. Say you manufacture two different types of dolls—one that uses high-end materials and is very expensive and the other low-end and quite inexpensive. The glamorous high-end doll sells magnificently in your local market, but the moderately priced doll is more appealing and affordable overseas. The only way to discover this is through extensive research of foreign countries.

If you start your market research and find out that there's no demand for dolls in France, you can always move on and pick another market. But stick to dolls, because that's what you manufacture and are comfortable with and knowledgeable about. Unless you've exhausted all of the options on your product of choice, it's best to stay as close to your original plan as possible—entertaining too many possibilities can put you off track and cause you to lose your confidence and enthusiasm.

If easy profits with minimal effort and exercise of business ingenuity are your priorities, you can just use your domestic market as a model. If you take a careful look at where, to whom, and why a product is selling well in your country and then locate markets abroad with similar demographics, chances are that the demand will be similar. A bonus: minimal product modification, if any, will be required.

Segmenting Your Product and Market

Another important aspect that will help you focus your research is categorizing or segmenting your product and target market by making lists of the relevant factors. Take the dolls, for example. What type of dolls are you going to export? Baby dolls? Antique? For boys? For girls? Talking? Educational? Under each product segment, list the categories of likely customers until you reach the end user for your product. Once you determine who your customer is, what she buys, when she buys, how often she buys, and why she buys, you've got a customer profile. For example, your customers for girls' dolls might include manufacturers, wholesalers, independent doll shops, big box stores, and e-commerce platforms, as well as private citizens. Push your lists as far as you can—it might take anywhere from one to ten categorizations before you can reach optimum segmentation.

Use a format like this for your list:

1. I'm going to export: _____ (product)

2. Specifically these types: _____ (type of product), _____ (type of target customer), _____ (type of buyer).

3. I'm going to export to: _____ (country)

Your completed list might look like this:

1. I'm going to export <u>"dolls"</u> (product).

2. Specifically these types: <u>"educational dolls"</u> (type of product), <u>"for girls ages seven to ten"</u> (type of target customer), <u>"to importing wholesalers of educational toys and direct via e-commerce"</u> (type of buyer).

3. I'm going to export to <u>"France"</u> (country).

Through this exercise, you will sufficiently narrow down search categories so that you are ready to conduct a search via Google, Bing, or Yahoo!. You will also be ready to send an e-mail to a trade officer to ask a specific question or set up an appointment with the Small Business Administration or US Export Assistance Center for help. Refer to your list and refer to it frequently to keep you on track.

Will Your Product Succeed in Your Market of Choice?

Once you have a good idea of what you want to export and where to, you can fill out your picture of market conditions by answering questions like these:

1. Who will buy your product and why?

2. What is the size of the market?

3. Who is your competition?

4. How competitive can you be?

5. How new is the product to the market you have selected?

6. Are there growth opportunities in the market?

7. What do the country's demographic profile, economy, and mass culture look like right now? (Its macroeconomic indicators such as GDP growth, employment, and birth rates will give you an overview of the state of the economy and population.)

8. Are there demographic, economic, or cultural trends that will shape the market in the future?

9. Does the country's government help or hinder the sale of imported goods? For example, are there any barriers to entry or to sales within the market?

10. Will the country's climate or geography present logistical problems for sales of your product of choice? For example, selling chocolates to countries with warm climates such as in Brazil.

11. Does the product have to be adapted to your target market by way of a physical reconstruction, a new package, or a change in servicing practices? (See Chapter 13 for more details on preparing your product for export.)

12. Will we need to translate or localize product labeling, packaging, collateral material and website immediately?

13. Does the product have the same use in the international market as in the home market?

14. Does the product require personal after-sales service and, if so, can you provide it in the prospective market?

15. Does the country's government have a trade agreement in place with your own country? For example, the United States currently has trade agreements in place with 20 countries and some still pending.

Tip Many new exporters look at where their competitors are exporting to and then investigate country and industry reports to identify the export trends and growing markets for their product or within their industry. Trade associations, US government online portals, and reports from other global organizations are an excellent source for this type of information. Because Canada and New Mexico border the United States and are a part of NAFTA, they are a good starting point for new exporters.

Use your own business sense and add to the list. Once you actually start your research, more questions will arise. This is all part of the process of turning your vague ambitions into a concrete strategy based on market realities, so the more smart questions you ask and answer, the better your chances of success.

Once you have narrowed down your options and answered all the questions, take the following steps, focusing on nine key areas (many of which—numbers 4 through 6—can be accomplished through the helpful guidance of a good logistics specialist):

1. Conduct a country assessment that examines the country's geographic, demographic, economic, cultural, political, and legal systems and infrastructure.

2. Perform a market assessment that examines the size, characteristics, and projected growth of the target market.

3. Examine your competitors' products, prices, marketing methods, and distribution channels.

4. Find out if there are any licenses or certifications needed to export to the country (refer to Chapter 22).

5. Learn about any tariffs and import regulations that will affect you (see Chapter 18).

6. Classify your product using one of the following commodity classification codes: Harmonized Tariff Schedule (HTS), Schedule B number (refer to Chapter 18), North American Industry Classification System (NAICS), or Standard International Trade Classification (SITC). Each of these classification systems allows you to assign a six-to-ten-digit code to commodities so that trade data can be collected and analyzed in a consistent manner. For help with any of the terms or concepts, visit export.gov's "Trade Data & Analysis" (`http://export.gov/trade-data/index.asp`).

7. Determine how you will distribute your product or service (using an agent, distributor, wholesaler, or e-commerce fulfillment—more in Chapter 17).

8. Figure out your global competitive advantage. What are you bringing to the marketplace that no one else has or can offer?

9. Test demand. Do a trial shipment to an interested customer, exhibit at a trade show, participate in a catalog-only show, or utilize a foreign-partner matching service. All of these methods allow you to sample test the market, determine interest, and find out whether people will buy your product.

Tip Don't rely entirely on the number of visitors to your online platform as a predictor of the e-commerce market demand for your product or service offering. Google's Adwords program can give you an idea of how many monthly searches there are for specific keywords, say "tablet cases," or phrases that relate to your product. A high volume of searches for one specific term does not necessarily ensure high market demand for your product, but it does provide a good starting point. Once you understand the market demand for products similar to yours, you can tailor your own Web site to meet the demands of consumers who may have an interest in your product. But again, this is all tied more to e-commerce and doesn't necessarily indicate the demand of those who don't use digital for purchases.

Keep Your Search on Track

Now you're ready to take advantage of export-information resources. A word of caution: Any time you dig into a complex subject, especially an unfamiliar one, you are at risk of being sidetracked no matter how intelligent and organized you normally are! Keep your search efficient and focused so you waste as little time as possible.

Remember that this search will be a messy and complicated one. You have seen that your search objectives are closely interrelated. To complicate matters even further, most of the resources I am about to list will have something to contribute to all three objectives: consumer demographics, market conditions, and customer lists. You might find it useful to set up an information form for each potential market with a blank line for the name of the country at the top, a list of all your questions (leaving room for the answers), and spaces for customer names and addresses. If need be, break all the questions on your list into subcategory questions so you can see how the details you're asking questions about belong to the larger picture you're trying to put together. It's a good idea to create this form on your computer or tablet. For one thing, it will allow you to print out blank copies as needed and bring spares with you (if you are doing an in-person meeting with an expert). For another, it will allow you to modify your question list easily and take all the room you need for filling in information. You might want to use the blank printed copies of your forms to make working notes and then type in your day's findings on your master file on your tablet. If you want, you can print out your complete listings for each country you research and tape them up to your wall to make a "map" of likely markets.

You might also find it useful to bring your tablet to your research location or laptop using Evernote, for example—see chapter 9—to keep you focused on one question at a time. If you are looking to find out whether your product is marketable in Istanbul, offensive to Russians, or competitive to leading brands of similar products in Indonesia, write the question down in Evernote and put it right in front of your face. It will come in handy later when you are immersed in details with no end in sight. You will be able to just look at the note—you might have answered your question hours earlier!

And save yourself unnecessary fatigue and frustration by making sure you go to the right organization for the information you want, whether on the Internet or in person. Fruitless trips are discouraging. Call ahead and ask your major questions first—it will save you a trip if experts at one of the places we will discuss don't have what you are looking for.

Now you're ready to begin exploring your export territory. In the next section we'll look at a variety of information resources on international trade, many of which can be accessed online.

Export Market Data: Where to Get It and How to Use It

The following resources offer a wealth of information on international trade. This list is not in any particular order; I recommend that you begin with whichever of your chosen resources is easiest to access. Once you've begun acquiring a body of knowledge, you'll have a better idea of where to direct your search. There are both physical locations and Web sites that offer information on international trade.

Physical Locations

We'll start with the physical locations where you can go to obtain information on international trade. Most of them are run by federal government organizations and have multiple branches in all of the states.

Small Business Administration

One of the most important places you should go, and many people's first stop, in order to seek high-powered export advice is your local Small Business Administration (SBA) office or the equivalent government-sponsored small business support group in your country. When you hit the bookshelves there (many directories are available online, but in person you have the benefit of the assistance of real people), you'll see directory after directory with intimidating titles like *Report FT 410* (the census), *HS Code Directory*, *Trade Profiles* (WTO Statistics Database), and so on. Luckily, the staff can help you navigate through them. Many of the people working at these organizations are retired from high-ranking positions in the corporate world and enjoy offering their years of experience to help others get a start. It's best to come armed with concrete questions to help them help you. Write down exactly what you want to know and what you want to use it for. Don't just throw up your hands and ask, "I want to export a product somewhere, can you assist

The export assistance available from the SBA includes training seminars and legal advice as well as answers to your questions. All export programs administered through the SBA are available through local branches. The SBA also serves as an administrative center for small business development centers; loan programs (funded by private lenders and backed by the government); and services for businesses owned by minorities, veterans, and women. Be sure to ask if you are eligible for these forms of assistance. In addition, each branch typically houses a business library, a computer center for business owners who don't own their own equipment, and an office of the Service Corps of Retired Executives (SCORE). The staff of SCORE, who work under the SBA's umbrella, can match up small businesses with mentors who have experience in foreign trade and help new or experienced exporters develop an export strategy.

Department of Commerce

Another stop should be your local branch of the Department of Commerce (DOC) , which houses twenty-one different Export Assistance Centers (EACs; find one by going to https://www.sba.gov/managing-business/exporting/us-export-assistance-centers) in the United States that link to one hundred US cities and more than eighty countries worldwide by providing a comprehensive global network. The mission of the EAC network is to deliver a comprehensive array of counseling and international trade services to US firms, particularly small- and medium-sized ones. The EAC offices have the appearance and feel of a private-sector export consulting firm, yet it is a federal agency that partners well with state resources and organizations that promote exports. Addresses and phone numbers for all district offices are yours for the asking. The centers give you access to the services of the US DOC, the International Trade Administration (ITA), the US Commercial Service, the Export-Import Bank of the United States, and the US Small Business Administration. Although the programs the organization offers are geared mostly toward experienced, export-ready companies looking to enter new markets, it also offers a boatload of trade and finance assistance to established small- and mid-sized businesses. One-on-one counseling is available. One of the simplest and handiest resources is the pamphlet *A Basic Guide to Exporting* issued by the US Government Printing Office (it can be purchased from http://export.gov/basicguide/). Although the guide focuses on exports from the United States, it also offers global advice on what is required to export from any point in the world. If the guide is not specific enough for you, check with the government programs that facilitate trade in your own country.

In addition to previously mentioned services, the DOC offers expert advice on export administration, trade adjustment assistance, travel and tourism, and minority businesses, to name just a few. Be sure to ask somebody about your specific situation, even if you don't see it covered here. More likely than not, there's someone who can help you. If not, you will be directed to other government service offices that can.

The following list is a sampling of information and services the DOC offers:

- Exporting seminars, webinars, podcasts, conferences, trade missions, and exhibitions
- Offering financial aid to exporters
- Providing information on emerging international-trade opportunities
- Furnishing information on export documentation requirements
- Exporting statistics

- Supplying readings on international trade

- Distributing information on licensing, patent, trademark, and protectionist practices abroad

- Providing counseling on general export marketing issues

- Offering services to help you make cross-border contacts and find agents and distributors (see Chapter 16)

US Commercial Service—An Exporter's Gold Mine

Ever wonder who gathers all that information on trends and actual trade leads? It's the US Commercial Service (USCS; http://export.gov/worldwide_us/index.asp). This wonderful resource is an exporter's gold mine.

There are more than 1,400 trade professionals, all eager and waiting to help you go global, who are working in USCS's 128 commercial offices, located in US embassies and consulates in more than seventy-five countries. Most of them have international experience, so they know what it takes to do business in the country in which they're stationed. They put their invaluable understanding of local culture and prospective customer contacts at the service of the small business owner interested in entering overseas markets.

I used this resource within the first couple of weeks of starting my business. It proved extremely effective. I contacted the American embassy with a specific question: I was seeking a list of reputable food-importing wholesalers that specialized in high-volume product movement throughout Japan. Within twenty-four hours I received a reply from an agriculture trade officer indicating that a list was being forwarded by airmail (well before the days of e-mail). When I received it, I was excited about its potential and began contacting the companies right away. It was an ideal way to get started.

Here are just a few of the services the USCS overseas staff will provide at no charge:

- Customer lists

- Sales representative and other agency-finding services

- Background checks on companies overseas

- Business counseling

Keep in mind that most state governments offer overseas business resource centers to help the small business executive tap into new markets. Check into these as well as the USCS—they usually work in tandem.

Web Sites Brimming with Trade Statistics

There are also many Web sites that offer a wealth of trade information.

TradeStats Express

TradeStats (`http://tse.export.gov/TSE/TSEhome.aspx`) provides the latest annual and quarterly trade data, including national trade data and state export data.

USA Trade Online

The Foreign Trade Division of the US Census Bureau hosts USA Trade Online (`https://usatrade.census.gov/`), which allows you to access current and cumulative US export and import data for more than nine thousand export commodities and seventeen thousand import commodities.

Market Research Index

Hosted by export.gov, Market Research Index (`http://export.gov/mrktresearch/`) provides a step-by-step guide on how to get started in market research. In addition, you can access the Country Commercial Guides written by US Commercial Service trade experts worldwide (`http://www.export.gov/ccg/`).

BusinessUSA

BusinessUSA (`http://business.usa.gov/`) is a centralized, one-stop platform designed to make it easy for businesses to access services to help them grow (through exporting) and hire, regardless of where the information is located or which agency's Web site, call center, or office they go to for help.

American National Standards Institute

The American National Standards Institute (ANSI; `http://www.standardsportal.org`) provides answers to the critical standards, conformance, market access, and trade-related questions that companies require to succeed in the U.S. and internationally.

National District Export Council

The National District Export Council (DEC; http://districtexport-council.org/) consists of 16 DEC members who have been elected to the National DEC by DEC members from each of the eight U.S. Commercial Service Networks. The mission of DEC is to encourage and support exports of goods and services that strengthen individual companies, stimulate U.S. economic growth and create jobs.

United States International Trade Commission

The Web site of the United States International Trade Commission (http://www.usitc.gov) aims to administer US trade-remedy laws; provide the president, the United States trade representative (USTR), and Congress with independent quality analysis, information, and support on matters relating to tariffs and international trade and competitiveness; and maintain the Harmonized Tariff Schedule of the United States. Its goal is to contribute to the development of a realistic US trade policy.

USEmbassy.gov

Run by the US Department of State, USEmbassy.gov: Websites of US Embassies, Consulates and Missions (http://www.usembassy.gov/) provides links to the Web sites of the diplomatic organizations in many countries and features business information specific to those countries.

World Trade Organization

The World Trade Organization (WTO; http://www.wto.org/) is an organization that focuses on opening up trade and sorting out trade problems as they arise. It is a forum for governments to negotiate trade agreements and a safe haven for them to settle trade disputes. It operates a system of trade rules.

Other Federal-Export Assistance Resources

There are also a handful of other organizations designed to assist you with federal exports.

Export-Import Bank of the United States

The Export-Import Bank of the United States (Ex-Im Bank; http://www.exim.gov/) is a government agency that is responsible for assisting the export financing of US goods and services through a variety of loan guarantees and insurance programs (see Chapter 20).

Foreign Agricultural Service

The Foreign Agricultural Service (FAS) of the US Department of Agriculture (http://www.fas.usda.gov/) provides a network of counselors, attachés, trade officers, commodity analysts, and marketing specialists to assist in making contacts overseas. Check with your state or regional department.

Additional Resources

There are also various other agencies that may come in handy during your search for federal-research assistance. Although you probably will not need to contact these agencies at the outset of your operations, you should know about them. They are: The Overseas Private Investment Corporation (OPIC; http://www.opic.gov/), the US Department of the Treasury (http://www.treasury.gov/Pages/default.aspx), USAID (the US Agency for International Development; http://www.usaid.gov/), Organization for Economic Co-operation and Development (OECD; http://www.oecd.org), and the Office of the US Trade Representative (http://www.ustr.gov/about-us/trade-toolbox/us-government-trade-agencies). Most of these resources are available through the office of your local chamber of commerce or Small Business Administration. Check the Web sites for further information.

Local Colleges and Universities

Another important resource is the colleges and universities in your state. Contact them to see what type of international assistance they offer to small businesses interested in expanding overseas. You'll find that nearly every major university offers what is referred to as a university outreach or partnership program, which extends university resources to individuals, groups, and communities. During the past few years, most campuses have focused on international development opportunities, offering services such as trade assistance, promotion of state exports, and trade research. Southern Illinois University Edwardsville (http://www.siue.edu/business/itc/), Michigan State University (http://globaledge.msu.edu/), and Bradley University (http://www.bradley.edu/academic/colleges/fcba/centers/turner/sbdc/), for example, all have programs in place. Michigan State University also offers a great resource called MPI (Market Potential Index: http://globaledge.msu.edu/knowledge-tools/mpi) to evaluate the potential of emerging markets as well as DIBS (GlobalEDGE Database of International Business Statistics: http://globaledge.msu.edu/knowledge-tools/dibs) that allows you to choose from thousands of variables in order to generate reports that synthesize and evaluate data from reliable sources.

In addition, many state and private educational institutions offer courses in exporting or going global. They may even cosponsor international trade seminars with federal agencies or private-sector organizations. If you cannot find a school in your area that offers this type of service, be sure to search the Internet.

Local Library—Yes, They Still Exist, and for a Reason

Today, even a small municipal-branch library has state-of-the-art computer terminals with a connection to the Internet, allowing you to access all kinds of information that will help you strengthen your position in the international marketplace. Reservations for a computer can be made at any library location or remotely for the library you intend to visit. Check with the head librarian on how best to approach your search—and plan on using the library's computer-cataloguing facilities to shorten your search time and get your hands on the right materials faster. The days of the painstaking, tedious card-catalog search with pencil in hand are gone! The typical public-access search terminal will enable you to type in one or more keywords and give you a listing of articles on those subjects. The entry for each article will include the title, author, name, and date of the periodical, and sometimes even an abstract of the article's contents so you can tell immediately if it will serve your needs or not. Better yet, more and more libraries have installed printers beside their search terminals so you can print out your list and take it with you. This makes a huge difference in convenience and efficiency.

Business Intelligence Companies

For those who find visiting agencies in person too intimidating, time consuming, or just plain old-fashioned, the following business intelligence companies arm you with critical and competitive information on US waterborne trade activity through an online searchable trade database, covering international trade activities throughout the world, for a fee: PIERS (http://www.piers.com), Datamyne (http://www.datamyne.com), and ImportGenius (http://www.importgenius.com).

■ **Tip** A little-known publication that is a huge source of trade data is the *Journal of Commerce* (JOC; http://www.joc.com). The magazine offers everything from a listing of the top hundred US exporters (including the top ten states exporting to China) to import/export trade leads and international trade news. What can you quickly glean from the data? Let's say you see a lot of container shipments being exported to Brazil. Why is this happening? What is the commodity? What should you be looking at or doing relative to that kind of movement?

Other Places to Look for Market Research Help

The following resources and tools offered by organizations provide advice and insight as well as statistics on international exporting:

Foreign Trade

Produced by the US Census Bureau, Foreign Trade (http://www.census.gov/foreign-trade/) is responsible for issuing regulations governing the reporting of all export shipments from the United States. It is the official source for US export and import statistics. If you're searching for import or export statistics, information on export regulations, commodity classifications, or a host of other trade-related topics, this is the place to get the information you need.

The Export Practitioner

The Export Practitioner (http://www.exportprac.com/) is a monthly magazine devoted to providing news and analysis about the export-licensing requirements and law-enforcement activities of the commerce, state, and treasury departments. The information provided in the advance reports will help you better understand an issue and, at the same time, avoid costly legal troubles.

The Global Trade Magazine

Global Trade Magazine (http://www.globaltrademag.com/) educates readers on ways to utilize the global marketplace to increase market share and corporate profits. They cover such industry segments as cargo transportation, banking, joint ventures, outsourcing, and expansion opportunities.

Ease of Doing Business Rankings

The Doing Business site, run by the International Finance Corporation and the World Bank, ranks economies on their ease of doing business, on a scale from 1 to 185 (http://www.doingbusiness.org/rankings). A high ranking on the Ease of Doing Business Index means the regulatory environment is more conducive to the starting and operation of a local firm. The index provides a bird's-eye view on the potential of exporting to a given economy, too.

The World Factbook

The World Factbook (https://www.cia.gov/library/publications/the-world-factbook/) is a reference guide produced by the Central Intelligence Agency that provides detailed information on history, people, government, economy, geography, communications, transportation, military, and transnational issues for 267 world entities.

US and World Population Clock

Produced by the United States Census Bureau of the US Department of Commerce, the US and World Population Clock (http://www.census.gov/popclock/) is a continuously updated population estimate based on earlier census figures, and serves as the leading source of quality data about the nation's people and economy.

World Bank Atlas Method

The World Bank Atlas Method (http://data.worldbank.org/about/country-classifications/world-bank-atlas-method) uses the Atlas conversion factor to minimize exchange-rate fluctuations in the cross-country comparison of national incomes.

Euromonitor International

Euromonitor International (http://www.euromonitor.com/usa) provides market research, business intelligence reports, and data and analysis on industries, economies, countries and consumers.

eAtlas of Global Development

The *eAtlas of Global Development* (http://www.app.collinsindicate.com/worldbankatlas-global/en-us), produced by the World Bank, is a sophisticated online interactive tool that maps and graphs more than 175 indicators from the World Bank's development database. It allows users to easily and quickly transform data into customized visual comparisons across time, countries, and regions.

International Trade Statistics Yearbook

The *International Trade Statistics Yearbook* (http://comtrade.un.org/pb/) is a multivolume publication produced by the United Nations Statistics Division and the Department of Economic and Social Affairs that is featured on the

International Merchandise Trade Statistics Web site. The yearbook provides information on the world trade of individual commodities in 2014 and features world-trade tables covering trade values and indices.

Bureau of Economic Analysis

A US Department of Commerce affiliate, the Bureau of Economic Analysis (BEA; http://www.bea.gov) promotes a better understanding of the US economy by providing timely, relevant, and accurate economic accounts data in an objective and cost-effective manner. The bureau's goal is to be the world's most respected producer of economic accounts.

Binational Societies, Councils, and Trade Associations

There are also binational groups that will put you in touch with citizens of a country where you'd like to do business. You can search the Internet for the local branches. NAJAS (National Association of Japan-American Societies; http://www.us-japan.org/), the US-China Business Council (https://www.uschina.org/), U.S.-Cuba Business Council (https://www.uschamber.com/press-release/us-cuba-business-council-elects-gutierrez-chair), and the US-India Business Council (http://www.usibc.com/), for example, all promote bilateral trade between the United States and the respective countries and also provide a stimulating social forum for people with common interests.

Check with your state to see if it has a foreign-relations or export council. Organizations like these usually assemble at least once a month, offering a forum for discussion about how to facilitate better international relations and expand trade.

Contacts made through business colleagues and associations can often also prove invaluable to exporters. Many states have associations that focus strictly on promoting world trade. Check with your local chamber of commerce to see which of these associations have chapters in your area and sit in on a meeting—and then sign up.

Additional Instant Resources

There are a number of additional online services that specialize in information about particular foreign markets, especially news about fast-breaking market opportunities in fast-changing parts of the world. When you use these services, don't forget to keep your segmentation schedule and your market-issues list close at hand.

- In addition to the previously mentioned ease of doing business rankings, the Doing Business site (http://www.doingbusiness.org/), run by the World Bank Group and the International Finance Corporation, provides objective measures of business regulations for local firms in 185 economies and selected cities at the sub-national level.

- When all else fails, you can go back to the days of picking up the phone and call the US Department of Commerce Trade Information Center at 1-800-USA-TRAD[E] (1-800-872-8723).

Creating an Action Plan

Once you've spent some time getting a picture of the international market for your product, you'll want to make a plan for how you're going to put your new knowledge to work. It's best to tailor your plan to your day-to-day operating style or that of your organization. If you are action oriented and like immediate and tangible results, then structure your export plan so that you'll see regular results or responses. If you are more methodical and conservative in your business habits, then structure your export plan to produce degrees of progress over a longer period of time.

Setting goals that will allow you to operate comfortably will generate regular signs of progress. For example, let's say you have no export business at present. Your goal might be to generate US$12,000 in international sales during one year. That's US$1,000 a month, or US$250 a week. When you break this annual goal down into regular increments, it begins to look reachable. There is no point in setting overambitious goals.

Tip Are you already exporting? Where to? Expanding into new markets is the next logical step. If you're currently exporting to Ireland, for example, then the United Kingdom might be a good complementary market to enter. Are you conducting business in Canada? Then try Mexico (due to NAFTA) since it's close in proximity to the United States. It's likely that similar conditions exist in other nearby markets too, indicating that your product or service could also be successful there.

Above all, your plan must be manageable for the person or persons who actually have to implement it. If you are beginning your export program as part of an existing company, it is particularly important to get and keep a top-to-bottom companywide commitment to the export project.

Once you determine the style in which you want to conduct your export activities, the sales goals you hope to attain, and how fast you want to achieve results, then draft your plan. Start with a short, specific statement that gives a comprehensive view of your program—you can break this down into more specific steps later. A simple plan might look like this:

- All Alone Becky New to Exporting, Inc.

"I am going to e-mail product offerings to all the customers on the lists I've compiled. At the same time, I am going to ramp up marketing efforts via all social networks. I hope to receive a dozen inquiries within two weeks and at least one order within a month. If my results are not achieved within this time frame, then I will contact the appropriate government agencies and begin plans to participate in a trade show."

If your company has a larger budget and more staff resources, your statement might look more like this:

- ABC Conglomerate Exporting, Inc.

"We are going to allocate 10 percent of our company's net profits to developing foreign markets. An export team will be appointed within three months. Informational and promotional brochures as well as pricing schedules suitable for exporting purposes will be developed during the following three months. Advertising and trade show activities will be implemented thereafter. Once market demand is identified, we expect to launch an e-commerce platform to sell to that specific overseas market."

Summary

As you can see, preparing market research doesn't have to be elaborate. It just has to be broken down into a series of manageable courses of action to be carried out during an estimated period of time. As you implement your plan, monitor it closely and expect to adjust it along the way to meet your objectives. And remember: the most important element of the plan of all is to keep trying!

So far, you've begun to learn about international markets for your product, to tap into the enormous network of export assistance that's available to you, and to plan how you're going to put these resources to work. Now you're ready to take more ambitious measures to get in touch with serious players looking to buy what you've got to sell. If you want to catch their interest, though, you must first make sure that the product you have selected for export meets the target market's local conditions. The following chapter gives a rundown on all the details you need to consider as you prepare your product for export.

Notes

i. "Jim Barber, President of UPS International, Talks Global Trade at the Discover Global Markets Conference," Bill Bryant, *Upside: The UPS Blog*, accessed March 28, 2016, http://blog.ups.com/2014/06/09/jim-barber-president-of-ups-international-talks-global-trade-at-the-discover-global-markets-conference/.

ii. Nolan Bushnell, Gene Stone, *Finding the Next Steve Jobs: How to Find, Keep, and Nurture Talent* (New York: Simon & Schuster, reprint 2014), XV.

iii. Walter Isaacson, *Steve Jobs (New York: Simon & Schuster, 2011),* 567.

Preparing and Adapting Your Product for the Export Marketplace

You may have heard the story that Coca-Cola translated into Chinese meant "bite the wax tadpole." (Some think it's an urban legend.) In fact, it's true, but the translation didn't happen in the way you might think."

—Phil Mooney, Coca-Cola Conversations[i]

How about when Braniff International translated a slogan touting its finely upholstered seats "Fly in Leather" into Spanish as "Fly Naked."

—"20 Epic Fails in Global Branding," Inc.com[ii]

© Laurel J. Delaney 2016
L. J. Delaney, *Exporting*, DOI 10.1007/978-1-4842-2193-8_13

Many business owners believe it is only packaging that has to be adapted in the overseas marketplace. That's a mistake. Adapting your product to meet the needs of an overseas market is a considerable undertaking and will likely require a substantial investment of time and money.

In the following pages, I talk about how packaging, labeling, and other product characteristics play a vital role in enabling international sales and what factors to consider when preparing your own product for export. I also include case study examples to better understand the process that goes along with modifying a product to succeed in the export marketplace.

This phase of business is very important because there are differences in both the cultural and physical environments across countries. You should expect that to some degree you will have to dive deep into your customers' culture to achieve your business goal and adapt your product to sell it outside domestic markets before you make your first sale. You'll be well situated to tackle this phase after you have availed yourself of the market information resources outlined in the previous chapter, consulted with local government market experts, and communicated with various sources overseas: prospective customers, wholesalers, agents, embassies, and so on.

■ **Tip** To help you get a better idea of your cultural preferences and style and how they differ from those of other cultures, take an online assessment: https://hbr.org/web/assessment/2014/08/whats-your-cultural-profile. Any big breaks that you spot between your style and others indicate the likelihood of misunderstandings and the need for you to be aware and adapt accordingly.

Studying competing products in the country where you wish to do business is a great way to target what works in that market. If you cannot visit the country and scan store shelves yourself, get in touch with the American Embassy and see if it can apprise you of what products are comparable to yours.

When it is not possible to sell the standardized products and services, a small business must adapt its product if it wants a global business. And although the changes might involve satisfying foreign countries' regulatory requirements, the biggest test is always with the end user—the customer—because that's who ultimately buys your product or service. If customers turn their noses up at your offering, even if you get regulatory approval, there will be no sales. Always keep the customer at the top of your mind and have empathy for others' point of view; it will lead to ideas for meeting cultural differences.

Case Study: Hershey's Yo-Man Satisfies the Sweet Tooth of Chinese Consumers

In 2013, Hershey introduced a candy to China. Known in English as the Lancaster and in Chinese as Yo-Man, it is a condensed-milk candy that Hershey expects will gain it a healthy share of an estimated ¥7.5 billion (in Chinese currency, which is equivalent to $1.2 billion) Chinese market. Premium-milk candy is considered the fastest-growing segment in China's candy market.

This is Hershey's first launch for a new brand beyond the US market. Hershey's goal is to expand its overall international sales to 25 percent of its global sales by 2017, up from its current 10 percent, which includes brand extensions and acquisitions. The candy company had sales of $6.6 billion (2012), aims to reach $10 billion annually by 2017[iii] and wants China to be its second-biggest market within five years.

Yo-Man will be manufactured in China by a local confectionary company in Hunan Province. Milk for the candy will be imported. Creating a new brand, and one that is specifically tailored for the Chinese market, is a good bet for Hershey. The company could have just as easily sold its Hershey Kisses and other related branded items without making any changes to the products, but that would send a message to the Chinese consumer that Hershey doesn't care enough to suit that population's particular taste buds. Or worse, the company might turn off the audience entirely by that move—forever—and open sweet opportunities for its competitors. It's a perceptive judgment call, and Hershey has decided not to take a chance wondering *what if* and instead is doing what is right for the Chinese market, its budget, and its resources.

Checklist to Prepare Your Product for Export

So how do you go about getting your product ready for a foreign market, much like Hershey has done? Grab a sample of your export-ready product, get out your tablet to keep you organized, and let's run through some rules of thumb to prepare your own product for export:

1. *The name, logo, or tag line of your brand or product might work well in your local market but could have negative connotations in a foreign market's local language.* For example, in the 1950s, there was a Swedish car magazine called *Fart*, which in Swedish means "speed." To Americans, however, the title meant a good laugh. Check to see what the translation of your brand's name means in the language of the country you are about to enter. If you don't, you will end up with a fiasco like Chevrolet had on its hands when it introduced its new automobile called the "Nova" in Venezuela—which in Spanish means, "Doesn't go!"

2. *The colors of your packaging need to take into account cultural sensitivities.* What do the colors connote in the country of destination? Vibrant, attention-grabbing red is often thought to signify warning or danger in the United States, but in Chinese culture it represents good luck. A slick black package with touches of embossed gold or silver conveys elegance and sophistication in the United States and some newly industrialized countries, but in certain parts of Africa, for example, it suggests death! Even if your design principles have been foolproof for products to be sold in the United States, expect to have to scrap them and start fresh when it comes to marketing products abroad.

3. *Look at the overall packaging and labeling design of your product. In addition to your color choices, your illustrations and graphics need to be appropriate, appealing, and understandable to your end user.* If there is any possible way you can get opinions on your package design from actual consumers in your target market, do so. Would they buy your product on the basis of the way it looks? For example, if you put a smiling face on your package, but they take the purchase of that particular product quite seriously in their country, would your labeling be seen as trivial, cheap looking, or even offensive? Details like this matter, and they need to be thoroughly researched and addressed before shipping anything of significant value to a foreign market.

4. *The size or quantity of your product itself needs to match the export country's expectations.* Your product's size might be perfect by US standards but way too large in Japan, where the size of the typical household is very small. One Whopper may feed one American, but that same burger sold in France may make a lunch for two, or the extra burger might be tossed in the trash. If too much of your product will go to waste, it's not economical or convenient for your consumer, and they won't buy it.

CASE STUDY: GIVE CUSTOMERS WHAT THEY WANT

One of my past clients manufactured a very successful premium ice cream. Supermarkets throughout the United States could barely keep the decadent treat in their freezers because the demand was so great. The company wanted to build on this success by expanding internationally. It chose Japan as its entry point into the international market. The Japanese are exacting about quality and would appreciate this premium ice cream, it was thought.

The test shipment fell flat.

What happened? My client looked deeper into the Japanese culture and discovered some very important differences betweens Americans and Japanese. First, Americans prefer gallon-sized containers, while the Japanese prefer individual-sized containers, which fit better into their smaller freezers. My client also discovered that the ice cream had too much sugar for Japanese tastes.

The company tried again; this time using a reduced-sugar recipe in individual-sized containers and shipping a twenty-foot freezer container to Japan monthly. Over time, that one freezer container a month grew to ten a month, and the company's business in Japan was assured.

5. *Weights and measurements vary from country to country.* You must label your product according to local standard measurements. The metric system is considered the global standard, but double check.

6. *The standard CE mark, which ensures consumer safety, is required on many products sold in EU countries.* A manufacturer that has gone through the conformity-assessment process may then affix the CE mark to the product. If you plan to do business in a country that is part of the EU, look into the benefits of securing the union's approval, which will make your product appear safer in your target audience's eyes.

7. *Look at how and where the product is sold.* Do most consumers like to make their purchases online in your export country? Or do they prefer to go to a local convenience store to make their purchases? It's not about doing it your way. It's about doing it in a way that the consumers of the home country prefer. Take the French cosmetics company L'Oréal, which is breaking the rules but with the hope of big payoffs. In Brazil, where women prefer door-to-door sales, L'Oréal will not be using

that approach. Instead, the company hopes its sales will increase by "creating six professional training centres - L'Oréal Professional institutes - in four Brazilian towns. These institutes aim to train and develop a new generation of contemporary hairdressers."[iv] Is L'Oréal attempting to make Brazilian women forget about that part of their culture? Only time will tell. Door-to-door vending is a long-standing custom in Brazil that has ushered millions of Brazilian women into the middle class. Some 2.5 million women, out of a total female workforce of 42 million, earn a living by doing direct sales in Brazil.[v]

Tip   To cash in on growth in emerging markets, Facebook is making adjustments to its social platform as it expands internationally. According to the *Wall Street Journal:* "[India] has about 100 million Internet users mostly through desktops. But the real focus for digital companies will be on the group of 900 million-plus mobile-phone users, most of whom will get Web access for the first time over the coming years."[vi] Think that Facebook will adjust and accommodate those folks? More than likely it will, especially if it fuels its own growth. Look for Facebook to offer free access to a select set of websites to those without internet access in India, but not without running up against resistance from regulators.[vii]

---

8. *Will you need to put a bilingual label on the outside of packages?* Canada requires a French-English label. Finland requires a Finnish-Swedish one. Most Middle Eastern countries require it to be in Arabic-English. You must find out! For some destinations, the first order or trial shipment requires only a sticker on the outside of the package in the language of the importing country. Generally, this sticker should state the importing agent's name and address, the weight of the package in the country's standard unit of measurement, an ingredient legend, and the expiration date if applicable.

Caution   Even a close translation of your product's name might not be close enough—"Jolly Green Giant," for instance, translates into Arabic as "Intimidating Green Ogre." Another example: Pinterest's "pins" and "boards" are understood in the United States because it's based on the concept of pinning things to a cork board. But in Brazilian Portuguese, for instance, users don't understand the reference because pins in Brazil means for an item used to fasten a diaper.

---

9. *Be careful of the cultural significance attached to the number of units you place in a box.* Anytime you have a relatively small number of products packed showcase style in their box, check beforehand to make sure the quantity is not considered unlucky in the overseas market. Some countries, particularly in the West, find seven to be a lucky number and thirteen to be unlucky. In Japan, the number four is the sign of death, so packing anything four to a box will be the kiss of death for your marketing venture! (Not that you need to worry too much about the number of cookies in a single box.)

10. *Put pictures of your product on the label of your package.* A picture tells a thousand words. When Americans read "pizza" on the outside of a box, they know what's inside. But will they know what it means in New Caledonia? Probably not. Keep this in mind when you develop packaging for worldwide sales. Illustrations are acceptable, two-color pictures look nicer, but four-color photography on the label shows it like it is. Put yourself in the shoes of the prospective customer. If you don't know what's being sold, why buy it? Get visual: Images speak every language.

11. *Don't skimp on packaging material.* If your packaging is behind the times in the United States, don't think you'll be able to unload it in the world market. Customers worldwide appreciate innovation and cutting-edge technology, and they *expect* it from the United States. Don't let your customers down. Keep informed on what is the newest and best in your packaging category.

CASE STUDY: KEEP AN EYE ON THE COMPETITION

My company used to export all-metal tins of gourmet nut snacks to Southeast Asia. We thought we were well received, until one customer asked why we didn't package our snacks like a major competitor did: that company used a composite of tin and cardboard, which was safer and lighter—desirable qualities in Southeast Asia. Once we found a supplier that could manufacture the composite tin, we ordered enough labels for both the domestic and international markets. Listening to that one customer and making that one change grew our sales in Southeast Asia more than 30 percent over one year.

12. *Look for ways to extend current product applications.* This is where a few months of actually living in a foreign country would really pay off. It would teach you how the locals do things and what they need to be able to do things better. You may find that if you changed the speed of a kitchen mixer, a food item in China would be made better and faster than ever before. Or you might want to reconfigure an existing vacuum attachment and it would be perfect for some out-of-the-way corners in Sri Lanka. Before you set out to do business in a particular country, ask some simple questions: How do the people there like to spend their time? What are their favorite foods? How do they clean their homes? How are their clothes laundered? If you aren't able to travel there, the information-gathering strategies outlined in Chapter 5 should give you some answers along these lines.

13. *Make sure your electrical products are suitable and compatible for international use.* If your wired product is not adjusted to the electrical standards in your target market, you'll have all sorts of problems, especially if you have already shipped the unacceptable product! A good resource you should know about is *Electric Current Abroad* (http://www. trade.gov/publications/pdfs/current2002FINAL. pdf), a publication of the US Department of Commerce. It provides everything you need to know about electrical standards worldwide. If for some reason you don't find the information you need, contact your local chamber of commerce or a government official in the country where you are about to do business.

14. *How will you handle warranties, guarantees, consignment sales, and service calls overseas?* Anticipate what it will take to put one of these features in place, not locally, but globally. Can it be done? If so, map out the logistics from start to finish and determine who will be responsible. If it's not feasible, then don't offer it.

15. *Determine how the physical environment affects your product.* Humidity, high energy costs, poor water supply, extreme hot or cold temperatures, or poor infrastructure can affect how your product holds up and works in a new market. You may only need to adjust your product to withstand a damaging environment, but if it's a lot more than that you should choose a market that's a better fit. If there are no roads to move your product, you can't get

anywhere. Period. Consider the differences between your home market and the foreign market. For example, when air conditioners are exported to Egypt, they must have special filters and the coolers must be sturdy enough to handle the thick dust and heat of Egyptian summers.

16. *Determine how the cultural environment affects how you market your product.* When Unilever bought Slim-Fast in 2000, it wanted to expand the company's market that existed outside North America, which accounted for more than 90 percent of its sales at the time. Unilever wanted to increase Slim-Fast's revenues fivefold by 2003. The company's strategy was to plug Slim-Fast into its global marketing and distribution system.[viii] According to Smriti Chand Marketing, "When Slim-Fast was first launched in Germany, its ads used a local celebrity. In the U.K., testimonials for diet aids may not feature celebrities . . . . [Also] in the U.K. banana was the most popular flavour but this flavour is not sold in continental Europe."[ix] This demonstrates the cultural effect each country has on a product and how vital it is to adapt to all the countries you export to in order to ensure that consumers love the product. Be aware of local customs and be willing to understand and accommodate any differences that can cause misunderstanding.

17. *Local product regulations need to be scrutinized.* In order to sell a product in retail stores or elsewhere, some countries require a statement on the product that indicates where it was made. Check with your prospective customers or a logistics specialist to determine if a country-of-origin label (see Chapter 22), for example, is required by law before you export a product to a foreign country.

Summary

It would be smart to determine if the anticipated export sales of your product will outweigh the expense of adapting it to the country's standards and to project how long will it take to recover the costs. You may find it more realistic, at least initially, to export your products to countries that will accept them as they are. From there, you can always grow and expand from your successes at your own pace. But keep a long-term perspective: being willing to make strategic changes to your product (a crucial attitude) will open doors to many more international markets. The risk is minimal compared to the risk of maintaining the status quo.

▓ **Tip**   It's crucial for your company to remain what it is (be it German, American, Japanese), but develop an understanding and willingness to accommodate cultural differences that exist. Follow that path, and great success in the export marketplace will come your way.

Now that we've spent a good deal of time looking at getting your product ready for export, we'll shift our attention to exporting a service.

Notes

i.   "Bite the Wax Tadpole," Phil Mooney, Coca-Cola Conversations, last revised March 6, 2008, http://www.coca-cola-conversations.com/2008/03/bite-the-wax-ta.html.

ii.   "20 Epic Fails in Global Branding," Geoffrey James, October 29, 2014, accessed March 28, 2016, Inc.com, http://www.inc.com/geoffrey-james/the-20-worst-brand-translations-of-all-time.html.

iii.   "Hershey to Buy China Candy Maker," Laurie Burkett, *Wall Street Journal*, accessed March 28, 2016, http://www.wsj.com/articles/SB1000142405270230477310 4579267634226586204.

iv.   "L'Oréal in Brazil," Euromonitor 2013, *Wall Street Journal*, accessed March 28, 2016, http://www.loreal.com/media/beauty-in/beauty-in-brazil/l'oréal-in-brazil.

v.   "To L'Oréal, Brazil's Women Need New Style of Shopping," *Wall Street Journal*, Christina Passariello, last modified January 21, 2011, http://online.wsj.com/news/articles/SB1000142405274870395170457609 1920875276938.

vi.   "India, A New Facebook Testing Ground," Amol Sharma, *Wall Street Journal*, last modified October 20, 2012, http://online.wsj.com/article/SB1000087239639 0443749204578048384116646940.html.

vii.   "Lessons from Facebook's Fumble in India," Bhaskar Chakravorti, *Harvard Business Review*, February 16, 2016, accessed March 28, 2016, https://hbr.org/2016/02/lessons-from-facebooks-fumble-in-india.

viii. "Unilever's Slim-Fast Goes From Juggernaut to After thought," Matthew Boyle, *Bloomberg*, last modified January 15, 2013, http://www.bloomberg.com/news/2013-01-14/unilever-s-slim-fast-goes-from-juggernaut-to-afterthought.html.

ix. "5 Major Product Communications Strategies Used in International Marketing," Smriti Chand Marketing, YourArticleLibrary.com, accessed October 24, 2013, http://www.yourarticlelibrary.com/marketing-2/5-major-product-communication-strategies-used-in-international-marketing/5834/.

Preparing Your Service for Export

Laughter is America's most important export.

—Walt Disney

Exporting services somehow doesn't seem as impressive as putting big things on ships and sending them abroad. It also may not create the kind of broadly shared prosperity that exporting manufactured goods can. But for now, it seems to be where the U.S. has a comparative advantage—and we should probably do whatever we can to maintain that.

—Justin Fox[i]

You don't have to be a manufacturer to export. As you take your business into the digital age, you'll find that keeping ahead of the competition takes more than just getting your product into world markets. You'll also need to export superior services to cultivate additional strength. In this chapter, I'll discuss exporting a service and how it differs from exporting a product. In addition, I'll provide a brief look at services that have the best potential for export success, a list of the best international market prospects, and a couple of case examples.

© Laurel J. Delaney 2016
L. J. Delaney, *Exporting*, DOI 10.1007/978-1-4842-2193-8_14

The United States is the largest global importer and exporter of services in the world. Export.gov indicates that more than two-thirds of US small- and medium-sized exporters are nonmanufacturers. Business services alone—such as financial products, software publishing, and telecommunications—employ more than double the number of US workers in the manufacturing sector. And these jobs are not just ordinary blue-collar positions. They are white-collar services that involve high wages, high skills, high technology—and high growth! Because of this, the United States is likely to retain these jobs.

When it comes to services—such as travel, banking services, royalties, legal advice and education of foreign students—we export far more than we import. In each of the past five years, our surplus in services has exceeded $200 billion.[ii]

Services are important because they account for most of the world economy and are steadily growing. Since 2000, their share of global output has expanded from 67 percent to 71 percent, while industry and agriculture have shrunk.[iii]

U.S. service exports continue to grow much faster than product exports, growing about 26% between 2010 and 2014, according to the World Trade Centre.[iv]

And there is every indication that the growth will continue in the years ahead, with many countries currently emerging from a period of economic weakness and showing a strong demand for American know-how as well as American-made goods. As long as countries' local currencies remain fairly stable and technology continues to advance, this demand will continue to rise, notwith-standing the ups and downs of the US dollar. Service exports typically don't face tariffs, as goods sold overseas often do.

AN EXAMPLE OF A SERVICE EXPORT: EDWARDS GLOBAL SERVICES PROVIDES EXEMPLARY SERVICES

Take Edwards Global Services (EGS), the winner of the 2015 President's E Star Award for export service. Presented by the Department of Commerce's International Trade Administration, the award is the highest recognition any US entity can receive for supporting export activity. EGS was recognized for using a proven, stepped process that assesses the global potential for US-based franchisors to successfully expand into international markets, develops a business plan for them to go global, and then implements the plan using their experienced U.S.-based executive team and in-country associate network in 32 countries.

EGS has been in operation since 2001. In 2011, EGS was first given the President's 'E' Award for export services, and four years later received another award as a result of continued, documented success for the US-based franchises their company represents.

There are, however, some nontariff barriers that do exist for service exports, such as safety standards, customs procedures, and regulatory hurdles (specific to investment trade), that can make it difficult but not insurmountable for an attorney, accountant, designer, or architect to work abroad.

Still, exporting a service attracts customers because the service usually offers original knowledge—and knowledge is power these days. People are starting new e-ventures every day, purely on the basis of a business model offering superior know-how and great ideas. Disseminating that knowledge aggressively and at a profit worldwide is a winning formula for global success. With technology advancing at lightning speed, and worldwide communications becoming faster and easier with every passing day, now is an ideal time to consider this business avenue.

■ **Fact** According Doris Nagel, President of Blue Sky Consulting Services, "Service[s] are the fastest growing exports just about everywhere. The U.S. is the largest single country services exporter, and depending on whether you believe the U.S. International Trade Commission or the International Trade Centre, the U.S. exports between $662 and $710 billion in services each year."[v]

How Technology Drives the Economy—by Fostering Competitiveness

Right now, a variety of technology-based industries, including communications, software development, cloud computing, and health care management, are booming. Take a look at the stocks traded on the NASDAQ—you'll spot the longtime movers and shakers in these industri es typically growing at a double-digit rate or more per year, with the young upstarts right on their heels. The good news for the prospective service exporter is that there is a strong correlation between technological advancements and the growing importance of knowledge. The greater the increase in the availability of technology, as is occurring now, the greater our need to learn how to use it and capitalize on it, fast. Time is of the essence if you want to stay at the cutting edge of your industry, and with current technology, particularly in the field of communications, not only can you count on being able to contact clients and colleagues worldwide in a matter of seconds, but you can also bet that it will cost you only pennies.

Exporting a Product vs. Exporting a Service: Is There a Difference?

Throughout this book, we have focused on exporting a product—one that you can see, hold, easily assign a monetary value to, and transport from Point A to Point B. Exporting a service, such as one that is business-oriented, professional, technical, financial, or franchise- or insurance-based, requires a somewhat different approach. Here's a quick rundown of the differences between a product and a service that affect the export process (again presenting the table we looked at in Chapter 1 in order to jog your memory):

Product	Service
Tangible	Intangible
Visible	Invisible
Measurable	Immeasurable
High perceived value	Low perceived value
Transportable—freight costs	Transportable—negligible freight costs
Negligible human interaction	High human interaction
Low maintenance	High maintenance
High standardization	Negligible standardization

To revisit our discussion in the first chapter, you cannot see or touch a service—it's invisible—and you often cannot assess its true value until after you have used it and discovered all the resulting benefits. A service is in many ways a tougher sell than a product, both at home and abroad. Each of the listed ways in which services differ from products creates a marketing challenge for the service exporter, perhaps the most crucial being the need to convince a distant customer to buy your service sight unseen and without any real idea of how he will benefit. This is why a service business depends first and foremost on people (refer to Chapter 4). Of course, when you export a product, you are also relying on a whole string of people to do their jobs—bankers to help you get paid, freight forwarders to move your goods, local distributors to get your product on store shelves—but exporting a service demands a special emphasis on human interaction, both at home and abroad.

People Power Drives Your Service Exports

Selling a service successfully requires even more people power than selling a product. When you export a product the traditional way, you offer it, clinch your sale, follow through, and troubleshoot as needed. Then, once the product is in your customer's hands, she oversees sales in her geographic territory and contacts you to order more of the product when she sells out. There is little need for communication between buyer and seller once the product is in the distribution pipeline and moving as it should.

By contrast, a service requires direct interaction with your customer, not just initially, but for the duration of the service contract. And for some services, of course, the quality of the interaction with your customers is exactly what they're paying for. This is why people with superior communication skills, diplomacy, and—this can't be emphasized enough—acute cultural awareness are the single greatest asset for delivering a quality service export. Having the technology in place to deliver the service is important, too!

Tip Never increase customer expectation, such as offering free expedited shipping or a discount on work, to the point where you cannot deliver on your promises! That does not make for a satisfied customer. It creates a ticked-off customer who never returns.

Which Services Are Best for Export?

As with a product, if your service is a success locally, it is a likely candidate to be successful elsewhere—but you'll need to do appropriate research to choose the new market most likely to respond well. (Also, just as with your product export, check the Export Administration Regulations [EAR] that can be found at the US Bureau of Export Administration [BXA] beforehand to find out if you need an export license [discussed in Chapter 22] to perform your service abroad.)

Your service should, of course, be relatively unique and difficult to come by in your target market. Services like a manicure at a beauty salon or a last-minute oil change at a car dealer, for example, are essential, but they are unlikely candidates for export because the skill level required to do them is very basic, plus the services themselves lack novelty. It's all too easy for local operators to duplicate these services, so why should customers seek them beyond their own borders?

The following highly skilled and specialized services offer infinite export opportunities because they are in demand worldwide:

- *Architectural, construction, and engineering services*: This sector requires special skills in operations, maintenance, and management with expertise in specialized fields, such as electric power utilities, construction, and engineering services.

- *Financial services*: These services include banking, insurance, securities, leasing, and asset management. US financial institutions, for example, are very competitive internationally, particularly when offering account management, credit card operations, and collection management.

- *Commercial, professional, technical, and business services*: This sector encompasses accounting, advertising, public relations, design, and legal and management consulting services. The international market for those services is expanding at a more rapid rate than the US domestic market. It is estimated that there are already 3.4 billion Internet users worldwide—but that figure represents only about 46.4 percent of the world's population.

- *Education and training services*: Management training, technical training, and English language training are areas in which US expertise remains unchallenged.

- *Entertainment and media*: Films that are made in the United States and music that is recorded in the country have been very successful in appealing to audiences worldwide.

■ **Tip** According to the Wall Street Journal, there's a bright spot for U.S. service exports. For example, when U.S. travelers spend abroad, that's counted as an import. When nonresidents spend in the U.S., that's an export, and U.S. exports of services are hitting record levels.[vi]

- *Environmental services*: The United States is the largest producer and consumer of environmental technologies in the world. Environmental technologies are generally defined as the goods and services that generate revenue on the basis of environmental protection (pollution), assessment, compliance with environmental regulations, pollution control, waste management, design and operation of environmental infrastructure, or provision and delivery of environmental resources.

- *Healthcare technologies*: Healthcare technologies "can be best described as the use of a suite of products and services designed to improve and coordinate patient care, address growing health costs, and confront the long-term burden of disease through the use of technology "[vii]

- *Retail and wholesale trade*: The wholesale trade sector is made up of establishments engaged in wholesaling merchandise. The retail trade sector comprises establishments engaged in retailing merchandise and may include integral functions such as packaging, labeling, or other marketing services.

- *Supply chain and distribution*: The United States wants to secure a more efficient and integrated approach to supply chain issues, which will involve leveraging the capabilities and resources of the US distribution network to bring competitive service offerings to other world markets.

- *Telecommunications and information services*: The United States leads the world in marketing new technologies and enjoys a competitive advantage in online services, computer consulting, and systems integration. This sector includes companies that generate, process, and export e-commerce activities, such as e-mail, funds transfer, and data interchange, as well as data processing, network services, electronic information services, and professional computer services.

- *Travel and tourism*: This industry is diverse and encompasses services in transportation, lodging, food and beverage, recreation, and purchase of incidentals consumed while in transit.

- *Transportation, shipping, distribution, and logistic services*: This sector encompasses aviation, ocean shipping, inland waterways, railroads, trucking, pipelines, and intermodal services, as well as ancillary and support services in ports, airports, rail yards, and truck terminals.

Figure 14-1 is a graphic depiction of the growth of commercial services by main sector, 1995-2014.

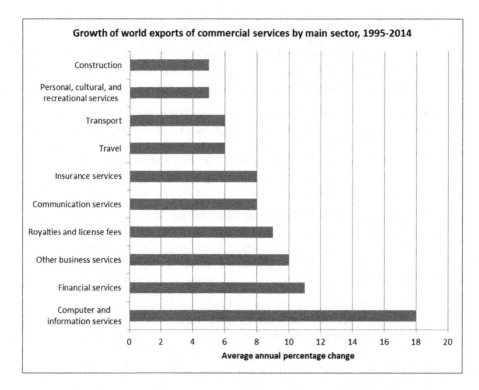

Figure 14-1. [viii]Growth of commercial services by main sector, 1995-2014 (Sources: WTO-UNCTAD-IT estimates).

There are also other services, such as passenger fares and royalties and license fees, for instance, that can be exported. For more information, visit the "Trade Data Basics" page on the International Trade Administration Web site at http://www.trade.gov/mas/ian/referenceinfo/tg_ian_001872.asp#P51_7855.

Top Service-Export Destinations by Volume

The Census Bureau indicates the following are the top ten countries receiving the largest amount of service exports from the United States:[ix]

- Canada
- United Kingdom
- Japan
- China
- Saudi Arabia
- Mexico

- Germany
- South Korea
- Brazil
- France

Targeting the countries that are known to be the most receptive to US service exports will allow you to capitalize on the strengths of particular countries, adapt accordingly, and succeed.

WHERE TO GET HELP

The same agencies that can help you get your product-export business up and running can advise you on marketing your service internationally. Start with the US Department of Commerce. If appropriate, it will direct you to export councils, US export assistance centers, or trade-development industry specialists. If, by some chance, these export-specific agencies are unable to help you, ask them for a referral to other government organizations or private-sector companies that have experience in service exports.

Financing a Service Export

Because of the intangible nature of a service export, it can be more difficult to finance a sale, in terms of knowing the amount to actually quote a customer, but you can nonetheless utilize the basic procedures for product exports I will outline in Chapter 20. It's important to involve your banker right at the beginning, before you attempt your first service export. As I have noted, it is hard to monitor a service, assess its value, and determine when delivery is complete—all of which makes it just as tricky for a bank to work out the logistics of financing this type of export as it is for you and your customer. Your best bet is to draw up a service agreement outlining delivery and payment terms to be signed by you and your customer. This will solidify the transaction and serve as a guideline for your banker to organize the financing.

Caution Don't get paranoid about how you are going to get paid on a service export. It's true that since a service doesn't have a form of collateral, financial institutions may be less willing to provide financial support to your company. However, many public and private institutions will provide financial assistance to creditworthy service exporters. Ask. By the way, try my method: Ask your customers for one-third of the payment upfront, one-third in the middle of the project, and one-third upon completion. This can be secured through your bank, provided you ask for help and have a legitimate business opportunity and a good credit history.

Planning for and Overcoming Market Barriers

Whether you are exporting a product or service, it is a given that you will have to confront numerous market barriers—governmental, practical, cultural, and economic. These barriers can be quite challenging, not to mention extremely frustrating, to a new-to-export service company. To overcome them and beat out the competition, you will need to plan on being aggressive and persistent and taking longer to establish a business presence than you may have expected to have to. If you cannot make any progress despite your best efforts, you may find you need to target another region or country for your export operation. Let's get acquainted with the barriers:

1. *Government:* Red tape, bureaucracy, bribes, infringements of copyrights, trademarks or patents, and special rules that only the natives seem to know about—these are just a few of the government-generated barriers you'll encounter. For example, you might discover that your target market has a labor regulation stating that whenever there is a locally funded project, local experts must be hired for any specialized services that are required. Or there might be restrictions aimed at a specific industry, like accounting, which tend to rule out foreign participation. Sometimes you will make dozens of solicitations that will go unanswered—and you'll never know why. The most notorious barrier is the governmental regulation that locals never comply with even though, for some reason, they're never caught. However, when you try to export, the regulation is enforced just rigorously enough to leave would-be exporters out of the trade loop. These slippery, elusive protectionist practices are very real, and they may well end up compelling you to take your business elsewhere.

2. *Local practice and custom:* Before you export your service, you must conform to global industry standards. If your service depends on scientific accuracy, for example, you need to perform any calculations using metric measurements and notation. If you don't, your proposal might get ignored because of your lack of compliance with local practices. Presenting your proposal in the local language is an obvious necessity if you want it to be read and understood. If you don't know the language, hire someone who does and get a high-quality translation.

3. *Cultural differences*: Sometimes differences between the types of media used in different cultures can present barriers if not used in a way valued by the other culture. Look closely at the photographs and print copy for an advertising campaign you are about to launch abroad, examine the materials you are about to use for an interior design project, and think through the pictures you have selected for your client's Web site. Are any of these items offensive in any way? If they are, then edit accordingly. If you don't know, find out from someone who does before you implement the service package.

4. *Economic*: One surefire giveaway that your target country is economically unstable is the situation where you are locked solidly into a deal and then find out that your customer is slow to pay or doesn't pay at all! Also, watch out for infrastructure factors that may apply in another country, such as astronomical prices for land, making it impossible to start a building project; undrinkable water, making it impossible to open up a tourist bar; or electrical service that is so scant and unreliable that additional power generators are needed to keep things running smoothly. All these factors present very serious barriers for your service business.

5. *Labor market issues*. While sectors other than services are typically capital intensive, the service industry is heavily reliant upon human capital. As a result, labor and skills issues (shortages, for example) can have a significant effect on the services sector, and thus on its ability to export.

6. *Investment*. Government policies affect investment decisions, particularly in highly regulated industries such as healthcare, financial, and environmental. If not designed and administered effectively, regulatory pacts could present barriers to investments needed to support services exports.

Seven Ways to Launch Your Service

When you set out to enter a market with your service export, you will face four critical questions: How are you going to get a foot in the door? How are you going to get noticed by prospective customers (for a discussion, see Chapters 6 and 10)? How are you going to keep your foothold once you're there? And how are you going to do it all inexpensively? Here are some ideas that may help you answer all four questions:

1. *Create new working relationships.* It may take a new working relationship to get your service business underway in another country. Find out who's already operating where you want to be, see what they can do for you, and figure out how you're going to make it an attractive proposition. Start by defining what you can share in terms of resources and what sort of partner you want. Look for individuals with a strong record of innovation and skills that can be combined with your own to create new opportunities.

2. *Consider an acquisition, joint venture, partnership, or franchise.* You can purchase, jointly own, partner with, or assign rights to a company that is operating in a country where you wish to do business. Discuss with your tax and legal advisors. If you can't work out one of these relationships, try working for the company as a consultant first, and then attempt to obtain an equity stake.

3. *Expand your services to your existing domestic clients that have a global presence.* One of the simplest ways to get a foothold in international markets is to follow your local customers to their international branch offices instead of starting an independent base of operations from scratch. It means a lot less risk for you, especially financial risk. If you'd like to try this route, find yourself a good confidant within a firm for which you are serving as a consultant. He can notify you well in advance of any future projects that may involve crossing national boundaries.

4. *Approach foreign companies operating in the United States.* If you have not yet performed a service for a global conglomerate, look for one that can take you where you want to go. If it has a presence in the United States, it is highly likely that it has already selected other foreign sites for further expansion.

5. *Learn the language of your target market.* You will have an incalculable advantage if you already speak your prospective customers' native tongue. You can at least be sure they will understand you! Try marketing your expertise in the area where your parents or grandparents were born. If you mention your ancestral ties to a prospective client, it may enhance her comfort level with you and make her more receptive to your solicitation.

6. *Seek representatives or agents.* Look for local professionals who perform a similar but noncompeting service, train them, and then hire them on a consultancy basis. Make sure your expertise adds value to their service package and vice versa—perhaps you can offer their specialization to your customers in the United States. It can be a global-sales and profit booster for you both as well as a relatively simple and inexpensive program to launch.

7. *Become a virtual consultant (also known as teleconsultant).* Market your knowledge and skills via telecommunications such as e-mail, Skype, Twitter, business apps, or the Internet. Don't dismiss any medium as obsolete—each has its own place in the business of global interaction and each will enhance your power to communicate, making you more efficient and responsive to your global customers. And don't forget to use digital platforms for marketing. For example, design yourself a Web site where private individuals as well as companies can read all about your service. Anyone who responds is a potential client!

An Example of a Service Export: A Wildflower-Nursery Business that Also Exports a Service

Neil Diboll runs Prairie Nursery (http://www.prairienursery.com), a nursery that sells wildflowers and other native plants that many people dismiss as weeds. These products are tough and well suited to climates like the Midwest in the United States, where temperatures in May, for example, can swing anywhere from as low as 40°F at night to as high as 80°F during the day.

Think Diboll can export a service tied to the nursery? You bet. And that's exactly what he has done so that he can operate a company that is more than a nursery. His team offers garden designs and customized advice that can be purchased from anywhere in the world, provided that person has access to the Internet. If you want an ecologically grown green roof or a backyard meadow, he will consult with you remotely or virtually via the Internet. Many product-based businesses have complementary services that can be exported.

To get the word out, use images—they have no language barrier. Every time Diboll does a great job creating a new garden for a client, he can take a picture and share it via Instagram, Pinterest, Facebook, and Google+. That's how his work gets discovered and how his service becomes in demand worldwide!

■ **Tip** The primary benefit of any virtual-service export is its lower cost and unlimited opportunity. You don't need to pay for travel and you don't have to limit your customer base.

Whichever strategies you apply, remember that every contact you make in the process of offering your service-export package can potentially refer you to another, and still another. Plus, word-of-mouth testimonies from happy clients are your best free advertising (you might ask them to provide an endorsement on social platforms such as LinkedIn and praise you on your Facebook page). As you work to put your network in place, you'll be doing more than building a strong base of operations—you'll be working up a healthy momentum that will generate future prospects.

TOP 10 INTERNET MARKETS

Here is a listing of Internet markets with the highest number of Internet users (as of November 2015, the latest available date). What this means is if you have a service export, these countries will be the most receptive to your offerings:[x]

- China
- India
- United States
- Brazil
- Japan
- Russia
- Nigeria
- Indonesia
- Germany
- Mexico

The Bottom Line: Maximizing Your Chance for Success

When you're running a service business abroad, you can't afford to become complacent. Stay focused and committed to your export service plan. Don't let your service offering ever become commonplace. Always work at becoming better and better at what you're doing. And be prepared to take aggressive measures to establish and protect your business presence. The following strategies are essential:

- Specialize, specialize, specialize. Find a type of service only you can deliver, enter a single market, and deliver it with a vengeance. Even if your customers have never heard of your service, make sure they see how they'll benefit from it. Don't just keep pace; be ahead of your time and ahead of the pack.

- Secure sufficient working capital to keep you operating over the long haul.

- Once you have staked out your territory, get the quickest, most extensive marketing exposure you can (reach out to key influencers—bloggers, Twitterers, and Facebookers alike who carry a huge fan base—via social media platforms).

- Use technology and rapid, inexpensive communications (e-mail, Facebook, LinkedIn, Google+, Twitter, Instagram, and Pinterest) to your optimal marketing advantage.

- Do whatever it takes to protect your copyright, trademark, or other intellectual property related to your service package.

- Even if your core business is in exporting products, consider developing a multifaceted export package involving both product and service components (such as Prairie Nursery does, as we saw earlier). This will enable you to create cost efficiencies and immeasurable added value for your customer.

- Once you have a hot export product and a customer lined up, take it a step further and offer your other resource: a marketing campaign geared to the local market to jump start your customer's sales of your product! Sound complicated? Sure, it will take some more R&D, but it will give you the creative edge you'll need to keep ahead of the competition and move freely within the world economy of the future.

- Don't forget about profitability. The biggest hurdle is usually that. Choose a business model that will work in the real world, move fast, and monitor the inflow of money. You want to dominate the market before your competitors do. When you are burning cash, you are at the mercy of others. When you are not, you are in control of your destiny.

Summary

As technology continues to grow, the market for service exports is only going to get bigger, making us all the more responsible and accountable for knowledge outcomes. Countries would benefit from adopting policies that increase service exports, improve productivity, and promote service-export performance. Breaking into export markets is a major achievement, but it's what you do once you're there that makes all the difference in whether you'll be an also-ran or an industry leader. Remember: if you're working hard on customer service, as I've been encouraging you to do, you're already a service exporter. See how far you can take it—and how far it can take *you*.

Notes

i.   "What the US Exports to the Rest of the World," Justin Fox, accessed April 3, 2016, https://www.ajot.com/news/what-the-u.s.-exports-to-the-rest-of-the-world-justin-fox.

ii. "What Trump and Sanders Get Wrong on Trade," Steve Chapman, Real Clear Politics, access date April 3, 2016, http://www.realclearpolitics.com/articles/2016/04/03/what_trump_and_sanders_get_wrong_on_trade_130172.html.

iii. Ibid.

iv. "5 Things You Should Know About Service Exports," Doris Nagel, LinkedIn, access date April 3, 2016, https://www.linkedin.com/pulse/5-things-you-should-know-service-exports-doris-nagel.

v.   Ibid.

vi.   "There's a Bright Spot for U.S. Exports (Hint: It's Not Goods)," Jeffrey Sparshott, November 4, 2015, accessed April 10, 2016, http://blogs.wsj.com/econom-ics/2015/11/04/theres-a-bright-spot-for-u-s-exports-hint-its-not-goods/.

vii.   "Healthcare Technologies Resource Guide," Export.gov, access date April 10, 2016, http://export.gov/indus-try/health/healthcareresourceguide/index.asp#P24_1438.

viii.   "International Trade Statistics 2015," World Trade Organization, access date April 3, 2016, https://www.wto.org/english/res_e/statis_e/its2015_e/its2015_e.pdf.

ix.   "U.S. Trade in Services by Selected Countries and Areas," Census.gov, accessed April 10, 2016, https://www.census.gov/foreign-trade/Press-Release/2016pr/02/exh20b.pdf.

x.   "Internet Users: Top 20 Countries, Internet World Stats," access date April 10, 2016, http://www.internet-worldstats.com/top20.htm.

Web Design with the World in Mind

A global gateway is the initial point of contact between your website and the world—it is, in effect, a web user's first impression. And as the old saying goes: You don't get a second chance to make a first impression. To truly welcome visitors to your website, you'll need a welcoming global gateway.

—John Yunker, cofounder, Byte Level Research[i]

A decade from now, I would predict, everyone reading this article will be able to converse in dozens of foreign languages, eliminating the very concept of a language barrier.

—Alex Ross, author of "The Industries of the Future" and the former adviser for innovation to the U.S. secretary of state[ii]

Why the meteoric rise of the importance of web translation? Because the majority of the world's population does not speak English. In fact, less than a third of the current Internet user base speaks English as a global language and this percentage, according to Yunker, will only decrease as the next billion

© Laurel J. Delaney 2016
L. J. Delaney, *Exporting*, DOI 10.1007/978-1-4842-2193-8_15

Internet users come online over the next several years. If English is your language, as it is mine, you're out of luck if trying to make, as Yunker puts it, "a good first impression" on the vast majority of international people. Globalizing your Web site offers an enormous revenue opportunity for your business.

Web globalization, a strategy that conveys cultural, linguistic, and business information to meet the needs of a target audience in an increasingly multicultural and multilingual world, is the next imperative for businesses, allowing them to gain traction and relevancy as a means to foster social engagement and enable online purchases. As more and more people access the Internet, English will become less prominent as the language of choice. What's holding companies back from translating to non-English languages? CEOs typically say it's because most of their audience only speaks English and then quietly mention budgetary constraints.

That sort of thinking offers a perfect lead into Theodore Leavitt's concept of "marketing myopia." Theodore Leavitt, a late marketing professor at the Harvard Business School, says, "Businesses will do better in the end if they concentrate on meeting customers' needs rather than on selling products."[iii] Marketing myopia is shortsightedness, or the inability to see the future. Could that be you when it comes to web globalization? Are you giving customers what they want in the language they want?

Make no mistake. As a Common Sense Advisory (CSA) report puts it, "Companies that are in favor of technology grow nearly three times as fast as companies that have mixed feelings about it or are against it."[iv] CSA also says, "the global market for outsourced language services and technology was $38.16 billion in 2015 and could soar to $49.8 billion by 2019."[v] The Bureau of Labor Statistics Occupational Outlook Handbook predicts the job outlook for interpreters and translators will grow 29 percent from 2014 to 2024, compared to an average growth rate for all occupations of 7 percent.[vi]

A Web site—or any online social platform, apps included—is a door to the world. "The Internet connects computers, but it is language that connects people,"[vii] as Byte Level's Yunker says. Without content customized for different regions, languages, and cultures, a digital presence can seem lacking. Translating your message makes a radical difference in how you get discovered on the web. Whether you think your target audience only speaks English, you lack the resources to translate a Web site, or you believe your products and services are inappropriate for the global marketplace, you are missing out on a huge chunk of business and are most likely leaving a lot of money on the table that will go to competitors who are willing to translate. To conduct business with most of the world, you must speak the language of your customers and ensure your Web site appears in the places where they are searching. It can't be said enough: globalizing your Web site offers an enormous revenue opportunity for your business. Further, author Alex Ross predicts machine translation will take markets that are now viewed as being too difficult to navigate and open them up[viii].

In this section, I discuss why you should design your Web site with the world in mind, the growth of Web globalization, the biggest challenges to Web site globalization, why Web globalization is essential to your Web marketing efforts, and what you can do now to get started. This information applies to translating marketing materials and campaigns on an as-needed basis as well.

Take it a step at a time, budget accordingly, and spend when and where you can. Perspective and a long-term horizon are what you need most, although you'll probably end up making the same mistakes that the rest of us make when first getting started. That's OK. We're in this together.

Caution   A site translated into another language will not compensate for a poorly built English-language Web site. For example, if your English site is lacking in clarity and content, or the e-commerce bells and whistles are broken for your English-speaking visitors, don't expect a translated version to work any better. So, fix the English site first to get the highest level of awareness and traffic that is possible before putting funds into developing a translated version. Then, when you can afford it, develop a foreign-language version featuring customized content unique to a specific market.

WHY TRANSLATE YOUR WEB SITE?

Here are twelve things Web site globalization will allow you to do:

1. Increase visitors to your Web site
2. Increase your international sales and profits
3. Improve your global web performance metrics
4. Broaden your reach and support
5. Gain global market share
6. Improve visitors' engagement and interactions
7. Become a more worldly brand
8. Outperform competitors
9. Deliver greater impact via an integrated strategy
10. Give customers the world over what they need and want and an easier read
11. Support a new market launch with the language that is spoken in that market
12. Lead globally by supporting languages that you can realistically and affordably support

The Growth of Languages Online: Selling to the Eighth Continent

The Internet is the eighth continent, where everyone who is online is a global citizen in a common space. To understand what's happening in web globalization alone, conduct a search using the keywords "web translation" and see what pops up. You'll most likely see Bing Translator (www.bing.com/translator), Free Translation (www.freetranslation.com), and Google Translate (www.translate.google.com). Now ask yourself this: Why would two of the world's biggest technology companies be so concerned about capturing your search results for web translation? Because at some point everybody needs help with quick translations, whether working online or with a document, or even just trying to decipher a word or phrase.

■ **Note** Automated web translation services are good for translating short, easy passages on the fly or in a pinch. But don't be fooled into thinking these tools will work effectively for Web site translations. They won't, for they are never as accurate as skilled human translators.

Only 25.9 percent of the world's Internet population speaks English, which presents you with a gigantic growth opportunity. The Internet is shifting from United States–centric and English only to more world-centric, with a multitude of other languages being spoken by more than 70 percent of Internet users. According to Statista, "In 2013, the global language services industry market size reached 34.78 billion U.S. dollars and was forecasted to rise to 47 billion by 2018."[ix]

Taking on the World One Country at a Time

The ability to offer more languages across multiple platforms and devices guarantees a company a greater global reach. And translation is just one of several important factors to consider in the process of globalizing your Web site.

■ **Tip** According to web globalization expert Yunker, a global gateway "is an umbrella term for the visual and technical elements you employ to direct users to their localized web sites and applications."[x] How's your global gateway working for you? Are you making a good first impression with a lasting impact?

The Top Ten Languages of Internet Users

More and more people are using the Internet every day in many different languages. You cannot afford to alienate your audience by not offering the right language to the right customer. What is the best language to translate your Web site into? Base it on the number of Internet users and the language they use while visiting your site. Web site translation gives customers the ability to access a site in their own language.

Top Ten Languages Spoken by Web Users as of November 30, 2015[xi]	
Language	Percentage of Internet Users Among the Total Population
English	25.9 percent
Chinese	20.9 percent
Japanese	3.4 percent
Spanish	7.6 percent
Portuguese	3.9 percent
German	2.5 percent
Arabic	5.0 percent
French	2.9 percent
Russian	3.1 percent
Malaysian	2.9 percent

Through these ten languages, you can reach and communicate with 78.2 percent of all the Internet users in the world, an ultimate incentive to consider web globalization. Although English is currently the top web language, as countries like China and Brazil continue to grow and get connected to the web, a non-English language might stand atop the list in the near future. CSA says that buyers of translation services should verify that they're not missing any popular languages that would allow them to appeal to a broader client base.[xii]

Biggest Challenges to Web Site Globalization

Once you have selected a language to translate your Web site into, other problematic issues come into play. The following is a list of the biggest challenges to Web site globalization along with the percentage of respondents who indicated that that was the most correct definition of the problem they were having. The survey was conducted by a company that monitors digital presence, Limelight, in August 2012.[xiii]

- Use of multiple platforms to manage sites and content: 57 percent

- Staffing/budgetary constraints related to creating regional content in local languages: 48 percent

- Lack of technical resources to build, maintain, and enhance regional sites: 29 percent

- Lack of staff and budget necessary to translate to local languages: 26 percent

- Giving staff located around the world publishing rights: 16 percent

---

Caution The previously stated results do not take into consideration translating and supporting content on social platforms (Facebook and Twitter, for instance) or on mobile sites and apps. At some point, these areas must also be translated into content that has the look and feel of an integrated, compelling, and seamless experience regardless of which digital device or platform a user is on. Take a look at Starbucks. It does a great job offering a multitude of Facebook pages in different languages and therefore widening its global reach.

The Web Globalization Approach

Here's how most companies approach web globalization. You create a Web site that I'll call www.organicdogcollars.com and it does well with English-speaking visitors. After a while, many of the inquiries you receive come from people who speak Spanish. You request that your IT technician or your web-hosting company uses IP-address tracking to determine exactly what part of the world the inquiries are coming from and find out that it is Argentina. That triggers the consideration to translate or adapt your Web site to accommodate the Argentinian market. From there, you designate an area on your site that reads, "Argentina Inquiries," where visitors can click to read content in their native language. This gesture takes them to an entirely new and different area that is translated into Spanish and takes into consideration Argentinian social customs. Task accomplished.

Not quite. While this provides an instant customized solution for visitors from Argentina, it doesn't offer a seamless and consistent user experience for visitors in other parts of the world who would want to receive the same-exact treatment for their native country and language. Let's say someone from Spain visits. Does he click on the "Argentina Inquiries" tab or do you go back and change that tab to read "Spanish-Speaking Guests," "Hispanic Visitors," or "Español"?

To optimize the potential for the greatest number of people to visit your site:

1. Decide on what you will be communicating (i.e., content plus design);
2. to whom (which target market); and then
3. translate (adapt) accordingly.

Much of the content you translate will be based on what your English-language visitors look at most, but you should concentrate on specific market needs. Brazil's colors might be radically different than those of the United States, for example, and South Africa's site might require more videos than Japan's. The point is that no two countries are ever alike. To master market needs, first familiarize yourself with internationalization and localization services. Let's go over both so you understand their place in web globalization.

Internationalization and Localization Services

According to Globalization Partners, internationalization involves "enabling the back end of a website to handle different languages, character sets, currencies, submit form data, site search capabilities, etc., and entails understanding what database and content management systems you are using to author, store and publish your site's content." Localization, on the other hand, involves "translating and localizing the front end of your website into different languages ensuring all content (text and graphics) is translated in an accurate and culturally correct manner."[xiv]

What is the subtle distinction between internationalization and localization services? Internationalization is the designing of a Web site so that it can be easily adapted for many different cultures and locales. It is a process that is generally only performed once, so it involves a one-size-fits-all solution that enables a site to be world ready.

Localization, on the other hand, involves more of the *adaptation* of a Web site for a particular area or culture (as in the case of Argentina). This includes translating the text into Spanish, making sure the design is culturally acceptable in Argentina (e.g., doesn't feature Hispanic images that will be perceived as stereotypical), and removing references that may not be relevant for Argentina.

Where internationalization is a process that is done only once, localization is performed each time you want to target a particular culture or language set, so you won't really hire translators until the localization stage in targeting a specific market.

THE 2016 WEB GLOBALIZATION REPORT CARD

According to "The 2016 Web Globalization Report Card," here are the top ten leaders in the globalization of Web sites, mobile Web sites, and apps.[xv] Use these as examples of how you might translate your own site. Granted, these companies are big, but you can still steal insights into how to create a great global gateway without breaking the bank.

1. Google
2. Facebook
3. Wikipedia
4. Hotels.com
5. NIVEA
6. Booking.com
7. Nestlé
8. Pampers
9. Adobe
10. Intel

■ **Tip** Yunker says that mobile is hugely important, particularly in emerging markets. More than 100 million smartphones were sold in India last year. The idea that emerging markets don't have Internet access is false. But it's important to note that emerging markets have slower networks, so mobile websites need to be lightweight.

Example of a Great Global Web Site

A quick visit to NIVEA.com and you will see a country list where you can select a local Web site. You can choose from seven different continents. Under each continent, there is a country listing. Country listings are in English, the country's native language, or both.

Explore. Go through the process slowly click by click. NIVEA gives you an enlightening web-globalization education on how each country's Web site differs in design to accommodate a market. Use the tour as an example on what you should be considering when translating a Web site to serve an audience in Tanzania, France, or Paraguay, for example.

A Step-by-Step Process to Web Globalization

To export to the world, a company needs to develop a Web site globalization plan. You can start out tactically ("We're targeting Argentina!"), but be strategic with your outlook ("Let's be world ready in five years"). Your plan might look like the following step-by-step overview.

■ **Caution**   What I have tried to do here is simplify the web globalization process into digestible chunks of information where you can read one point, think on it, let it stew, and then move on to the next. Web globalization is a complex, not linear, process. The following is by no means an all-inclusive list of things that need to be addressed, but it is a start—a primer. Solutions can be found. Use my list as a guide and then scour the web for more answers.

Target Your Market

Where are you going to get the biggest bang for your web globalization buck? Once you decide on a market, speak the same language as that market! You can either research the market in advance (as you did in Chapter 12) or wait for visitor inquiries to come to you to determine the best place to target. Let's hope your research and inquiries match up, where, for instance, you find that Argentina is the best market for your products and, lo and behold, inquiries through your Web site are all from Argentina. That makes it easy to figure out where to go. Don't try to do too much too quickly. To keep things simple, take it one country and one language at a time.

Hire the Right People

When you're ready to start the process of building a site, hire the right people or service provider, get that person or company on board, and then develop guidelines. Who will translate your web platforms and who will be responsible for overseeing the process to make sure that everything gets done perfectly? You need external experts who are experienced in web globalization and you need internal people who are trusted and respected to do any work that needs to be done. The internal people should not be merely order takers; rather, they should be people who are professional, accomplished, and enthusiastic, and can provide insights into how the project should be managed. It can only help that the people you work with not only understand your products and industry, but also understand your target customers and how to best communicate with them.

Freelancers can also be used in a pinch. I regularly hire a handful of freelancers, for example, who I trust beyond measure, have been with me for years, and do magnificent work. And just as we talked about earlier in the book (Chapter 2), you need to get a companywide commitment to the internationalization effort, including one from the higher-ups. That buy-in should come fairly early in the game. Get the team on board quickly and effectively by developing guidelines or a standard operating procedure that everyone follows—from how the translators will work with your team to how the savvy technology folks will be a part of the grand plan. Consider having at least two translators on board—one to translate and the other to edit. Leave no stone unturned in terms of outlining how things will be handled.

Give the "Skunkworks" Project a Name

A skunkworks is a small group of people who work on a project in an unconventional way. Usually, they are separate from other operating groups, at least in large companies. Nothing is more drab than referring to John Smith as heading up "that Canada Web site project" or Mary Jacobs by saying, "Oh, she's spearheading the web globalization effort for the firm." For goodness' sakes, give the project a name that everyone can identify with, shows opportunity, and charges them up and gets them going to make it happen! Try "Global Seabiscuit," "Code Global," "NWR!" (New World Ready!), or "TOA" (Take On Argentina) as project names.

Build for Growth

The next step is to pick a site structure and build for growth. According to the Google Webmaster Central Blog, to start a multilanguage site, "the first thing you'll want to consider is if it makes sense for you to buy country-specific top-level domains ... for all the countries you plan to serve. So your domains might be ilovebackpacking.co.uk (.uk for the UK), ichlieberucksackrei-sen.de (.de for Germany), and irdemochilero.es (.es for Spain)."[xvi]

The key question to ask, then, is how well known your top-level domain (TLD), service, product, or company is. If it's comparable in popularity to Mickey Mouse, for example, you might want to buy one TLD and use it for what is to become your multilingual site (see the second bullet point below), which is the easiest and least expensive route. Meanwhile, if you haven't already, you might want to consider additionally purchasing the other types of TLDs using the same domain name (known, when you buy country-specific domain names, as geo-targeting) to ward off competitors from snatching them in the future. You have the options of using:

- Subdomain (www.spanish.mickeymouse.com, www.french.mickeymouse.com, or www.german.mickeymouse.com)

- Subdirectory (www.mickeymouse.com/spanish, www.mickeymouse.com/french, or www.mickeymouse.com/german)

- TLD (for Spanish, www.mickeymouse.es; for French, www.mickeymouse.fr; or for German, www.mickeymouse.de)

■ **Note**   There are a variety of ways to phrase domain names that appear in different languages. You can use mickeymouse.com/es, mickeymouse.com/spanish, or mickeymouse.com/espanol, for example. To be safe, consult with an experienced web globalization expert.

Whichever route you take, build for growth. Make sure you have the technology bandwidth to support each and every different country you may move into. You may start in Argentina and a year from now expand to India. Your site structure must enable that global-growth expansion plan.

■ **Caution** We have a long way to go to come up with a clear standard on how to handle branding for localized international sites because it varies from company to company and country to country. Don't be intimidated. Everybody is in the same boat when it comes to understanding web globalization rules and regulations.

Here is a sampling of how companies feature country-specific information (in this case, Spain):

- Engadget: http://es.engadget.com/
- Mars: http://www.mars.com/spain/es/
- Dodge: http://www.dodge.com/es

When you visit these sites, notice the consistency in colors, images, font styles, amount of content, design layout, and flow. When you are making your own site, do a similar assessment of the country you're going to cater to.

A professional web developer can help you with understanding subdomains, subdirectories, and TLDs, but you want to provide her with a consistent way to handle creating subdomains and adapting content to each country's language and culture. This method is easier to handle when updating and maintaining your site.

Invest Only in What You Can Afford But Don't Ever be Cheap

You will need to not only adapt your Web site, social platform, or app to an overseas audience, but also to invest in properly maintaining and managing your localized online properties. That requires people power. Some companies get in a cost-conscious mode (cheap) when it comes to translation, delivering poor-quality multilingual websites, which can have severe consequences: offending and dissuading non-English visitors more than English-only ones! Invest only in what you can afford but don't ever be cheap. Count on continuous updates and improvements throughout the duration of growing your world-ready business. And one last thing to think about here: will you need on-the-ground support in the country where you are serving customers?

Welcome Visitors in a Way That Speaks to Them Directly

You also need to craft the type of welcome gateway you will have on your site that lets foreign visitors see what local content is available to them and directs them to where they need to go. Will the name of the country be in English or in the native language of the country—for example, Spanish for Argentina? Will you show separate visual icons, such as the flags of countries with listings of native languages, for visitors to click on to enter their portal? Or will you feature one map or small globe where visitors can click on their part of the world? Before you decide, check with someone skilled in linguistics to make sure your choices don't offend anyone.

On this topic, Yunker says a key factor in your decision should be whether you intend to keep adding languages and countries to your Web site in the future or only support a small number over a limited period of time. If you are going to stay small, perhaps you only need a visual element that displays the user's current language or country setting, which gives him the ability to change this setting.

Get Started Translating

The next step is to choose a portion of content on your Web site to translate. You don't have to translate every aspect of your English Web site into another language. You might decide to only translate products and services that make sense for a specific market. Take NIVEA, for example, where every one of its local sites feels like its own and no one else's. On the USA site (http://www.niveausa.com/), for instance, you see photos of NIVEA products along with a couple affectionately embracing, whereas on the Bahrain site (http://www.ar.nivea-me.com/), you see a photo of a woman's face but you only get a view of a limited portion of her body. That's because in Muslim countries it is not acceptable to show skin in public. Whatever you decide to do, don't give any hint that your Web site has been translated. What I mean by that is you want visitors to feel as if the content was written and designed just for them! Then, begin the process of translating that information to meet their needs.

Track Metrics

After doing the basics, you will need to establish a way to track metrics. Most hosting companies offer a way to track visitors or page views. Check with yours. Google offers Google Analytics, which can be added to most online platforms. The point of tracking is to see how your translations are measuring up in terms of the quality of content, visitors, returning visitors, inquiries, and sales from a certain part of the world.

Create a User Experience

It is important to create a user experience for your site visitors. This can be done by creating a personal design on the site (an infographic, for example, showing how to design the perfect tabletop setting using your company's candles), making visually appealing transitions between content areas, or developing an interactive story that surprises the user by describing how to enjoy your product or service in a way they never imagined. Maximizing the user experience can be a powerful tool for unleashing the full potential of an application, product, or service offering by allowing an engaged user to look at what you are offering in a holistic way. The goal is to put users first. Determine what they want and what they need. Then, translate accordingly to meet those requirements in a fun and inspiring manner. Whether visitors are in North or South America, using a PC or a smart phone, you must provide a consistent look and feel along with a flawless experience. Deliver the content in the native language of the customer.

Keep It Simple

Keep the translation process simple. Even if your Web site is aimed at an English-speaking audience in Hong Kong, it still needs to be professionally translated in a culturally appropriate way. Stay away from generic translation sites as mentioned earlier. It is not enough to translate a Web site from one language to another. Your translation to the native language must sound natural and not as if it's a Web site that started out in English. To reach any new overseas visitor online, your site should be reviewed for both cultural customization and accuracy and be localized with the target language for the locale.

■ **Tip** Poor efforts in the level and quality of the translation can cause more harm to your business than had you made no effort at all. You don't want to alienate, offend, or reject visitors altogether or look foolish (remember, first impressions matter). It's all about usability and customer satisfaction!

Set a Schedule

At this point, you need to determine how material will get translated and published and at what times. Just as we talked about a companywide commitment in Chapter 2, you need a similar international commitment for web globalization. Take it a step or country at a time. Match your target country to your product or service offering, your capabilities, your budget, and your objectives. Appoint a chief champion or project manager, a lead translator (a human is preferable over a computer), an astute multicultural designer, and a top-notch tech person to oversee each translation project. And remember, it's not just about translating words; there are other translation factors that must be addressed, such as design, currency conversion, customer service support, and transportation costs. This is where the external web globalization team needs to shine with experience and provide answers.

Test, Test, Test!

Before going live, you need to test your site locally in the overseas market. Use different browsers to do so. And don't forget to test your site extensively on mobile devices, because that's where the growth will be in the future.

Consider the User's Search

Another essential step to take before the site goes live is to optimize the content for search results. Consider search engine optimization for each language you're translating into (referred to by Google as multilingual AdWords). Figure out how local search engines will recognize your translated material or hire someone with experience in international search engine visibility. Match English words, for example, with high-ranking translations in other languages, which can be found through Google Trends.

Go Beyond Translation

It is necessary to adapt—not merely translate—your Web site and blog to the global marketplace, just as it is with graphics. Pay attention to how people read in different countries. Failing to do so will negatively affect readability on your site. Do they read from left to right, as we do in the United States, or from right to left (RTL), as they do in Arabic-speaking countries? In this instance, adjust the text accordingly by making the RTL direction the default text direction on your Web site.

Measure Specific Results

Now that you've done everything there is to do to localize your site, you need to use the metric tracking you have set up to measure the return on your investment for your efforts. Track four key areas: web traffic, leads generated from that traffic, leads that translate into actual business (revenues and profits), and e-commerce sales increase.

> **Tip** Start reading! There are a couple of really good books on web globalization. Conduct a search for "web globalization books" and the most popular will rise to the top, such as John Yunker's *The Art of the Global Gateway*. Many of these books offer a good primer to understanding what is involved with web globalization.

Web Globalization: Getting Started

There are a couple of places to look for external guidance in getting started with web globalization efforts. I caution you to work with a firm that has a proven history of success in adapting Web sites for international markets (Get references!) and understands the key roles that database-driven Web sites and dynamic architecture play in web globalization. Each firm takes a different approach to web globalization. Some offer software solutions in the cloud (something we haven't covered here but need to be aware of the emerging presence of), while others don't. Find out what the firm does, how it does it, and how much it will cost. For the layperson, this can be a complex process, but for a firm that has vast experience, it's a walk in the park. Don't forget your primary focus before you dive in: know your audience, because you are about to get even closer to them!

Web Globalization Service Providers

Here are some service providers I culled from a variety of sources:

- Eriksen Translations: http://www.eriksen.com/. Eriksen provides translation, interpreting, typesetting, project management, web localization, and cultural consulting in over one hundred languages.

- Euroscript: http://www.euroscript.com. Euroscript provides global content management solutions.

- Globalization Partners International (GPI): http://www.globalizationpartners.com. GPI provides Web site translation, documentation translation, and software translation.

- Hewlett-Packard's Application and Content Globalization (HP ACG): http://www8.hp.com/us/en/business-services/it-services.html?compURI=1079061. HPACG provides language solutions for applications and content.

- LanguageLine Solutions: http://www.languageline. com/. LanguageLine offers interpretation, translation, and localization services.

- Lionbridge: http://www.lionbridge.com. Lionbridge provides translation, online marketing, global content management, and application-testing solutions.

- Moravia: http://www.moravia.com. Czech Republic-based Moravia provides translation, localization, language services, and a full range of other globalization services, including testing and engineering to prepare products for a successful global market launch.

- RWS Group: http://www.rws.com. RWS Group provides intellectual property translation, filing and search services, and technical and commercial translation and localization

- SDL International: http://www.sdl.com. SDL delivers an integrated localization solution and translation services to connect with customers worldwide.

- STAR Group: http://www.star-group.net. Translator and language service provider STAR Group is represented globally, with 51 locations in more than 30 countries, allowing for project managers, translators, and experts to have expertise on site in a local market.

- Translations.com: http://www.translations.com. Translations.com, a TransPerfect company, specializes in a variety of Web site translations, including specialization in legal, patent, certified, and software translations.

- Welocalize: http://www.welocalize.com. Welocalize specializes in both translation services and analyzing cultural characteristics to ensure that a company's web offerings are more accessible worldwide.

- TransPerfect: http://www.transperfect.com/. TransPerfect provides language services and translation-related technologies for companies ranging from small businesses to global enterprises.

- Sajan: http://www.sajan.com. Sajan is a global translation service provider offering localization solutions and language translation management system technology.

- adaQuest: http://www.addaquest.com. adaQuest helps you take on the whole world with your localization goals.

- Language Services Associates: `http://www.lsaweb.com`. Language Services Associates delivers a full range of language translation services and language interpretation services to companies across the globe.

- U.S. Translation Company: `http://www.ustranslation.com`. U.S. Translation Company provides interpretations and translation services in over 100 languages.

Consulting Companies Specializing in Web Globalization

The following companies offer support services in web globalization to individuals and businesses—from translation, to interpretation, to localization projects. If you want an unbiased expert opinion on the service providers previously mentioned, for example, these two companies should be able to assist you. Prior to entering into a consulting arrangement, double-check as to whether the company has any commercial ties to the organization listed.

Byte Level Research

A longtime front-runner in web globalization, Byte Level Research (`http://www.bytelevel.com`) is a research and consulting firm that helps companies create and improve their Web sites to successfully speak to the world. In addition, for more than eight years BL has published *The Web Globalization Report Card* (`http://bytelevel.com/reportcard2013/`) annually. It is a much-sought-after, in-depth analysis of the world's leading global Web sites, language trends, and best practices.

Common Sense Advisory

Common Sense Advisory (CSA; `http://www.commonsenseadvisory.com`) supports firms in the areas of translation, localization, interpreting, internationalization, globalization, marketing, international strategy, market intelligence, web content, and procurement.

Additional Considerations

Whichever company you decide to work with, in addition to the basics, make sure it covers nitty-gritty details, such as legal, statutory, and privacy issues, as well as providing customer service support through e-mail, global site registration, and so forth. All of those things can be problematic if you don't have an in-house expert. Consult with your international attorney throughout the process to ensure the legal requirements are satisfied, including but not limited to local domain names, privacy, data restrictions, and online terms and conditions.

Additional Resources: Associations

- **European Language Industry Association (ELIA):**
  http://www.elia-association.org. Members of ELIA
  include a large number of European translation agencies.

- **Globalization and Localization Assocation (GALA):**
  http://www.gala-global.org. GALA is an international
  association whose members are major players in translation and interpretation with a focus on new technologies.

- **American Translators Association (ATA):** http://
  www.atanet.org. ATA members include freelance translators and translation companies.

- **Association of Language Companies (ALC):**
  http://www.alcus.org. ALC is a professional organization for American translation companies.

- **Chambre Nationale des Entreprises de Traduction
  (CNET):** http://cnetfrance.jimdo.com. CNET is a
  professional organization for key players in the French
  translation market.

■ **Tip** Translators Without Borders (http://translatorswithoutborders.org) is considered the world's leading nonprofit translation organization. It facilitates the transfer of knowledge from one language to another by managing a community of NGOs that need translations and professional, vetted translators who volunteer their time to help. Two other translation organizations that come to mind are PerMondo (http://www.mondo-lingua.org/) and ITC Global Translations (http://itcglobaltranslations.com), an affiliate partner of SDL International. If you run a nonprofit organization and need translation help on your web initiatives, check to see whether the service providers mentioned earlier offer a discounted rate or special service packages especially for nonprofits.

How Much Will it Cost?

According to Globalization Partners, there are many factors involved when determining how much web globalization efforts will cost. These include the number of words; the number of target languages; the web-graphic require-ments; the requirements of the devices you're catering to, whether PCs, apps, or digital technology; the number of publishing platforms; the content manage-ment system used; the markup and scripting languages; and so forth.[xvii] That said, a proposal is generally required so that a package can be tailored to your specific needs.

Word on the street says that for a simple translation project, fees can average anywhere from ten cents to thirty cents per word (and possibly more depending on the nature and scope of the project). One must not forget about the additional cost of technology to support the project and other related elements in the Web site design that must also be adapted.

Jack Welde, the CEO of Smartling, says, "Typically, professional translation involves one or more translators plus an editor/reviewer. You might also find additional costs to write a style guide for translating your site, to develop a glossary of standardized terms, and to do linguistic Q&A, to review the final product."[xviii]

Creating a global presence for your Web site is not easy and is likely to be a costly undertaking, but to play the global game competitively, you must buy the services required to keep your brand understood, strong, and enjoyed by the world.

Vigdis Eriksen, the founder and president of Eriksen Translations, says, "To reach out to the world for business, your website should be flexible enough to adapt to other languages in the future. Build for scalable global growth and success."

Summary

Your Web site is oftentimes the first and strongest impression visitors have of you. If you want international customers to find you, stay longer on your Web site, and buy something from you, then create content that is communicated in their native language. You don't have to leap into this—you can "lean in," as Sheryl Sandberg, COO of Facebook, would say. You can take baby steps to get where you desire to go (say by satisfying the needs of Argentinian visitors to start with). The core challenge is this: Do you want to remain a sleepy small business serving only English-speaking customers for the rest of your life, or do you want to wake up and learn how to outcompete the companies in your category by offering multiple languages and serving the world? The latter requires the right architecture, the right information, the right technology, the right people, and the right integration.

Now that you are poised to sell to the world, one language, country, or globalized Web site at a time, you are ready to serve customers. In case customers don't discover you, we'll go find them!

Notes

i. http://bytelevel.com/books/gateway/, accessed April 17, 2016.

ii. "You Will Speak Every Language," Alex Ross, The Wall Street Journal, accessed April 17, 2016, http://www.wsj.com/articles/the-language-barrier-is-about-to-fall-1454077968.

iii. "Marketing Myopia," Theodore Levitt, *Harvard Business Review*, last modified July 2004, accessed April 17, 2016, http://hbr.org/2004/07/marketing-myopia.

iv. "Language Service Provider Growth Factors," Common Sense Advisory, last modified November 2010, http://www.commonsenseadvisory.com/AbstractView.aspx?ArticleID=736.

v. "Monterey: The Importance of Being the 'Language Capital of the World,'" Marie Vasari, Monterey Herald, accessed April 17, 2016, http://www.montereyherald.com/article/NF/20160402/NEWS/160409939.

vi. Ibid.

vii. "Frequently Asked Questions About Byte Level Research and Web Globalization," John Yunker, accessed April 17, 2016, http://bytelevel.com/about/faq.html.

viii. http://www.wsj.com/articles/the-language-barrier-is-about-to-fall-1454077968.

ix. "Global Language Services: Market Size 2009-2018," Statistic, accessed April 17, 2016, http://www.statista.com/statistics/257656/size-of-the-global-language-services-market/.

x. "The Ultimate Guide to Global Navigation," accessed April 17, 2016, http://www.globalbydesign.com/2010/09/09/the-art-of-the-global-gateway/.

xi. Adapted from "Internet World Users by Language: Top 10 Languages—World Internet Statistics," Internet World Stats, accessed April 17, 2016, last modified November 30, 2015, http://www.internetworldstats.com/stats7.htm.

xii. "The Top 10 Languages That Reign Online," Stephen Henderson, Common Sense Advisory (CSA), accessed April 17, 2016, http://www.commonsenseadvisory. com/Default.aspx?Contenttype=ArticleDetAD&tab ID=63&Aid=36478&moduleId=390.

xiii. "Limelight CMO Survey Confirms That Globalization of Digital Presence is a Strategic Priority," Limelight Networks, accessed April 17, 2016, last modified August 23, 2012, https://globenewswire.com/news-rele ase/2012/08/23/483584/10002888/en/Limelight-CMO-Survey-Confirms-That-Globalization-of-Digital-Presence-is-a-Strategic-Priority.html.

xiv. "Language Globalization Guidebooks," Globalization Partners International, accessed October 29, 2013 http://www.globalizationpartners.com/ser-vices/guide-books.aspx.

xv. "The 2016 Web Globalization Report Card," ByteLevel Research, accessed April 17, 2016, http://bytelevel. com/reportcard2016/#top25.

xvi. "How to Start a Multilingual Site," Google Webmaster Central Blog, last modified August 7, 2008, accessed April 17, 2016, http://googlewebmastercentral.blogspot. com/2008/08/how-to-start-multilingual-site.html.

xvii. "Website Translation and Localization Services," Globalization Partners, accessed April 17, 2016, http:// www.globalizationpartners.com/services/web-site-translation.aspx.

xviii. "How Much Does It Cost to Translate a Website from English into German, French, Spanish, Japanese, Korean, and Chinese?," Jack Welde, Quora, accessed April 17, 2016, last modified February 25, 2011, http://www. quora.com/How-much-does-it-cost-to-translate-a-website-from-English-into-German-French-Spanish-Japanese-Korean-and-Chinese.

Developing Sales and Distribution Capabilities

Finding Cross-Border Customers

The purpose of a business is to get and keep a customer. Without customers, no amount of engineering wizardry, clever financing, or operations expertise can keep a company going.

—Theodore Levitt, late marketing professor at the Harvard Business School[i]

In the future, our customers will create greater value for us. They not only generate income for us, they can also help us evolve.

— Zhu Bin, CEO, GuangDong Create Environment & Technology Co., China[ii]

Finding customers for your export product and services can be accomplished through a range of programs, largely government sponsored, including trade shows, trade missions, and related trade-networking services. I'll introduce a number of these services to you and explain how you can take advantage of them. I'll also revisit how to use social media and networking to attract potential customers worldwide.

© Laurel J. Delaney 2016
L. J. Delaney, *Exporting*, DOI 10.1007/978-1-4842-2193-8_16

This section is one of my favorites because, as Levitt says, you can't keep a company going without customers, and most books on international trade never provide a specific course of action on how to find them. I've been in your shoes and know the struggles that come with starting an export venture, so use me as a resource to help you get started. Get out your customer compass (sounds like a great new product idea!), and let's go. I want this part to be fresh, fun, relevant, and accessible to everyone everywhere.

Define Your Cross-Border Customers

As we discussed in Chapter 12, the goal of the export research you did is to help you select a likely market for your products, envision your end user, and refine your product or marketing strategy, if need be. This usually involves learning the demographics of your targeted consumer in the country you are about to enter and considering how to reach them in the most efficient manner.

■ **Caution** By now, you'd better know what is important to a consumer when she makes a purchasing decision related to your product or service, because if you don't (and if Theodore Levitt were alive today, he would most likely agree), your best intention will not satisfy, or woo, the extremely selective, busy, and value-conscious visitors to your online properties.

Learning about consumer trends is another means of helping you to determine where your product belongs and predict how successful it will be. Another goal of your research has been to assemble information about your first tier of customers—in other words, the intermediaries or end users who will actually purchase your product. Regardless of whether you are selling direct or indirect, your customers will tend to fall into one of six categories, which I will get to later.

However you move your product, it's important to be aware of how many intermediaries will be involved in getting your product or service to your consumers. Each one will add his markup to the price of your product in order to earn his due profit. You need to take this into consideration when you price your product, so that it won't end up being excessively expensive by the time it actually hits store shelves or arrives at a consumer's door. The most attractive import won't be able to compete with local products if it costs more than a consumer is willing to pay.

Caution When you set up an e-commerce shop (look back at Chapter 8), you must decide what type of customers your transactions will primarily involve: business to business (B-to-B), business to consumer (B-to-C), consumer to consumer (C-to-C), or business to government (B-to-G). If your target customer is B-to-B, the analysis in this chapter applies because B-to-B describes commerce transactions between two businesses, such as between a manufacturer and a retailer, a manufacturer and an overseas agent, or a manufacturer and a distributor. It also works with a B-to-C target.

There are six different categories of customers I will talk about in this chapter: the distributor or importing wholesaler, the overseas agent or representative, the overseas retailer, the overseas end user, the trading company, and the e-commerce customer (your Everyday Joe who might buy a single belt, for instance, at your e-commerce site for himself).

Let's start first with the large-volume customer.

Distributor or Importing Wholesaler

A distributor buys products from you (the seller, or exporter in this case) in large volumes, and then warehouses, distributes, and resells them to its customers. It also takes care of after-sales service. It is the most common first-tier buyer you will find and can offer the most efficient and profitable way to get your product to the consumer.

Note Don't get too bogged down with titles and terminology. They vary from country to country. In Japan, for example, distributors are referred to as wholesalers.

When evaluating prospective distributors, look for the following critical characteristics:

1. They trade in the geographic areas where you want to sell your product.

2. They have experience in importing, selling, marketing, and promoting your type of product.

3. They have distribution channels in place that will reach your targeted consumer.

4. They distribute products that are similar to yours but are noncompeting.

5. They are large enough in size to accomplish the desired results.

6. They have the financial strength to meet the demands of your business over the long haul.

7. They have a substantial number of sales outlets and a successful sales performance.

8. They have facilities to warehouse your products.

9. They have a reputation in the marketplace for scrupulous honesty, reliability, and regular customer service.

10. They deliver the kind of after-sales follow-through you'll be proud to have associated with your product.

11. They understand local culture, know how to negotiate the ins and outs of government regulations, and might even have helpful political connections.

After you find a distributor or two that match this criteria, I recommend that you meet with each one—preferably in person, or via Skype if you are conserving expenses—and decide which one comes closest to sharing your views on market penetration.

You will be establishing an important and long-term relationship, ideally, and that means you should find out everything you can about them well before you structure any contract. When you interview them, use the following list of questions as a guide:

1. How long have you been in business?

2. Can you share a few success stories about similar yet noncompeting products you have sold?

3. Have you represented other foreign companies? Explain what you did.

4. How long has your relationship lasted with the top three companies you represent?

5. How will our line fit in or complement your existing portfolio of products?

6. What's your game plan for building our brand in your country?

7. Do you have good market coverage, including a trained and educated sales force?

8. What specific territory, customer type, or product range are you interested in covering (either exclusively or nonexclusively)?

9. Can you deliver on pre-agreed sales targets?

10. Where do you see our brand in three, five, and ten years?

Tip Conducting serious due diligence on a distributor who intends to buy a large volume from you consistently over the course of years can spare you from headaches later on. You don't want to doubt your partner throughout the relationship. The relationship should be fluid, trusting, adventurous, and growth oriented. For more information, read, "Pre-Screening Overseas Distributors: 50 Questions: http://importexport.about.com/od/DevelopingSalesAndD istribution/a/Pre-Screening-Overseas-Distributors.htm.

In the case of exclusivity, as referred to in number eight, Dan Harris, an expert on Chinese law and the publisher of the *China Law Blog*, says this: "If you grant an exclusive, you should be sure to set sales quotas and performance targets [as noted in number nine] that will allow you to terminate the contract if not met." He goes on to say, "Setting adequately high minimum sales quotas will protect you from getting stuck with an under-performing or non-performing distributor. Clearly defining the sales quotas and performance targets is essential. The typical provision mandates a certain minimum dollar value of sales or a minimum number of units sold. Failure for a distributor to meet the minimum for a certain period might result in termination or, alternatively, it might just lead to it losing exclusivity."

Harris also cautions, "If you are going to sell your product into a new international market (whether through a distributor or otherwise), you absolutely must register your trademark in the country before doing so and you absolutely must register that trademark in your name, not that of your distributor." Control over intellectual property rights is important!

He finishes with, "A good distribution contract makes clear what happens upon termination because doing so greatly improves your chances of smoothly transitioning to a new distributor. Is your distributor allowed to sell down its remaining inventory of your product or must it cease sales immediately? Are you required to buy back the inventory and, if so, at what price? You want to put in your contract that the distributor must inform you of any pending and future sales. Lastly, where will your disputes with your distributor be resolved, and by whom?"[iii]

CASE EXAMPLE: TAKE YOUR TIME AND ALWAYS PARTNER WITH SOMEONE YOU HAVE GOOD INSTINCTS ON

Founder Alison Larson of WorldBlazer Consulting LLC, who has managed such big-name fashion brands as OshKosh B'Gosh and Carter's, says: "The worst partner I can remember was a company from Turkey and the UK who wanted to roll out our [fashion] brand throughout Europe. They gave us a business plan with huge sales numbers and pushed us to begin immediately (the first bad sign). Although my instincts said "Run!," the plan was too big to ignore and the company wanted to go forward. It wasn't long before the market went south, the company went bankrupt and the owner disappeared with the money of some of his customers."[iv] She goes on to say, "… you can never turn a bad partner into a good partner no matter how hard you try." Don't rush into any deal and always go with your instincts.

Prequalifying Distributors

Once you have found a distributor, how do you prequalify it beyond your interview process to ensure that it is a reputable organization? These 10 helpful resources will give you some tips:

1. *Country Riskline Report*: (http://www.dnb.com/risk-management/international-risk/14909183-1.html). A Dun & Bradstreet (D & B) service that provides an in-depth analysis of political, commercial, and economic risk covering of doing business in a single country.

2. *The Million Dollar Database*: (MDDI; http://www.mergentmddi.com). Also put out by D & B, this database provides a flexible gateway to a database of 1.6 million international business records from outside the U.S. and Canada.

3. *USEmbassy.gov: Websites of U.S. Embassies, Consulates, and Diplomatic Missions*: (http://www.usembassy.gov). This Web site provides a list of US embassies in other countries. Contact the one in the country in which you hope to do business and run your prospective customer's name by the people there, just in case they know anything. You'll be surprised at how willing they will be to help.

4. *International Business Credit Reports from Experian.com:* (http://www.experian.com/b2bglobal). Experian provides global information on a wide range of businesses from more than 225 countries. The suite offering consists of three products: the *United Kingdom Risk Report,* the *European Company Report,* and the *International Developed Report.* Pricing varies based on the complexity of the inquiry and the country.

5. *ICP:* (http://www.icpcredit.com/). International Company Profile provides international credit-status reports, company profiles, and business information on companies all over the world, especially in the emerging markets. Pricing varies based on the region and delivery time, but generally starts around US $75.

6. *U.S. Commercial Service's International Company Profile:* (http://www.export.gov/salesandmarketing/eg_main_018198.asp). The U.S. Commercial Service's ICP provdes financial reports on companies in more than 80 countries. Pricing varies based on the complexity of the inquiry and the country.

7. *GloBIS:* (http://www.glo-bis.com). GloBIS provides business credit reports, market intelligence, and databases in China and everywhere else around the globe. Delivery times and pricing vary by region.

8. *LexisNexis:* (http://www.lexisnexis.com/risk/products/instant-identity-verification.aspx). LexisNexis lets you verify professional credentials instantly by tapping more than 34 billion public and proprietary records.

9. *Global Verification Network:* (http://globalverificationnetwork.com). GVN, formerly a RedRidge verification service, screens applicants and conducts investigations for private sector financial transactions.

10. *Onfido:* (http://www.onfido.com). Onfido can verify anyone in the world within seconds.

 Tip   Managing Director Louise M. Kern of GloBIS says that at the very least you should request from all key business distributors their: full name, name in the local language, business registration number, address, and contact numbers. Once you have that data, conduct your own Internet-based due diligence search in your native language and in their language—include search terms such as "scam" or "fraud" – to reaffirm truths or uncover discrepancies. Statements from your distributors always need to be verified and consistent with reality.

Other Ways to Prequalify Distributors

The following should be used in addition to, not in lieu of, the above listed resources.

- WHOIS Search for Domain Registration Information, Network Solutions: (*www.networksolutions.com/whois-search/TYPECOMPANYDOMAINNAMEHERE*). When a company registers a domain name, the Internet Corporation for Assigned Names and Numbers (ICANN) requires the domain name registrar to submit personal contact information to the WHOIS database. Once a listing appears in the online directory, it is publicly available to anyone who chooses to check the domain name using the WHOIS search tool. You can find out when a company was established and registered, and who the listing is under. For a small monthly fee, a registrar can also elect to keep their listing information private so that instead of showing their contact information, Network Solutions's contact information will be featured.

- Check all social media platforms such as Facebook, LinkedIn, Twitter, or a blog to see if company information is current and consistent with all other information a distributor has provided.

Once you have qualified several prospective distributors and found a good one that can carry out your export action plan, you're ready to discuss an export business contract. Consult with your international attorney to set up a contractual agreement that establishes terms of mutual cooperation and assures you of an exclusive market, product type, or customer type for a specified period of time, with defined sales performance targets. Cross-border specialist, attorney, and Harvard Business School alum Randall Lewis believes you need to control mechanisms in your distribution partnership, such as distribution channels, key account management, and annual sales volumes, in order to achieve full market entry penetration levels.[v] Commit to a minimum of one year so that you have time to see how well you and the distributor work together. You should also monitor sales performance closely during this time. If sales are satisfactory and both parties are agreeable, you can extend the agreement as often and as long as you wish. As Harris adds, clearly defining the sales quotas and performance targets is essential because failure of the distributor to meet the minimum for a certain period might result in termination, which could later become your way out if the relationship is not working.

Overseas Agent or Representative (Importer)

An overseas agent works on a commission basis (ranging from 2.5 to 15 percent) to locate buyers for your product, which is considered indirect exporting (more in Chapter 17). It involves selling to an intermediary, who in turn arranges the sale of your products either directly to customers or to importing wholesalers. Once a buyer is found, however, customer service and all transaction logistics, including setting up payment and arranging transportation, become your responsibility. The agent oversees your work, stays in close contact with the customer, and will step in to assist on behalf of either party if needed. The advantage of this type of working relationship is that you have a fair degree of control over price and who your customers are.

Since overseas agents, sometimes considered foreign country brokers, typically have a vast knowledge of a target market along with solid relationships with customers, they can easily identify and exploit opportunities for your enterprise, from tracking demographic trends, to announcing radical customer shifts, to identifying emerging hot new products in any given country. The trick to working effectively with agents or reps is to stay in close contact by e-mail, telephone, or Skype and set expectations in writing right at the outset.

To find agents, work with the US Commercial Service; check online sourcing platforms such as Alibaba (http://www.alibaba.com), Global Sources (http://www.globalsources.com), EC21 (http://www.ec21.com), and TradeKey (http://www.tradekey.com); inquire with the international trade team at your bank for recommendations; reach out to industry trade-show executives who have access to the exhibitors and buyers who attend; and conduct a search via the Internet by typing in "Sales agent, UK, pet supplies," for example. Many of the ways to find an overseas agent are similar to those that I will look at in Chapter 17 in my discussion of export management companies (EMCs).

■ **Note** Using a company's own sales force will exert the most international control, but often for small businesses it is at a cost that is not affordable. Using overseas agents, representatives, and distributors is a prudent stepping-stone for testing the market and learning whether your product and services can be sold successfully first through someone who knows the market better than you do.

Overseas Retailer

You can also sell your products directly to overseas retailers, such as department stores, supermarkets, or mail-order houses on either an exclusive or nonexclusive basis. However, retailers are generally small in size, service only a regional location, and have limited warehouse space. This means that their purchases are usually small and they can only give your product limited geographic distribution. Larger retailers like Costco, Walmart, and Tesco have the capability to import directly but rarely do because of the challenges it presents (local culture and tastes vary from country to country), so you will still need to appoint a local agent or distributor to service the local on-demand needs of the small and big firms alike.

Alternatively, small businesses with ties to major domestic retailers (Toys "R" Us, Costco, and Target, for example) may also be able to use them to sell abroad. Many large American retailers maintain local buying offices and use these offices to sell abroad when practical.

Overseas End User

You can also sell your products directly to certain types of end users, such as hospitals, universities, or original equipment manufacturers. They, in turn, may resell your products to their customers or incorporate them into their own manufacturing processes.

Buyers can be identified at trade shows, through international-trade publications, or through your local US Export Assistance Center (http://export.gov/eac/). When you sell directly to an overseas end user, you are responsible for shipping, collecting payment, and after-sales service unless other arrangements are made.

Through e-commerce, you can also sell directly to anyone, anywhere in the world through a B-to-C transaction, as discussed in Chapter 8.

Trading Company

As I note in the next chapter, you can sell your products directly through a trading company, which resells them to its customers. Trading companies such as Jardines (Hong Kong, and one of the original Hong Kong trading houses that date back to Imperial China) and Mitsui & Co. (Japan) have long histories as import intermediaries in the development of international trade between countries. They are virtually identical to export management companies (EMCs), but they tend to function on a more demand-driven basis; that is, the demand of the market compels them to buy specific commodities. Trading companies usually have long-standing customers for whom they source products on a regular basis, and these customers can be located not just in one country but all over the world. Nowadays, some people refer to trading companies as global B-to-B traders that specialize in one commodity and in one market with strong logistics capabilities. (An example would be eTransWorld [http://www.lexecongroup.com/etransworld.php].)

Trading companies, better known in Japan as *sogo shosha* companies, are useful for establishing contacts or making introductions for you, but they are rarely qualified to do extensive marketing of your product. This is because they tend to be huge, loosely structured organizations that lack both the appropriate investment funds and the focused commitment to bring a product to market. Their efforts show very little continuity, which means poor repeat business. If you use a trading company and it develops some business for you, consider meeting the customers it finds in person, taking responsibility for the sales, and doing the marketing and distribution yourself. It could be a great way to lay the groundwork for future direct sales.

■ **Note**   Many large trading companies maintain buying offices in the United States and use these offices to sell abroad when practical.

---

e-Commerce

The proliferation of smart phones, tablets, and other portable and wearable devices is driving the growth of e-commerce. More and more companies are using this method of distribution and marketing for selling and, as a result, more and more individuals are buying via e-commerce. Technically, e-commerce is a form of direct selling. However, due to the unique issues associated with this form of commerce and distribution, it needs to be placed in a direct-method distribution class of its own. Sales of e-commerce are those to the second type of customer I mentioned earlier, your Everyday Joes.

E-commerce happens on three primary types of sites:

1. *Transactional site:* This type of site is one where people buy directly (Apple, Coach, and Sunglass Hut, for example).

2. *Information site:* Here, people visit a site but are led to buy elsewhere (e.g., eBay, Amazon)

3. *E-Marketplace:* On this type of site, people browse thousands of products, shop, and buy online (Zazzle and Etsy, for example).

Now that you know who your customers are, let's talk about how you're going to meet them.

Making Customer Contacts—Composing Your Inquiry

When a large-volume customer, such as an overseas wholesaler, contacts you or you contact him either by snail mail or over the Internet, always respond promptly and completely. Include the following materials and information:

1. *A cover letter:* It should establish your credentials as a reliable and reputable supplier in the industry. I always suggest e-mailing a scanned, signed copy of the letter and then sending the original via airmail, especially if you have attractive letterhead and marketing materials. (If snail mailing, attach your business card.)

2. *Product specification and pricing sheets:* These should provide enough information for the customer to make an intelligent decision as to whether or not he wants to continue communicating with you. Your letter to the customer might look like this:

Dear [Name of Customer]:

Thank you for your interest in our _____ product line. We have enclosed product catalogs and special export pricing for your review. Additional information can be found at our Web site called _____, located at _____, on our Facebook page at _____, on our LinkedIn page at _____, and on our Google+ page at _____. You can visit us on Twitter, too: _____.

Our company was established in 1974 and has been serving customers worldwide with quality products since then. We have the manufacturing capacity to keep up with demand. In addition, we only require a fourteen-day lead time to produce any quantity you might wish to order.

We look forward to your reply and the opportunity to do business with you.

Sincerely,

[Your Name]

Your goals here are very basic: to identify yourself, to reference the inquiry, to provide the information requested, to establish yourself as a solid, reputable institution, and to respectfully express your interest in entering into a relationship with the company. A lot of this information might already be featured on your Web site, but when it comes to specifically tailored information, such as pricing, it's best to respond directly and with a personal touch.

I've already discussed a number of sources from which you are likely to obtain lists of likely customers in the course of your market research. Start e-mailing inquiries to the customers on your lists and keep adding new names. Meanwhile, the following are some high-powered services and activities that can put you directly in touch with people who are actively seeking products like yours.

Next, I'll cover some valuable US Department of Commerce's International Trade Administration programs that help companies succeed in export markets around the world.

Gold Key Matching Service

Start with the most useful program: the Gold Key Matching Service (http://export.gov/salesandmarketing/eg_main_018195.asp), a US Commercial Service.

For a small company with a reasonable budget, the Gold Key Matching Service (GKMS)—which is run by the US Department of Commerce, US Commercial Service—is one of the most efficient ways to meet with prescreened potential cross-border business associates, whether you are seeking an agent, distributor, or joint-venture partner. The service arranges individual meetings, most taking place at the US embassy in the host country. Many companies say that this is a wise investment because you pay only for your airfare, lodging, and entertainment and have a series of productive meetings already set up.

Many businesses could benefit from learning more about the GKMS. Every year, the US Commercial Service helps thousands of national companies navigate the challenges of exporting goods and services worth billions of dollars. Located in 109 cities across the United States and in US embassies and consulates in more than seventy-five other countries, its global network of trade professionals opens doors that no one else can. First and foremost, it can connect US companies with international buyers worldwide. After all, isn't that what you are after: *finding customers the world over?*

The GKMS will also help you with:

- Creating custom market reports and industry briefings to target the best trade prospects and opportunities with the help of trade specialists

- Conducting market research that pertains to a specific country and examines cultural issues, analyzes market potential and size, and includes market-entry strategies for your product or service offering

- Performing due diligence on foreign competitors

- Setting up appointments with prospective trading partners in key industry sectors

- Conducting effective debriefings with trade specialists and assisting in developing appropriate follow-up strategies

- Booking international travel, accommodations, interpreter service, and clerical support

- Arranging participation in trade shows sponsored by state and federal agencies

---

■ **Tip** If you are operating on a shoestring budget and cannot afford to travel internationally, the GKMS also offers a video service whereby you can receive all the same benefits but you meet your potential business partners via videoconferencing instead of in person. Inquire.

Gold Key Service in India

Let's say you are interested in visiting India with the intention of eventually doing business there. (In calendar year 2014, the United States saw exports of nearly $37.2 billion to India, a 4.3 percent increase over 2013.[vi]) First, you would need to brush up on India (to do this, you could go to http://export. gov/india/doingbusinessinindia/index.asp) and then review the "Frequently Asked Questions" and look at "I am an American company and want to export to India. Where do I start?" (http://export.gov/india/ frequentlyansweredquestions/index.asp). Next, you would get in touch with the Gold Key Service for India (http://export.gov/india/contactus/index.asp), which will assist you in identifying attractive opportunities tailored to your business and arrange appointments with prescreened key players in the Indian market.

The service can help you set up appointments with your choice of agents and distributors; importing wholesalers in your industry; key governmental officials; service experts (e.g., bankers, consultants, and lawyers); potential Indian partners' trade associations; joint venture specialists; and major end users. It's up to you and what your business needs are. GKS makes it easy to enter the market and does most of the work, if not all, at a modest fee.

Fees vary depending on company size and the scope of service, but for standardized services they typically are as follows (the prices are as of 2016): $350 for small- to medium-sized new-to-export companies that are using the service for the first time; $700 for a small- to medium-sized company; and $2,300 for a large company.

Other Helpful US Government-Sponsored Programs

The Gold Key Matching Service isn't the only useful program. Here are some of the others.

The US Export Assistance Centers

The US Export Assistance Centers (EAC; http://www.sba.gov/content/us-export-assistance-centers) are staffed by professionals from the Small Business Administration (SBA), the US Department of Commerce, the US Export-Import Bank, and other public and private organizations. They can provide the help you need to find reputable distributors to compete in today's global marketplace.

Trade Leads Database

The Trade Leads Database (TLD; http://export.gov/tradeleads/index.asp) contains prescreened, time-sensitive leads and government tenders gathered through US Commercial Service offices around the world. You can search leads and receive notification when new leads are posted.

Platinum Key Service

The Platinum Key Service (PKS; https://build.export.gov/main/salesandmarketing/eg_main_018196) allows US companies to take advantage of longer-term, sustained, and customized US Commercial Service assistance on a range of issues. The fee-based service can include a range of issues including but not limited to identifying markets, launching products, and developing major project opportunities. Ongoing service is available for six months, one year, or a specified time frame based on the mutually agreed upon scope of work. To request this service, inquire with an EAC (http://www.sba.gov/content/us-export-assistance-centers).

International Buyer Program

The International Buyer Program (IBP; http://export.gov/ibp/) recruits thousands of qualified foreign buyers, sales representatives, and business partners to US trade shows each year, giving exhibitors an excellent opportunity to expand business globally.

International Partner Search

International Partner Search (IPS; http://export.gov/salesandmarketing/eg_main_018197.asp) will put its trade specialists, located in more than eighty countries, to work finding you the most suitable strategic partners. All you do is provide marketing material and company background information, and IPS does the work!

Business Intelligence Companies

No matter what business you are in, you will benefit tremendously from studying your competitors and working to lure their customers by offering better products or services. The following business intelligence companies offer searchable trade databases, covering international trade activities throughout the world, for a fee. They are a fantastic source of tracking what companies are exporting and to where.

As you review these sites, you must know what to look for. For example, if you want to export refurbished computers, study your competitors to find out: Are they growing? Do they have websites, blogs and other social media platforms? Do they make the news? Are they global? This doesn't mean copying every move they make. It means analyzing what your competitors are doing and then understanding why they are doing it so that you can tap into lucrative opportunities just as they are—but with a better, stronger, or new-and-improved version.

Find out where all their exports are going. You can either steal away business from them by exporting to the same location, provided you have a competitive advantage or a better value proposition (vastly improved quality, design, or price on a refurbished computer, for instance), or you can predict where they might go next and enter that market before they do. (Tread carefully here, because you are on your own, carving out a new unproven market—can you do it profitably?)

If you duplicate a competitor's strategy, tweak it to accommodate your strengths and then execute it better. And don't forget to utilize the transparency of social media and social networking. See what people are saying about your competition. If there is a thread of discontent, capitalize on it with a new product or differentiate an existing product in the market where the competitor is weak. Two critical key points: Find out what works, and do it better. Find out what doesn't work, and avoid it. A few good sites to review your competitors and their strategies are the following:

- *PIERS:* (http://www.piers.com). Whether you need to conduct market research, generate sales leads, or find buyers, PIERS is a comprehensive source of US waterborne import and export trade data online.

- *Datamyne:* (http://www.datamyne.com). This site provides real-time data about US exporters and export movement.

- *Import Genius:* (http://www.importgenius.com). This site provides real-time data on containers that enter the United States.

- *Journal of Commerce:* (http://www.joc.com). The JOC provides trade data and offers everything from a listing of the top hundred US exporters (including the top ten states exporting to China) to import/export trade leads and international trade news.

- *Panjiva:* (http://www.panjiva.com). If you desire to grow your market share, gain new insights, or reduce costs in your global supply chain, Panjiva provides solutions in these areas by providing shipment, company, and location data from more than 600 million shipment records and spanning more than 10 million companies.

- *Export Abroad:* (http://www.exportabroad.com). Whether it is identifying sales targets or staying up to date on compliance issues, Export Abroad helps you keep track of markets around the world and alerts you to new opportunities as they occur.

Tip Revisit Chapter 12, because all the market research resources I list there can also help you find customers—from the Small Business Administration, to world trade centers, to American embassies. All you need to remember is to ask: "Help me put together a list of potential customers in _____(fill in country) for _____ (fill in your product or service offering)."

Other Ways to Snag Customers Worldwide

You can do all the social networking in the world to find potential international buyers for your product or service offering, but one surefire way to corral people to one central location in person is to exhibit at a trade show. You can do this either locally or internationally.

Domestic (Local) Trade Shows

A good first step and a low-cost way to generate international sales—for both the large-volume customer and Everyday Joe—is to exhibit at a domestic trade show in your industry that offers an "international buyer" exhibit area. This will allow you to keep your transportation expenses to and from the show low. If the show's local, you can even drive to it and sleep at your own home each night.

It may sound counterintuitive to make international sales without leaving the country, but the fact is that international buyers are attracted to large trade shows in the United States. And let's not forget the draw of Las Vegas, Chicago, Miami, and other big trade show venues.

For example, many years ago, I exhibited at the International Home & Housewares Show in Chicago, where I am based, to tap into its international buyer audience and number of global member benefits. Afterward, I was able to use the directory in order to prospect customers.

After you generate national interest and sales success, you can think about exhibiting overseas at a show that brings in worldwide buyers in your industry. From there on, and as discussed in Chapter 10, others in your industry will expect to see you there every year as long as you're in business. If you exhibit once and then disappear, they'll think you gave up on the market or went out of business.

For a listing of domestic trade shows, many of which will be within driving distance of your city, visit the ExpoPromoter Web site at http://www.tradeshowsusa.com/.

■ **Tip** Instead of exhibiting at a trade show, you can organize your own program anywhere you choose—call it what you wish—to bring customers all over the world to you. In 2015, we did exactly that with our first ever Global Small Business Forum (http://globalsmallbusinessforum.com) held in Chicago at the famous Navy Pier. We plan to host the forum every year to meet with new customers and suppliers in person, educate them on the latest trends, better understand their needs, and develop solutions together.

International Trade Shows

When you decide to exhibit internationally at a trade show, you incur transportation, food, hotel, and exhibition-related expenses. Yet those additional costs are often more than offset by the potential of finding customers on the ground from all over the world.

Many big international trade shows, such as Hannover Messe in Germany (https://texaswideopenforbusiness.com/news/texas-joins-largest-ever-us-business-delegation-hannover-messe-2016), offer a US Pavilion, where the actual cost of the exhibit is subsidized by our government, offering a substantial discount from the regular exhibit rate (inquire with your state's US Export Assistance Center). The pavilions are strictly for the American exhibitors. Market experts from the US Embassy are typically on hand at the show to help national firms make connections and further establish themselves in a new market.

For a listing of international trade shows, try these sites (but also conduct a web search on your industry—automotive, technology, or food, for example—to find out when and where the next overseas trade show will take place):

- *Trade Show News Network*: http://www.tsnn.com/
- *BizTrade Shows*: http://www.biztradeshows.com/
- *Events Eye*: http://www.eventseye.com/
- *export.gov*: http://export.gov/eac/trade_events.asp

Tip The US Commercial Service has what is called a trade fair certification program. It is a cooperative arrangement between private-sector trade show organizers and the US government for the purpose of organizing a US pavilion. The goal is to increase US exports and expand national participation in overseas trade shows.

Government-Sponsored Trade Mission

Trade missions serve US firms that want to explore and pursue export opportunities by meeting directly with potential clients in their respective markets. They typically offer one-to-one meetings, networking events, site visits, briefings, and media coverage.

Certified Trade Missions (CTM; http://export.gov/ctm/index.asp) are overseas events that are planned and organized by private- and public-sector export-oriented groups outside of the US Department of Commerce. They are designed for new and experienced exporters to establish sales and set up representation abroad at a low cost. CTMs typically bring representatives of US companies into contact with potential agents, distributors, joint venture partners, licensees, local businesses, and government contacts.

Binational Societies, Councils, and Trade Associations, and Chambers of Commerce

As I discussed in Chapter 12, it is important to search the Internet for local binational groups that will put you in touch with customers in the country where you'd like to do business. The National Association of Japan-America Societies (http://www.us-japan.org/), the US-China Business Council (https://www.uschina.org/), and the US-India Business Council (http://www.usibc.com/), for example, all promote bilateral trade between the United States and their respective countries and also provide a stimulating social forum for people with common interests. In addition, they can help with prospecting for export customers. You just need to ask.

Check with your state to see if it has an export promotion agency, or a foreign relations or export council. Organizations like these usually assemble at least once a month and offer a forum for discussion about how to better facilitate international relations, expand trade, and acquire new customers.

Contacts made through business colleagues and associations can often prove invaluable to exporters. Find someone who is successfully exporting and doesn't compete with you, and buy her lunch and pick her brain. Many states offer associations—such as The International Trade Association of Greater Chicago (http://www.itagc.org/), Monterey Bay International Trade Association (http://www.mbita.org/) and the International Trade Association of Southwest Ohio (http://www.mvita.org/)–that focus strictly on promoting world trade. Check with your local and international chamber of commerce to see which of these associations have chapters in your area and sit in on a meeting—then sign up. There are American chambers of commerce located all over the world.—for example, in China (http://www.amchamchina.org), India (http://amchamindia.com) and Japan (http://www.accj.or.jp)—each with the goal of promoting trade with the United States.

All of these are ways to scout for new, promising customers in export markets, and each can be a valuable source of knowledge.

Tap Local Clients for Their International Reach

One of the easiest ways to quickly enter a new foreign market is to partner or form an alliance with a company (it could be a client—Brother International, IBM, or American Express, for example) who is more powerful than you and is already conducting like-minded yet noncompeting business in that market. Before you consider this avenue, I caution you to consult with tax and legal advisors to learn what type of partnership you should form, if you form one at all, what compliance issues need to be addressed, and whether or not you will be required to file tax returns in the host country. Please note that not all partnerships need to be formalized. Sometimes a trusting relationship and a handshake is all it takes to get started.

Most companies decide to partner because they sense that there is great synergy between two specific companies—a mutual need and desire to share risk in achieving a common objective. I'll go into more detail about partnerships and alliances in Chapter 17 when I discuss methods of exporting, but for now I'll just say that partnering can open doors to new markets by enabling the acquisition of export customers at a faster rate. Inquire with your global clients. Ask for an introduction to the individual who heads up the in-country office. Take it one country at a time.

CASE EXAMPLE: PARTNER WITH A DOMESTIC CLIENT THAT HAS A GLOBAL PRESENCE

When I first started exporting foodstuff, I contacted one of the largest Japanese trading companies in the world: Mitsui & Co. The company had a local office in Chicago and did a significant amount of exporting to Japan. I approached the company about piggybacking my products with those it carried. Since I had the suppliers and the company had the established distribution channels and customer base, it was a good match. By combining my company's gourmet food items with Mitsui's beef products, we were able to provide extra value to customers throughout Japan. We went on to export container loads of product every month for many years. That experience taught me the importance of partnering in growing a business internationally—especially for small businesses!

Find Customers Through Advertising

If you've done a good job of marketing your business by implementing a variety of tactics over a long period of time and have placed a strong emphasis on organic search engine marketing, the world will find you. If that's working, you should not have to spend money on public relations or advertising—a far more costly way to market your business. However, if those Everyday Joe customers are not beating down your online door, here are a few options for profitably acquiring customers through advertising. Note that these are merely a sampling of what's available.

- *Search engine ads*: Focus on search engine marketing by purchasing ads on search engines. All companies have the possibility of using the same tactic. Thus, you are competing against everyone else who wants to spend money on advertising to get customers. For service providers, try Google AdWords, Microsoft Bing Ads, and Yahoo Gemini Ads.

- *Affiliate and performance-based marketing*: If you have a product or service that others want to promote, get your constituency base involved by asking them and explaining how you can reward them with each visitor or customer they bring to you through their efforts. This can be affordable, scalable, and controllable. For affiliate programs, try CJ Affiliate, ClickBank, and LinkShare (a Rakuten Affiliate Network).

■ **Caution**   No amount of money spent on advertising will make up for a poor customer experience.

- *Retargeting*: This process works by keeping track of people who visit your site and then retargeting your ads to them as they visit other sites. This advertising only works for sites that already have traffic, so if you already have visitors and want to leverage and increase traffic, give it a try.

    Here's how it works: Let's say an individual visits your site to buy a special Irish bracelet. She stays for a bit and then leaves to look elsewhere on the web for a similarly styled bracelet at a better price or better quality. When that person shops other sites on the web for Irish bracelets, your retargeted ad will appear on their screen showing the Irish bracelet with a special discounted offer. If this sounds a bit complicated, work with a vendor to provide you with a marketing solution that fits your needs. For retargeting providers, try Criteo, FetchBack, Quantcast, AdRoll, and MediaForge (a Rakuten Affiliate Network).

- *Display ads:* This type of ad allows you to target a specific demographic, extend your reach, and build your brand. It can be a video, banner, wallpaper, company logo, or other similar graphic. For display ad providers, try Google AdWords, Burst Media (a RhythmOne company), AOL, and Yahoo.

■ **Tip**   Many social media and networking platforms have targeted advertising programs in place to help you acquire new customers for your business. Facebook claims you can reach more than 1.4 billion people with its targeted advertising and will help you choose the right ones. LinkedIn offers targeted self-service ads as well, where you can pay by clicks or impressions and control your ad campaign from beginning to end. Inquire.

Summary

Finding customers for your export product and services can be easily accomplished through a wide variety of methods, including but not limited to social media and networking best practices, government-sponsored programs, trade shows, trade missions, and related trade-networking services. You can even advertise to acquire customers. But it's not simply one tactic that will bring export customers to your door. It's several different things in combination, and each part must be done exceptionally well, including becoming fluent in each market's cultural sensitivities (as we will get to in Chapter 24).

As a result of your diligence, you will get customers. Now, we're on to the easy part—determining your best export-sales strategy. How will you serve your customers?

Notes

i. Theodore Levitt, *The Marketing Imagination* (New York: Free Press, 1983).

ii. "Disrupt or be Disrupted," Jane Hiscock, accessed April 24, 2016, http://insights-on-business.com/gbs-strategy/disrupt-or-be-disrupted/.

iii. Dan Harris, publisher of the *China Law Blog*, www.chinalawblog.com; used with permission.

iv. "10 Critical Errors That Fashion Companies Make When Going Global," Alison Larson, accessed April 24, 2016, http://www.worldblazer.com/wp-content/uploads/2013/10/worldblazer-ebook.pdf.

v. "A Guide to Controlling International Distribution Relationships: A Checklist for Success," Randall Lewis, Pulse LinkedIn, accessed April 22, 2016, `https://www.linkedin.com/pulse/guide-controlling-international-distribution-checklist-randall-lewis`.

vi. "Doing Business in India – the second fastest growing market in Asia," accessed April 24, 2016, `http://export.gov/india/doingbusinessinindia/index.asp`.

Methods of Exporting

Direct, Indirect, and Collaborative Sales Channels

[Be] prepared to change your strategy or combine several options as your business needs evolve. By opening your mind to the full range of possibilities, you broaden perceived opportunities, sharpen your strategic decisions, and enhance global performance.

—Pankaj Ghemawat, Anselmo Rubiralta Professor of Global Strategy at IESE Business School in Barcelona, Spain[i]

There are several factors to consider when determining whether a direct, indirect, or collaborative sales strategy is best for you—the most important are the extent of your resources, the degree of control you wish to exercise over your export ventures, and other in-country issues. The following analysis will help you to make a decision that is tailored to your needs.

First, let me emphasize that timing is everything. Readiness to seize an opportunity is more important than having your whole strategy nailed down beforehand. If you get a promising inquiry for your export product, go for it. Don't analyze it to death until after you've responded to the inquiry. If there's one thing I'd like you to take away from reading this particular section and entire book, it's the exporter's habit of action: It's better to do something—anything—that will

© Laurel J. Delaney 2016

L. J. Delaney, *Exporting*, DOI 10.1007/978-1-4842-2193-8_17

put you in the export marketplace than to expend enormous amounts of time researching and debating options and wondering what other people would do if they were in your place. When an opportunity comes, you must be ready to operate via any sales channel, be it direct, indirect, or collaborative.

Methods of Exporting

Let's look at the two primary methods of exporting: direct and indirect.

Direct Exporting

Direct exporting means you export directly to a customer interested in buying your product. You are responsible for handling the logistics of shipment and for collecting payment.

The advantages of this method are:

- Your potential profits are greater because you have eliminated intermediaries.

- You have a greater degree of control over all aspects of the transaction.

- You know who your customers are.

- Your customers know who you are. They feel more secure in doing business directly with you.

- Your business trips are much more efficient and effective because you meet directly with the customer responsible for selling your product.

- You know whom to contact if something isn't working.

- The feedback you receive from your customers on your product and its performance in the marketplace gets to you faster and more directly.

- You get slightly better protection for your trademarks, patents, and copyrights.

- You present yourself as fully committed and engaged in the export process.

- You develop a better understanding of the marketplace.

- As your business develops in the foreign market, you have greater flexibility to improve or redirect your marketing efforts.

The disadvantages of direct exporting:

- It takes more time, energy, and money than you may be able to afford.

- It requires more people power to cultivate a customer base.

- Servicing the business will demand more responsibility from every level of your organization.

- You are held accountable for whatever happens. There is no buffer zone.

- You may not be able to respond to customer communications as quickly as a local agent can.

- You have to handle all the logistics of the transaction.

- If you have a technological product, you must be prepared to respond to technical questions and to provide on-site start-up training and ongoing support services.

Indirect Exporting

Indirect exporting refers to selling your products to an intermediary, who in turn sells them either directly to customers or indirectly to importing wholesalers. The easiest method of indirect exporting is to sell to an intermediary in your own country. When selling by this method, you normally are not responsible for collecting payment from the overseas customer nor for coordinating the shipping logistics.

An export management company (EMC) is one such intermediary. A good one will, in all respects, act as a global extension of your own sales-and-service presence—more or less executing your intentions on behalf of the product. These companies offer a wide range of services, but most specialize in exporting a specific range of products to a well-defined customer base in a particular country or region. For example, one of these companies might specialize in exporting agricultural products to restaurant customers in Europe. An EMC is highly market driven, representing your product along with other companies' noncompeting products as part of its own import "product line" aimed at the customer base it has created. Generally, it buys the product from a manufacturer and marks up the price to cover its profit. This is called a buy-resell arrangement. Other common compensation structures include commission and buy-and-resell, start-up payment, project fee only, fee plus commission, and buy-and-resell. An EMC will carry out all aspects of the export transaction. Fees vary depending on the services rendered and risks accepted but can range anywhere from 1 to 7 percent of sales value.

■ **Tip** An example of an EMC is Provisions International (`http://www.provisionsinter national.com`), which exclusively sells and markets well-known brands internationally for major companies.

Finding a good EMC is not that difficult. You can conduct a search through Google or Bing with the keywords "Export management company" to access a list of them. For each company, make note of how long it has been in business, the number of employees it has, the products in which it specializes, and the countries to which it exports. Start your own select list of companies that export products that are similar to yours but don't act as competition to it. Then consult the following resources for more referrals to add to your list:

- *A local trade association with an international focus*: Attend a few meetings and talk some shop—somebody's bound to know of an EMC or even run his own.

- *The international division of your bank*: The division is likely to have an inside line on which EMCs are reputable and doing well.

- *A conference or trade show that specializes in a particular industry, such as agricultural, construction, or hunting and sporting goods*: Attend a show or even consider exhibiting so you can access a list of exhibitors and buyers who attend. As you walk through the show, ask questions. Find out who is using whom for export movements.

- *As always, your local Chamber of Commerce or small business assistance center*: It generally knows who has been in the export trading business for a while. At the very least, it can point you to a good exporting resource.

- *Freight forwarders*: They might be able to provide you with the names of EMCs that use their service. Because you probably haven't made a sale at this point, you probably don't have a working relationship with a transportation company. Ask someone you know who uses a freight forwarder regularly.

- *Social media, trade magazines, and newspapers*: In addition to tracking what's going on in your industry by way of social media, trade magazines and international newspapers, you can also place a paid ad or conduct an outreach effort indicating "distributor wanted" or "representative wanted" on your specific product line in an overseas market. Vet all inquiries (refer to Chapter 16) to ensure respondents prequalify and can do the job.

You might also use the services of an export trading company. ETCs are virtually identical to EMCs, but they tend to function on a more demand-driven basis, according to which the demand of the market compels them to buy specific goods or commodities. They usually have long-standing customers for whom they source products on a regular basis. For example, they might get a request from a customer to find a supplier of canned corn who can provide twenty container-loads a month for a given number of months. The ETC will then seek out a reputable manufacturer that can handle the demand at an economical price and arrange for the transport of the goods to the customer. You can track down a good ETC using the same channels recommended above for finding an EMC.

Indirect exporting can also involve selling your products to an intermediary in the country where you wish to transact business, who in turn sells them directly to customers or other importing distributors (wholesalers). Under these circumstances, you will not know who your end consumers are. When selling by this method, you are normally responsible for collecting payment from the overseas customer and for coordinating the shipping logistics. In some instances, the overseas agent might request that it be allowed to handle the shipping, usually because it receives special transportation rates from carriers with whom it has done volume business for years. In this case, you will need to arrange for the cargo to be ready by the shipment date. You must still collect payment from the customer, but your actual involvement in the transaction is minimal. It is nearly as easy as a domestic sale.

The advantages of indirect exporting are:

- It's an almost risk-free way to begin.

- It demands minimal involvement in the export process.

- It allows you to continue to concentrate on your domestic business.

- You can learn about export marketing as you go rather than needing to master it immediately.

- Depending on the type of intermediary with which you are dealing, you don't have to concern yourself with shipment and other logistics.

- You can field-test your products for export potential.

- In some instances your local agent can field technical questions and provide necessary product support.

The disadvantages are:

- Your profits are lower.

- You lose control over your foreign sales.

- You very rarely know who your customers are and thus lose the opportunity to tailor your offerings to their evolving needs.

- You are a step removed from the actual transaction, causing you to feel out of the loop.

- The intermediary might also be using your product to test the market for her own products that are similar to yours, including ones that are directly competing with it. They might be selling their products to the same customers instead of providing exclusive representation.

- Your long-term outlook and goals for your export program can change rapidly, and if you've put your product in someone else's hands, it's hard to redirect your efforts accordingly.

Questions to Use for Deciding on the Method of Exporting

Only you can determine which strategy suits your needs. Your choice will depend on your goals, your available resources, and the type of business you run. I do recommend that you choose the method that makes you most comfortable and lets you focus on your own core competencies or business priorities, so that you aren't wasting your energy worrying that something isn't working. At the same time, though, I think I've made my bias in favor of direct exporting abundantly clear—it's the only way to maximize control, profits, and market presence. I urge you to move in that direction as soon as you feel able.

Tip If at all possible, go the direct marketing route. It's the best way to learn, grow your presence in the market, and maximize profits.

Let's start with a list of questions to consider before you decide which method of exporting will be best for you:

1. *How big is your company?* A larger company will have more people power to dedicate to the task of achieving direct sales than a small firm or a solo operator, who may find the indirect route to be more readily within his reach.

2. *How big do you (or your company or division) want to get?* If you want to be the size of Siemens AG someday, tackling direct sales now will help you build the foundation for that blockbuster future. But even if you prefer to continue doing business as a one-person operation, you'll want to establish some direct channels as your business develops.

3. *How much time and money do you have?* If you have deep pockets and all the time in the world, then you have nothing to lose by selling direct. If time is of the essence because you don't have unlimited funds, indirect channels are more likely to bring you a fast sale.

4. *Will your product require extensive on-site training and support?* Look at Apple, one of the world's largest producers of smart phones. It wants to maintain a reputation not only for making high-quality, expertly designed products, but also for improving its customers' lives. The only way to express this commitment to them is by staying right in their faces all over the world and constantly improving upon and updating existing products. Would Apple rely on local agents or set up a joint venture to cultivate the high degree of customer satisfaction it's after? Unlikely. The more complex and technical your product, the greater the importance of on-site customer service. In Apple's case, this involves retail stores featuring only its own products, staffed by highly trained company employees. But if you're exporting a product that comes without instructions, you'll do your customers no disservice by going indirect.

5. *Do you feel like you know what you're doing and where you want to go? Do you have a strong heart, mind, and stomach?* If you can honestly answer yes to these questions, then go direct. If not, start off indirect and slowly move into developing collaborative relationships.

■ **Caution**　Early in my career, I worked with an export trading company that purchased goods from my company so it could export them to Japan. I, in turn, was acting as an export trading company for the manufacturer, who thus had two intermediaries between itself and its foreign customers. Imagine the high retail price the consumer paid once the product landed in his country! If you are two or three times removed from a direct relationship with your customers, think twice—or even thrice!—about how you might get to them directly. After all, the name of the export game is to generate your own network of customer relationships. The sooner you begin building this foundation, the sooner you will have a flourishing export business.

In-Country Factors that Can Affect Your Distribution Choice

To ensure you make an intelligent decision regarding whether to export directly or indirectly, confront the following issues. Going in with your eyes wide open will help enable success in an overseas market.

- *Your potential costs and profit margins can help you determine whether it is more profitable to sell directly or indirectly.* In some emerging countries, competition in large cities is so fierce that costs are low and margins thin. On the other hand, particularly in rural areas, the lack of capital can cause just a handful of big, established companies to grow significantly, often gaining monopolies. Hence, the large companies in these areas get away with charging higher prices and achieving wider profit margins. As a potential exporter, determining the competition you will face will help you figure out whether selling directly will truly be profitable, or if it makes more sense to do it indirectly.

- *The competition you face in your export area can affect your choice of entry.* Is the market you are about to enter saturated with lots of competitors? Will you end up a "me too"-type product with no key differentiator to spur sales? Or do you have a value proposition (better pricing, design, or quality, for instance) that will disrupt the market and allow you to become a market leader?

- *The length of a sales channel can affect distribution choice.* In Japan, for example, the traditional distribution system adds many layers to get a product transported to a consumer. In this country, perhaps it would be better to work directly with a big retailer than to go through an importer that might sell to three other intermediary companies to get the product in the hands of the end user.

- *The reach or availability applied to your product line can affect whether it is profitable to bring it into a new market.* Is there an existing distribution system for your type of product in the country you are exporting to, or must it be established? Does the government have any restrictions to direct sales on your product line, sales to intermediaries, or limitations on licensing requirements? The more established the system for bringing your product into the country and the fewer restrictions, the less time and labor will be required to export the product.

- *The channel of distribution affects how a product enters a market.* If there is no distribution system to be found in an export country or it is blocked, it will be impossible to enter the market. Or perhaps your product can only be sold door to door or through street stands and the country you wish to enter does not support that method of selling.

- *The product inventory needs to be handled, paid for, and stocked.* Nothing is worse than having lots of interest and demand for your product, only to find out later that it is out of stock at the factory. Get a feel for power, control, and competition in a market. If you see or hear of any distribution company dominating a market (distributing to many middlemen across the country), it's a sign that it will be a tough market to crack unless you get that company on your side. Go elsewhere.

- *Barriers to entering a country, whether real or imagined, can influence a market-entry strategy.* Certain economic or political trade controls and restrictions can cause impediments to an import. Two of the key controls are tariff and nontariff barriers set up to reduce imports that might compete with locally produced goods. It's a form of protectionism. Others include: embargoes, sanctions, export license requirements, entry time restrictions, restrictive government policies, high entry and exit costs, and weak infrastructure.

- *Distance can matter.* According to Pankaj Ghemawat, writing in the *Harvard Business Review*, "By distance, I don't mean only geographic separation, though that is important. Distance also has cultural, administrative or political, and economic dimensions that can make foreign markets considerably more or less attractive."[ii] Make sure you evaluate the many dimensions of distance and how they can impact opportunities in a foreign market, allowing you to decide whether it will be profitable to export directly to a country.

The bottom line is: you need to spend as much time as you need surveying the market before you decide on your method of exporting.

Other Methods to Entering an Export Market: Collaborative Sales

Now that we've looked at direct or indirect exporting, let's examine other means for entering an export market: global strategic initiatives, or what I refer to as collaborative sales. Each of these new styles of selling enables you to enter an overseas market faster to expand your existing sales or operations into a foreign country and improve your competitive position. And none of them are mutually exclusive. Rather, these options should be considered along with, or in addition to, direct and indirect exporting. You can, for example, export if a market permits it and has a licensing arrangement in place or form a joint venture. Once you form a new relationship, you reduce domestic dependence and increase export revenues and profits worldwide. I'll start with the most widely used initiative first and then drill down as best I can from there.

Tip All global strategic initiatives involve an attempt to achieve outcomes that are acceptable to all parties involved. Keep it clear in mind what you are seeking to gain from the initiative but don't lose sight of the valuation creation opportunity either, select the right type of relationship, and choose a partner whose contribution will enable you to achieve those goals. Most important, seek international legal (for agreement help) and financial advice. Consult with your export dream team before taking formal action.

Partnership

If you've gotten about as far as you can on your own in charting your export strategy, it's a good time to consider partnering with another company that is located in a foreign country where you are already doing business or would like to be doing business. First, it's important to understand exactly how a partnership works and what it can and cannot do for you.

A partnership is a commitment (voluntarily made) by parties to work collaboratively rather than competitively to achieve mutually desired results in a complex endeavor. A partnership does not necessarily involve a formal contract. It can be formed with a handshake and be based purely on trust. "You do this. We'll do that." Done.

Partnerships can be project based, narrowly defined, or spelled out with a definite time frame. It depends on what needs to be accomplished. If the arrangement is relatively long in duration, say five to ten years, some refer to that as "strategic partnering."

In a partnership, each side knows and commits to the goals of the project and to those of one another, but independence is generally retained. In other words, each party may individually suffer or gain from the relationship.

The biggest downside or disadvantage to a partnership is conflict resolution or the question of who takes responsibility should a crisis arise. The biggest advantage is you can get a partnership going rather fast by minimizing risks while maximizing your leverage in the marketplace.

Global Strategic Alliance

There is no precise definition of a global strategic alliance (GSA). There have been many different versions put forward by thought leaders with the focus on what it achieves. In my experience, a GSA is usually established when a company wishes to edge into a related business or new geographic market—particularly one in a country where the government prohibits imports in order to protect domestic industry. Strategic alliances can come in all shapes and sizes—from an informal business relationship based on a simple contract to a licensing or joint-venture agreement that spells out what needs to be done. Typically, these alliances are formed between two or more corporations in the same or complementary businesses, each based in its home country, for a specified period of time. They are formed between a group of companies that would benefit equally from the partnership. The arrangement can create a win-win environment—or a big-time lose—for all parties. The common goal, however, is for all parties to achieve their objectives more efficiently, at a lower cost, and with less risk than had they acted alone.

The cost of a GSA is usually shared equitably among the corporations involved, and the alliance is generally the least expensive way for all concerned to form a partnership. An acquisition, on the other hand, offers a faster start in exploiting an overseas market but tends to be a much more expensive undertaking for the acquiring company—and one that is likely to be well out of the reach of a solo operator. While a global strategic alliance works well for core business expansion and utilizing existing geographic markets, an acquisition works better for immediate penetration of new geographic territories. Hence, an alliance provides a good solution to export marketers that lack the required distribution to get into overseas markets.

A GSA is also much more flexible than an acquisition with respect to the degree of control enjoyed by each party. Depending on your resources and the type of relationship you form, you can structure an equity or nonequity alliance. Within an equity alliance, each party can hold a minority, majority, or equal stake. In a nonequity alliance, the host-country partner has a greater stake in the deal and thus holds a majority interest.

Yet the right choice of a partner is arguably more important than how the alliance is structured. When it gets down to business, you want a partner who will have an active contribution to make and who is flexible and able to resolve conflicts as the alliance evolves. Even more important, however, is that you have a clear idea of what you are seeking to gain from the alliance, what the value creation opportunity is, and that you have chosen a partner whose contribution will enable you to achieve those goals.

■ **Tip** The whole point of a healthy collaboration is to draw out new and diverse knowledge. Cast a wide net. Partners can provide a different perspective and opportunity for reframing rather than merely confirming expectations or assumptions. Seek variety. It is the spice of business and fosters innovation.

What do alliances look like? Starbucks, once a small business, opened its first store in Seattle in 1971. Since then, it has created more than twenty-four thousand stores in more than seventy countries[iii]. It was strategic partnerships that enabled it to advance a lot of its growth. "Starbucks partnered with Barnes and Noble bookstores in 1993 to provide in-house coffee shops, benefiting both retailers."[iv] A couple of years later, Starbucks partnered with Pepsico to bottle, distribute, and sell the coffee-based drink Frappacino. Soon, they will be working with Microsoft to develop their Starbuck's Windows phone app[v].

In 2010, Intuit, which serves millions of small businesses around the world with its financial software, and Nokia (soon to be a part of Microsoft), which sells hundreds of millions of devices each year, announced an alliance to develop and deliver an innovative new mobile and web-based marketing service. This service has catered to small businesses around the world, bringing their respective expertise to bear for a wider audience than had they not partnered up.[vi]

The world's biggest shipping lines, China Ocean Shipping Co. (Cosco), and China Shipping Group, plan to form a new shipping alliance that helps them control around 26 percent of the trade between Asia and Europe, the world's busiest container shipping hub.[vii]

Forming an Alliance: Where to Look

You might be surprised to find that you can build mutually advantageous alliances with some unlikely allies. Many companies make conscious decisions to form partnerships with complementary or even competing companies that can offer them a market share in countries they have been struggling to break into for years. South Korean technology company Samsung and American-based Best Buy, for example, have entered into a broad global strategic alliance that involves setting up 1,400 ministores called Samsung Experience Shops, selling Samsung products in Best Buy and Best Buy Mobile locations across the United States. The locations feature Samsung's laptops, connected cameras, and accessories, giving Samsung a presence in Best Buy locations, previously held only by Apple. By using their complementary strengths and expertise, these companies ensure their mutual survival and foster continued growth in their respective industries.

Even if you're not an international technology company or one of the world's leading retailers, you can follow the example set by Samsung and Best Buy and see which of your contacts, colleagues, peers, or competitors in the international market might have compatible needs and objectives. You'll probably feel most secure with a company that you already have a reasonably long-standing business relationship with, especially if you have achieved substantial sales growth together. It could be your distributor in Athens, a manufacturer that took on distribution of your product in Vietnam, or that trading company in Japan that can't keep up with consumer demand. Any one of your contacts with a problem you can solve or a need you can fulfill might serve as a potential partner.

Advantages of a GSA

There are many specific advantages of setting up a GSA. It will allow you to:

- Get instant market access, or at least speed your entry into a new market
- Exploit new opportunities to strengthen your position in a market where you already have a foothold
- Increase sales
- Improve competitive position
- Create value
- Gain new skills and technology
- Shape and sharpen the innovation opportunity
- Develop new products at a profit
- Originate new conversations
- Share fixed costs and resources
- Enlarge your distribution channels
- Broaden your business and political contact base
- Gain greater knowledge of international customs and culture
- Enhance your image in the world marketplace

Disadvantages of the GSA

There are also some inevitable trade-offs of a GSA to consider:

- Weaker management involvement or less equity stake in the larger company
- The dreaded market insulation—an inability to see the realities of the market—due to the local partner's presence
- Less efficient communication within the company
- Poor resource allocation
- Difficult to keep objectives on target over time
- Potential loss of control over such important issues as product quality, operating costs, employees, and customer service.

For example, if you enter into a GSA with even a little less equity stake—say, 49 percent—you lose managerial control. You may end up with that equity percentage because the host government only allows up to 49 percent for an outsider, because you could only negotiate that amount, or because you were willing to accept a minority stake in exchange for gains (e.g., responsibility for R&D) that you thought important during the negotiation phase. Whatever the reason, what are you going to do if profits plummet, product quality deteriorates, or customers are dissatisfied? You do not have enough interest in the venture to take action. Your 49 percent can swiftly depreciate when it comes to exercising any control. In any partnership, the majority-interest holder tends to dominate, putting its needs first and its partner's last. The ideal situation is a fifty-fifty partnership, which allows both parties to share the decision-making. If you do settle for a minority interest, make sure you maintain enough control to accomplish your objectives in the target market.

■ **Caution**   There are always exceptions to the fifty-fifty partnership being the ideal scenario. In the United States, for example, there can be advantages to a business having 51 percent ownership by women, minorities, or service-disabled veteran-owned firms. This can be used to gain contracts or preferential treatment in the marketplace. The Small Business Administration, for example, offers many special programs and services to help these designated groups who have 51 percent or more stock ownership succeed.[viii]

It's also critical to explore all the legal and financial implications before entering into an alliance with an overseas company. Seek legal counsel from those who are well experienced in international trade, acquisitions, joint ventures, and divestitures and ask them to go over the best- and worst-case scenarios with you. You should hire counsel both in your own country and in the host country for maximum protection of your rights. You are not only seeking to ensure the fundamental integrity of the partnership, but also to work out crucial entitlements and obligations, such as copyrights, trademarks, patents, taxes, antitrust, and exchange controls.

You will also need to keep informed about the host country's political and economic stability. Get in touch with the local economic development offices within that country. They should be able to assess the country's future investment climate and to provide you with past, present, and future growth trends. This will give you a better idea of what kind of risks you will incur, if any, if you go ahead with the alliance.

As an exporter, it's only a matter of time before you consider a GSA as a logical step in expanding your business. It's not enough to expand domestically; that is not an exporter's core business. Your core business is the world. Up until now, you may have single-handedly cemented strategic alliances with a network of agents and distributors to maintain access to markets worldwide, but you are currently finding that this is no longer enough to remain competitive. You may feel that you've gotten about as far as you can on your own and want to explore alternatives for kicking your export business into high gear. You're prepared to exchange a limited measure of creative control if it will get you established in highly lucrative new business territories.

So you've decided to create a GSA. Now what?

Negotiating a Deal for the GSA

In negotiating a deal for a GSA, your main concern should be that you and the other party share the same goals and see the deal-making process in the same light. The knowledge and experience each partner brings to the table should complement a firm's core knowledge base and provide the underlying basis for mutual learning.

During the initial phase of negotiations, rather than discussing an agreement point by point, you might be better off outlining in draft form how you would like the joint venture to work. This keeps the draft-in-progress simple and provides a tangible way for the other side to see your ideas. Then expand on each point in your outline and make sure that each party understands the objectives and implications. You can accomplish this by presenting each issue in draft form and having a representative from each side write a synopsis of her understanding of it. If there are any discrepancies or disagreements, you can clear them up at this point, prior to putting together a final draft agreement.

After you submit your draft, it's up to the other party to make a counterproposal that sets out its own conceptual framework for a GSA. This method allows for shared control of negotiations and gives the parties an opportunity to offer alternate ways of setting up the venture. With each proposal and counterproposal, the parties will narrow the gap and come closer to a viable agreement.

Retaining Autonomy and Independence

A good GSA allows for both parties to retain a fair degree of autonomy and independence with minimal restrictions on complementary business opportunities. Ideally, the two parties will form a whole that equals more than the sum of its parts. So, it's important to spend a significant amount of time getting to know the party with which you are considering joining forces.

Problems usually occur when there is poor communication between parties or when there is a staggering difference in strengths and management philosophies. Without a clear-cut mission statement that clarifies goals or objectives from the beginning, things can take a disastrous turn when business gets well underway. For example, it might initially seem that an alliance between a company that has a stronger management team and one with a weaker one offers enormous opportunities for the weaker partner, but in the long run it turns out that the weaker party becomes a drain on resources, forcing the stronger management team to carry the entire weight of the alliance. In the end, the strong partner buys out the weaker one. It's a no-win situation.

To have a reasonable chance of success, the merging parties should both have six vital elements: (1) good communication skills, (2) matching corporate cultures or at least awareness of cultural incompatibility, (3) matching corporate philosophies and commitments, (4) accurate capability and contribution assessment, (5) credibility as a good partner, and (6) compatible strategic ambitions. If you do not see these elements operating during the time of negotiations, you never will. Cut your losses and look for a more compatible partner.

Considering the GSA: What Can We Learn?

Before you decide to enter into a GSA, make an excruciatingly honest appraisal of your own goals, strengths, and limitations. Determining at the outset if you're really ready to form an alliance or not and what you can realistically expect to accomplish will save you losses down the road. Appraise your potential partner just as carefully. And remember, no two deals are alike; the final structure of any alliance depends on what each party has to offer the other and what each hopes to gain.

Expect cultural factors to complicate the smooth running of business. For instance, if your partner-to-be behaves in a way you experience as flat out weird in that it goes against the grain of your own culture, or they take forever to get back to you, factor that in and consider it very carefully while you are reviewing the upside and downside of the deal. This odd behavior could mean trouble waiting to happen. Picture yourself living with the alliance you've made for a long, long time. Make sure you can live with your partner before you sign on the dotted line.

As a longtime independent businessperson, you might approach such an arrangement with ambivalent feelings and dread the potential headaches of working out all the details. But if the arrangement is structured properly, thoughtfully, and equitably, a GSA can pay off handsomely for both parties in terms of greater growth, higher profits, and excellence in export business. I recommend that you review and consider all the options I have talked about and then harness your newfound skills and direct your efforts exactly as you see fit.

Joint Venture

Just as GSAs allow companies with complementary skills to benefit from one another's strengths, a joint venture can do the same. When two companies invest money into forming a third jointly owned enterprise, that new enterprise is called a joint venture. For a joint venture to work, there should be a nice give-and-take, a codependency, or a shared management arrangement. The joint venture can receive market knowledge (customer and distribution, for example), assets, and financing from both parent companies without altering the condition of the parent company. The new venture is an ongoing enterprise whereby the parent companies—"parents"—own the joint venture and share in the profits (or losses) it generates.

A joint venture spells out a defined project that each of the respective parties involved agrees to and carries out. Again, I repeat: Not only do the parties share in the venture's profits, but they also share in the losses. Each parent company has an equal voice in controlling the project, which means there is more than one parent. Oftentimes they each can be powerful and visible.[ix]

Tip Oracle founder Larry Ellison purchased the Hawaiian island of Lanai. He was cited in an interview in the *Wall Street Journal*, saying, "We have the right climate and soil to grow the very best gourmet mangos and pineapples on the planet and export them year-round to Asia and North America. We can grow and export flowers and make perfume the old-fashioned way—directly from the flowers, like they do in Grasse, France. We have an ideal location for a couple of organic wineries on the island."[x] The big question is this: Should Ellison do this on his own or elect to go the sales collaboration route and negotiate with Dole on the pineapple side and Chanel or Estée Lauder on the perfume side? If Ellison is eager to get to market and doesn't mind giving up a piece of the action, collaborating with other companies who have been there, done that will speed up the process. If not, he can launch on his own, take as much time as he wants and reap 100 percent of the rewards. Knowing Ellison, I think he will go it alone. It'll be fun to watch his progress.

One illustration of how a joint venture might work would be a situation in which you currently export a ton of stuff to a particular overseas market. The importer asks you if he can make the product in his market and reexport to other contiguous markets. That's how the seed is planted. You form a joint venture, and that newly formed enterprise spells out intent, and it starts to service customers in other parts of the world. You continue exporting to the importer, but he has a new obligation or role and vested interest, as you do, in the success of the newly formed organization.

Tip Two classic articles on the subject of joint ventures worth a read are: "How to Make a Global Joint Venture Work," by J. Peter Killing (*Harvard Business Review*, May 1982, `http://hbr.org/1982/05/how-to-make-a-global-joint-venture-work/ar/1`), and "Launching a World-Class Joint Venture" by James Bamford, David Ernst, and David G. Fubini (*Harvard Business Review*, February 2004, `http://hbr.org/2004/02/launching-a-world-class-joint-venture/ar/1`).

International Franchising

International franchising is a strategic way to reduce dependence on domestic demand and grow new future revenue and profit centers worldwide. Extending a brand globally through franchising involves a lower risk than doing it through more hands-on exporting, requires minimal investment, and offers a huge upside potential on scaling capabilities. Let's look at what international franchising is, its benefits, examples of companies that have successfully franchised internationally, how to get started in franchising, and where to look for additional help.

What Is International Franchising?

Franchising is a pooling of resources and capabilities to accomplish a strategic marketing, distribution, and sales goal for a company. It typically involves a franchisor—potentially you—granting an individual or company (the franchisee) the right to run a business or sell a product or service under its successful business model and giving the other party the right to be identified by its trademark or brand.

The franchisor charges an initial up-front fee to the franchisee, payable upon the signing of the franchise agreement. Other fees, such as marketing, advertising, or royalties, may be applicable, and are largely based on how the contract is negotiated and set up. Advertising, training, and other support services are made available by the franchisor.

Benefits of International Franchising

In addition to entering new overseas markets with additional customers, international franchising can also offer franchisors the opportunity to use what are called foreign-master owners, rather than franchisees. These individuals are typically natives of the country and understand the political and bureaucratic problems in their country far better than any outsider. Foreign master franchise owners pay a hefty up-front fee to acquire a designated geographic area or, in some instances, an entire country, where they operate as a mini- or sub-franchise company, selling franchises, collecting royalties, training the owners, and overseeing all other related matters. They can even open units by themselves. In general, a specified number of franchises must be outlined to gain the exclusive right to use the business model in an entire country.

Examples of Successful International Franchising

Domino's Pizza International began serving consumers outside the United States in 1983 when the first store opened in Winnipeg, Canada. Since that time, Domino's Pizza International has extended its global reach to include more than seventy international markets, serviced by more than 10,000 corporate and franchised stores.

The company claims, "The success of Domino's Pizza outside the U.S. is due to the collaborative relationship between our exceptional franchisees and the corporate team that supports them. Together, we continuously strive to support a policy of 'One Brand—One System' in order to be the best pizza delivery company in the world."[xi]

Another fast-food giant, McDonald's, does business in 118 countries around the world. For those countries where McDonald's does not already have a presence (Afghanistan, for example), the company does not have any firm plans to open locations. The company says it is instead focusing on the markets where it already has a presence.[xii]

Many of these companies weren't huge when they started their overseas operations, yet little acorns grow into mighty oaks. A friend and colleague of mine, Shelly Sun, CEO and cofounder of Illinois-based BrightStar, has visions of having her company follow such a path: The company was established in 2002 as a full-service health care staffing agency serving corporate and private clients. Sun has big plans to use the franchise model to take her company international. Currently, her firm generates $350 million annually and has more than 300 locations throughout the United States and Canada, and she has plans to expand it further within Canada as well as to the UAE and Australia in 2016. She wants to first make sure she has a solid base of franchisees and an equally solid basis of royalties coming in before going global. "If we had expanded internationally prior to 2012, we would not have had the resources to invest in the high level of support, which we believe is indispensable in a successful international expansion strategy," says Sun. Future growth will occur in the United Kingdom and Asia.[xiii]

Getting Started in International Franchising

The best place to find out how to get started is the International Franchise Association (http://www.franchise.org). It can help you with the first steps to take and tell you what opportunities are available in the global marketplace. As in any new international expansion, there will be challenges: cultural differences, legal considerations, contract negotiations, and intellectual property issues, to name just a few. For a snapshot on what is involved, see the article "Dealing with the Complexities of International Expansion."[xiv]

Tip For information on preparing your franchise to go global, such as choosing a deal structure for international franchise expansion, and negotiating an international franchise agreement, visit the International Franchise Association's International Toolkit Courses: http://www.franchise. org/InternationalToolkit.

Where to Look for Franchising Help

Here are a couple of resources that will guide you in the international franchising area:

1. *International Franchise Association:* (http://www.franchise.org/). This site is considered the go-to source on anything to do with franchising—from country profiles to international franchising articles and information on international franchising laws.

2. *Franchising World:* (http://www.franchise.org/franchising-world-digital-version). The International Franchising Association site offers digital versions of current Franchising World issues and archives of past articles.

3. *3. DLA Piper's FranCast Series:* (https://www.dlapiper.com/en/us/insights/publicationseries/francast/). The FranCast Series is put out by DLA Piper. DLA Piper is considered the number one global law firm in the area of franchise law by *Who's Who Legal* and is ranked the top practice in the United States by the respected research firm Chambers & Partners.

4. *Grow Smart, Risk Less: A Low-Capital Path to Multiplying Your Business Through Franchising*: Written by Shelly Sun, this book provides a road map to guide you in franchising your business.

5. *International Franchising: A Practitioner's Guide*: Written by Marco Hero, this book is a practical guide for all those involved in planning and operating an international franchise program, describing a range of topics from in-house counsel, to managing directors, to those in private practice.

For other book selections on franchising, try the IFA Publications and Book Store: `http://www.franchise.org/ifa-publications-and-book-store`

Establishing a Foreign Office or Acquiring an Existing Company

When companies want to quickly gain access to markets or a new area of expertise (technology, for example), they usually form a partnership or GSA. They can also open a foreign office or acquire a smaller company with those assets in the targeted market.

To maintain better control of your exports, you can establish a foreign branch office, subsidiary, or joint venture, in which you make the decisions and staff it with local people who receive the imported goods (your exports) and see that they are properly distributed to the intended customers and serviced thereafter.

The advantage of this type of arrangement is that the branch office can serve both as the initial link in the marketing channel in the foreign market and can facilitate customer loyalty for the brand. The biggest disadvantage is that you have higher setup costs and the potential for higher credit risks at the beginning stages of operation.

Acquiring a smaller company, on the other hand, offers a faster start in exploiting an overseas market and might avoid getting a trade restriction (which blocks an export or makes it cost prohibitive to sell a product at a profit) but tends to be a much more expensive undertaking for the acquiring company—one that is likely to be well out of the reach of a smaller enterprise.

Due to uncontrollable economic factors, many companies can be forced into establishing a foreign branch office if they want to maintain a market presence. This often happens when companies are doing well with their exports in a foreign market, only to discover later on that the government has raised the tariff on their particular commodity from 20 percent to 70 percent. As a result, they must decide to either stay in the market, take the hit, and hope for the best—thereby remaining competitive—or beat the system by acquiring a company in the foreign market that can make and distribute the product, in which case they will enjoy a definite cost advantage by eliminating the tariff. Obviously a lot depends on competition (if you are the only one in a market, you might be able to sustain the tariff increase), customer demand, funding, human resource capability, and long-term outlook.

Whatever route you take, keeping track of regulations that constantly change, not to mention having the experience needed to run an operation and distribute products through the distribution chain, can be complicated. Before you consider this option, check with your international attorney and tax accountant. Make sure the opportunity you see or anticipate justifies the investment.

With ever-changing compliance issues and new country alerts appearing frequently, you will need to be kept informed of issues that can impact your overseas operations. Will your office staff handle this, or will you need to appoint an outside person to manage the foreign operation? This is sometimes necessary because seemingly routine tasks, such as issuing payroll or taking care of back-office mail and supplies, can absorb huge amounts of time, particularly when dealing with different time zones, multiple languages, and a wide variety of service providers.

Take into consideration these ten points before establishing an office overseas:

1. Who are your core customers?

2. Where is your best talent pool located?

3. Is the market attractive enough?

4. What are the legal structure, especially as it pertains to establishing a business entity, and regulatory climate of the other country like?

5. Are there any legal restrictions on foreign investment in the target sector?

6. What are the preliminary tax consequences?

7. Is there any intellectual property (IP) protection strategy in place?

8. Should you consider locating your business in a free trade zone area (refer to Chapter 3)?

9. How will cultural differences impact your enterprise?

10. Do you speak the language?

Licensing

Where laws prohibit the establishment of a foreign branch office, subsidiary, or joint venture, licensing can prove useful to an exporter. Licensing is different from obtaining an export license, which is covered in Chapter 22.

Licensing is a contractual arrangement where the firm—the licensor—offers some proprietary assets (a trademark, a patent, marketing know-how, technology, or an established production process, for example) to a foreign company—the licensee—in exchange for royalty fees or other kinds of payments. The licensing agreement can be long term or on a per-project basis.

Companies like HP[xv] and Oracle[xvi] license some of their software technology to companies in other parts of the world to jointly create better products, speed up time-to-market, and generate lucrative royalties fees. To allow customers to legally use its images for their projects, Getty Images licenses its stock photos, illustrations, and archival images to individuals and companies worldwide.[xvii]

Royalty fees for licensing can range anywhere from one-eighth of 1 percent of the gross-sales revenue stream to 15 percent or greater. Before you sign on the dotted line, consider these factors: you must account for currency conversion, how royalties will be paid, geographic jurisdiction, what taxes might be applied, and how progress will be monitored and audited.

Licensing can be very beneficial to small companies that lack the resources to invest in foreign facilities. Compared to exporting, licensing can also offer an entry mode that requires a low commitment of capital and allows you to navigate around import barriers while still providing you with access to markets quickly that might otherwise be closed to imports.

As in all modes of entry into the market, there can be risks with licensing. The biggest one I see is—as the licensor—serving as a feeder to a potential future competitor. Once an agreement expires, the licensee can run with your idea. That brings us to—once again—the ever-important issue of consulting with your international attorney about how to protect yourself against the risks of licensing arrangements. When evaluating prospective licensees, look at the list of characteristics to look for in distributors and the list of questions to ask them that follows, provided in Chapter 16.

Summary

When all is said and done, the best strategy for export market expansion is one that makes you feel like you have the whole world in your hands. Although most companies begin their foray into foreign markets through exporting, the best long-term global-market entry strategy is a diverse one—employing direct, indirect, and collaborative initiatives—to ensure you don't rely on one single channel for export growth. The collaborative initiatives we've looked at in this chapter are options to be considered along with, or in addition to, direct and indirect exporting.

Once you've decided what type of exporting method you are going to use, you must figure out how to put the deal together and make the export sale happen. Next, I'll show you how to choose safe, prompt, and cost-effective transport; arrive at an appropriate price-per-product unit; and work with a freight forwarder to prepare your final quotation. Read through these next two chapters carefully and refer back to them often. You want to be on top of all the information you'll need at each stage of the process.

Notes

i. "Managing Differences: The Central Challenge of Global Strategy," Pankaj Ghemawat, *Harvard Business Review*, March 2007 `http://hbr.org/2007/03/managing-differences-the-central-challenge-of-global-strategy/ar/1`.

ii. "Distance Still Matters: The Hard Reality of Global Expansion," Pankaj Ghemawat, *Harvard Business Review*, September 2001, `http://hbr.org/2001/09/distance-still-matters-the-hard-reality-of-global-expansion/ar/1`.

iii. `http://www.starbucks.com/business/international-stores`.

iv. "Examples of Successful Strategic Alliances," Je' Czaja, *Chron*, accessed October 27, 2013, http://smallbusiness.chron.com/examples-successful-strategic-alliances-13859.html.

v. http://www.fool.com/investing/general/2016/04/16/microsoft-and-starbucks-are-finally-working-togeth.aspx.

vi. "Nokia and Intuit Form Global Alliance to Create Mobile Marketing Services to Small Businesses," Intuit: Press Releases, September 15, 2010, http://about.intuit.com/about_intuit/press_room/press_release/articles/2010/NokiaAndIntuitFormGlobalAlliance.html.

vii. "Shipping Lines Take New Global Alliance to Regulators," Costas Paris, The Wall Street Journal, accessed May 1, 2016, http://www.wsj.com/articles/shipping-lines-take-new-global-alliance-to-regulators-1461100105.

viii. "Woman Owned, SDVOSB, and Minority Owned: Are Business Designations Necessary?," SBA.gov, accessed May 1, 2016, https://www.sba.gov/blogs/woman-owned-sdvosb-and-minority-owned-are-business-designations-necessary.

ix. See "How to Make a Global Joint Venture Work," J. Peter Killing, *Harvard Business Review*, May 1982, http://hbr.org/1982/05/how-to-make-a-global-joint-venture-work/ar/4.

x. "Larry Ellison's Fantasy Island," Julian Guthrie, *Wall Street Journal*, June 13, 2013, http://online.wsj.com/article/SB10001424127887324798904578529682230185530.html.

xi. "International Franchising With Domino's," biz-dominos.com, accessed May 1, 2016, ,https://biz.dominos.com/web/public/international/international-franchising.

xii. "International Franchising," the About McDonald's Web site, accessed October 27, 2013, http://www.about-mcdonalds.com/mcd/franchising/international_franchising.html.

xiii. Shelly Sun, CEO and co-founder, BrightStar, email exchange April 25, 2016.

xiv. "Dealing with the Complexities of International Expansion," Bachir Mihoubi, International Franchising Association, published in *Franchising World*, March 2011, http://www.franchise.org/Franchise-Industry-News-Detail.aspx?id=53325.

xv. "HP Intellectual Property Licensing," HP, accessed May 1, 2016, http://www.hp.com/hpinfo/abouthp/iplicensing/.

xvi. "Global Pricing and Licensing," accessed May 1, 2016, http://www.oracle.com/us/corporate/pricing/index.html.

xvii. "License Agreements," gettyimages, accessed May 1, 2016, http://www.gettyimages.com/Corporate/LicenseAgreements.aspx.

Managing the Transaction

Transport, Logistics, and Fulfillment Options

The number one thing you can do is figure out how to ship to people globally.

> —Joanne Bethlamy, former director, Cisco Internet Business Solutions Group[i]

The container is at the core of a highly automated system for moving goods from anywhere, to anywhere, with a minimum of cost and complication on the way. The container made shipping cheap, and by doing so changed the shape of the world economy.

> —Marc Levinson, author, *The Box: How the Shipping Container Made the World Smaller and the World Economy Bigger*[ii]

© Laurel J. Delaney 2016
L. J. Delaney, *Exporting*, DOI 10.1007/978-1-4842-2193-8_18

People have been trading with each other, between countries, across roads and oceans, for thousands of years. According to the International Maritime Organization, "We live in a global society which is supported by a global economy—and that economy simply could not function if it were not for ships and the shipping industry. Shipping is truly the lynchpin of the global economy: without shipping, intercontinental trade, the bulk transport of raw materials and the import/export of affordable food and manufactured goods would simply not be possible."[iii] Since export shipment involves moving goods from one country to another—a somewhat riskier and more complicated enterprise than domestic shipments—it is extra important to find a company that offers safe, reliable, quick, and cost-effective transport services.

In this chapter, I discuss a range of air and ocean transport choices (containerized shipments, for example), including special state-of-the-art vehicles for cargo with special handling requirements, and a variety of methods for loading your export shipment. In addition, I'll introduce you to global freight forwarders, logistics specialists, and third-party logistic providers (3PLs)—the all-around experts who will become an indispensable part of your export transport operation.

The quantity, value, and perishability of your product; your customer's location; how fast the shipment is needed; and how much you are willing to spend will determine which method of transportation you should use. Oftentimes, a compromise among these factors takes place. Product movement between neighboring countries, such as the United States and Canada, is relatively simple and economical, and you can always ship overland by road, by conventional rail, or by double-stacked trains, whichever your customer prefers. Product movement over water is somewhat more complicated and expensive. Accordingly, I'll focus on air and ocean shipping options. I'll also take a look at third-party logistics providers that support e-commerce sales.

SHIPPING HAZARDOUS MATERIALS OR GOODS

Always remember that if you are shipping hazardous materials or goods, such as products packaged in aerosol cans or containing dry ice, you must notify your transportation company. This type of shipment requires special transit treatment and is carefully regulated by the US Department of Transportation under the US Code of Federal Regulations, Title 49. These regulations determine which products may or may not be transported via air and offer guidelines for preparing the product for safe export. Whether shipped by air or ocean, hazardous goods must be properly certified, marked, and labeled and must be packed and handled with appropriate care. Should your transport company, freight forwarder, or 3PL provider be unable to guide you through the process of shipping a hazardous product, contact the US Department of Transportation (DOT) or International Air Transportation Association (IATA), or conduct a Google or Bing search with the keywords "Shipping hazardous material internationally" to obtain more information.

Air Transport

Shipping by air used to be an emergency strategy, used only when a customer needed a product immediately, but with the proliferation of international air delivery services such as Federal Express, DHL, UPS, and soon to be Amazon, it is now easy and economical to move your product around the world, even overnight. You'll generally pay a higher price per kilo than you will for ocean shipment, but in some expense categories you'll actually rack up some savings. For example, packing costs tend to run less for air transport. One major consideration is the weight of your cargo. Are you exporting feathers? If so, air transport would be cheaper, provided you don't use cartons that take up a lot of space. Tractors, on the other hand, should be transported via ocean.

If exporting highly perishable items is your business, you'll want to familiarize yourself with carriers that offer affordable worldwide express shipments of chilled, frozen, and fresh foods, such as seafood, meats, and produce. You will see more and more demand for this service as the market for organic, fresh, and convenience foods expands. I suggest you call the US Department of Agriculture's international marketing office for additional help. It usually has directories, workbooks, and guides to assist exporters of highly perishable products.

The International Air Transport Association (IATA; http://www.iata.org) represents 260 airlines worldwide and more than 400 strategic partners. When these members reach agreement on a fixed rate, they file a tariff with the US Department of Transportation (DOT; http://www.dot.gov). Tariffs define the rate, rules, and regulations governing air cargo deliveries for a given carrier or conference. Only when an exporter is charged by a shipper a cost that is beyond the maximum amount specified in the tariff (unless it is under a service contract) will she need to notify a regulatory agency to complain.

There are two major types of equipment used in air transport:

1. *Air cargo containers*: These types of containers are loaded by hand or forklift. They come in more than a dozen different styles and sizes.

2. *Air cargo pallets made of wood or plastic (corrugated plastic is used but not recommended) with netting*: These are also loaded by hand or forklift.

Which type of equipment you use depends on the type and quantity of the cargo you are shipping. To determine the absolute best way to ship your cargo, always discuss your situation with your transportation company. And don't forget to find out the distance from your customer's door to the closest seaport or airport. If one delivery destination is closer than the other, you'll save your customer time but not necessarily money in the case of shipping to the nearest airport, because air cargo can be expensive.

The top two considerations when choosing air vs. sea freight are transit time and the cargo itself. It usually takes a product a couple of days to arrive by air, whereas sea freight takes anywhere from twelve to fourteen days. The cargo itself, whether delicate in nature (fine art, for example) or large in size (as is heavy equipment), forces you to make the best decision for your cargo shipment.

■ **Caution** Always check with your shipping specialist to verify the pallet requirements for your destination country. Some countries, for example, require certain types of wood packaging to be treated with chemicals or heat before being allowed into their country.

Ocean Transport

Shipping by ocean takes much longer than shipping by air, but it is nearly always much less expensive. That is why it will generally be your overseas customers' preferred method of transport. Whereas with air shipment, the greater the volume of your shipment, the more expensive it becomes, with ocean shipment a greater volume of shipment actually decreases the cost. Ocean transport is less simple, though, because it involves many more choices that you may know very little about. These include the choice between terminals, vessel types, container loading options, and so forth. You'll have to rely on your transport company to give you advice.

When choosing a transport company, you'll want to find out the following:

1. The frequency that the vessels sail
2. The transit times
3. The reliability measures
4. The ports served by the steamship line
5. The company's safety record
6. The computerization for cargo management

The last point, computerized cargo management, is vital these days. You want to be able to track your cargo at any given point. If it gets lost, you want to know that the transport company can find it. Cargo management is an important part of the package you offer your customers, so anytime you find a new and better way to serve them in terms of cargo, jump on it.

Shopping for an Economical Transport Package

Shipping lines—whose vessels are still commonly referred to as "steamships" although the days of steam-powered shipping are long gone—can be classified as either independent or conference. Independent lines tend not to have as many ports of call, which can cause shipping delays. Sometimes, while comparison shopping, you will find an independent line that quotes you a rate that is cheaper than what the conference lines are offering. However, when using an independent line, you can't be sure of your shipper's timeliness or reliability.

Conference lines, on the other hand, guarantee similar standards and rates. If you can contract with a conference line on an exclusive basis, rates are usually cheaper than, or at least competitive with, those offered by an independent line. The guarantee on rates during a specified period of time is a savings that you can then pass on to your customer or use to pad your own profit margin. Other types of ocean transport companies that have evolved over the years are NVOCCs, or non-vessel-operating common carriers, and shipper's associations. NVOCCs book space on vessels and then sell the space to shippers with smaller cargoes in smaller-volume units. They consolidate these smaller shipments into container-loads under one bill of lading, and as a result can pass on more favorable rates to the small cargo shipper. You can also take advantage of a larger shipper's economies of scale to move your smaller loads more cheaply. Shipper's associations, similarly, were formed to pull together several different shippers' cargoes to achieve greater volume and hence lower rates.

Don't forget that ocean and air shipping itself is only part of the transport package you'll need to assemble. To get your product to an ocean-going vessel for loading, you must also transport your cargo overland by truck or rail. How do you do this without spending an arm and a leg? The most advanced and efficient transport mode currently available to exporters to handle this problem is intermodal transportation. This is a start-to-finish transport package that takes your cargo from its point of origin to its point of destination (commonly described as "door-to-door") under a single bill of lading. It involves the use of at least two different transportation modes—rail and ocean, for example—to cover the overland and overseas movement of the cargo. The company that offers the package is liable for getting the cargo from the point of origin to the final destination, and it will charge you a "through rate" to do so. The rate represents a substantial savings over what it would cost you to engage separate carriers for each leg of the trip. An added bonus: The company can issue a computer-generated bill of lading within hours of the cargo's receipt at an inland terminal or immediately after the vessel has left port. This means faster turnaround time in collecting payment from your customer. Some intermodal service packages also offer container freight stations, which save you time and drayage (local transportation) costs by bringing their service closer to your door.

■ **Tip**   With the Internet and the advent of e-commerce sales transactions for B-to-C transactions, most international carriers and third-party logistics providers now offer all-inclusive door-to-door landed costs (meaning they include the price of the product, the delivery charge, taxes, duties, customs, all in a currency your shoppers understand) on single-product shipments delivered to a consumer. In 2009, this was unheard of. What a difference seven years makes!

If you are an exporter of refrigerated commodities, most sophisticated transportation companies can offer cost-efficient transport via refrigerated vehicles. For example, there are railcars equipped with individual generators to ensure the preservation of perishable products during transit. Some companies offer what is called a "motorbridge" (trucking) service to exporters of frozen meat and other perishables, which entails a through transportation rate from the producer's door to the customer's door. Other companies offer multipurpose vessels for more cost-effective shipment of noncontainerized cargo, such as tin, tea, equipment, and grain. These vessels are usually smaller in size than those found in a regular containerized ship, allowing them to travel safely through rough seas and narrow channels. They also make the difficult portside dockings at newly industrialized countries easier.

It's imperative to shop around and compare rates to get the best possible transportation package for your customer. Don't be shy about questioning a transportation company or freight forwarder at length and in great detail about its service and rates. That is what it is there for, and you don't owe them anything until after you've hired them. Always inquire about the latest and most advanced methods for moving goods overseas. Even as you read this, improvements are underway. Keeping current with the transportation industry will help you offer your customers the most innovative and cost-effective service and equipment options.

Break-Bulk and Container Loading

What kind of vessel you choose to ship your cargo, and what special handling, loading or storage apparatus, if any, should be used, will depend on the type and quantity of your goods. Here are a variety of common options and techniques for loading your shipment.

Break-Bulk

Better known as less-than-container-load, or LTL shipment, break-bulk shipment is the most likely option to be used by new exporters, whose first orders are likely to be small. It allows your customer to test the product in his market before committing to a large quantity, such as a full container-load or more. The shipper can still load the goods into a container, but the container will be delivered to a consolidation point (port of exit) where other shippers' goods will also be stowed in the container. The advantage of this method is that it allows smaller, low-volume exporters to have their cargo containerized, although it is not as desirable as a sealed door-to-door container, as I will discuss.

To control the expense of small-quantity shipment, find a transport company that specializes in break-bulk. Naturally, when you are shipping a small trial order and hoping for repeat business, it will be to your advantage to control your customer's costs by offering them the best rate possible. When shipping LTL, you'll need to take extra care in packing and marking your cartons. (I'll discuss carton marking in greater detail later.) Break-bulk shipments are commonly packed using the following materials:

- *Pallets:* Wood pallets must be strong enough to be stacked on racks and reused numerous times. *Never* let your cartons overhang a pallet. Your whole load might collapse! As previously mentioned, some countries require certain types of wood pallets to be treated with chemicals or heat before allowing the shipment to cross its borders. Check with your transportation specialist.

- *Slipsheets:* Used to pull your cargo to the point of loading, these sheets are usually made of fiberboard or plastic. They must be strong enough for the forklift operator to clamp onto and pull. Slipsheets cost less than pallets and eliminate the expense of transporting pallets back to the shipper for reuse. Cartons placed on slipsheets must be cross stacked, shrink-wrapped, or secured with extra-strength strapping.

- *Crates:* Wood crates are still popular with some shippers due to their strength and resistance to humidity, at any temperature and at any point in transit.

All onboard packing aids should be recyclable or reusable. Use the minimum amount of material necessary to protect your product. Pallets, slipsheets, and crates are loaded using the following methods:

- Bulk loading by machine or hand (for bulk commodities, for example)

- Hand loading using individual shipping containers, with or without pallets

- Unit loading using palleted or slipsheet stacks into containers with forklifts

Container Loading

Shipment by container-load continues to be the preferred method for exporting goods because each container is sealed (allowing it to stay closed from the factory door to the customer's door), strong, theft resistant, and stackable. Containers are also easy to load and unload; transport by truck, rail, or ship; and store. The only time the container may be opened while in transit is for the customer's inspection, so the transport of the goods becomes nearly bulletproof concerning safety and pilferage issues.

> *"It's a simple steel box, but it revolutionized trade and made globalization possible. Today, around 95 percent of goods transported around the world see the inside of a shipping container at some point."*[iv]

■ **Note** According to Journal of Commerce senior editor Joseph Bonney, US containerized exports are to rebound in 2016. "Although global economic growth is expected to increase in 2016 and China's growth remains strong by world standards, China's double-digit growth appears unlikely to return soon. Eleven of the 12 economists surveyed by Bloomberg last week said they expect China's economic growth to continue to decelerate at least through 2018."[v]

Containers are available in various volumes and in a number of specialized constructions to accommodate various cargo types. Typically, shipping companies provide containers, but you can also rent or buy them new or used. If you want to do so, try eBay, contact a local shipping company to inquire about used shipping containers, or contact the Container Alliance (http://www.containeralliance.com/), a network of portable storage and shipping container providers.

A container can cost anywhere from $1,500 (used) to $8,000 (new). Rental costs range from $75 to $295 per month. You can also expect to pay delivery and pickup charges on any of these scenarios. The twenty-foot container, the most popular volume, works well for starting up with exports. The forty-foot container is the second most popular choice. It's important to resist the temptation to overload this larger container or you won't be able to move your cargo over land! For large loads, a forty-five-foot container is an attractive bargain because it gives you a 27 percent increase in interior capacity over the forty-foot unit for the same handling costs. Containers come as large as forty-eight feet, but these are comparatively rare.

Just as you conducted market research on where the best market is for your product using a variety of sources, keeping track of where all your exports are going provides a good basis for asking yourself, "Should we be looking at these markets since there are so many containers going to that part of the world?" Take *The Journal of Commerce's* annual ranking of the top fifty world container ports for 2014.[vi] Here is a snapshot of the top ten container ports, which shows heavy concentration in China (Asia):

1. Shanghai, China

2. Singapore, Singapore

3. Shenzhen, China

4. Hong Kong, China

5. Ningbo-Zhoushan, China

6. Busan, South Korea

7. Qingdao, China

8. Guangzhou Harbor, China

9. Jebel Ali, Dubai

10. Tianjin, China

The port of Shanghai handled 35.29 million twenty-foot-equivalent container units, and is considered the busiest container port in the world in 2014[vii].

High-cube containers (referred to as HQ; they include twenty-foot, forty-foot, and other measurements) are oftentimes shipped at the same rate as a standard container but offer more cargo space and are typically one foot taller. Garment containers have a movable track system, so that prepressed and prelabeled garments can be shipped on their individual hangers, unloaded, moved right into a showroom, and racked for sale. Open-top containers, designed for awkward, oversize goods, such as heavy equipment, can be loaded from the top by crane. This reduces handling costs. Refrigerated containers come in high-cube and wide-body dimensions and offer temperature-controlled environments that can be monitored by means of an exterior temperature recorder, a central shipboard control, or even satellite transmission. Bulk-hatch containers, used for commodities such as corn and grains, can be loaded from the top or the rear for easy access and minimal handling. Vented containers allow for appropriate ventilation and thus eliminate potential condensation, preventing damage to moisture-sensitive goods like tobacco, spices, and coffee. Flat-rack containers, designed for moving huge goods, such as heavy equipment, lumber, and pipes, can be loaded from the top or the side, thus reducing handling costs. An expandable chassis accommodates a variety of box sizes and allows for easy offloading from ship to train or truck.

■ **Tip** If you are interested in learning more about shipping containers and who invented containerized cargo (hint: an American by the name of Malcolm P. McLean), read the article "The Truck Driver Who Reinvented Shipping,"[viii] and try *The Box: How the Shipping Container Made the World Smaller and the World Economy Bigger,*[ix] by Marc Levinson. Both are fascinating reads!

Having shown you what's entailed in getting your shipment underway, I'd like to introduce you to one of my favorite solutions for the shipping phase: the freight forwarder.

The Global Freight Forwarder: Your One-Stop Transport Pro

Global freight forwarders serve as all-around transport agents for moving export cargo, typically transporting it from a factory door to your customer's warehouse or storage facility. Their service saves you lots of time, effort, and anxiety and is available for a very reasonable fee, usually under US$200 per transaction—an expense that you'll include in your price quotation to your customer and recoup when you collect payment. These are just some of the things a freight forwarder will do for you:

- Handle all shipping arrangements on the basis of your specifications

- Take legal responsibility for the shipment

- Pay up-front costs to move the product

- Arrange for a carrier to arrive at your factory door at a specified date and time

- Book space with transportation carriers

- Handle all documentation and see that it is properly processed

- Arrange insurance, if requested

- Present documents to your bank in a timely fashion to meet your payment terms

- Suggest or make on-the-spot packing adjustments, if needed

- Move the product from the factory door to the port of exit, either by common carrier or rail

- Take responsibility for getting the cargo on the vessel in time to sail on schedule, thus enabling you to meet all the terms and conditions of your payment agreement

- Monitor the shipment from beginning to end and keep you informed throughout

- See to it that the shipment arrives safely at the foreign port of entry and proceeds from there, depending on the delivery terms that you quoted to your customer

If you were to undertake the transit of goods yourself, you would probably be overwhelmed by all these logistics, and you would certainly not achieve the savings that forwarders can, given the networks of service providers that they have in place and the volume and frequency of shipping that they do. You can find freight forwarders by conducting a web search using the keywords "Freight forwarders, international transportation" or you can check for listings in trade magazines or other international directories. You should find hundreds of them. In some instances, they will be categorized by the geographic area they serve, the type of commodity in which they specialize, or the transport modes they offer, such as air or ocean—most forwarders offer both. Pick two or three that seem like a good fit for your product and shipping destination. Some may be located near your office or by an airport or port facility that you expect to use often.

The Kings and Queens of International Shipping: UPS, FedEx, DHL, and TNT

Logistic experts UPS, FedEx, DHL, and TNT have long been considered the best in international shipping. Check with each of these companies in regard to their areas of expertise, including whether they not only ship worldwide, but also handle fulfillment needs and collecting payments from customers worldwide.

- *UPS Global Trade*: http://www.international.ups.com/

- *FedEx Small Business Center*: https://smallbusiness.fedex.com/international

- *DHL*: http://www.dhl.com/en.html

- *TNT*: http://www.tnt.com/express/en_us/site/home.html

■ **Tip** The electronic filing of export information, formerly done with the Shipper's Export Declaration (SED) form, is the system used by US companies to electronically declare exports with the US Census Bureau. The process, now called electronic export information (EEI), is done through what used to be AES*Direct* (http://aesdirect.census.gov/), but has now been transitioned over to Automated Commercial Environment (ACE) (https://www.cbp.gov/trade/automated), and becoming the single window for facilitating the importing and exporting of goods. The filing is required for items valued over $2,500 or on products requiring an export license. Most sophisticated carriers can take care of the electronic filing on your behalf for a small fee and provide options for you to self-file or provide your own company's completed EEI. Check with each international carrier. Refer to Chapter 22 for more information.

Two Freight Startups To Watch For in the Internet Age

A freight forwarder's work touches much of global trade, but what is missing is the integration of new technology, which enables online booking and tracking of cargo shipments. These startup companies are revolutionizing the freight cargo industry and are worth a watch.

1. *Flexport:* http://www.flexport.com
2. *Freightos:* http://www.freightos.com

Third-Party Logistics and Fulfillment Centers

Exporting represents a significant opportunity for online small business retailers. Setting up an e-commerce site automatically puts you in front of a potential 3.4 billion online customers.[x] To service even a fraction of those customers, you've got to get up to speed on how to package and ship your products internationally.

A third-party logistics company (abbreviated 3PL) provides logistics services for part or all of your supply-chain-management functions. They can warehouse, pack, and ship your products to customers all over the world, for example. Some will even produce or procure goods for you. Many of these services can be scaled and customized to your needs.

Further, 3PLs allow you to leverage their industry expertise, achieve volume discounts, and realize other benefits (better carrier rates, for instance). To get up and running, many service providers require you to have a good technology program developer on board to install appropriate applications. Prepare accordingly.

▒ **Note** Typically with a 3PL, you'll need to integrate your e-commerce platform closely with that of the 3PL's provider. Major carriers like UPS and FedEx, for example, offer tools or even application programming interfaces (APIs) that make it possible to calculate the landed cost and integrate shipping tools into your e-commerce platform. Consult with them on how to incorporate their APIs within your existing e-commerce platform.

In Chapter 8, I discussed e-commerce platform providers and challenged you to ask whether your provider can not only calculate the international shipping costs on transactions, but handle the fulfillment part on B-to-C transactions as well. Decisions must be made on who will put your product in a box, label it, insert the appropriate commercial invoice (used as a customs declaration form), calculate shipping charges (including tariffs, duties, and taxes), and ensure the product arrives to a customer's final destination timely, economically, and safely. These are things a 3PL will do for you. It may be worth investigating one or more from the list we will look at to make the fulfillment part of e-commerce easier on yourself and your customers as well.

Third-Party Suppliers

Here is a short list of third-party suppliers (3PLs) who specialize in helping businesses ship internationally and deal with the customs, tariffs, and currency conversions worldwide. The whole point of using 3PLs is to enable you to reach customers globally and take on new customers by using existing technology systems—all without hiring extra employees. Shippers agree that 3PLs provide new and innovative ways to improve logistics effectiveness, and that they are sufficiently agile and flexible to accommodate future business needs and challenges.[xi]

1. *Pitney Bowes: Global Ecommerce*: (http://www.pb.com/ ecommerce/). Pitney Bowes helps you extend your e-commerce all over the world by providing a seamless international checkout process (including the benefit of a landed price calculation on international shipments)—the last step in completing an online transaction and making a sale for your online retail environment. As of June 2015, they also own Borderfree (http://shop.borderfree. com).

2. *UPS: Order Management and Fulfillment:* (http://www.ups.com/content/us/en/resources/techsupport/alliances/application_order.html). With the help of UPS, you can select from a list of approved service providers who integrate UPS technology into their business applications and software solutions. Note: Using these companies might require the assistance of a technology program developer to get the application installed and up and running. Note: UPS also owns cross-border e-commerce shipping specialist i-Parcel (http://www.i-parcel.com).

3. *Amazon Services: Fulfillment by Amazon:* (http://services.amazon.com/fulfillment-by-amazon/benefits.htm). With FBA, you can store your products in Amazon's fulfillment centers and have them picked, packed, and shipped by the company. The company also provides customer service for your products.

4. *Shipwire:* (http://www.shipwire.com/). With warehouses in the United States, Canada, the United Kingdom, The Netherlands, Australia, and Hong Kong, Shipwire will work with your existing order-capture systems, including automating order submission, real-time shipping rates, and inventory status. Shipwire's warehouses process and ship orders typically the same day and are strategically located to reach customers worldwide within a few days. When the company contacts a customer, it determines the best carrier, service, and packaging to get your product to its destination efficiently, while allowing you to control your order, inventory, and supply chain operations across its warehouses.

5. *Bongo International:* (http://www.bongous.com/). Bongo was established to enable consumers worldwide to purchase and receive goods irrespective of their physical location or payment method. The company was acquired by FedEx in 2014. So if customers want to buy something online and the store doesn't accept their preferred international payment method, Bongo will. Membership is free. It focuses on enhancing your cross-border shopping experience and reducing the cost of international transportation. Not quite the supersize of UPS or Amazon, but growing, Bongo International currently services 200,000 international consumers globally through their five distribution centers on each US coast, the UK, Belgium, and Peru.

6. *Fulfillrite*: (http://www.fulfillrite.com/). Fulfillrite's order fulfillment software directly integrates with all major e-commerce shopping carts, including but not limited to: Shopify, BigCommerce, Magento, 3DCart, eBay, Amazon, Paypal, and others. Similar to the other companies listed, upon receipt of your merchandise, Fulfillrite inspects and sorts it. It then enters your merchandise into its system, which you have access to via the web portal. It does the order picking and packing and ships to any international destination via a carrier of your choice: USPS, UPS, FedEx, or DHL Global (Fulfillrite's software is compatible with each of theirs).

7. *Ingram Micro*: (http://www.ingrammicro.com/). IM is a large wholesale distributor that primarily handles technology and is a global leader in IT supply chain, mobile device services, and logistics solutions. I am including it in the list just so you can get a glimpse of who the giants— Apple, Cisco, Hewlett-Packard, Wal-Mart, Amazon, IBM, Lenovo, Microsoft, Samsung, among others—use to distribute and market their technology and mobile products. IM also claims to work with companies of all sizes, in more than 170 countries, that can't afford to manage procurement and distribution.

8. *Speed Commerce*: (http://www.speedcommerce.com/). A recent partnership between Speed FC and Navarre, Speed Commerce provides distribution, third-party logistics, supply chain management, and other related services for North American retailers and their suppliers. It does everything from distribution and sales, to supply chain management, to packaging services.

9. *Mercent*: (http://www.mercent.com/). The company designs e-commerce marketing software for retailers. It does this by providing compelling online e-commerce innovations and technology leadership.

10. *Ally Commerce:* (http://www.allycommerce.com). AC is a complete e-commerce outsourcing solution for branded manufacturers selling direct to consumers. The company provides web design, marketing, pricing, customer service and sales support, warehousing, inventory and order management, fulfillment, and returns management. UPS has an undisclosed amount of investment in AC.

■ **Tip** Some people shy away from putting all their eggs in one basket. In the case of selling, distributing, and marketing your products worldwide, you might want to consider a master logistics provider that does it all. That way, you develop a strong relationship and achieve efficient distribution with fewer touch points (meaning fewer people handling your product), letting you focus on perfecting your sales and marketing methods.

Simple Methods to Improve Logistics and Boost Sales

There are a few other factors to consider before getting started with international carriers or 3PLs. Here are some steps you can take to improve your international e-commerce results:

1. *Comparison shop between carriers and the various carrier-shipping-fulfillment options.* Saving even pennies on each package you ship internationally can save you big bucks later on, and those savings can boost your bottom line. Use various online calculators (USPS, UPS, or FedEx, for instance) to get an idea of what it might cost to send your package to China as an example of the costs.

2. *Audit your shipping and fulfillments costs quarterly.* See if you are making or losing money. If you are losing money, switch carriers or take an entirely new approach toward the product you are exporting, the market you are entering, and the carrier you are using.

3. *Scrutinize the rates of different carriers to decide whether to opt for a flat-rate price on each package or go by weight or measurement (whichever is greater) on the calculation.*

4. *To ship free or not to ship free? That is the key question.* Free shipping is a growing trend in e-commerce. The most popular offer is free shipping in exchange for a minimum order in dollars. Second to that is free shipping for a limited time only, such as three weeks prior to a Valentine's Day shipping deadline. I've always fallen for the free shipping offers, especially when I need a product and it's coming from overseas, showing that it does have a positive psychological influence on consumers, resulting in increased sales. If you offer free shipping, make sure you don't lose money on those sales!

▓ **Tip**   To quickly determine how easy or troublesome it might be to export to a particular market, go to the United States Postal Service's international Postage Price Calculator (http://ircalc. usps.gov/), click on the country you wish to export to, and select the type of package and weight (like "Package" and "Two pounds"). Then, click "Continue," select the next option based on your preferred delivery date, and click "Customs Forms" and "Other Service" to get an idea of what documentation is required. Make a note on any prohibitions and restrictions for that country. Bottom line: if you see anything that raises a red flag, whether messy customs restrictions or lengthy paperwork filing, cross the country off your list for doing business.

> 5. *Consider an international mail consolidator service.* As your shipping volume grows, you may wish to consider using this type of company to gather thousands of international mail packages from clients and deliver them directly to the postal system of each destination country. Depending on the services you use, an international consolidator can speed your package processing and provide good postal rate discounts. To find consolidators, conduct a search using the keywords "International mail consolidators." You will find dozens of companies that offer this service. Or a good listing of providers can be found on the "Shipping Consolidators" page of the USPS Web site at https://www.usps.com/business/shipping-consolidators.htm.

▓ **Caution**   No customers on your e-commerce site? You might ask individuals to buy from the countries you're targeting on your Web site on a test basis. Then, examine what could be preventing consumers from purchasing more from you online (e.g., language barrier, glitches, pricing too high, and so forth)—and then carefully address all the reasons behind their reluctance. All things being equal, if you think you are doing everything right, only your customers can tell you how you are not meeting or exceeding their expectations.

Summary

You now have some guidelines telling you what transport and fulfillment methods are available to get your product to your customer and how to make a cost-effective choice. As you move on to put together a price quotation for your customer, including price per unit, total transport, and incidental charges, you'll see exactly how valuable working with a good global freight forwarder, logistics expert, or fulfillment company can be in making the sale and delivering the goods.

Notes

i. "Cisco Exec on Growth of Worldwide Ecommerce, Cultural Differences," Practical Ecommerce, June 10, 2011, http://www.practicalecommerce.com/articles/ 2841-Cisco-Exec-on-Growth-of-Worldwide-Ecommerce-Cultural-Differences.

ii. Marc Levinson, *The Box: How the Shipping Container Made the World Smaller and the World Economy Bigger* (Princeton, NJ: Princeton University Press, 2006).

iii. "The Role and Importance of International Shipping," International Maritime Organization, accessed October 31, 2013, http://www.imo.org/KnowledgeCentre/Ships AndShippingFactsAndFigures/ TheRoleandImportanceofInternationalShipping/ Pages/TheRoleAndImportanceOf InternationalShipping.aspx.

iv. "The Whole World in Boxes," Deautsche Welle, accessed May 9, 2016, http://www.dw.com/en/ the-whole-world-in-boxes/g-19231681.

v. "JOC Economist: US Containerized Exports to Rebound in 2016," *Journal of Commerce*, accessed May 8, 2016, http://www.joc.com/ international-trade-news/trade-data/ united-states-trade-data/joc-economist-us-con-tainerized-exports-rebound-2016_20151215.html.

vi. "The JOC Top 50 World Container Ports," *Journal of Commerce*, accessed May 6, 2016, http://www.joc. com/port-news/international-ports/joc-top-50-world-container-ports_20150820.html.

vii. http://www.joc.com/port-news/interna-tional-ports/joc-top-50-world-container-ports_20150820.html.

viii. "The Truck Driver Who Reinvented Shipping," Anthony J. Mayo and Nitin Nohria, Harvard Business School: Working Knowledge; the Thinking That Leads, accessed October 3, 2005, http://hbswk.hbs.edu/item/5026.html.

ix. Levinson, *The Box*.

x. "World Internet Usage and Population Statistics," Internet World Stats: Usage and Population Statistics, page updated April 27, 2016, accessed May 8, 2016, http://www.internetworldstats.com/stats.htm.

xi. "2014 Third-Party Logistics Study, John Langley, Jr., Ph.D., and Capgemini, accessed May 8, 2016, https://www.capgemini.com/resource-file-access/resource/pdf/3pl_study_report_web_version.pdf.

Pricing and Preparing Quotations

A company's job is to find the market's acceptable price.

—J. Willard Marriott Jr., founder, Marriott International, and
Robert G. Cross, chairman and chief executive of Aeronomics Inc.[i]

*What the customer pays for each piece of the product has to work out as
Y dollars for us. But how the customer pays depends on what makes the
most sense to him. It depends on what the product does for the customer.
It depends on what fits his reality. It depends on what the customer sees
as 'value.'*

—American management consultant, author, and educator,
Peter F. Drucker[ii]

Pricing a product or service for the export market, determining its landed
costs (the total cost of a product once it has arrived at your buyer's door,
for example), and presenting the costs in quotation form are critical steps in
the international sales operation. Price determines revenue. Presenting the
pricing and providing the quotes for your goods or services in the right way
are both crucial for a successful and ongoing export business. Prices must be

© Laurel J. Delaney 2016
L. J. Delaney, *Exporting*, DOI 10.1007/978-1-4842-2193-8_19

high enough to generate and sustain a reasonable profit, yet low enough to penetrate a market, gain market share, attract customers, and be competitive in export markets.

In this chapter, I'll discuss several pricing strategies: how to establish an exporter's markup; how to develop export pricing (which differs from the preceding strategy); and how to work with a freight forwarder, logistics specialist, or fulfillment operation to arrive at good shipping rates that will please your customers. I will also show you how to use these figures to put together a pro forma invoice, a key document in every export transaction.

There are differences in pricing a product when you are a manufacturer's rep vs. when it's your own manufactured product. There is also a difference in pricing a product vs. a service. Be sure to distinguish between each of these pricing tactics as you read through the following pages.

■ **Note**   Selling products in a B-to-C transaction using e-commerce requires the same rigorous pricing strategy outlined in this chapter, but instead of preparing a pro forma invoice, as you would do in the case of large-volume orders or service export, the computation of the total price can be automated by a software service provider. (Refer to Chapter 18 for a listing of companies that provide this type of service.) Automated price computations simplify the process and guarantee that the customer receives an accurate calculation of the total landed price on a single item (including duties and taxes), and that she will not pay more than she is supposed to. Watch out for future growth of the automated landed-cost capability, especially in the B-to-B marketplace.

Pricing for Product Exports

Let's look at the three areas of concern related to pricing for exporters.

Representing Exports for a Manufacturer: Product Markup

In Chapter 11, I talked about deciding to export a product that you currently manufacture. I also talked about finding a product and a manufacturer for export when you don't have one of your own or see an opportunity to do so. When you represent exports for a manufacturer, you must determine your breakeven points, where your exporter's commission on a product shipment covers your business operating costs. Theoretically, of course, if you have a customer, say Jane Doe Importing Wholesaler, willing to buy, you can price your product at almost any level, provided it doesn't exceed what the customer is willing to pay or what the market will bear. This assumes the manufacturer has granted you authorization to set any price. Just keep in mind that you don't want to alienate the customer or make it easy for your competitors to undercut you!

Typically, exporters take between a 10 and 15 percent markup on top of the cost the manufacturer charges them for the product. In other words, if your supplier charges you $1 per unit for his product, you might mark it up to anywhere from $1.10 to $1.15 per unit. That markup becomes your profit or commission. Consider the following criteria to determine just how high or low you can go on your markup. This also applies when you manufacture your own product for export, which I will cover later.

1. *Uniqueness*: If the product is a market "first," you can afford to charge a higher price.

2. *Quality*: Is the product's quality upscale? Or marginal? Price up or down accordingly.

3. *Your cost*: If the manufacturer has already priced the product high, keep your markup low. If a major manufacturer (which are those that achieve considerable economies of scale in production) is able to give you a low offering price, then you can afford to set your commission slightly higher. Be careful here, as this scenario can be deceptive. If your cost is low to begin with, it might mean that the product is a mass commodity rather than a specialty offering, and that the market is already flooded with similar "me-too" items. If so, you have to keep your profit margin very tight.

4. *Newness*: Is the product already established or is it new to market? Sometimes you can price higher when a product is new to market just because your customers need and want novel product offerings. But novelty also has its downsides. A new-to-market product doesn't have the brand recognition, image, and popularity that overseas customers tend to look for when they want a product with surefire consumer appeal.

5. *Customer contact*: Who's calling the shots, you or the customer? Did the customer ask you to find the product or did you approach the customer and offer it? This makes a difference. A customer who has asked you to source a product is usually more receptive to a slightly higher price because she really needs the item. Don't lose your head here, though; never, ever get greedy. Your customer knows a rip-off when she sees one.

6. *Product positioning*: Positioning your product in the best possible light determines the price at which you will be able to sell it. Use the product's pricing in the equivalent sector of the domestic market as a guide to your overseas profit margin. For example, if your price for a product is $1 and you are targeting the upscale specialty market overseas, the suggested retail price at a local upscale store could be $8.99, so you take a higher profit margin.

▓ **Caution**   Export and domestic pricing always differ due to a variety of factors. The difference in overseas market conditions, costs, volume, brand support, quoting formats, certification if required, and currencies all affect what you should charge for your products or services in a foreign market.

---

7. *Direct (includes e-commerce) or indirect sale*: If you are selling directly to an end user, you can afford a higher profit margin. If your product is handled by a series of intermediaries—say, an export trading company, an importer, and a wholesaler—before it gets to the retailer and end user, remember that each of these middlemen will tack on his due percentage, and most likely without your consent, which can jack up the price substantially. If you price high at the beginning, your product will be priced right out of the market by the time it gets to the end user. Nobody wins.

8. *How desperate are you for income? Are you in a mood to see what you can get away with?* If this is the case, I won't stop you. But realize you may be making a big mistake from which you won't be able to recover—and thereby losing a customer altogether. You may really need income and feel you have nothing to lose, but don't forget the priorities of a successful exporter: the customer relationship comes first.

9. *Competition*: Price your products to stay in the global game. If you're up against unlimited competition, make sure you're offering comparable prices along with some extra form of value for your customers.

10. *Government policies*: Government policies can have both direct and indirect impact on pricing policies. Examples of factors that have a direct impact are taxes and tariffs. Examples of factors with an indirect impact are country deficits (spurring high interest rates) and currency fluctuations.

11. *Are you associated with an internationally known celebrity?* That makes a world of difference! No matter what you are offering, fans will buy your product at any price just because star power is attached. Stars whose meteoric success has allowed them to launch successful enterprises (with the help of enterprising people like you) include Jennifer Lopez with her perfume and clothing line sold through Kohl's, Jay Z with his Rocawear, and Jessica Alba with the Honest Co. The more popular your celeb is and the more difficult it is to get the product, the higher you can price it. Mainstream pop culture is the best marketing tool there is—look at Mickey Mouse and Andy Warhol! Consider yourself fortunate to be working with a celebrity, and go for the higher price!

How Pricing Works: Example Where I Represented the Exporting of a Chocolate Manufacturer

Here's an example of how I set pricing when representing a chocolate manufacturer in Chicago: I looked at my American supplier's pricing schedule and saw that a box of chocolates cost $3.00 wholesale (with a US retail price of $15.95 a box). I wanted to make a substantial profit right from the start.

First, I asked the supplier for a 25 percent discount off its standard domestic-price schedule based on a minimum order of a thousand boxes (with twelve units to a box). Hence, the supplier (manufacturer) could achieve economies of scale in production (large production runs that reduce per-unit costs) whenever it produced our overseas orders. It agreed to the price discount.

Next, I conducted market research to determine what the market would bear (including a thorough assessment of competition). Because there was nothing like our chocolates that existed in the market we were entering—Dubai—I decided to keep it clean and simple and price the product 10 percent lower than the standard domestic wholesale pricing, or $2.70 per unit ($32.40 per case), even though we were actually getting a 25 percent discount from the supplier. That meant the price to the customer now included our 15 percent commission.

The price still could have been considered high, but the product had unique characteristics—the chocolate was of superb quality and would be available in an exotic flavor. Because I knew that most overseas consumers would love to try it, the packaging was beautifully done, and the retail price point was equally high here in the States, I was convinced that the product could be put into a luxury category. In addition, the product was ideally suited for special occasion celebrations and gift-giving seasons such as Christmas and Valentine's

Day, or the equivalent in other parts of the world. All of these reasons assured me that upscale, affluent consumers overseas would be willing to buy such a product whatever it cost. The truth of the matter is that price is important, but it is not the only selling point in a deal.

■ **Tip** When you have a unique product or service, you can sell it at a high price. This is known as skimming. But you need to make sure what you are selling is unique, for otherwise you will price yourself right out of the market.

I contacted a freight forwarder and asked how much it would cost to ship a container-load of boxed chocolates (about a thousand cases) overseas. I was given an estimate of $3,600 (a refrigerated container would be needed during summer months, making the transport price higher than usual), plus another hundred dollars or so for transaction costs. I figured in these transportation costs along with the cost per box to the customer and realized the landed cost of the chocolates was now up to $3.44 per box or $41.24 per case. I'll thoroughly cover how I arrived at this later on.

Then, I made an offer to my foreign customer on behalf of the manufacturer, and he agreed. I had a sale and was delighted that my research had paid off. Now, it was a matter of exceeding the customer's expectations in all respects and developing a great relationship that would grow into other opportunities to export to the same customer in the future.

Going It Alone: Establishing Product Pricing and Markup for Your Manufactured Product for Export

There's a big difference between pricing a product as an export representative and pricing your own manufactured product for export. When you represent a company for export, the company has already factored in all its direct and indirect costs related to the production of the product. You merely add on your commission in order to offset your operational costs and generate a profit. However, when you price a product that you manufacture for export, you must take into consideration all of the above plus factor in middlemen and apply the following accounting methods:

- Add in all the direct material, labor, and overhead costs involved in producing the goods. Isolate and allocate all the costs.

- Deduct all costs unrelated to an export order (marketing and legal or domestic advertising, for example).

- Add in all of the out-of-pocket costs related to making the export sale happen (including but not limited to an export manager's salary and benefits, travel, legal, market research, promotional material, logistics fee, product modification, and translation costs).

- Set a slim margin (a minuscule percentage of the total costs) of error. Meaning, mistakes will happen when you are dealing in uncharted territory. Anticipate them by buffering your pricing to absorb fluctuations (such as higher shipping fees, currency fluctuations, fees for a payment method or early discount).

Caution Don't forget to factor fluctuations in currency into the price. If you plan to sell in currencies other than US dollars, although the exchange rate percentage may be small for converting to US dollars, it can add up over multiple shipments on a regular basis and erode profit margins.

- Make money. You are in the export business to grow and be profitable. Allow a reasonable markup and profit margin, but never lose sight of getting the best market penetration as fast as possible (revisit point number nine in the "Exports for a Manufacturer" section).

Tip Many small business owners use what is called a cost-plus method of pricing. That's when you add up the total costs involved in producing a product, including all expenses related to getting export ready, and then add on a markup to cover an appropriate share of overhead costs plus a fair profit margin that will yield an adequate return on investment. This is usually expressed as a percentage of the cost. Other business owners use penetration pricing, which is based on standard domestic pricing with a slight discount predicated on the anticipation of volume purchases. When doing penetration pricing, be sure to state an expiration date on your price schedule and indicate that prices are subject to change due to market conditions and the final pricing proposal. In either scenario, monitor results after the fact to ensure you make money.

A good international accountant is always helpful in determining the type of accounting data that should be used in planning and implementing a pricing strategy for the export activity of manufactured products. Your goal is to analyze and control costs to ensure you make a profit. The five key drivers in determining the best export price are: cost, demand (customers), distribution, competition, and government policies.

Test your price out on one of your customers (just as I did with the chocolates) with whom you have cultivated a strong relationship and to whom you've presented your product's positive sales attributes. See what reaction you get and then negotiate from there. If you priced the product with only a slim margin built in for yourself—so slim you cannot afford to go any lower—and your customer still balks at the price, consider renegotiating with your supplier. Oftentimes, if you explain that the only way to sell the product overseas is to price it more competitively, the supplier will agree to go back to the drawing board and see if it can rework the numbers. Don't attempt this too often though, because if you continue to have price problems the supplier will sooner or later catch on that you haven't properly checked out what the foreign market will bear.

Small business owner Caron Beesley, who also serves as the community moderator for the Small Business Administration, says, "Not charging enough is a common problem for small businesses simply because they often don't have the operational efficiencies of larger companies and frequently find that, whatever they sell, their costs are higher than they anticipated. Small businesses do have one advantage, though, and it's one that justifies charging a higher price—service!"[iii] Keep this advice in mind as you price for export.

Complete Your Quotation with a Competitive Shipping Rate

Let's say you've given your product a markup of 15 cents on the $1 total cost per unit. By the time it lands at your customer's port, it costs her $1.25 per unit. How does that happen?

Just as in a domestic sale, you will be billing your customer for the costs of shipping when exporting your product. To finish your price quotation, you must first contact a freight forwarder, which will provide you with a competitive shipping rate. But before you contact the freight forwarder, collect the information in the sidebar and keep it right at your fingertips. If you don't have this information when you call, e-mail, or submit your inquiry online (a capability that most of them provide you), the company will require that you get it.

FOURTEEN QUESTIONS YOU WILL BE ASKED BY A FREIGHT FORWARDER

1. *What is your commodity? Is it perishable or nonperishable?*

2. *What is your product's commodity number?* You can look this up in the appropriate directory at your local international Small Business Administration office. A commodity number, generally known as an "HS/Schedule B product description," allows for easy

classification by customs officials. It's important to be as specific as possible in determining your product classification, because transportation rates vary widely, even among products you would expect to fall under the same category. For example, there's a big difference between the transportation rates for computer hardware and computer software. If you are unable to determine the appropriate number, the freight forwarder will calculate an accurate shipping quote based on your product description.

If your product is already a standard export but you are sending it to a new market, a freight forwarder will take your commodity number and assign an appropriate tariff number. That number will then be filed as the industry standard for all subsequent exports of that commodity to that location. Every time you export that product to that country, you must use the assigned tariff number to ensure the same rate.

Tip   To get a leg up and determine your own tariff number, or tax at the border, that certain foreign countries will collect when your product crosses into their country, use the FTA Tariff Tool, which now includes the latest information on tariffs in TPP: `http://export.gov/fta/ftatarifftool/`

---

3. *Are you shipping by air or by ocean?*

4. *How many cartons do you plan to ship?*

5. *What is the size of the cartons?* This needs to be assessed both in linear dimensions (height, length, width) and in cubic meters.

6. *What are the net and gross weights of the cartons in kilograms?* (The net weight is the weight of the product on its own; the gross weight adds the weight of the cartons to that of the product.)

7. *Do you plan to stack the cartons on pallets? If so, how many will be loaded on each pallet?* Your freight forwarder should be able to guesstimate how much weight and cubic space each pallet will take up and calculate the total weight and volume of the shipment accordingly.

8. *Do you have enough product to fill a container?* Full loads of cargo are generally known as "containers" (see Chapter 18) and average between twenty and forty-eight cubic feet. Once you have your total number of cases and total weight calculated, your freight forwarder should be able to tell you if you have enough product to fill a container. If you do, it's an advantage. Your product will be loaded into the container all by itself rather than being consolidated with other companies' products in order to fill the container, and a seal will be put on the door of the container. This means that nobody else will have access to your goods when they arrive at the port of destination,

except your customer and his designated agent. This safety measure guards against potential theft, pilferage, and product tampering.

9. *From what location will the product be moved?* Usually, this is the manufacturer's factory door.

10. *To what port does your customer want the goods delivered?*

11. *Will your shipment require an export license?* (See Chapter 22 for a complete discussion of export licensing. To avoid shipping delays, it's best to make this determination as soon as you know what kind of product you'll be selling.)

12. *Are there any time constraints involved in getting the product to a customer?*

13. *Is insurance required for the shipping of your product, and, if so, who will be responsible for it?*

14. *Who will collect the payment on the transaction, and is there a preferred method?*

Having given the company all this information, you can expect a bit of a wait for its response. Generally, an efficient freight forwarder can get back to you with a quote within a few hours. If it's a large firm and a busy time, expect a callback or e-mail the next day. The forwarder should give you a very detailed analysis as to how it arrived at its rates. If there is anything you don't understand, stop and ask about it. Also, ask for a rate confirmation number so that when you call back, whether in a week or several months, the company will have a record of the quote and a way to access it. And don't forget to ask how long the rates are valid! After you've called a few forwarders, sit down and compare quotes.

■ **Tip**   Many international shipping companies (UPS, for example) have a designated area on their site for calculating shipping costs and estimated delivery times to targeted countries. You will need to provide information about your shipment in required online fields, including destination, origin, shipment date and weight.

How Does the Freight Forwarder Arrive at a Rate?

Besides the physical logistics of your actual shipment, here are some extraneous factors that will affect how your freight forwarder calculates your shipping rate:

1. *The tariff on your product:* Unless the company files a new rate for your product and destination, as discussed in the second item of the "Fourteen Questions YOU will be asked by a Freight Forwarder" sidebar, freight forwarders use rate books to determine the tariff.

2. *The amount of traffic to and from your destination point.* Competitive container port areas such as China and Singapore, for example, can create overcapacity situations in the container port sector, shipping delays, and higher prices on transportation.

3. *How the industry as a whole is performing*: One factor the freight forwarder might look at is whether demand is exceeding available transportation services or the other way around.

4. *Exchange rates*: These rates are a major factor in the transportation calculation. They will be reflected in your quote as the CAF, or currency adjustment factor. Let's say a freight forwarder quotes you a rate of $1,800 for shipping a twenty-foot container-load from a West Coast port in the United States to Tokyo and lists the CAF as 57 percent. That means you must add 57 percent onto the base rate to arrive at a total rate of U.S. $2,826.

Selecting the Best Freight Forwarder for Your Needs

Once you've got a few quotes, you'll need to compare more than the numbers to determine which freight forwarder offers the best value. Ask your customer which of the following should take priority:

1. Low-cost transportation
2. A timely delivery
3. Safe handling of product
4. Choice of transportation method
5. All of the above

Try to select a couple of forwarders that offer the last choice, all of the above, are always pleasant to talk with, and are financially solvent—and then stick with these companies through thick and thin. You do want to double-check the company's financial solvency, because if it goes out of business during the transit of one of your shipments, you are liable for the consequences. If, on the other hand, your customer needs a timely delivery to happen, then select the forwarder that specializes in speed, and so on.

Every time you have a customer who wants a quote, it pays to shop through your list, because you never know when the quality of service might change, the prices might go up, or the company might discontinue service to certain ports. Check and double-check on behalf of your customers. Always offer them the absolute best value you can find, because it makes them want to keep coming back.

Reading Your Quotation

When your freight forwarder gives you a quote, the total charge will be broken down into line items, as shown in Figure 19-1:

Inland transport:	$_____
Ocean transport:	$_____
CAF ___ percent:	$_____
Documentation:	$_____
TOTAL:	$_____

Figure 19-1. Export quotation worksheet

Inland transport refers the cost to move the product from a factory door to a port of exit within the same country. Ocean transport is the cost to move the product from the port of exit to the port of entry of the country of destination. CAF stands for currency adjustment factor, which is the going rate of exchange from one currency to another; for example, from the US dollar to the Chinese yuan. Documentation represents the freight forwarder's fee for handling all documentation associated with the shipment, including letters of credit.

Terms of Shipment

You should also familiarize yourself with the following terms of shipment, which are the ones that are the most commonly used. These are known as *Incoterms* and, according to the International Chamber of Commerce, "have become an essential part of the daily language of trade."[iv] They have also been incorporated in contracts for the sale of goods worldwide. These terms of shipment will affect the final numbers on your export quotation as well as your financial responsibility for the shipment:

CIF

You are responsible for paying the cost, insurance, and freight (CIF) costs in advance to a named overseas port. You will collect these later, at the point when you invoice your customer. Normal practice is to insure a shipment for 110 percent of its CIF value. Let's say you are insuring a shipment to the Far East (Japan, Korea, Taiwan) at a rate of $0.6175 per $100 (which includes war risk insurance and "special perils" coverage). The details are shown in Figure 19-2:

Invoice Value:	$ 12,000.00
Freight:	$ 1,200.00
Clearance/Handling:	$ 100.00
TOTAL:	$ 13,300.00
110% of TOTAL:	$ 14,630.00
INSURANCE:	$ 90.34
CIF TOTAL:	$ 14,720.34

Figure 19-2. Calculating CIF (cost, insurance, and freight) totals

Here's how you arrive at the CIF total: Add the invoice value (cost of the product), freight charges (typically includes fees for both inland/ocean shipping and CAF), and clearance/handling charges. Multiply this total by 110 percent for the cost of the insurance, and then divide by 100. Take the resulting figure and multiply it by $0.6175, which will result in your insurance charge of $90.34. Add this to your previous total of $14,630 for a CIF total of $14,720.34. It's good to know how this is done, but you won't have to concern yourself with this calculation or the actual issuance of the certificate if you use a freight forwarder. All you have to do is ask the freight forwarder to quote you insurance coverage at the 110 percent CIF rate.

CFR

The CFR, or the more widely used CNF term, refers to the cost and freight. The exporter is responsible for paying the freight costs to the named port of destination and collecting the charge from the customer later on.

Note An import duty is payable based on CIF prices, or what is considered the transaction value of invoice. For further clarification, check with the "Technical Information on Customs Valuation" page on the World Trade Organization's Web site (http://www.wto.org/english/ tratop_e/cusval_e/cusval_info_e.htm).

FAS

FAS, or free alongside ship, refers to getting the goods shipside and ready to be loaded, all of the costs of which are the exporter's responsibility. The costs of loading the goods into transport vessels at the specified place and all other costs from that moment onward are the customer's responsibility.

FOB

The exporter must take care of all paperwork and/or expenses necessary to collect the goods from the supplier and place them on an international carrier. The buyer is responsible for all costs from the moment the goods are placed on board the vessel and onward, which is known as FOB, or free on board.

Ex-

Terms beginning with "ex," such as *ex-factory* or *ex-dock*, indicate that the price quoted to your customer applies only at the specified point of origin (either your own location, your supplier's factory, or a dock at the export point). This term means that you agree to place the goods at the disposal of the customer at the specified place within a fixed period of time. As the seller, you do not need to load the goods on any collecting vehicle. That is also the responsibility of the buyer.

In order to accommodate the ever-increasing use of the electronic data interchange (EDI), Incoterms have been revised to reflect new shipping methods, such as free carrier (FCA), carrier paid to (CPT), carriage and insurance paid to (CIP), delivered at terminal (DAT), delivered at place (DAP), and delivered duty paid (DDP). Be sure to ask your freight forwarder how each of these terms of the transaction affect the ultimate price of the shipment as well as the logistics of shipping or contact the International Chamber of Commerce (ICC) for additional guidance.

Preparing the Cost Analysis and Pro Forma Invoice

Your next step is to add the itemized charges that appear on your invoice form, which becomes a pro forma invoice. A pro forma invoice is considered a pre-advice document and serves as a guide to action on what the expectations are on an export sale. It sets the stage for the negotiation process.

Here are some ways in which a pro forma invoice is helpful:

- Serves as a legal, binding agreement

- Minimizes errors

- Outlines all relevant information pertaining to the export transaction

- Is a widely accepted form of a sales document structure in the export industry

- Enables banks to establish a payment method on behalf of the importer

Your document will have all the familiar components of an ordinary domestic invoice: a description of the product, an itemized listing of charges, and sales terms. Let's say you want to get your customer a landed-price quote for a shipment of candy to her port of entry, in this case "CFR Tokyo."

If you have one hundred cases of candy, packed twelve units to a case, and each case is priced at $120, or $10 per unit, the total cost for the order would be $12,000. Figure 19-3 shows the invoice you would make up:

Pro Forma Invoice # _____	
Date: _____	
Selling price	$12,000 (FOB, with the origin being the factory door in the United States)
Inland transport	$ 700
Ocean transport	$ 1,500
Duty	$ 300
CAF	$ 1,250
Documentation	$ 125
TOTAL LANDED PRICE (or Total CNF Tokyo):	$ 15,875
We certify that Pro Forma Invoice No. _____ is true and correct	
The country of origin is _____	
This quote is valid for thirty days	

Figure 19-3. Pro forma invoice for a shipment of candy to Tokyo

The selling price is your cost to buy the product from the manufacturer plus your markup. Add to that figure the total shipping costs and divide that amount by the number of cases of candy. That gets you your landed price per case. Then, divide that figure by the number of units in a case. This will give you your landed price per unit.

So, if the total landed price for shipment were $15,875 (CFR Tokyo as shown above), and you divided this amount by one hundred cases of candy, you'd come up with $158.75 as the landed price per case. You'd then divide that price by the number of units in a case (twelve) to come up with $13.23 as the landed price per unit. Remember, the selling price is your cost to buy the product from the manufacturer plus your markup.

You have now finalized your price quotation and created a pro forma invoice. Don't forget to specify a precise time period during which your quote is valid (by including, "This quote expires on __/__/__," for example), and to add the freight forwarder's quote reference number.

Three additional critical steps on the pro forma invoice are: (1) Make a statement certifying that the pro forma invoice is true and correct, (2) make a statement that indicates the country of origin of the goods, and (3) mark your invoice clearly with the words "Pro forma invoice."

Once your customer approves the pro forma invoice, it will become your actual invoice for the order. The customer will also use the pro forma invoice to obtain any necessary funding (payment) or import licenses. Your customer should communicate acceptance (usually via fax or e-mail) in a short written sentence or two with a signature, as is done in the following: "We accept your pro forma invoice No. 1234 against our Purchase Order number ABCD." You will then respond: "We acknowledge and confirm your P.O. number ABCD against our pro forma invoice number 1234."

■ **Tip**   Regardless of whether it has been requested or not, it is wise to prepare a pro forma invoice showing the cost of getting the product to the overseas buyer for any international quotation. Use the Incoterms correctly when quoting. You don't want to get stuck absorbing shipping costs only because you didn't understand how to use the sales terms correctly.

Pricing for Service Exports

Now, at this point, you might be saying, "That's all well and good, but I'm exporting services." Selling a service successfully requires even more people power than does product sales. Pricing a service, such as one that is professional, technical, financial, or franchise or insurance oriented, entails a somewhat different approach because a service requires direct interaction with your customer, not just initially but for the duration of the service contract. And for some services, the quality of your interaction with your customer is exactly what they're paying for.

Whether pricing a product or a service for export, the fundamentals remain the same: you need to first conduct market research on the competition, the ease of entering a new market, the maturity of the industry, the uniqueness of the offering, and so forth.

But let's not get ahead of ourselves. Here's a look at the other factors that are important to consider concerning pricing a service export:

- You need to differentiate your service offering from existing offerings or convince a prospective customer to hire you to do something that's never been done before.

- Make sure you look at all costs associated with the service offering, including taxes, establishing a foreign branch office, sales visits, translation, IP protection, and so forth.

- Examine and factor in the amount of time that will be spent on the proposal (presales effort) and allocate your schedule accordingly.

- Pay close attention to cultural business practices specific to a country. Will you be pricing your service per hour, on a fixed-project basis, or in some other negotiated format that fits the protocol of the country's standards?

- Make sure to determine how you will account for after-sales nurturing and follow-up costs.

- You'll need to comply with applicable international standards. Learn the tax and legal implications for providing your service in an overseas market well in advance of submitting a proposal to a client.

- Make sure you factor in any promotional costs associated with supporting your services in the overseas market.

- Determine what the impact on your domestic business will be in terms of hiring additional staff, whether it be on the ground in the country in which you wish to conduct business or locally to support the new business.

- Select barrier-free markets for your service export. The Trade in Services Agreement (TISA; https://servic-escoalition.org/negotiations/trade-in-ser-vices-agreement) has the potential to create trading conditions that enable services industries to achieve their full export potential.

■ **Tip** Set a benchmark price that reflects your brand and its values and capabilities. Tuck away a slim margin that can be used later for negotiating purposes if need be (offering a new client a one-time courtesy discount, for example). Bear in mind you might be competing against more well-known and well-heeled competitors, but if your offering is unique, you've got as good a chance as anyone to land the business.

Pricing Model for a Service Export

I've said it before, but I'll say it again: consult with your international accountant to determine your best service export pricing strategy, especially one that favors healthy profits and minimal tax exposure.

■ **Tip** There are other pricing methods, such as variable cost pricing, skimming (as mentioned earlier), and penetration (also touched upon earlier). The decision of which pricing model to use is largely based on the level of competition, innovation, market conditions, and available resources. Consult with your international accountant and also conduct a web search to learn more about each method.

Calculating "cost plus" pricing requires a complete understanding of your total costs (hence, the consultation with your accountant) for delivering your service into a target overseas market. To do that you must:

1. *Know all costs, margins, and expenses to get the service export out the door.* Don't forget to allocate for the after-sales service part of the contract.

2. *Realize you might not be competitive in all markets.* (Adjust your pricing accordingly, but if you find you can't be profitable, go someplace else where you can be).

3. *Align your service export price with its perceived benefits in the target market.* This holds true whether you are pricing a product or a service.

Once you establish the cost, add a margin (return on your investment) to cover profits and to reflect a price that is in line with your perceived market position (think along the lines of Apple providing a technology-export-service proposal vs. ABC Tech House doing so. Apple's pricing will be higher due to its prestige in the marketplace, and ABC Tech House's will be lower due to its unknown name and desire to get a foot in the door.) It is important that you have an understanding of the average margin in the export market for your industry and that you price your service offering competitively to guarantee two things—that someone will purchase the product or service you are offering and that you make money.

Just as on a product export, you need to finalize your pricing by preparing a pro forma invoice. You don't, however, have to concern yourself with Incoterms because you are not shipping products, nor do you have to establish a harmonized code to categorize your service, or prepare documentation for customs purposes. The pro forma invoice will come in handy later when you discuss with your client how you will get paid (refer to Chapter 20).

Last Thoughts on Market Differences

Here are a few final thoughts on export pricing. Calculating a different price for each overseas market and segment of a market can be a seemingly daunting experience, but it might be necessary because:

- *Customers vary.* In Ireland, for example, you might be selling to distributors that sell to end users, while on your e-commerce site you sell directly to end users. In Dubai, you might sell to small independent retailers and a handful of big box retailers directly. Each of these examples calls for developing specially tailored pricing that meets the needs of the marketplace and provides profits for your business.

- *Markets vary.* Some countries have a five-step distribution method (where the product changes hands five times before an end user purchases it) and others might only have a door-to-door sales concept.

- *Competitors vary.* Tracking your competitors is not only prudent; it's beneficial for determining just how high or low you can set your pricing.

The bottom line is: you need to adapt and adjust.

In the export marketplace, you can never compete on price alone. While price is important, it is seldom the only factor in the buying decision. You need to compete on several different levels. The majority of customers worldwide take into account a combination of factors and look for the whole package before making a purchasing decision. Do your homework. Because the whole purpose of an export business is to gain new business, you need to have the winning combination in overlooked and unlikely market spaces and make money. Use pricing strategy as a spark to enhance export performance, and don't forget to charge what your products are worth.

Summary

You have learned how to coordinate a sale. You are now ready to enter the export business. From this point on, no additional changes should be made to the transaction by you or your customer until after the expiry date given on the pro forma invoice. Before you release the order for your product or the contract for your service, though, you and your customer must negotiate terms of payment. Read on for an overview of the most common—and the most secure—methods of arranging a payment for export goods and services as well as an array of export financing sources.

Notes

i. Peter Krass, *The Book of Management Wisdom*. New York: John Wiley & Sons, Inc., 2000.

ii. Peter F. Drucker, *The Essential Drucker*. New York: HarperCollins, 2001.

iii. "How to Price Your Small Business' Products and Services," Caron Beesley, SBA.gov, accessed May 15, 2016, last modified May 10, 2016, http://www.sba.gov/community/blogs/how-price-your-small-business%E2%80%99-products-and-services.

iv. "The Incoterms® Rules," International Chamber of Commerce: The World Business Organization, accessed May 15, 2016, http://www.iccwbo.org/products-and-services/trade-facilitation/incoterms-2010/the-incoterms-rules/.

Getting Paid

Terms, Conditions, and Other Financing Options, Including Mobile Payments

Since 2009, the Export-Import Bank [of the United States] has financed $235 billion worth of export deals for American companies, including more than 5,000 small businesses.

—The Business Journals[i]

The most important thing to negotiate before closing on an export sale is how payment will be made. In this chapter, I outline several strategies so that you can get paid in full and on time while minimizing risks. I also offer a brief overview of other nontraditional ways to finance an export transaction, should you find yourself unable to work out a standard method of payment.

Traditional Payment Methods

Remember the two types of customers I talked about in Chapter 16? The first was the distributor, overseas agent, wholesaler, or retailer—the big-volume purchasers—who will use the more traditional payment methods I am going to talk about in this section. The other type of customer is your Everyday Joe—the overseas end user—who buys your product from an e-commerce site or mobile device or through an app, which I will explain in greater detail later.

L. J. Delaney, *Exporting*, DOI 10.1007/978-1-4842-2193-8_20

Let's start with the large-volume customer. To make a point fast, I want to share an experience I had when trying to establish a payment method with a new customer. It went like this.

In an early stage of my business, I had been communicating with a customer in Japan for several weeks. His company was large and established and had a solid reputation in the food industry. He was interested in our line of cookies and he placed a $21,000 order.

I responded to his inquiries with a pro forma invoice showing all the pertinent data. In addition, I stated that payment was to be made by a confirmed irrevocable letter of credit[ii] (L/C) opened in favor of AB Cookie Kingdom Company (real name withheld for confidentiality reasons) through JP Morgan Chase. A few days later, the company gave the go-ahead to start producing the order. I assumed that it had accepted and approved our pro forma invoice and was about to open the L/C as requested.

A few more days went by.

I scheduled the production of the order. I faxed (that's how we communicated back then!) the company again with the production details and an inquiry as to when I would see a copy of the L/C.

No response. More days went by. Finally, I started to wonder about the customer. I sent another fax asking him exactly what was causing the delay on the L/C. The company finally replied that it had opened the L/C a week ago and that I should be receiving it any day. I phoned the bank and talked to a key contact in the international division. I asked that it keep a special lookout for an L/C coming in from Tokyo.

Still more days went by. The order was produced. The manufacturer invoiced me immediately. The balance was due in full thirty days from the invoice date.

My contact at the bank called me up and reported that he had received an L/C from AB Cookie Kingdom Company with the account number at the top. The bank couldn't understand a word of it, though. It was in Japanese. Note: This had happened to us more than once. We had a similar situation with a customer in Germany on a smaller transaction amount, so pay attention to the lesson we learned the hard way to ensure you don't make the same mistake!

I faxed my customer and asked that the company forward an English-language copy of the L/C so we could make sure we were complying with the terms and conditions.

The customer faxed us another copy of the L/C in Japanese. The inexplicable confusion persisted for several weeks. After we finally received the L/C in English, we found that a condition had been included in the text, stating that the shipper could not consolidate our product with other products to make up a full container-load. This left us with a wide-open payment risk, since shipping companies don't want to sail with a half-empty cargo hold, and our chances of meeting this condition were slim.

We faxed the customer again and asked him to amend the L/C (costing us money, I might add). The company responded by saying that we had instructed it on what to do and it had done that. We tried to tell the people there nicely that they had erred by including the clause prohibiting consolidated shipments.

More time went by. Our manufacturer was calling repeatedly and asking us when we were going to release the cargo. We didn't want to release it without secured payment from the customer.

The customer finally faxed again and requested that we ship "open account," whereby payment is not required until the goods are manufactured and delivered. By then, we were exhausted and desperate (a position you never want to put yourself in!) because we had produced goods that were sitting in a plant waiting to be released—and overwhelmed with frustration at having spent several weeks trying to accommodate our customer with a payment method when what was wanted all along was an open-account status.

We shipped open account. You should most emphatically *not* do that. Why? Many months later, and even then only with the help of the Embassy of the United States in Tokyo, we collected payment.

I learned a great deal from this transaction. Agree on the terms of payment in advance, and never ever sell on open account to a brand new customer. No ifs, ands, or buts. Just don't.

Red Flags

While reading the above account, you probably realized early on that I wasn't dealing with a customer. I was dealing with a noncustomer pretending to be a customer. This story is fortunately not typical, but it does highlight what can go wrong in setting up terms and conditions for an export sale. I caution you to beware of overseas contacts who:

- *Fall off the face of the earth for long periods of time.* A good customer communicates often and conscientiously. If a customer doesn't or can't communicate in an honest and responsible manner, he is not a customer.

- *Ignore instructions.* Get approval and acceptance of your terms and conditions in the form of a signature from a top executive—preferably the owner—of the company with which you are about to do business. If she's reputable, she'll be willing to be held accountable for the terms of the sale.

- *Force you to become lax on your terms and conditions.* A customer who pretends to be a special case, for some contrived and dubious reason, isn't. Don't fall for it.

- *Slip in new terms or information at the latest point in the negotiations without advance discussion.* This is, quite bluntly, the tactic of a con artist. Steer clear.

- *Make you feel desperate (as the Tokyo customer had done with us) or as if you have lost control of your own business.* Let this customer go with a clear conscience. It's better to find one good customer than a hundred bad ones.

These characteristics define what a customer should not be. But once you have found a good customer and have worked your way through the pro forma phase, you can arrange a form of payment that is satisfactory to both parties. In the following section, I will discuss the most common methods of export financing: payment in advance, payment by L/C, and the risky open account.

Choosing a Payment Method—Factors to Consider

Many circumstances and priorities will influence your choice of payment method. A lot will depend on how much you know about financing a sale and how willing your customer is to accept your terms and conditions. Other factors include:

- Your cash flow needs

- Your relationship with your customer

- The political and economic conditions in the country to which you are exporting

- Interest rates and currency adjustment factors

- The type of product (stock or custom)

- Your customer's creditworthiness

- Your customer's reputation

- The terms your competitors are offering

- The availability of other buyers and sellers

- Your supplier's demands

- The physical location of buyer and seller

- The urgency of the transaction, whether you are under time constraints, and the size of the transaction

Whatever terms of payment you negotiate, you must always (1) make sure they are understood by all parties and (2) have your customer sign a document that indicates acceptance, such as the pro forma invoice that I talked about earlier. This prevents some unpleasant surprises later on and reduces your shipment liability exposure.

To minimize risk with an overseas customer, you should consider which payment method in Figure 20-1 is mutually advantageous for you as the exporter, and your customer.

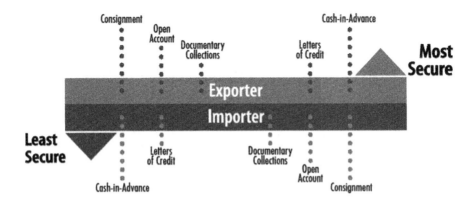

Figure 20-1. Payment risk diagram[iii]

Payment in Advance

Payment in advance is obviously the best of all payment methods for an exporter (seller) since you can prevent possible collection problems and you have immediate use of the money. I use the advance payment method when I know absolutely nothing about the customer, when the speed of handling will make or break the sale, and when the transaction is less than $5,000. The only difficult part of this financing method is actually making it happen.

When your customer agrees to this arrangement, he accepts the full risk of the financial transfer. If he does accept it, ask him to make a wire transfer from his bank account to yours or issue a certified check made payable to you in US dollars, preferably sent by courier. It's reasonable to ask for half of the total sale in advance, with the balance to be paid thirty days from the bill-of-lading date. This reduces your customer's risk, thus helping to maintain goodwill. Make sure, though, that the advance amount covers your out-of-pocket costs.

▓ **Note** Never accept cash for a high-value transaction. This poses a risk and could send a red flag to export regulatory officials.

▓ **Tip** To get cash in advance, you must ask. Let's say a customer in Yugoslavia wants to import a thousand of your flash drives. So, you prepare a detailed pricing proposal showing all costs involved. Within the proposal you state in bold letters: "Method of Payment: Wire transfer in advance for full amount of order and payable in US dollars." Your customer wire transfers the full cost of the transaction plus your profits, paying a small wire transfer fee. In effect, you not only fronted the funding on the production of goods, but you also built in a healthy profit margin to use for funding future growth.

Letters of Credit—Security with Flexibility

After payment in advance, securing payment with a letter of credit (L/C) is the next best option. It's a more expensive and complicated arrangement, but it's worth it. An L/C is a commercial document issued by a bank at your customer's request in your favor and is based on the seller's instructions outlining desired terms and conditions. It guarantees you'll get paid, as long as the terms stated in it are fulfilled.

▓ **Tip** To supplement this chapter (and expand your export resource data bank at the same time), I recommend that you contact a few banks, beginning with your own, and see if it will e-mail you its international banking directory at no charge. Nearly every large bank publishes one. For example, Bank of America Merrill Lynch publishes "Solutions for Exporters" (https://gems-pp. bankofamerica.com/documents/16303/74434/exporter.pdf.) It's usually a slim volume but as good as a fat encyclopedia for showing you every imaginable way to finance an export sale. Such a directory can be very useful for reference should your customer ask you a technical question about how her financing will work.

The Letter of Credit Process

There are four participants in an L/C transaction—two businesspeople and two banks:

1. *The buyer:* That's your customer. He opens the L/C.

2. *The opening bank:* The bank normally issues the L/C, so it is sometimes referred to as the "issuing bank." It assumes responsibility for the payment on behalf of the buyer. The opening bank can contact a corresponding bank near the

seller in the United States to advise it on the opening of the L/C. If the L/C is confirmed (the buyer must make this request when submitting the application for the L/C; this is a request and not a requirement, for the advising bank may decline for whatever reason), the US correspondent bank can confirm and pay on behalf of the buyer provided exact documents required for the L/C are provided and match up.

3. *The paying bank:* This is the bank under which the drafts or bills of exchange are drawn under the credit.

4. *The seller:* That's you—the global marketer, exporter, shipper, beneficiary—to whom the credit is issued.

Note There can be other parties and roles in the L/C process: Examining, confirming, reimbursing and negotiating bank but the above are the most common.

To summarize the process: Once you and your customer agree on payment by L/C, it is the customer's responsibility to take your pro forma invoice to her bank or to complete the process of setting up the L/C online, with the invoice attached to the application, and opening the L/C in your favor. Once the opening bank has all the appropriate information from the customer, it advises you, the seller, that the L/C has been opened. Oftentimes this will be done by wire to the paying bank. Your bank then forwards that information to you. The L/C is final and subject to correction only for errors in transmission.

Although we live in an era when rapid data transmission by fax or e-mail or in the cloud has become the norm for business communications, some opening banks still prefer to wire advice of an opened L/C and then notify you by telephone (if you have a good international banking officer), e-mail, or snail mail, of its arrival. When you are expecting an L/C to be opened in your favor, it's prudent to call your bank to notify it to be on the lookout for the L/C or to check the status of it. However the information gets into your hands, review it immediately by checking the terms and conditions against your pro forma invoice.

It is not unusual to find differences between the L/C and the pro forma invoice, such as incorrect product descriptions or reference numbers or an impossibly early shipment date. Once you have confirmed that your invoice is correct, you can try to preempt some of these errors by e-mailing the buyer what is called an L/C template (see `http://www.key.com/pdf/sampleloc.pdf`) to show him what the completed version should look like. You may find that he ignores it and opens the L/C in the standard format he uses. If that happens and you notice substantive discrepancies, bring them to your bank officer's attention at once. If you find that you cannot make adjustments to accommodate the customer, you must request an amendment to the L/C. This, unfortunately, costs money. Your bank officer can request that the opening bank contact your customer about the amendment or you can bypass the banks and contact your customer directly. Bypassing the bank will save your customer the charges for the amendment but doesn't always provide the safety you still need to maintain the security of the transaction.

If you do communicate directly with your customer, you will need him to acknowledge the discrepancy and state whether or not he will take action to modify the L/C. Buyers generally accomplish this by alerting their bank to the discrepancy when the documents are presented by the bank for approval and then formally waiving that discrepancy. If the customer cannot be relied upon to do this, you get stuck! So always consult with your banker before attempting any informal deals like this.

Accuracy in all details of your L/C is critically important. One of the most exasperating delays I've ever experienced was caused by a discrepancy our bank found between our company name and address on the L/C that I had just presented. It looked like this:

GLOBAL TRADESOURCE LTD

6807 N LAKEWOOD, UNIT LL

CHICAGO, ILLINOIS 60626

UNITED STATES OF AMERICA

On our commercial invoice, we had given our address as follows:

Global TradeSource, Ltd.

6807 N. Lakewood, Suite LL

Chicago, IL 60626

United States of America

Would you believe that, from the bank's standpoint, the differences in upper/lower letters, spacing and punctuation were sufficient to indicate a different beneficiary altogether? The bank said it could not present our documents unless we corrected the errors and made everything exactly the same as in the L/C. What choice did we have? We fixed it. We even went so far as to put everything in capitals the way the issuing bank had. Pay attention to the details so nothing will stand in the way of your getting paid!

This synopsis ought to give you some idea of the typical steps taken—and the typical delays—in the L/C process. Don't be surprised at what seems like an unreasonably long turnaround time.

Types of Letters of Credit

There are a number of different types of L/C; two are important enough to distinguish up-front and the others offer more payment flexibility.

Irrevocable Letter of Credit

An irrevocable L/C is a commercial document that the customer requests a bank to issue in your favor. Once issued, it cannot be modified without both parties' consent. In this case, "irrevocable" means that the bank must pay you even if your customer defaults, provided the documents presented are "clean." Clean documents are in complete compliance with the language of the L/C and are presented to the bank prior to the expiration date. It's the most secure method of payment and one that I suggest you use as often as possible. You can also request that the L/C be confirmed by any US office of the issuing bank prior to submission. This arrangement provides the greatest degree of protection because the bank must pay you even if your customer's bank defaults. If the L/C is unconfirmed, the US bank must wait until it receives funds from the foreign bank before it will credit your account.

Banks usually charge about one-eighth of 1 percent (based on the bank's policy and the relationship between the exporter and the bank) of the total transaction cost as a processing fee. Although many exporters complain about this expense, I am convinced that the payment security this document offers far outweighs the negligible fee.

Unless otherwise stipulated in the L/C, all banking charges, including charges outside the buyer's country, are for the account of the applicant. If any of these charges are for the beneficiary's account, they are normally deducted from the face amount of the drawing at the time of payment. Upon receipt of an L/C, read through it carefully because fees such as pre-advice, advising, confirmation, amendment, document examination or negotiation, disrepancy, reimbursement, and even cancellation, to name just a few, can all add up.

Revocable Letter of Credit

A revocable L/C is a commercial document that your customer requests a bank to issue in your favor that can be modified without both parties' consent at any given point in time. Once this L/C has been issued, you have the following assurances as the beneficiary: the bank can assure you that, yes, your customer has arranged for the bank to pay you such an amount, and, yes, your customer is known and respected, and has been banking with the bank for decades. Unfortunately, you cannot rely on this type of L/C since the bank is under no obligation to cover it if your customer defaults. You may as well just run a credit check on the customer and ship using an open account. It's almost the same risk.

A letter of credit may be modified or restricted in a variety of ways. The most common arrangements are outlined briefly here. If you get stuck negotiating payment terms with your customer, check this section to see if you can find a mutually agreeable option. If you still can't resolve the matter, turn to your international banking advisor for guidance—that's what she's there for. Be creative and cooperative in investigating payment arrangements that will accommodate your customer, but always make sure *you* end up with a secure and timely payment.

Payment Timetables

You may extend varying payment terms within your L/C, ranging from a demand for payment on sight to an allowance of up to 180 days before payment is due. Let's look at each term.

Sight-Draft Payment

The time required to receive funds under an L/C drawing depends on the terms and the location of the paying bank. A sight draft is a payment instrument that requires your customer to pay the amount in full upon receipt of the documents—that is, "on sight"—before title to the goods can be transferred to him. A sight draft is not guaranteed by a bank, so it is vital to get payment before releasing cargo. This payment method is of obvious advantage to you.

Time-Draft Payment

If an L/C calls for a time draft, it is handled by a bank somewhat like a sight draft at the time payment is due; however, a time draft allows your customer some time, usually 30, 60, 90, or even up to 180 days, to pay the amount in full after title to the goods is transferred to her. Customers generally prefer this payment method, but obviously it can compromise your cash flow.

Banker's Acceptance

Once a time draft has been accepted by a bank, it becomes a "banker's acceptance." Since this acceptance is now the bank's liability, it holds payment in safekeeping until maturity and then pays you automatically. Banker's acceptances can also be used to obtain financing by selling the acceptance to the bank at a discount, although this practice is fairly rare.

Special Types and Uses of Letters of Credit

These are some specialized L/Cs that might gain you additional flexibility and security in financing your export transactions:

1. *Transferable L/Cs:* These L/Cs permit you to transfer your rights in part or in full to another party. They are typically used when the original beneficiary (you) acts as a middleman between the supplier of the merchandise and the buyer. The supplier is thus assured of payment for the goods even though it is not dealing directly with your customer. Keep in mind that no credit line is needed here since you are using your L/C as collateral. Once you transfer an L/C, there will be a nominal transaction fee involved.

2. *Assignment of proceeds:* This is very similar to a transferable L/C. The difference is that whether or not an L/C is issued in transferable form, you may request the paying bank to pay the proceeds guaranteed under the letter of credit to a third party. Again, no credit line is needed in this transaction, but you will be charged a nominal transaction fee. The assignment of proceeds, on the other hand, has no monetary value to the third-party assignee until the proceeds (the actual payment by the bank) become available. Therefore, if you neglect to ship merchandise as ordered or fail to submit proper documentation, no payment will be made to the assignee even if he can present the letter of assignment.

3. *Revolving L/Cs:* If you have a customer who intends to give you ongoing business, you may wish to open a revolving letter of credit. You can ask your banker for this, but you may not get it. Banks need to book the entire transaction amount, and for a revolving account, they have no idea what that amount will be. If you are fortunate enough to be extended this lenient credit arrangement, the amount of the L/C is automatically reinstated after a drawing of funds or after a specified period of time. The purpose of a revolving L/C is to limit shipments of merchandise, and consequently drawings under the L/C, to limited quantities within a certain period of time. A revolving L/C has the effect of renewing the original set of payment terms and conditions so you don't have to renegotiate each time. Revolving letters of credit are set up differently depending on the particular requirements of each transaction, so always consult with your banker.

4.　*Back-to-back* L/Cs: This setup is used fairly often by trading houses or middlemen that do not have the funds necessary to purchase the merchandise or the capital resources needed to obtain an unsecured loan from the bank. Its purpose is to extend indirectly the commitment of the issuing bank beyond the beneficiary to another party, usually the supplier of the merchandise. A back-to-back L/C is quite different from a transferable L/C or an assignment of proceeds in that it is an entirely separate transaction from the original or the master L/C. All parties involved must therefore rely on the successful completion of the original letter of credit. Since this is a more complex form of credit, a consultation with your banker is suggested.

5.　*Standby L/Cs:* These serve as assurance that your customer will fulfill her obligations under a contract. In other words, you draw funds under the standby L/C only when your customer fails to meet his obligations. This type of L/C is generally used to repay money borrowed or advanced. It often works well to assure payment of invoices for sales made on open account. Standby L/Cs can cover financial, performance, or trade-related transactions.

Special Payment Structures

Even though I personally have never had occasion to use any of these special payment structures for an L/C, it is important to let you know that they're available. Consult your banker to find out how they might work for you and your customer.

- *"Red clause"*: Under a red-clause L/C, you are able to obtain advances against the credit in order to purchase and process merchandise. The red clause within the letter of credit outlines a specific payment arrangement over a specific period of time.

- *Installment payments*: Under an installment L/C, you can draw a portion of the credited amount by presenting a sight draft, accompanied by shipping documents and a promissory note for the full credited amount.

- *Progress payments:* A progress-payment L/C allows for you to draw funds against the L/C for amounts proportionate to the progress being made in the production of goods. Proof of progress can be in the form of an inspection

certificate issued by you, your customer, or an independent party. This type of L/C is usually used to finance
large, long-term projects, such as an economic and real
estate development or sales of costly goods, such as large
machinery. The balance of the credit becomes available
to you once compliance with the terms of the L/C is
complete.

- *Advance payments:* This arrangement for the L/C allows
  for the exporter to receive funds in advance that might
  be necessary to purchase or process merchandise for the
  buyer.

- *Deferred payments:* This arrangement calls for sight drafts
  specifying that the draft is payable at a later date. These
  payments can be confirmed or unconfirmed.

- *Discounted payments:* This structure allows you to boost
  profits for your business with an L/C while satisfying
  your customer's payment preference. (I am elaborating
  on this method here because although it is rarely known
  or practiced, it can be an effective cash flow accelerator
  for your business.) You can elect to receive payment at
  sight provided the provisions of the letter of credit are
  met against an L/C to boost cash receivables and profits.
  However, this method hurts your customer's pocketbook
  because he has not, at this point, had a chance to sell the
  goods you just sold to him. As such, it can be a fairly big
  cash outlay for him. Alternatively, you can elect to receive
  a deferred payment (as previously noted), say after 180
  days, to allow your buyer a grace period for payment.
  In that case, there's no boost to your profits or bank
  account until six months have passed, but your customer
  will be happy that you've given him more time.

- There is another option in the way of discounted payments that can benefit both the seller and buyer. In this
  arrangement, once the bank that opens the L/C has
  accepted the documents and drafts you present, it may
  discount the amount it owes you and pay you, the beneficiary of the L/C, in advance of the maturity date (a fixed
  or determinable future date) provided that you indicate
  that you want this to be done in the agreement. What
  that means is this: you can allow your customer 180 days
  after the sight of the original bill of lading to pay her bank,
  but you collect the money involved in the transaction
  immediately.

- The interest rate on discounted payments for early payment varies anywhere between 6 and 18 percent of the total transaction bill. It is your responsibility as the seller to absorb it, but it is generally based on the annual rate of interest on a loan, the risk of the country in which the bank opening the L/C is located, and the reputation of the bank. The end result is that you get cash fast from the export sale and your customer gets the 180 days she needs to pay.

- *Mixed drawings*: Sight and time drafts may be specified under the same L/C. For example, the L/C may call for payment of 50 percent at sight, 25 percent sixty days thereafter, and 25 percent ninety from then. The bank oversees and pays the procedural duties when they are due.

The Worst Method of Export Financing: Open Account

An open account transaction means that payment is not required until the goods are manufactured and delivered. Documentation covering the shipment of goods is handled outside of the typical banking channels. This method of payment is fine if your customer is easily accessible. However, in the international business arena, where your customer can be fifteen thousand miles away, this method of payment cannot be used safely unless you are 100 percent certain that the buyer is creditworthy, and unless the country of destination is politically and economically stable. Otherwise, it's a huge risk to the seller (as I pointed out earlier with my Tokyo noncustomer). This is why I keep pushing for the L/C method. Or, at the very least, back up your open account terms with a standby L/C. You might also consider export-receivable insurance, which costs about the same as opening an L/C—about 1 percent of the transaction—but gives you the option of offering your customer open-account terms and retaining some protection. Your banker can assist you here.

But even the most compelling reasons for granting an open account are short-sighted at best. Many books on international sales propound the doctrine that export wannabes should always consider shipping on an open account basis, especially when you're first starting out and a major recognized company is interested in purchasing your products. For example, let's say an international conglomerate called Big Cheese LLC e-mails you a request for $25,000 worth of bicycle parts to be shipped immediately by air. How could a small shop like you, Little Cheese Export Enterprises, resist the chance to win an account like Big Cheese LLC? But we've all heard stories of what can happen to small, growing suppliers who deal with the big players. Conglomerates like our hypothetical Big Cheese LLC have been known to give high-volume business to small firms, enabling them to grow like mad. Then, virtually overnight, they switch vendors—and poof! Poor Little Cheese Export Enterprises bites the dust. It wouldn't be only the loss of the account that would do your company in, but also the delayed payment on the last order. In fact, some of my own worst payment experiences have been with huge companies that thought they were entitled to pay whenever their accounting department decided they should. I'd find myself waiting two months, three, six. Eventually they'd pay up, but was it worth it? Only if I had a good cash flow and a supplier that was willing to work with me. If you find yourself in circumstances in which you can afford to sweat out big-ticket deficits and you feel certain that somewhere down the line you'll get your money, then go ahead. But how many small-business owners—or beginning exporters—can comfortably operate this way? Take stock of your own situation and proceed accordingly.

If you find yourself in a position where none of these arrangements are possible and you cannot close a sale, you might explore a few of the following financing alternatives. Keep in mind that each industry has its own special government financing programs, so check with your industry associations at both the local and national level to see what they have to offer.

Noteworthy Export Noncash Payment Considerations

Consider the following additional ways to finance an export deal when other means are unavailable:

- *Countertrade*: In countertrade transactions, which involve trading in goods and services as opposed to money, cash does not change hands. Some business owners elect to use this payment method when there is a shortage of hard currency, surplus activity, lack of experience, or lack of credit. The benefits include but are not limited to: entering into difficult markets, increasing sales, overcoming credit problems, and gaining a competitive advantage. The downside is that it can be time-consuming and complex to negotiate.

- *Bartering (a type of countertrade)*: This involves a direct exchange between two parties of goods or services that have an equivalent value without using a cash transaction. In simple terms: it's a swap of one product for another product without the use of any money. The parties involved still must value the goods or services exchanged in the transaction as if they were cash. Doing so will be necessary for tax and customs purposes, so you need to be sure to comply with governmental requirements and accurately complete and file appropriate forms. Barter houses are often called on to assist companies of all sizes to convert what they have into what they need without any cash changing hands (conduct a web search to find ones that specialize in your industry and in a particular overseas market). Barter houses provide information and find potential buyers for goods received. They are particularly useful to the small exporter.

- *Consignment:* This involves an exporter (the seller) selling to a consignee (customer #1) but maintaining ownership of the goods and the consignee only taking possession of the goods in a foreign country. The consignee markets the goods and, when she makes a sale, the title transfers simultaneously from the exporter to customer #1 and customer #2 (the consignee's customer). It's only when the goods are sold—meaning that customer #2 pays customer #1, who in turn, pays the exporter—that the exporter gets paid. The exporter has the main role and is responsible for getting the product to the consignee. Consult with your international attorney to discuss the best terms and conditions for this type of contract arrangement for export sales.

■ **Caution** Transacting business in multiple currencies spanning several countries might be beneficial to a big operation interested in hedging against currency fluctuations, but for a small business, if not managed well, it can hurt the bottom line. It's best to negotiate terms in your own country's currency (US dollars, for example). This transfers the risk to the other party—the customer.

Regardless of payment method, it's important to try to keep the international payment process simple.

Export Financing Assistance

There are several federal agencies that offer financial assistance to exporters. These are just a few of the programs and types of assistance that are available to small businesses. Contact your bank to see if it is approved to underwrite any of these programs.

- *Small Business Investment Companies*: (http://www.sba. gov/content/sbic-program). These privately owned companies provide financing, equity capital, and long-term loans to small businesses.

- *International Trade Loan Program*: (http://www.sba.gov/ content/international-trade-loan). This program offers loan financing of up to $5 million for fixed assets and working capital for small businesses in a position to either expand existing export markets or develop new markets. These loans are also available if your small business has been adversely affected by import competition and you can demonstrate that the loan proceeds will improve your global-competitive position.

- *Export Working Capital Program*: (http://www.sba.gov/ content/export-working-capital-program). This program provides advances up to $5 million to fund export transactions. You can use the loan proceeds to finance suppliers, for work in process, or for production of export goods and services.

- *Export Express Loan Program*: (https://www.sba.gov/ loans-grants/see-what-sba-offers/sba-loan-programs/general-small-business-loans-7a/special-types-7a-loans/sba-export-loan-programs/export-express-loan-program). Considered the simplest export loan program, SBA Export Express offers financing up to $500,000, either as a term loan or a revolving line of credit. To qualify, you must have operated your business for at least twelve months (there are exceptions, so be sure to ask) and must demonstrate that the loan proceeds will be used to support export activity. You can use the loan proceeds to finance export orders, expand your production facility, purchase equipment, participate in overseas trade shows, or translate marketing material for foreign markets.

- *7(a) Regular Business Loan Program*: (http://www.sba.gov/ category/navigation-structure/loans-grants/small-business-loans/sba-loan-programs/7a-loan-program). The Small Business Administration offers this long-term loan with a guarantee for small businesses that might not have been able to secure funding through normal lending channels.

Tip Find more SBA export lenders: https://www.sba.gov/managing-business/exporting/export-loans/export-lenders.

- *Foreign Agricultural Service:* (http://www.fas.usda.gov/topics/export-financing). Run by the US Department of Agriculture, this service provides financial support to food exporters. Check with your state or regional department.

- *Overseas Private Investment Corporation:* (http://www.opic.gov/). OPIC educates small businesses about the benefits of expanding into developing markets and offers a number of products (political risk insurance, for example) and services to address their specific needs. OPIC's Small Business Center offers qualified small businesses with annual revenues less than $35 million the opportunity to utilize the organization's streamlined loan approval process.

- *Minority Business Development Agency:* (http://www.mbda.gov/). MBDA operates more than forty business centers throughout the United States. These organizations, in turn, provide business consulting, procurement matching, and financial assistance (relative to exporting) to minority-owned firms.

Tip Consult the *Trade Finance Guide: A Quick Reference for U.S. Exporters* (http://export.gov/TradeFinanceGuide/) in English or in Spanish (http://export.gov/tradefinanceguide/eg_main_063270.asp). It's very useful. And if you are trying to raise instead of obtain flexible financing for your export-driven company, you might consider TradeUp Fund (http://www.tradeupfund.com), which allows you to access critical gap capital to export and expand in international markets.

- *United States Trade and Development Agency:* (http://www.ustda.gov/). USTDA links US businesses to export opportunities by funding project planning activities, pilot projects, and reverse trade missions. USTDA is an independent US government foreign assistance agency that is funded by Congress.

Export-Import Bank of the United States

The Export-Import Bank of the United States (Ex-Im Bank; http://www.exim.gov/smallbusiness/) is responsible for assisting the export financing of US goods and services through a variety of loan guarantees and insurance programs. The goals of this agency are to offer superior service and to make a difference by providing exporters with needed support and providing taxpayers with enhanced value. The bank also assists exporters by serving as a liaison between US and foreign banks.

In 2015, Ex-Im Bank supported 109,000 American jobs, $17 billion in exports at no cost to American taxpayers, and more than $3.1 billion of exports from U.S. small businesses, of which nearly 90 percent directly supported U.S. small businesses.[iv]

Ex-Im Bank's top five eligibility requirements for small business exporters to receive a loan are that they:

- Be located in the United States

- Have at least one year of operating history along with a positive net worth

- Have services that are performed by US-based employees

- Ship products from the United States to a foreign buyer

- Export products with more than 50 percent US-made content based on all direct and indirect costs

The following list describes just a few of the many programs and products offered by the Ex-Im Bank to exporters. Be sure to inquire further.

- *Working Capital Guarantee*: (http://www.exim.gov/smallbusiness/smallbusprod/Working-Capital-Guarantee.cfm). This is a 90 percent loan-backing guarantee offered to commercial lenders to facilitate small exporting businesses securing the crucial working capital they need to fund their export activities.

- *Global Credit Express*: (http://www.exim.gov/sites/default/files/managed-documents/fly-wcg_03_global_credit_express_exporters_05nov2013.pdf). This program delivers short-term working-capital loans directly to creditworthy small-business exporters. It adds liquidity to the US small-business export market by financing the business of exporting rather than specific export transactions.

- *Letter of Interest*: (http://www.exim.gov/tools-for-exporters/applications-forms/letter-of-interest). This letter states Ex-Im Bank's willingness to consider financing for an export transaction and serves to help small businesses secure financing and make the online application process fast, simple, affordable, and secure prior to export.

- *Small Business Multi-Buyer Export Credit Insurance*: (http://www.exim.gov/products/exportcreditinsurance/). This credit insurance can be purchased from Ex-Im Bank, either through an insurance broker or directly from the bank, to reduce foreign risk. It offers a variety of policies tailored to cover particular risks and situations; for example, extend credit terms to foreign customers, the failure of an overseas customer to pay his credit obligation, and competitive payment terms.

- *Express Insurance*: (http://www.exim.gov/what-we-do/export-credit-insurance/express-insurance). An easy and fast-to-get product which helps small business exporters insure their receivables. This product improves the chance of getting bank financing because the business owner borrows against their insured receivables.

- *Single Buyer Insurance*: (http://www.exim.gov/what-we-do/export-credit-insurance/single-buyer-insurance). This policy "specifically covers payment for products or services that are delivered/rendered on open terms to approved buyers. The insurable loss events are insolvency/bankruptcy of the buyer or slow payment. A claim is filed when either of these events occur,"ᵛ says David Barrett, a sales agent for Euler Hermes North America, a leading provider of trade-related insurance solutions.

- *Working Capital Loans and Guarantees*: (http://www.exim.gov/smallbusiness/moreinfo/Working-Capital-Loans-and-Guarantees.cfm). These loans and guarantees of commercial financing are available to overseas buyers of US capital goods and related services. They offer a low interest rate, cover up to 85 percent of the export value, and generally give repayment terms of one year or more. In addition, they provide repayment protection to creditworthy buyers of US capital goods and related services for private-sector loans.

Since it is impossible to list all the programs offered by Ex-Im Bank, I suggest calling the regional export finance center closest to you (http://www.exim.gov/contact/headquarters) or visiting a center in person (http://www.exim.gov/contact/regional-export-finance-centers). Its purpose is to help expand local support to small businesses. Use it!

■ **Tip**   Escrow services allow both exporters and importers to protect a transaction by placing funds in the hands of a trusted third party until a specified set of conditions is met. Shipments are tracked to ensure the seller shipped and the buyer received the merchandise. This is a variation on cash in advance and can be a beneficial method of payment on international trade transactions but like any transaction, there are risks involved. It can, however, fill the gap between open account trade and cash in advance and is generally less expensive than an L/C. Escrow.com (https://www.escrow.com/why-escrowcom/security.aspx), for example, offers this type of service.

Online Payment Methods: E-Commerce and M-Commerce

We've already talked about payment options to use with large-volume customers; now let's look at the ones to use for Everyday Joe who only buys online. How will you collect money from him, especially if, for instance, he lives in Brazil? It depends. From this point on, proceed cautiously, because no online payment—whether through a Web site, mobile device, or mobile app—will work effectively unless the country you're dealing with accepts it! It's vital to keep that at the top of your mind along with everything else you are about to read. It's also important to take consumers' online preferences into consideration before integrating a payment plan into your e-commerce and m-commerce platforms

---

■ **Note**   By the time you read this, many banks will have launched a mobile payment service that could potentially grow to rival those of credit card companies, especially if these payment methods receive financial institution backing. If these efforts are successful, it could challenge the business model for credit card companies such as Visa, American Express, and MasterCard, which rely on customers to use their branded credit cards for online payments. Watch closely for how this develops and how it might impact your business, because the expanding digital payment arena, including wearable devices that make mobile payments, is just beginning to take off. We're living in fast-changing, ultra-tech-savvy times.

Credit, Debit, Global Prepaid Cards, and Third-Party Providers

The majority of online payment is done with credit or debit cards, and a high penetration of people use PayPal in conjunction with their own banks. That said, payment methods still can vary from country to country. How do you know which countries accept which payment method? You can find out by doing the following:

1. Check with your international banker.

2. Inquire with someone who lives in the country with which you desire to transact business.

3. Conduct an online search using the keywords "Preferred online payment methods, _____ [country]." Your search entry might look like this: "Preferred online payment methods Norway." As of January 2014, the results would show that 67 percent of online buyers in Norway prefer to make debit or credit card payment, 14 percent prefer using invoices, 14 percent prefer PayPal, 3 percent go with online bank payment, and 2 percent fall into the category of other/unsure/don't know.[vi]

4. Check About-Payment's "All Popular Online Payment Methods" (https://www.about-payments.com/ knowledge-base/methods).

Credit Cards

Most US companies offer credit card payment options online because they offer the capability to conduct business throughout the world. Among the credit cards accepted are American Express, VISA, Mastercard, and Discover. All of these work for online transactions, provided the banking system within the country accepts them and they are secure. Many credit card companies charge anywhere from a 1.95 to 3.5 percent service fee on the total transaction price. If a country does not accept a particular credit card, find a comparable service used by the country to fill in the gaps. The greater the global reach for a card, the easier it will be on you for collecting payments.

In addition, several credit card companies now offer country-specific credit cards and other payment services, made possible by special payment features that collect "regional" global payments. These include Maestro, offered by Mastercard for use in multiple countries; Dankort, offered by Visa in Denmark; Visa's Carte Bleue, used in France; Skrill, which facilitates global e-commerce; and debit cards for use in China, to name just a few.

Here is a list of the more popular and commonly used mobile payment methods used in this country:

- *Mastercard PayPass*: (https://www.paypass.com/). PayPass lets you accept everyday purchases quickly and safely through a MasterCard or Maestro-enabled card or device. Buyers can search worldwide for merchants—like you—who accept MasterCard PayPass. Note: Before implementing PayPass, check first with the card's bank to see which countries accept it as a payment method.

- *Visa payWave for Mobile*: (https://developer.visa.com/paywavemobile). This is a mobile payment system available for Visa issuers, mobile network operators, mobile device manufacturers, and third-party wallet providers looking to develop proprietary applications. According to Visa Developers, PayWave "enables Visa cardholders to simply wave their card or mobile device in front of a contactless payment terminal to make a payment."[vii] Buyers can make payments, including credit, debit, and prepaid products, for both online and offline contactless transactions.

- *Square*: (https://squareup.com). This online service allows you to start accepting credit cards in a heartbeat at 2.75 percent per swipe. Once you sign up, Square mails you a free Square card reader.

- *PayAnywhere*: (http://www.payanywhere.com). This credit card reader and free app lets people pay anywhere using Visa, Mastercard, American Express, Discover, and debit cards. You can download it at the App Store, Google Play, and Blackberry App World. PayAnywhere was created by the multibillion-dollar credit-card-processing company North American Bancard, which has more than two decades of merchant-payment-processing experience. The processing fees are competitive: 2.69 percent per swiped transaction. However, for a keyed-in transaction where you type the credit card number, the rate shifts to 3.49 percent plus a $0.19 transaction fee. There is no monthly fee, minimum required, or cancellation fee. PayAnywhere is compatible with iPhone, iPad, iPod touch, most Android phones or tablets, and Blackberry smart phones, and the company offers 24/7 live customer support through a toll-free number.

- *China UnionPay:* (http://en.unionpay.com/). The leading banking-card association in China is the third largest payment network by value of transactions processed, after Visa and MasterCard. The cards can be used in 150 countries and regions outside China. The company gives Chinese shoppers with UnionPay cards the option to make online purchases at the Web sites of participating Discover Merchants. What that means is that UnionPay cardholders have a safe and secure way to make purchases online around the world. In addition, China UnionPay provides access to Discover's services at all ATMs and electronic-payment merchants in Mainland China.

- And there's more. UnionPay recently partnered with PayPal to allow card members in China to use PayPal to shop online. That represents a phenomenal new opportunity for international retailers to sell to a larger base of Chinese customers.[viii]

Debit Cards

Debit cards, where accepted, can be used instead of cash when making purchases. In some cases, they can be assigned exclusively for use on the Internet.

Caution The development of debit cards, unlike credit cards, has generally been country specific, resulting in a number of different systems around the world. Be sure to check what type of payment system a country uses or prefers to use before establishing an online payment method. You'll also want to consider the fees associated with every payment option.

Global Prepaid Cards

Inasmuch as U.S. banking credit cards are used widely, not all countries accept them. That is why global prepaid cards are increasingly important for global commerce and are quickly gaining popularity among the millennial generation (Generation Y). Global prepaid cards allow users to preload money and later make purchases and complete payments via American Express, Discover, MasterCard, and Visa cards, ATM networks, private networks, and the Internet. For travelers, prepaid cards are a more secure alternative to the once-popular traveler's checks or large sums of cash.

Payment-Processing Methods Offered by Third-Party Providers

We will look at the payment-processing methods offered by different third-party providers in this section. The companies' methods will guide you through the payment implementation process for e-commerce and m-commerce transactions. (Some are specific to e-commerce and others require a mobile app, so be sure to double check what they can and can't do). Most charge a service fee ranging from zero to 2.9 percent, some tack on an additional per-transaction fee (thirty cents, for example), and others charge a monthly fee. Review their terms carefully.

Before you enter into an agreement with any company, find out which countries it services, the fees it charges on each transaction, how it handles disputes, what happens on charge-backs (the process where the cardholder's issuing bank requests a reversal of charges on behalf of the cardholder), what verification system it uses to minimize fraudulent activities, and how to terminate a plan, if need be.

There are many ways to get paid via third-party m-commerce and e-commerce companies. A few payment options offered by companies are given in the following list. There is also some information on the lesser-known payment options. Before making a decision, check reviews and chat rooms about these payment services to learn what users are saying.

- *ACH Payments:* (http://www.achpaymentsolutions.com/). ACH payments are electronic transfers made from one account to another. ACH processing allows you to use the Automated Clearing House (ACH) network to collect payments. Many large banks offer these payments. Bank of America Merrill Lynch is one. PNC, Chase, and Citibank also offer them. Check with your bank.

- *Amazon Payments:* (https://payments.amazon.com/). This service operates through your web browser, allowing other Amazon customers to e-mail you money and you to receive it using the accept-payment information in your Amazon.com account. On sales up to $2,999.99, fees are 2.9 percent plus $0.30 per transaction or less. On transactions of $3,000.00–$9,999.99, fees drop to 2.5 percent plus $0.30 per transaction and so on. Volume discounts apply. Inquire.

- *PayPal:* (http://www.paypal.com). PayPal allows you to set up a merchant account, through which you can make an online payment to or receive money from any person with an e-mail address. You can use it via the Internet or a mobile device, or in store. The company charges a 2.9 percent transaction fee on the total sale amount plus a $0.30 fee per transaction. The international charge is 3.9 percent transaction fee plus a fixed fee based on the currency received.[ix] When you buy something, it is free of a service fee. Transferring money is free, too. PayPal's big advantage is its reach—it is in 200 markets and allows customers to get paid in more than 100 countries, withdraw funds to their bank accounts in 57 currencies and hold balances in their PayPal accounts in 26 currencies.[x]

- *Bill Me Later:* (https://www.billmelater.com/index.xhtml). A PayPal service, Bill Me Later offers buyers the option of buying now and paying later. It is available as a method of payment at many online stores, and once added to your PayPal account, it can be used almost everywhere PayPal is accepted. It's essentially a reusable credit line without the plastic. BML works well for larger-ticket items where providing financing for a certain period of time, such as six months, will enable a sale. Interest charges apply and accumulate at an APR of 19.99 percent starting from the date of purchase, a significant rate that is important to keep in mind when selling or buying using BML. PayPal tracks purchases and payments done with BML, and provides you an online statement showing all charges.

- *CyberSource:* (http://www.cybersource.com/). Offered by Visa, CyberSource is an online payment service that accepts many payment types preferred in local markets (including Bill Me Later and PayPal), transacts payments in more than 190 countries, and funds in more than forty currencies. It can be integrated into most major commerce platforms with the help of a savvy tech programmer. In addition, it provides real-time tax calculation for sales originating worldwide so you can provide accurate totals for your customers at checkout. Costs (not listed on site) include set-up and implementation fees based on your specific billing requirements. A monthly usage fee will be charged based on either transaction or revenue volumes

- *Dwolla:* (https://www.dwolla.com/). This payment network allows anyone in the U.S. to send and receive money at no cost. Setting up the account is free, and there are no per transaction fees. The site offers a variety of options, from a Plus, Premium or Custom account, with prices ranging from $25 to $1,500 a month based on the solution you need.

- *Intuit Payment Network*: (https://ipn.intuit.com). From the makers of QuickBooks, Intuit Payment Network allows users to send and receive payments over the Internet. As the payer, it's free to send money, and your financial information is never shared. The catch? The receiver's bank shells out $0.50 per transaction. One advantage of IPN is that QuickBook users can include a payment link on invoices so customers can pay conveniently online. The site also provides the option to add pay buttons with fixed or variable amounts on your existing web or e-commerce site. And since it is integrated with QuickBooks, if you are already a QuickBooks client, the ability to streamline your financial management system might make it worth considering. Check reviews online before signing up to gauge its effectiveness.

- *Adyen*: (http://www.adyen.com). Adyen is a global provider of online, mobile and point-of-sale payment solutions. They have a presence on six continents and currently provide advanced payment solutions to more than 4,500 customers, including Facebook, Dropbox, and Airbnb. Adyen charges a setup and subscription fee, which varies based on volume. Inquire.

- *WorldPay:* (http://www.worldpay.com). WorldPay operates across 146 countries and is considered a world leader in payments processing technology and solutions for merchant customers. On a typical day, WorldPay "processes 31 million mobile, online and in-store transactions – that's about 360 a second."[xi] The organization offers a pay-as-you-go plan, monthly subscription service, or volume pricing model. Inquire.

- *Global Payments:* (https://www.globalpaymentsinc.com/en/us/). Operating in more than 29 countries throughout North America, Europe, the Asia-Pacific region, and Brazil, and with more than eleven billion transactions processed, Global Payments, a registered ISO of Wells Fargo, is a worldwide provider of payment technology services. The fixed fee per credit card transaction is $0.19, with a gateway transaction fee of $0.29.

- *Google Wallet:* (http://www.google.com/wallet). "With the Google Wallet mobile app, you can make your phone your wallet." That's the claim Google makes about Google Wallet, a free digital wallet that securely stores credit cards, debit cards, offers, and more. With GW, your customers can buy in your store and online, and send money. Transactions are fast. There is no setup fee. Receiving money is always free. The fee for sending money using a credit or debit card is not prominently noted on Google's site, other than "There is a small transaction fee."

■ **Note**   Google's Android Pay (https://www.android.com/pay/), launched in September 2015, has been adopted by Wells Fargo, Citibank, and Bank of America. The U.K. became the first country outside the United States to support the mobile payment system, but others are likely to follow. Apple Pay (http://www.apple.com/apple-pay/where-to-use-apple-pay/), on the other hand, is already used in many countries. Banks are expected to carry the burden of the service—so the more major banks that support Apple, the more global Apple will become. Like Google's Android, consider Apple Pay's international roll-out ongoing.

- *Authorize.Net:* (http://www.authorize.net/). A CyberSource solution and a wholly owned subsidiary of Visa, Authorize.Net enables Internet merchants to authorize and accept online payments via credit card and e-check. The site manages the routing of transactions in a similar way to the traditional credit card swipe machine you find in brick-and-mortar stores. However, instead of using a phone line, it processes the charges over the Internet. Retail merchants can integrate Authorize.Net's payment service via a third-party POS (point-of-sale) payment solution. In addition, the site provides a free Authorize.Net Verified Merchant Seal that can be added to a merchant's Web site to establish trust and build consumer confidence.

  Authorize.Net has been providing payment-gateway services since 1996, and as a wholly owned subsidiary of Visa, its reliable reputation makes the company a good choice, but at a price.

- *Stripe:* (https://stripe.com/). San Francisco-based Stripe makes it easy for developers in particular to accept credit cards on the web. The key differentiator?

You don't need a merchant account or gateway to set up, but you do need a bank account. Stripe stores cards, subscriptions, and direct payouts to your bank account. The fees range from 2.9 percent per transaction plus a $0.30 per transaction fee. The firm also accepts ACH and Bitcoin payments, which are capped at $5—payments above $625 cost $5. An interesting tidbit: the company is backed by PayPal founders Peter Thiel, Elon Musk, and Max Levchin. Stripe currently supports the United States, Canada, and seven other countries. Check to see if your country is supported or if it is in open beta mode: https://support.stripe.com/questions/what-countries-does-stripe-support.

At the bottom of their website, it states: "We're actively working on adding support for other countries. You can sign up to be notified when Stripe is available (https://stripe.com/global) in your country."

- *Braintree, a PayPal Company*: (https://www.braintreepayments.com/). This company, founded in 2007, offers another way to accept payments online (including foreign currency) and on mobile apps. It provides a merchant account, a payment gateway, recurring billing, and credit card storage. Your first $50K in card processing is fee-free. After that, fees are 2.9 percent of each transaction plus a $0.30 per transaction fee. The company accepts PayPal, Apply Pay, Android Pay, Venmo, Bitcoin, and whatever's next. There are no additional fees and no minimums. Braintree works with most of the leading e-commerce and billing platforms. Check to make sure yours is covered.

As a result of PayPal's acquisition of Braintree in 2013, the world is your oyster in terms of accepting payments from buyers almost everywhere. Get a better understanding of what might be available to you if you choose to set up and accept payments from any of the regions Braintree services: https://www.braintreepayments.com/products-and-features/global.

Caution Fraudulent activity is a pervasive issue when it comes to online payment activity. Be vigilant. Consult with your bank or credit card company to determine the best practice for preventing and managing online payment fraud.

- *Simply Commerce*: (https://www.simplify.com/com-merce/). Owned by MasterCard, Simply Commerce (MSC) accepts e-commerce and mobile-commerce payments regardless of the payment brand (meaning, it doesn't just work with MasterCard) in a matter of minutes. It's developer friendly, in that it gives merchants, especially small businesses, the code instructions for accepting electronic payments. MSC serves as both a merchant account and payment gateway in a single, secure package deal. Fees range from 2.85 percent for each transaction plus a $0.30 per transaction fee. There are no setup or monthly fees. MSC also works with most of the leading e-commerce (Magento, for example) and billing platforms (OpenCart, for example).

  The biggest benefit of MSC is the MasterCard name, which projects security and reliability. Note: As discussed earlier, MasterCard also has PayPass (http://www.mastercard.com/sea/consumer/paypass.html), a payment method that lets you use your phone as your wallet to make everyday purchases without having to swipe the magnetic strip on your credit card or provide your signature.

Many third-party logistics and fulfillment suppliers (3PLs), discussed in Chapter 18, specialize in helping businesses ship internationally and collecting payment. Inquire.

 Final note   The information that I have shared in this chapter regarding online payment methods is just the tip of the iceberg. Watch for tremendous strides and breakthroughs in e-commerce and m-commerce payment methods for smart phones and tablets during the coming months—not years—which will bring new options to consumers worldwide.

Summary

Remember what I said earlier: The most important thing to negotiate before closing on an export sale is how payment will be made. Knowing that these solutions exist will allow you to fund, grow, and succeed in the export marketplace.

When you have wrapped up your export sale, either by finalizing secure payment terms or arranging a creative-financing package that satisfies both you and your customer, it's time to move your cargo. After a final review of every-thing you have put into place thus far, you're ready for the export wrap-up: booking, packing, marking, and insuring your shipment to make sure it arrives in the best condition for your customer and preparing export documentation. The following chapter will outline the most essential documents as well as the less common types you might be required to present. After a final thorough review of terms of payment and documentation, your export goods will be on their way!

Notes

i. "Export-Import Bank Fred Hochberg says exporters need Senate to give his trade credit agency a quorum," Kent Hoover, The Business Journals, accessed May 15, 2016, updated April 8, 2016, http://www.bizjournals.com/bizjournals/washingtonbureau/2016/04/export-import-bank-back-in-business-but-not-for.html.

ii. An irrevocable letter of credit is a commercial docu-ment that your customer requests your bank to issue in your favor. Once issued, it cannot be modified with-out both parties' consent. "Irrevocable" means that the bank must pay you even if your customer defaults, provided the documents presented are "clean," mean-ing that they are in complete compliance with the lan-guage of the L/C and are presented to the bank prior to the expiration date. I discuss L/Cs in depth later in the chapter.

iii. "Trade Finance Guide: A Quick Reference for U.S. Exporters," Export.gov, accessed May 15, 2016, http://www.export.gov/tradefinanceguide/.

iv. "EXIM Bank Releases its FY 2015 Annual Report," January 14, 2016, accessed May 22, 2016, http://www.exim.gov/news/exim-bank-releases-its-fy-2015-annual-report.

v. "International Trade Credit Insurance," Laurel Delaney, About.com: Import & Export, accessed October 30, 2013, http://importexport.about.com/od/Financing/a/International-Trade-Credit-Insurance.htm.

vi. "Digital Buyers in the Nordic Countries Differ on Preferred Payment Methods," eMarketer, August 15, 2014, accessed May 22, 2016, http://www.emarketer.com/Article/Digital-Buyers-Nordic-Countries-Differ-on-Preferred-Payment-Methods/1011126.

vii. "Visa PayWave for Mobile," Visa Developers, accessed October 30, 2013, https://developer.visa.com/paywavemobile

viii. "PayPal Announces Partnership With UnionPay, Launches Its New China Connect Service," Kapron Asia, June 8, 2015, accessed May 22, 2016, http://www.kapronasia.com/china-payments-research/paypal-announces-partnership-with-unionpay-launches-its-new-china-connect-service.html.

ix. "PayPal Fees For Purchases, Getting Paid and Personal Transfers," accessed May 22, 2016, https://www.paypal.com/us/webapps/mpp/paypal-fees.

x. "About PayPal," accessed May 22, 2016, https://www.paypal-media.com/about.

xi. http://www.worldpay.com/uk/about/company-overview.

Booking, Marking, Labeling, and Insuring

Beware of little expenses. A small leak will sink a great ship.

—Benjamin Franklin

Many US companies lose more business in moving products overseas than in any other phase of the export process. In this chapter, I'll explain what the reason for this is and take you through the final steps of sending off your large-volume shipment. I'll also show you how to book your order with a global freight forwarder and how to pack, mark, and insure your cargo for a safe and timely delivery to your customer.

As I discussed in Chapter 18, an experienced global freight forwarder is worth its weight in gold because it will spare you the need to master all the complexities required to send off a shipment. Further, an experienced freight forwarder will let you work "on your export business" (thinking beyond what

© Laurel J. Delaney 2016
L. J. Delaney, *Exporting*, DOI 10.1007/978-1-4842-2193-8_21

the day-to-day reality of your business calls you to do)ⁱ as opposed to working "in your business"—a classic line by Michael E. Gerber, who wrote *The E-Myth Revisited.*ⁱⁱ In other words, you don't want to get buried in minutiae that some-one else with experience can easily handle; instead, you can spend your time working on getting more export business. Too many details can make you crazy, so my intent here is not to overwhelm you. Rather, it's to provide you with the fundamentals of moving products overseas. After that, it's up to you to use the information as a guide while you work with transport experts to export your products.

A quick note: This section is not about the Everyday Joe who buys a single product online. In this chapter, I will cover big customers—those who buy from a couple of cases to thousands of cases at a time.

Ready? Let's move it!

Booking Your Order

Once you have a legitimate order and finalized terms of payment, it is time to call your freight forwarder and give it the go-ahead to book your shipment. The company should pull up your quote reference number and reconfirm the quote first. Once it books your shipment, it will give you a booking confirma-tion number. *Write it down* or track it somewhere safe (Evernote.com, for example), because if there's ever a problem later on, you will need to refer to that number constantly.

By now, after my warnings about the necessity of negotiating payment terms to minimize your risk, you're probably a bit nervous about sending off the shipment. What do you do if the payment terms you set up with your cus-tomer fall through at the last minute? You do have a means of escape, but it'll cost you. All the way up until it gets loaded onto the vessel, you can ask your forwarder to hold your shipment, but remember, you are liable for all freight costs even if the shipment never leaves port. If your cargo leaves port and you still don't have a guaranteed payment method from your customer, request that the cargo not be released to your customer when it arrives at the port of destination. Normally, it wouldn't be released anyway because your customer needs to produce certain documents in order to clear it—which he won't have received unless payment has been settled—but you never know. When in doubt, always take extra precautionary measures to reduce your risks.

▓ **Caution**   The scenario where a shipment leaves port and you still have not secured payment illustrates how an export can go wrong. Secure your payment term upfront to ensure you are not left holding the bag.

Let's say you have been assigned the booking number FAN 31063. (The book-ing number enables the steamship line or freight forwarder to keep track of your shipment from the point of origin to the final destination.) The freight forwarder then gives you sailing information that looks like this: "Dresden Express, V14E30; sailing out of Oakland on 8/19 with ETA Hamburg, Germany 9/20." The forwarder will also tell you the absolute latest you can have your goods ready at your factory door in time to meet the sailing date. You must prepare the necessary shipping documents before then. Pay careful attention to that date, because it's critical information, especially if you are shipping against a letter of credit (L/C) that has an unreasonable expiration date—in this case, September 20. If you miss that August 19 sailing date, you miss meet-ing one of the conditions of your L/C. When that happens, you lose your guarantee of payment from your customer! Naturally, you want to avoid this at all costs.

■ **Tip** You can find global sailing schedules at JOC Sailings (`http://www.jocsailings.com/`). There, you can filter search results by port locations, carrier, vessel type (break-bulk or container, for instance), departure and arrival dates, and so forth. I use it to do a fast check on transit times to port destinations worldwide. If I were to receive a client's order on July 19, as in the previous example, I would know that I have less than a month to produce goods in time to meet the sailing date out of Oakland. It works the same if a customer says she wants goods delivered to her port of entry by the middle of November. You can check the schedule to see when you need to get goods produced in time to meet the sailing date.

One of the first documents your freight forwarder needs is an Electronic Export Information data, formerly known as Shipper's Export Declaration Form 7525-V, which now must be filed electronically (EEI; `http://export.gov/logistics/aes/index.asp`). An EEI is required anytime you use a freight forwarder or export directly using a steamship line or air carrier. This document specifies your product's commodity number, reaffirms what you have already communicated to the freight forwarder, and formally instructs the company to carry out the shipment. The freight forwarder will refer to the EEI to verify that the ocean bill of lading is prepared exactly as your cus-tomer specified in the originally accepted pro forma invoice and to confirm the method of payment. The document also helps customs to keep track of exports and to monitor the type of license being used to cover each shipment. It is also used by the Census Bureau to compile statistics on US trade patterns and for export control purposes. It must be prepared prior to shipment and presented to the carrier.

Whoever is handling your shipment will be able to provide the online link to the form and, in some cases, can even prepare the document on your behalf provided you authorize the company to do so with a power of attorney form (transport companies typically have this form template online for easy access). If the company does not provide it to you, the EEI can be electronically filed at the new Automated Commercial Environment (ACE) https://www.cbp. gov/trade/automated. Ask your freight forwarder or shipper how to prepare the form if you are unsure and the company will walk you through the process.

■ **Tip**   When in doubt about anything, ask. Be fearless about getting answers. When you see a required field on the EEI, Port of Export code (where your shipment is leaving the country), for example, be sure to consult with your freight forwarder, because this field can easily generate errors, penalties and delays in your export shipment if filed incorrectly. In fact, according to U.S. Customs Border Patrol (CBP), it is considered one of the top mistakes they issue penalties for!

Details, Details, Details: Preparing Goods for Overseas Shipment

Let's say you're an exporter specializing in handcrafted figurines and you're all set to move a carton of porcelain angels to your customer in Argentina. Piece of cake, right? Think again! Here are some of the logistics you will have to attend to before this shipment can get out the door:

1.   How sturdy is the carton? Tip: a new box is recommended.

2.   How secure is the seal that holds the carton together?

3.   Is the inside packing strong enough to keep the porcelain undamaged if the box is thrown into a truck?

4.   What is the weight of the carton?

5.   Is your product a temperature-sensitive export (ice cream, chocolates, or fresh fruit, for example)?

6.   What markings should you show on the outside of the carton?

7.   Is it important that the package arrives at your customer's doorstep by a certain date?

8.   Is any special documentation required to accompany the package?

9. Is it acceptable to leave the shipment outside your customer's factory door should he not be there when it arrives?

10. Do you require that your customer be notified one way or several different ways prior to delivery?

11. Do you require a confirmation of that delivery?

12. What about insurance? If the package gets lost or is damaged in transit, then what?

Caution   I once had a client in Chicago who was shipping cookies to Japan in early September in a regular twenty-foot container. The weather is typically cool in Chicago around that time of year, but as it turned out, the temperature abruptly went up to 90°F the week the shipment was leaving. Although warned about the unsuitable weather conditions, the client decided to stay with the regular twenty-foot container to save money instead of using a refrigerated one. When the cookies arrived in Japan, they were a mushy mess due to the unusual heat during transit. It took us weeks to figure out how to correct the situation, a tricky issue since the client had also elected not to insure the shipment. Needless to say, we did come up with a solution, but not without experiencing a lot of stress, needless aggravation, and delays. This illustrates two more examples of what can go wrong on an export shipment—those being the wrong choice on the mode of transport and a bad decision on insurance coverage!

Fortunately, not all products will be as much of a headache as porcelain figurines can be. But every export shipment calls for appropriate attention to the packing and shipping process so that your customers will receive their goods in perfect order. You need to pack your goods carefully so that they will survive the trip undamaged and mark your packages liberally with all the information necessary to ensure proper handling and tracking. You also need to envision the route step by step, from the time it leaves the factory door to the time it gets to your customer, and provide for all contingencies.

Carton Markings for Export

To pack your product effectively for export, you must provide complete, appropriate, and accurate package markings. There are several considerations that govern your shipment marking. First, you must make sure that whatever markings you put on the outside of a carton can easily be read by anyone, anywhere in the world. Second, you must meet shipping regulations and ensure the proper handling of your goods. Finally, you must know when it is appropriate to mark the outside of your cartons with what is truly in the inside—there are times when that's the last thing you should do. Your customer should be your best advisor as to how to mark your cartons for export, but if she seems ill informed or cannot be reached for consultation, the following guidelines ought to cover most situations.

If you are shipping a container-load or more, simple identification of your cargo should be enough, but take extra precaution so that reading your package is easy on the cargo handlers. Pretend the lights are out and your flashlight is dead—and you have to read your cartons. If you were in a gloomy warehouse trying to identify the contents of a stack of cartons, what would you hope for? That whoever prepared the cartons for shipment would have given some thought to making sure their goods could be identified even in the worst-case scenario and marked them accordingly. Mark your cartons with big, bold letters that can be read even at a distance and in poor light. Think about moisture; think about dust; think about accidental grease splattering all over your cartons. Use waterproof markers or waterproof labeling with durable adhesive. The more aggressive and durable your markings, the better your chances of avoiding misunderstandings and delays in shipping.

If you are shipping a smaller quantity of goods, such as a single carton or several cartons to be placed on a pallet, you also need to provide much more detailed identification on the outside of the carton, including the following:

1. *A shipping address label:* Your consignee's (customer's) name, address, and key contact person, and preferably also a telephone number, e-mail address, and fax number should be placed on your shipping label, along with the customer purchase or order number. As an extra added measure of security to your packaging process, put an extra label inside each carton. Then, if the outer label cannot be read or becomes detached, your information will be intact.

2. *A return address label:* Your company name, address, key contact person, and communications numbers (telephone, fax, and/or e-mail) should be placed on each carton, so that if a problem arises en route you can be notified immediately.

3. *The country of origin:* Your return address label should show your country in which you do business, which may not be the actual origin or place where the goods are manufactured. Check with your customer, transport company, or local consulate to see how the country of origin should be represented on the carton. This marking supports all your documentation and streamlines processing at the port of destination.

4. *A description of the contents:* What's included in the package should be marked on the outside—unless you're shipping a product in high demand. If you're shipping a low-price product that you consider a commodity item—canned peas, for example—you might think it's all right to mark the outside of your carton "Canned Peas," right? Not always! If the demand for the product in the importing country is phenomenal and the country can't keep up with it locally, you could be asking for theft or hijacking. Talk to your customer about substituting a different product identification on your carton to make your goods less tempting. For example, if Malaysian consumers love peas and hate green beans, you and your customer can agree ahead of time that, for purposes of your shipment, "Canned Green Beans" means "Canned Peas." This practice, sometimes referred to as blind marking, is simple but effective. However, you and your customer must change your code names every so often or else you'll attract the notice of the smarter and more organized thieves who keep track of what is moving in and out of the ports. More obvious high-value products, such as cameras, computers, or televisions, can also be shipped under blind markings. In all other cases, of course, it's best to mark the outside of your carton with exactly what's inside. That minimizes confusion for customs, your customers, and intermediary handlers at every stage of the shipment.

5. *Markings that are in English:* Unless notified otherwise, everything you write on the outside of your package should be in English. Your customer or your transportation company should be able to tell you whether it is required to provide any carton markings in the language of the importing country as well. If such markings are required, call up a local translator and have the necessary language rendered appropriately. Better yet, contact the country's local consulate to help you—they are always eager to facilitate trade, and it may even provide the service at no charge. But be sure to get your translation approved by your customer. You don't want to be too eager to finish up the labeling chore, only to find that your translation is inaccurate, ambiguous, or even offensive! Note: Foreign law might dictate the need for a translation in the foreign country's language, especially if the item is a hazardous substance. Be sure to check.

6. *Phrases and symbols for immediate identification of packages needing special handling:* There are numerous standard international phrases that signal the need for careful handling of hazardous or breakable products, such as "This side up," "Fragile—Handle with care," "Flammable," and "Keep dry." The International Organization for Standardization (ISO) provides a set of graphical symbols to help overcome language and other barriers (refer to "The International Language of ISO Graphical Symbols," `http://www.iso.org/iso/graphical-symbols_booklet.pdf`). In addition, you might also conduct a keyword search for "shipping marks and symbols" to find additional information on material handling in the context of shipping marks, labels, and symbols. Be sure to also find out which international symbols apply to your product. When in doubt, label your cartons with both words and standard symbols.

7. *An identification of the number of cartons you are shipping:* This should be written on each carton. For example, number each of the respective cartons "One of three," "Two of three," and "Three of three." This ensures that all of the cartons in your shipment will arrive—together—at the port of destination.

8. *A marking on all sides of the package:* If possible, have your cartons marked on five sides—that is, on all four sides and the top. Stay away from seams and folds. If your plant or transport company cannot do all sides, have markings placed on at least two of them—the long and short ends. But, again, the ideal strategy is to mark five sides. That way, no matter how your cartons are positioned, they can easily be read from any direction. Also, don't forget to remove any old markings. You do not want to create confusion for the receiver of your package.

9. *Weight and measurement markings:* Make sure that your container is marked with the net and gross weight and measurements (dimensions) on the outside and in the appropriate system of measurement, which is generally accepted to be metric.

■ **Caution** A lot can go wrong on a shipment when you are in a hurry, because the focus generally tends to be on the quality of the product and how excited the customer will be when he receives it. There's more to getting an export shipment from Point A to Point B. To minimize risks, always take your time and do your homework to avoid awkward surprises that can cause delays, nonpayment, or a customer refusal.

Insure, Insure, Insure!

Insurance is as vital to your product delivery plans as safe vehicles and good sturdy cartons. When you ship important cargo many miles away and it is completely out of your control, you do not want to take any chances on your vessel foundering in a massive midocean storm or your airline simply losing track of your cargo altogether. If situations like these occur, you must be compensated for your cargo's value.

Insurance coverage for export shipments is traditionally provided either through your airline or freight forwarder or by an insurance company specializing in ocean and air cargo. There are three types of coverage commonly provided for export shipments: perils, broad-named perils, and all-risks. Since most transport companies offer an all-risks plan and few, if any, shippers are likely to want to skimp on coverage, I will concentrate on this type of coverage here.

An all-risks policy covers all physical loss or damage incurred by any external occurrence, excluding loss or damage caused by an extenuating circumstance such as war, riots, strikes, or civil disobedience. This type of policy generally costs between 1 and 2 percent of the declared value of your shipment. Coverage varies according to your product type and your destination point— you can get coverage for a portside-to-portside shipment or from the factory door to the customer's door, for example—so be sure to ask your policy provider which type best suits your needs and those of your customer. Keep in mind, though, that no insurance coverage protects you against your customer refusing your cargo or against her failure to secure a required import license delaying shipment clearance, so plan accordingly.

Here are four points to consider when securing air or marine insurance:

1. *Get enough coverage.* Talk to your transportation company about what amount of insurance coverage you will need should your cargo get lost or destroyed. Many people ask for coverage of 110 percent of their transaction value, including freight costs and the insurance. The extra 10 percent is to compensate for your lost time, profits, and any legal or other expenses you might incur from the ordeal. You do not want to find out later (insurance claims typically take anywhere from one to six months to settle) that you are only covered for 20 percent of your transaction value!

2. *Decide who will secure the insurance.* How much control do you want as the exporter (seller) should something go wrong with your shipment? Your terms of sale usually determine this. Your liability ends at the point at which

the title to the goods changes from seller to buyer. If you are guaranteed payment for your shipment regardless of its condition upon arrival, you might be more easy-going about letting your customer handle insurance. In addition, if you are shipping open account, I recommend that you not only secure the insurance yourself, but also do so through a US company to see that any claims will be settled expeditiously. Don't forget: Your customer is usually the first to discover damage or loss of cargo. He must take all reasonable measures to minimize the loss or damage and to keep the merchandise as evidence for claim settlement.

3. *Decide who pays for it.* Sometimes your customers will request the insurance and offer to pay for it, and sometimes they won't. How you and your customer assign financial responsibility for insurance depends on the cost of the coverage and how the expense will affect each party's bottom line. Negotiate the point to achieve a win-win situation.

4. *Leave a paper trail.* No matter who arranges and pays for the insurance, there are specific documents you must be prepared to present in the event of filing a claim. These include a letter of claim along with a copy of the bill of lading covering the shipment; a copy of an insurance certificate (prepared by your transport company or if you purchased insurance through an independent carrier, by you); and a survey report issued by a claim agent, plus an invoice showing the amount of damage or loss. Timeliness is of the essence—do not miss filing deadlines.

One export shipment that doesn't reach your customer's door is one too many! You could sustain severe financial loss as a consequence; maybe even the collapse of your enterprise. So, protect your business, your cargo, and your customer's interests before releasing merchandise by securing the appropriate insurance coverage.

Summary

At this stage, you will be able to sit back and congratulate yourself because your export goods are on their way! But don't get too comfortable. Within a week, you'll need to prepare all necessary export documentation to ensure that you get paid and that your customer receives the cargo without undue delay. In the next chapter, I will cover the most essential documents as well as the less common ones you might be required to present. In addition, I will talk about the two types of export licenses, when a license is required, and how to procure it. After a final review of terms of payment and documentation, your export transaction will be complete.

Notes

i. "Michael E. Gerber Companies," accessed May 27, 2016, `http://michaelegerbercompanies.com/megcompan ies13/`.

ii. Michael E. Gerber, *The E-Myth Revisited: Why Most Small Businesses Don't Work and What to Do About It* (New York: Collins Business, 2005).

22

Documentation, Export Licensing, and Other Procedures

One day there will be no borders, no boundaries, no flags, and no countries and the only passport will be the heart.

—Attributed to Mexican-American musician Carlos Santana

Export Enforcement is committed to working with industry to help identify threats, facilitate licensing decisions and party screening, and mitigate penalties where companies have taken the appropriate actions to manage export compliance.

—Assistant Secretary of Commerce for Export Enforcement
David W. Mills[i]

© Laurel J. Delaney 2016
L. J. Delaney, *Exporting*, DOI 10.1007/978-1-4842-2193-8_22

In these past several chapters, I've walked you through the somewhat-complex process of getting your export shipment together with the help of your global freight forwarder. In this chapter, I'll go over another set of painstaking but critical details—the preparation of shipping documentation to coincide with your transport and payment methods. I will also address the often anxiety-producing (but needlessly so!) issue of the exporter's licensing responsibilities. Finally, I will provide a checklist for a final inspection of your documentation to make sure everything's letter perfect.

Export Documentation

The first step in preparing export documentation is to carefully list the shipping arrangements you have just made for your customer. You want your export sale to be a complete success, and this is a critical phase. The documentation for an export follows the same pattern as that for a domestic sale. When you sell your widgets to your customers across town, you invoice them, right? That's where you start with your overseas customers as well. Where your local customer sometimes has special requirements for the order, such as a packing list or specified outside markings on each case shipped, your export transaction will have special documentation requirements, too. These will vary according to the country of destination and the type of goods shipped.

If you've selected a freight forwarder that has a history of shipping your type of product, the company should be right on the ball about the current documentation requirements and also offer you the option to process most if not all documentation online. Take the initiative, though, and ask a lot of questions. Use the company's expertise to your advantage.

Nine times out of ten, you will need the following basic documents to complete an export sale:

1. A commercial invoice

2. A packing list

3. A certificate of origin (where applicable)

4. Three original ocean or air bills of lading and copies of them

5. A payment instrument

Other important documents required for some destinations and some commodities:

- A quality-inspection certificate

- A consular invoice

- An import or export license

- An insurance certificate

- Dock and warehouse receipts

- A health inspection certificate

- An IATA (International Air Transport Association) shipper's certificate for restricted or dangerous products

I will review each document thoroughly so you will feel comfortable preparing it. Be aware, too, that there are software programs available that will execute your export documents online efficiently—Unz & Co. offers one (http://www.unzco.com/software/unzexpdoc.htm). As your business grows, you might consider installing one of these programs. Most freight forwarders provide these documents online as well. Whenever you need to review a document to see what it looks like, just conduct an online search to pull one up.

■ **Tip**   The exports I talk about in this chapter are all ongoing, but that won't always be the case. If you have temporary exports, say if you are exhibiting at a trade show (look back at Chapter 16) in a foreign market and need to send cases of product samples for display, you might consider getting a Carnet. A Carnet is an international customs and export document that is used to clear customs without the need to pay any duties and taxes on merchandise that will be used for trade shows and sales solicitations to prospects. You can learn more at Boomerang Carnets: http://www.atacarnet.com/.

Commercial Invoice

A commercial invoice (for an example, see http://www.unzco.com/forms/commercialinvoices.htm and the commercial export combination http://www.unzco.com/forms/commercialinvoices.htm#cec) usually describes what you are exporting and references important transaction numbers. Your invoice must be prepared exactly as you and your customer agreed upon in your pro forma invoice. If both of you agreed on a change in the sale terms later on, record that change on your invoice. In addition, always include the following information, even if it isn't asked for:

1. The names of the buyer and seller. If consigned to someone else, the names of the shipper and receiver

2. The description of merchandise—the more information you provide, the better, including the name of the product, brand, symbol and numbers that identify the product being imported

3. The customer-reference purchase order number for the pro forma invoice

4. The method of payment, including any and all reference numbers pertaining to it

5. The shipping terms from your price quotation (for example, cost and freight [CNF] Tokyo, free alongside ship [FAS] Seattle, free on board [FOB] New York)

6. The currency in which the transaction will be made (US dollars, Japanese yen, French francs, etc.) and the purchase price for each item sold

7. The country of origin

8. The bill of lading number

9. The container number, if shipped by container

10. The quantities in weights and measures—if you fail to disclose the weight and measure of the goods necessary to assign duties, the importer of record pays expenses incurred to obtain this information in advance of release of the merchandise from Customs Border Patrol custody

11. The ports of exit and entry

12. Marine or air transit instructions: the name of vessel or aircraft, voyage or airway bill number, date of departure, and date of arrival at destination

13. The invoice and all related documents must be in English

Packing List

A packing list (for an example, see `http://www.unzco.com/forms/packing_envelopes.htm#packinglist`) is used to inform transportation companies about what they are moving as well as to allow the customer and others involved in the transaction to check what has been shipped against the pro forma invoice. It's a good safeguard against shipping incorrect cargo! To prepare your packing list, delete all the prices on the invoice and double-check to see that the number of cases; weight (net, gross, metric); and measurements appear on the invoice. Then rename the document "Packing list," and write it in big, bold letters, and you're all set.

An export packing list should be clearly marked "Packing List Enclosed." Shippers and forwarding agents determine the total weight and volume of the shipment, and whether the correct cargo as indicated is being shipped—all based on the packing list.

Your freight forwarder, bank, and customer should indicate how many copies they will need and where each copy will need to be attached (outside of each shipping container in a waterproof envelope, for one) and distributed to the appropriate parties to the transaction (along with your other original documents in line with the terms and condition of the sale), some weeks in advance of when the shipment takes place. I always make three to four extra copies for my file just in case.

Certificate of Origin

Not all export shipments require a separate certificate of origin (for an example, see http://www.unzco.com/forms/certoforigin.htm#General). Often, merely stating the country of origin on your commercial invoice is sufficient. When a certificate is required, it's usually because the country to which you are exporting allows some preferential treatment for shipments like yours, such as a lower duty rate under a trade agreement with the United States, which must be detailed in a separate document. (For example, Mexico, Israel, and Canada have preferential arrangements with the United States if a shipment is intended to be duty-free.) The certificate also protects customers from unknowingly bringing in goods from countries with which trade is prohibited by embargoes, cartels, or other political or economic factors.

Composing the document is utterly simple. Just type up your own sample form for the certificate claiming that your goods are of a certain origin. It would look like this:

> We hereby certify that the goods reflected in our Invoice No. _____ dated _____ were produced and manufactured in the United States of America on _____, 20__.
>
> XYZ Export Co.
>
> _____
>
> Ms. Betsy MacDonald, President

Bear in mind that there are two components to determining the country of origin: (1) the goods must be shipped from that country, and (2) a substantial percentage of the value of the product must be added in that country.

Your customer might request that you have this document certified by your local Chamber of Commerce. To have this done, send the Chamber your prepared certificate along with a letter requesting the certification and three copies of your commercial invoice. If you email the documents, be sure to indicate which documents you would like to be certified. The Chamber will take the statement that you provide, retype it verbatim on Chamber letterhead and certify it with notary seal and signature. Most Chambers charge a flat fee ranging from $15 to $25 for this certification. If you are a member, the fee might be waived or reduced. Be sure to read the fine lines of your customer's terms and conditions to determine whether or not you need to have this done. Turnaround time can be as short as twenty-four hours, but you may want to call in advance if you are setting up a shipment in a hurry.

Certificates of origin for goods that are manufactured in the United States, as well as abroad, can also be obtained by contacting eCertify: http://www.ecertify.com.

■ **Tip** For more information on a Certificate of Origin, read, "What Is a Country of Origin Certificate?": http://importexport.about.com/b/2011/03/31/why-is-a-country-of-origin-certificate-important.htm.

NAFTA Certificate of Origin

Check with your carrier to find out if your product qualifies for a reduction or elimination of duty under the North American Free Trade Agreement (NAFTA). For information regarding eligibility, contact your local US Customs and Border Protection (CBP) office (http://www.cbp.gov/trade/nafta). If it qualifies, the NAFTA Certificate of Origin form (for an example, see http://www.unzco.com/forms/certoforigin.htm#CBP434) should be used to receive the benefits of reduced duty, which will be passed along to your customer. Sample forms can be found at the CBP site (http://www.cbp.gov/trade/nafta/certificate-origin).

■ **Tip** Transactions valued less than $1,000 do not require the NAFTA Certificate of Origin, but you will still be required to make a statement on your commercial invoice to the effect of: "I certify that the goods referenced in this invoice comply with the origin requirements specified for these goods in the North American Free Trade Agreement, and that further processing or assembly outside the territories of the parties has not occurred subsequent to processing or assembly in the NAFTA region." The statement should be handwritten, stamped, and typed on or attached to the commercial invoice. If you do regular shipments of the same group of commodities to the same destination over the course of the year, you can ask your freight forwarder or transport specialist if you can complete a blanket NAFTA Certificate of Origin so as not to have to complete the form for each and every shipment. My theory is, whenever you find something is a royal pain in the #%@, ask how to simplify the process!

Bills of Lading

Depending upon how fast you want to get cargo to your customer and how much she is willing to spend, you will either ship by ocean or by air. Accordingly, there are two types of bills of lading, the ocean bill of lading (for an example, see http://www.unzco.com/forms/billsoflading.htm) and the airway bill (see http://www.ups.com/aircargo/using/services/supplies/airwaybill.html).

An ocean bill of lading serves both as a receipt for the cargo and as a contract for transportation between you, the exporter, and the carrier. It also symbolizes ownership; accordingly, if it is in negotiable form, it can be bought, sold, or traded while the goods are in transit.

When you use air freight, an airway bill is issued in lieu of a bill of lading. It serves as a through bill of lading, which covers domestic and international flights moving cargo to a specific destination. Your air transportation carrier will advise you of the house airway bill number (shipper's document of receipt) and the master airway bill number (freight forwarder's document of receipt) assigned to your shipment. You must be sure to communicate these to your customer along with other transportation details. Airway bills of lading serve functions similar to those of ocean bills, but they are only issued in non-negotiable form. This means that you and your bank have less protection because you lose title to the goods once shipment commences. Be sure to refer back to Chapter 18 if you are shipping hazardous goods. Special forms are required.

I will describe ocean bills of lading in further detail because ocean freight is the most economical—and therefore the most frequently used—method of export shipment. To have one made up, you must prepare and submit a Shipper's Letter of Instructions form to your freight forwarder so that it can issue it accurately. This form indicates if the transaction is being made against a letter of credit (L/C), whether insurance is required, where to send documents, and so forth. Once you've finalized terms of payment with your customer, you need to furnish these facts to your freight forwarder. Most bills of lading are issued with three originals and several copies.

There are numerous different types of ocean bills of lading, but you will find that the following are the most commonly used:

- *Straight (non-negotiable):* This type of bill of lading provides for delivery to the person whose name appears on it. It must be marked "Non-negotiable." Only the person named can claim the goods upon arrival. A straight bill of lading is usually used for goods shipped on an open-account payment basis in cases where the exporter is not concerned about the importer receiving the goods without payment.

- *Shipper's order (negotiable):* This type of bill is used when you want to impose conditions on the delivery of the goods, such as requiring an acceptance of a draft. This type works well when payment has been secured by a L/C because you can make sure that the terms of the letter of credit are met before the goods are released.

- *Clean:* This type of bill is issued when the shipment is received in good order. If there is any damage or a shortage of product is found, a clean bill of lading will not be issued.

- *Onboard:* This type is issued when the cargo has been placed aboard the named vessel. It is signed and certified by the master of the vessel. For a L/C transaction, an onboard bill of lading is required in order for you, the exporter, to get paid.

Most of my customers ask for a shipper's order bill of lading, which authorizes their bank to take title of the goods should they default on payment. The bank does not release title of the goods to the buyer until payment is received. The bank will also not release these funds to you, the exporter, until all conditions of the sale have been fulfilled at your end.

Payment Instruments

As I discussed in Chapter 20, getting paid is an essential part of the export transaction. Numerous criteria are applied by businesses when determining which payment instrument to offer as a term of sale. A payment instrument in this case refers to documentary collections such as a sight or time draft, which is widely used in international trade. A documentary collection is the collection by a bank of funds due from a buyer against the delivery of specific documents relating to an export sale. The seller (exporter) sends a draft or other demand for payment with the related shipping documents to the buyer's bank. Compared to open account sales, the documentary collection offers more security to the seller (exporter), but less than a letter of credit.

Other Important Documents

Over the years, I have found that the following documents have also been required from time to time. This is not a complete listing, but it will give you an idea of what to expect in the way of special documentation requirements. Note: I am providing a more comprehensive approach to the Import and Export License section to resolve any potential confusion or questions you might have on this topic.

Quality-Inspection Certificate

When shipping high-value products or when you are dealing with a very conscientious customer, an inspection certificate might be requested. An inspection certificate provides proof that what you are shipping is, in fact, what the customer ordered and is also of good quality. If a customer requests this document, agree to it—but see that he covers the administrative and inspection fees. Also, ask him to recommend an independent inspection agency to perform the review at your end. If he doesn't have one, ask your export resource bank for a suitable contact.

Tip I once had a customer in Tokyo who asked to have an inspection of his goods done prior to their leaving the factory in Chicago. He requested that his close friend, living in Chicago, conduct the inspection. When the goods were ready for dispatch, my customer's friend arrived at the plant and opened a few cartons here and there to ensure that we were not shipping inferior merchandise. Then, she eyeballed all the cartons to see that they were marked on the outside in the way her friend had requested. Finding everything in order, she signed the inspection certificate and copies we had prepared in advance. In this case, the inspection didn't cost the customer a cent, everything was certified as A-OK, and we were all happy!

Consular Invoices

A few countries still require consular invoices, which are special forms that must be legalized by a consulate of the country to which you are exporting. If required, copies are available from the destination country's embassy or consulate in the United States. This procedure prevents under- or overpricing and also helps the consulates pull in a little extra revenue. Be sure to discuss with your buyer who will bear the costs of the expense.

Import and Export Licenses

Recently, I received an e-mail from a woman who works at a small manufacturing company. She explained that her company had recently exhibited at a jewelry show in the United States and a German man had expressed interest in a product at her booth. He had said he would buy ten thousand of her pierced-earring backings if she could ship to the port of Hamburg within sixty days. He had a big fair coming up and knew he could preview the holders to his customers and garner much interest.

She was thinking through the details but was very apprehensive about getting involved in exporting because people had told her that it's hard to get an exporting license. "What is this 'license'?" she asked. I could tell by her message that this single issue was worrying her more than any other aspect of the export transaction requirements I've covered thus far. And, to tell you the truth, I didn't have an answer for her, so I said I would check with the Export Administration Regulations (EAR) and get back to her.

We all fear the unknown, and government bureaucracy is especially scary. Most of us don't want to add more phases to a business process, like exporting, that's already complex enough—especially ones that might slow the project down indefinitely. But don't let an obstacle like this cause you to give up on a good overseas lead! You can find your way around export licensing with less trouble than you think. Let me show you how. As for the woman with the pierced-earring backing holders, it turns out she did not need a license because most exports from the United States do not require a license, and may be exported under the designation No License Required (NLR).

First of all, don't worry—just because you have to apply for a license does not mean that there is a possibility that your application will be automatically denied and you'll be barred from exporting your shipment. The licensing process is undertaken for specific governmental purposes, primarily to monitor outbound shipping traffic. There are two types of export licenses: a general license (GL) and a validated license (VL). A general export license is a standing permission given by the government to export a certain category of products. Individual exporters do not need to apply for one. A validated export license, on the other hand, is assigned to a specific exporter for a specific product, either for a designated period of time or for a single transaction. Exporters should know that failure to comply with the regulations surrounding either type of license carries both civil and criminal penalties, so pay close attention.

Determining Which License You Need—General or Validated

The Bureau of Export Administration (BXA) maintains the EAR, which includes the "Commerce Control List" (CCL). The CCL includes items such as software, commodities, and technology, which are subject to the export licensing authority of the BXA. Once you know what you are exporting, where it is going, who will receive your item, and what your item will be used for, you can consult these materials to determine which export license you need and find out whether any restrictions apply.

■ **Note** The "Export Administration Regulations" page on the US Bureau of Industry and Security Web site includes downloadable files on everything mentioned in this section—from the "Table of Contents" for the EAR, to the "Index," to the "Commerce Control List," to "License Exceptions." Bookmark it for future reference: http://www.bis.doc.gov/index.php/regulations/export-administration-regulations-ear.

When you export any good valued (the value, for example, designated on the export license that corresponds to the commodity being exported) at over $2,500 (or requiring a license), you must submit information on the shipment to the Automated Export System (AES). You can get help on filing AES and classifying merchandise, regulations, and trade data by calling 1-800-549-0595.

Some sections of the EAR (http://www.bis.doc.gov/index.php/regulations/export-administration-regulations-ear) to check out include:

> *Part 732, Table of Contents:* "Steps for Using the Ear" is a step-by-step guide to general license obligations.

> *Parts 738 and 774:* "Commerce Control List Overview and the Country Chart," Part 738, and the "Commerce Control List," Part 774, will tell you which country group your export destination falls into. Don't let the numbers and abbreviations scare you. Once you're looking at the EAR, getting to the right section isn't terribly difficult.

> *Supplement No. 1 to Part 738:* This supplement to the country chart offers comprehensive instructions on using the chart along with a detailed example. If your country of destination is not listed here, you do not need a validated license unless your commodity meets one of the technical exceptions noted within the export commodity control number (ECCN; an item that may be subject to a short supply control, for example).

> *Part 774, in reference to the country destinations that require a validated license:* In addition to listing your country grouping, the "Commerce Control List" in Part 774 also lists country export destinations that require a license. If your product is on the list, an "X" appears next to the country you intend to export to. The next step in the export process is to apply for an appropriate license electronically through the Simplified Network Application Process Redesign (SNAP-R). Everything you want to know about SNAP-R can be found at http://www.bis.doc.gov/snap/ and https://snapr.bis.doc.gov/snapr/docs/snaprFAQ.htm. Before applying for a license, check with your customer on what documentation is required.

Part 748: The "Application Classification Advisory and License," featured in this part, allows you to find the ECCN assigned to your type of product yourself if the Department of Commerce can't help you. For items subject to the EAR but not listed on the CCL, the proper classification is EAR99. This number, which appears at the end of each category in the CCL, is a "melting pot" classification for items not specified under any CCL entry.

New, Web-Based Tools for Exporters

In conjunction with the government's ongoing Export Control Reform Initiative, The Bureau of Industry and Security (BIS) at the Department of Commerce offers some new and useful web-based tools for exporters to determine if their products are subject to EAR regulations. This list is by no means comprehensive. It only highlights some of the most important regulation changes that have taken place via the Export Control Reform (ECR).

- **Simplified Network Application Process Redesign (SNAP-R):** https://www.bis.doc.gov/index.php/licensing/simplified-network-application-process-redesign-snap-r. SNAP-R allows users to submit export license applications via the Internet. It also allows you to obtain a Company Identification Number (CIN) and user account.

- **System for Tracking Your Export License Application (STELA):** https://www.bis.doc.gov/index.php/licensing/track-your-application-stela. You can check the status of your export/re-export license applications and classification requests.

- **Commerce Control List Classification:** https://www.bis.doc.gov/index.php/licensing/commerce-control-list-classification and under that is the Export Control Classification Interactive Tool: http://www.bis.doc.gov/index.php/export-control-classification-interactive-tool. The CCL determines whether or not authorization is required to export a specific good. The Export Control Classification Interactive Tool helps you identify the steps to follow when reviewing the CCL in Supplement No. I to part 774.

- **Guidance on re-exports:** https://www.bis.doc.
  gov/index.php/licensing/commerce-control-
  list-classification. If you are outside the United
  States and want to re-export or transfer (in-country) a
  good that is of US origin, this section guides on determining whether your good is subject to the EAR.

To determine if your item is specially designed or not, including how the
review of the term relates to the larger CCL (see Supplement No. 4 to Part
774 of the EAR—Commerce Control List Order of Review) visit: http://
www.bis.doc.gov/index.php/specially-designed-tool.

Never use these tools as substitutes for carefully reading the EAR regulations
and seeking advice from your freight forwarder or international attorney who
is knowledgeable of regulations and knows how to deal with government
agencies when there is something that you do not understand. Review the
Export Reform Control (ERC) FAQs: http://www.bis.doc.gov/index.
php/2012-03-30-17-54-11/ecr-faqs.

You can contact the Office of Exporter Services at your local department
of commerce (DOC) by phone or e-mail to go over these steps. If it can't
help you, do the research on your own and then visit one of the DOC counselors to confirm your findings. Check with your international attorney on
specific export transactions, because the EAR is complicated; the index to the
"Commerce Control List" alone is seventy-five pages.

A brief alert: Various requirements of the EAR depend upon your knowledge
of the end use, end user, ultimate destination, or other details of the export
transaction. If you can discuss your transaction in good conscience with DOC
counselors and with complete confidence, then there should not be any cause
for an agency intervention. But, as mentioned earlier, if you cannot explain
whom you are selling your product to, why the customer is buying it in the
first place, or what she will do with it once it is purchased, you've got a problem. If this is the case, you should refrain from pursuing the transaction, advise
the BXA, and wait. The BXA is there to help you, not hurt you. Its role is to
prevent exports and re-exports that go against the national security and foreign policy interests of the United States. It is good to consider it our duty
as citizens to work in partnership with the agency to maintain the highest
standards of protection for our country.

Caution   To comply with export law, map out an export-compliance strategy. This is vital. But
keep it simple and easy to understand, because you don't want to accidentally end up exporting a
product that will be used for other wrongful purposes later on. US export controls help protect our
country by keeping products and technologies away from countries of concern, persons who might
use the products against us, or terrorists. Violations of this nature can result in both criminal and

administrative penalties. Assigning one person to track the complete export process carefully and always address the how, what, when, where, why, and originating party of every export is a start to meeting US exporting regulations and keeping our country safe. For more information, visit the US Bureau of Industry and Security (`http://www.bis.doc.gov/index.php/compliance-a-training/export-administration-regulations-training`).

Must You Obtain the Import License for the Destination Country, Too?

Obtaining an import license is not your responsibility. It is your customer's. If you have secured payment with him, for example, with an Irrevocable Letter of Credit, it is up to your customer to take the appropriate measures to determine whether he needs an import license. If he does need a license and neglects to apply for it, and you ship against the L/C, you are still entitled to payment because you took care of things at your end. The customer, however, will not be able to clear the product at the port of entry until he clears up the licensing problem. If he fails to get an import license and you ship on open account, you may not get paid until weeks or months later. That said, it is a good idea to find out from your customer if an import license is needed, even though it is not your responsibility to arrange it. Whether or not the license is needed, be sure to secure payment.

Other Port-of-Destination Requirements

It's important to be aware of the standards and regulations of the importing country. Ideally, your customer will be knowledgeable about possible barriers to entry, but it helps to be aware of shipping restrictions and documentation requirements yourself. For example, if you are exporting food, medical, or electrical goods, your customer may not be able to import these items until she conducts an inspection to see that the goods meet local standards. Most developed nations have organizations comparable to the US Food & Drug Administration that monitor product safety. So, before your customer imports so much as a cheese sandwich, she will have to check with the organization that is equivalent to the FDA in her country to make sure the product can be imported. Once you've made sure that there is no reason why your product should be barred from entry, you may be ready to ship.

Shipping Under a General License

If you've checked the EAR and confirmed with your department of commerce that you do *not* need a validated license (VL), you can proceed with your shipment under a general license without having to apply for a formal license. The good news is that the majority of products exported are covered by a general license.

You should still check to see, however, if your shipment requires Electronic Export Information (EEI, formerly Shipper's Export Declaration (SED), which helps US customs to monitor shipment licensing.

Shipping Under a Validated License

On the other hand, you might have found out that the country you want to export to requires a VL for your product. Usually, the following types of products are subject to export controls and will require a VL:

1. Goods that pose potential harm to your own country's security

2. Goods that cause a shortage of supply in your own country

3. Goods that affect your country's foreign policy

To ensure a smooth license application process, tell the truth (full disclosure is best), know your customer,[ii] and determine well in advance of filing whether there are any red flags.[iii] Should you make a mistake (e.g., failure to register; unauthorized shipment), own up to it, take corrective action, and come up with a solution to the problem. And above all else, learn from your mistakes so you avoid repeating offenses.

Applying For An Export License

If an export license is required, you may submit an export license application through the online Simplified Network Application Process Redesign (SNAP-R). Visit the SNAP-R section of the BIS website for more information on signing up to be a SNAP-R user: `https://www.bis.doc.gov/index.php/licensing/simplified-network-application-process-redesign-snap-r`.

In the SNAP-R system, you, as the exporter, may prepare a commodity classification request or application for export or reexport. Part 748 of the EAR details requirements for submitting a license application.

BIS conducts a complete analysis of the license application along with all documentation submitted in support of the application. You may check for the status of your pending export or re-export license application by visiting their System for Tracking Export License Applications (STELA) at: `https://www.bis.doc.gov/index.php/licensing/track-your-application-stela`.

If your license is approved, you will receive a license number and expiration date to use on your export documents. A BIS-issued license is usually valid for 24 months.

I recommend that you inquire with your international attorney, your local DOC, and your local EAC for further ins and outs of licensing and also to get some hands-on experience in using the reference materials discussed here.

■ **Tip** There are license exemptions or exceptions that authorize you to export or re-export items subject to the EAR (see Part 740), under stated conditions, where they would otherwise require a license. Check with the Bureau of Industry and Security at the U.S. Department of Commerce at https://www.bis.doc.gov/index.php/forms-documents/doc_view/986-740.

■ **Caution** EAR license exception can be a painstaking exercise, and if you run afoul of the exception requirements, then an EAR export control violation may occur. Monitor your export-control compliance efforts carefully to maintain a compliance rate as close to 100% as possible.

Insurance Certificate

If the customer requests that you provide insurance, then you must issue an insurance certificate evidencing the type and amount of coverage for the cargo being shipped (refer to Chapter 21). Be aware, though, that some countries prohibit insurance coverage issued in the United States, so check in advance with your freight forwarder before making any insurance commitment to your customer. The forwarder will quote you insurance coverage at the 110 percent CIF (cost of goods, insurance, and freight) value and prepare the certificate for you. The company probably knows that the certificate should be made in negotiable form and must be endorsed before it is submitted to the bank.

In some instances, an airway bill can serve as an insurance certificate for a shipment by air. Be sure to check with your shipping company.

Dock and Warehouse Receipts

The dock receipt is issued once the export product has been moved by the domestic carrier to a port of exit and left with the next responsible carrier, which will then take it from the port of exit to the overseas destination. The receipt proves that a transfer has been made from one carrier to another. The warehouse receipt lists the goods received for storage at a warehouse.

Health Inspection Certificate

It is important to know about the destination country's health and sanitary regulations that pertain to the product you are about to export. The best way to find out about these regulations is to contact officials in the Office of Food Safety and Technical Services (OFSTS) at the Foreign Agricultural Service (FAS) located in Washington, DC. This office is largely responsible for overseeing manufacturing, production, and shipping practices that affect food safety, such as food additives, product standards, and packaging.

If you are exporting an agricultural product, you might need a Phytosanitary Certificate detailing inspection. This certificate is issued by the US Department of Agriculture (USDA) to satisfy import regulations for foreign countries. It indicates that a US shipment has been inspected and is free from toxic plant and pest diseases. In addition to the Phytosanitary Certificate, the USDA issues the Export Certificate for Processed Plant Products and the Certificate of Quality and Condition. If a processed plant product cannot be given a Phytosanitary Certificate but has been denied entry to one or more countries for lack of a health certification, an Export Certificate can be issued. Some products in this category are bulk nuts that are salted, roasted, or vacuum packed (in or out of their shells); soy-fortified products; and meal extracted from seeds by solvent. The Certificate of Quality and Condition is offered by the USDA's Processed Products Branch following official inspection and grading of canned, frozen, and dehydrated fruits and vegetables and related products. This certificate is available on a fee basis and can be tailored to meet your specific export needs.

Some countries require that health certificates be notarized or certified by a chamber and legalized by a consulate.

International Air Transport Association (IATA) Shipper's Certificate

An IATA shipper's certificate for restricted or dangerous products is required for all dangerous goods shipments transported by air carriers and air-freight forwarders (http://www.unzco.com/forms/interndangergooddec.htm#IATAdec). The exporter (shipper) is responsible for accurately completing the information on the form per the instructions of IATA (http://www.unzco.com/forms/instructions/DG_IATA.pdf) and ensuring that all requirements have been met through IATA's Dangerous Goods Regulations (http://www.iata.org/publications/dgr/Pages/index.aspx). Compliance measures include, but are not limited to, packaging (shipping carton is adequate, for example), marking (the product exported is identified correctly), and required information related to the product exported.

Get It Right the First Time, So That It Is the Only Time

Even a minor documentation problem can cost you and your customer time and trouble. Once, a very upset Greek customer faxed me about a documentation problem on a shipment he had just received. He complained that I should have prepared the commercial invoice to match up exactly with the pro forma—yes, I know I've just been lecturing you on the importance of doing that, but back then I didn't realize just how important it really was. My customer told me that the local customs officials would not allow clearance of the goods because of that particular discrepancy. Although I was a little confused by the extra data they wanted included on the commercial invoice, I reissued it within minutes, not just in one new version but in three, just in case the first one didn't suit the people at customs. As it turned out, all three of them worked, so they settled on the one that best suited their needs and cleared their shipment.

Fortunately for me, that mistake was easily resolved. In fact, to this day—twenty years later—the customer still brings up this story because he never had a supplier go to such great lengths to get it right the second time! Now, my guiding principle is to go to great lengths to get it right the first time so that it is the only time. It should be yours, too.

Tip Most transport companies can alert you to documentation problems and take care of them on your behalf. The only thing that might be required is your approval on a reissuance of a document and perhaps a signature (online or offline).

Summary

Hopefully this chapter has alleviated any concerns you might have relative to what is essential when preparing shipping documentation to coincide with your transport and payment methods. You're well on your way to becoming a successful exporter.

I have emphasized again and again that the world of international business is driven by relationships. If you want to succeed in building your own network of relationships, you may need to rethink the way you do business and make a comprehensive commitment to customer service. I will talk about establishing exceptional export service and the strategies that work to make success happen in the next chapter. Much of this has to do with communicating regularly, following up to ensure satisfaction, following through on promises, and becoming a valued participant in your customer's business and professional growth.

Once you've got the basics down, I will introduce you to cross-cultural learning, making a point to express points of cultural intelligence that will help you to further establish your competence and trustworthiness. This will set you apart from your competitors and make you memorable—both of which will strengthen your global network and help keep export business coming your way!

Notes

i. http://www.bis.doc.gov/index.php/forms-documents/doc_view/1005-don-t-let-this-happen-to-you-071814.

ii. "Know Your Customer Guidance," Bureau of Industry and Security, accessed May 29, 2016, http://www.bis.doc.gov/index.php/enforcement/oee/23-compliance-a-training/47-know-your-customer-guidance.

iii. "Red Flag Indicators, Bureau of Industry and Security, accessed May 29, 2016, http://www.bis.doc.gov/index.php/enforcement/oee/23-compliance-a-training/51-red-flag-indicators.

Keep Building Your Business

In Pursuit of Exceptional Export Service

Strategies for Success

The "value added" for most any company, tiny or enormous, comes from the… Quality of Experience provided.

—Tom Peters, author, *Re-Imagine!*[i]

Give customers what they want—and a little more. Let them know you appreciate them. Make good on all your mistakes, and don't make excuses, apologize. Stand behind everything you do.

—Sam Walton, founder of Walmart[ii]

The relationship between you and your overseas customer shouldn't end when a sale is made. If anything, it requires even more attention. Once you've completed the initial export transaction, you must expect to provide a broad spectrum of "free" or "value-add" services in order to encourage repeat business. It's the kind of follow-up I refer to as the "care and feeding" of customers and suppliers, which is done to keep them coming back, the premise of this chapter.

© Laurel J. Delaney 2016

L. J. Delaney, *Exporting*, DOI 10.1007/978-1-4842-2193-8_23

Thanks to the Internet, customers have more say so, limitless options, and higher expectations on product quality. They also take responsive service into account when considering a purchase. The challenge for exporters is to capitalize on this by increasing value for the customer without sacrificing profits.

So, why deliver good customer service? Repeat business; fans raving about you to others; employees, your biggest resource, feeling inspired because they work at a caring company; and growth. These are just a few of the many ways a business benefits by providing exceptional customer service. Good customer service is smart marketing—something to be proud of when delivered well. You might have the greatest product or service for export, but if you don't treat customers like they are gold, they will go elsewhere. Good customer service can make or break a business. People do business with people they like, can trust, and can grow with.

Exceptional Export Service Philosophies

This chapter is devoted to a list of fifteen strategies I've come up with that have helped my business and my clients' businesses achieve successful employee, customer, vendor, and colleague relationships the world over. To achieve exceptional export service, you must plan for it and then act on it. Consider the following tips your "commonsense blueprint" when developing your own in-house set of principles for great customer service. As you will see, many of these actions should be taken both before and after a sale. Note: These traits apply to both your Everyday Joe and big-buying customers.

■ **Tip**   Remember how I emphasized getting the right people on the export bus in Chapter 4? I explained how best to serve customers and suggested firing people who are not on board with your values. Life is too short to waste one second with Debbie Downers or Dave Disruptors (unruly people who have the capability, if given sufficient attention, to take the organization down due to their rogue behavior).

Communicate with Your Customer

The relationship truly begins after the sale. It is important to reach out to the customer once the sales transaction has been completed because your first ambition is to serve them. Customers like approachable and easy-to-find exporters, knowledgeable follow-up, and a show of heart. Expand the relationship in a way that lets additional possibilities fall into place. Ask how everything went and what more you can do for them. Follow up with them in a week or two with a list of new ideas designed to foster the relationship. These might concern how the product they imported can be used for other purposes or how showing the product in action via a YouTube video might increase sales. Growth is vital to sustaining a long-term relationship, and it also creates the conditions for superior results.

You need to find out how your customer feels about you and your company after he buys your product. Only then can you determine if a customer is satisfied or if you can fix a problem. Start asking today or set up an online survey (using SurveyMonkey or MailChimp, for example) that allows customers to weigh in and evaluate the experience they had with your company. They will see that you are trying to improve your service.

Resolve to practice a "no surprises" policy with your customers. Surprises are seldom good. Nobody likes to hear bad news (more on this later) via a grapevine, so make sure you communicate with your customer on any important information that will impact your relationship.

Stay away from canned responses via social media channels when it is obvious a customer is angry. A canned response might be: "Thank you for choosing ABC Company for your stay. We appreciate your business!" And this could be after a firm or a person wrote: "Your accommodations were deplorable. I will never stay at your facility again, ever." To build the relationship and learn as much as you can, strive for personal interactions with your customers to ensure each customer is treated as a priority and taken care of in the way she expects. Remind each employee that part of their job is to serve as a "brand ambassador" for the firm.

Care About and Support Your Customers

Take a humanistic approach to handling all inquiries. Show some love. And if you can't fix the thing that made the customer unhappy, refer him to someone else who can. Remember, based on the type of product or service you export, you might need on-the-ground support in the overseas market to help your customers better understand how to sell your offering to their own customers. Always let your customers know that this extra value is available.

And listen to both what's said and what's not said. I once had a client whose only child had gone off to college, and I could tell it impacted him by the delays in our communications and short responses when he did reply. After asking how he was doing and how his son was coming along, he poured out to me in an e-mail what it was like to send your only child off to school and have an empty nest at home. Sometimes putting the elephant on the table or opening up a discussion with your customer about what's going on in each other's lives can be both cathartic and an emotional bonding opportunity that strengthens a relationship. It also shows heart and support in a time of need.

Pay Attention to Details Pertaining to Your Customers

What might seem mundane to you can make a world of difference to your customer.

Your customer likes jazz? The next time she visits you at your home office, take her to a jazz experience like no other. To you, it might seem basic or mundane, but she will be thoroughly impressed that you remembered and cared enough to do something special for her. Or maybe you have an overseas customer who loves San Francisco. When he returns to his homeland, send him off with a beautiful picture-book of San Francisco showing all the great places along with a historical perspective.

Get Everyone on the Same Page About Your Customers

The customer service mentality should permeate your entire organization. What is your commitment to customers? Does everybody in the company understand this commitment inside and out? Do you provide exemplary service? Friendly service? Accessible service? The service goal of online retailer Zappos is "Delivering happiness."[iii] Define yours and carry through on it every step of the way. Ask yourself these questions to frame it:

1. What is our customer service plan (what do we stand for)?
2. Why is it important?
3. Who is responsible for it?
4. How will it get done?
5. How will it be measured?
6. How will we celebrate our customer service successes?

Tape the following motto to your wall or use it as a sign-off on your e-mails: "Everything we do is to help our customers compete more effectively and win in their marketplace." Also, create your own statement about what you want to make happen for your customers and then offer some extra-value or even "free" perks related to it. Based on the statement "I want to allow distributors to win an all-expense-paid trip to the company's home base if they bring us X amount of business in a quarter," you could sign the distributors up for your company newsletter, feature them on your blog, produce a video offering tips on how to use your product or service in ways they didn't think of, and direct them to where they should go for reorders.

> **Tip** Use your existing customers to gain new ones. The shortcut to achieving that type of growth is to *ask*. If you've done a good job with your service, a customer will be more likely to give you leads on new customers. Referrals are potent opportunities to move fast on getting new customers, provided you do everything just right as outlined here.

Set Up a Mother Ship Service Counter for Your Customers

All customers need a home base to revert to in good times and bad. Set up a "mother ship" center for handling them. It can be one person in the company who holds down the fort or it can be a hundred-person effort. Train all of your employees to anticipate and respond to customer inquiries with care and to take every inquiry seriously. Make them responsible for handling e-mail inquiries, phone calls, social media inquiries, and so forth.

> **Tip** Should any of your employees ever make a mistake with a customer, have her admit it to the customer, apologize, correct it, promise it won't happen again, and do something special as a courtesy (highlight him on your blog, for example), and then move on.

Treat Your Customers like Your Partner or Spouse

Ever hear the expression "How a man treats his mother is how he will treat his wife"? The same theory applies to business owners and their employees. How a business owner treats her employees is an indication of how she will treat her customers. If treated well, employees will be more likely to go the extra mile in their work with customers. If treated badly, they'll be less likely to put forth great care and work ethic.

Let's take a time where a customer visited me in Chicago and asked me to accompany him on a tour of a supplier's facilities in Boston—on a day's notice. It's standard procedure to accompany your customer to the supplier's plant, so I immediately got on the phone to book the flight. Lo and behold, there were no seats. My customer said it was not a problem and that he would make the trip alone. Then I checked another airline and found that it had a red eye at 4 a.m. I booked the flight but decided not to tell the customer. I arrived at the plant much, much earlier than his appointment time. You should have seen the look on his face when he showed up and saw me there! He thought it had to be too good to be true. My point: I treated this customer as if I were meeting my spouse at an important event—and I did so without hesitation.

Create an Experience for Your Customer

When you buy a cup of coffee at Starbucks, it's not just about the coffee; it's about the experience—who you might see, who might see you, what work you might do on your laptop, what music might be playing, or what news is circulating in the neighborhood. Or maybe you want to have private, unrushed time all for yourself. Yes, the coffee tastes good, but if everything else were terrible, would you go back for that great cup of coffee? According to Dori Jones Yang and Starbucks Chairman and CEO Howard Schultz, "The underlying foundation of this company [Starbucks] is not about growth. It is about the passionate, soulful connection we have with our people, our customers, and our shareholders."[iv] The spirited human connection, sanctuary-type experience, and great cup of coffee are what keep customers coming back to Starbucks.

You are not exporting a product or service. You are exporting an experience for your customer that comes in a bundle that includes access to and interaction with you. Eliminate or reduce one part of the bundle and the customer will leave you and take his business elsewhere. I strongly believe, as Tom Peters says, that a "quality" customer experience correlates to customer loyalty, so get it right! You can run your export business as a "transaction-based experience" where you just get the deal done or you can run it as an "experienced-based brand" where every touch point relates to the superiority of your product or service. If it's the latter, what will that entail?

Think back to Vosges Haut Chocolate that I talked about earlier in the book. With a slogan of "Vosges Haut-Chocolat invites you to travel the world through chocolate," a mission of "Peace, love and chocolate," and the invitation "Ring our chocolate concierge" all posted in the "Contact Us" area of the site, Vosges is most definitely an "experienced-based brand" offering exceptional service at every point of interaction with the company.

Caution   Over time, as customers gain familiarity with a product or service, they might find an exporter's support program to be of declining value. Their buying decisions then become more price sensitive. You can shop for more inexperienced customers or you can kick it up a notch with the experienced customers by providing stronger marketing, improved account-management resources, and additional value by helping to develop new applications for existing product or service offerings.

Create a High Standard for Your Customer Service

Raise your own expectations of what you believe your customer should get from you. Set up a high standard involving a heightened set of expectations for customer service and then meet them effectively. Give your employees ways to reward customers and show them how much you care.

Maybe your customer needs delivery within a month. Reduce the time it takes for her to get the product to three weeks and maintain that on future orders. Or maybe your customer needs a special loading configuration where the product is delivered in a container. Follow her instructions and do the shipment to her liking.

Give Time to Your Customers

One of the most undervalued benefits that we can give a customer is our time. Set aside a certain amount of time each day, week, or month to devote to your customers. Ensure that their needs are being met personally and promptly. Your time is valuable. They know that. When you give your time, you show customers they are worth it.

My general rule for responding to customer communications is to do so within twenty-four hours. What's yours? When customers want to see you, get an e-mail from you, or speak with you, devote time to providing them the service they require. It's a valuable commodity to customers.

Stay Away from the Status Quo with Your Customers

Once a good customer relationship has been established, it's easy to get comfortable. As the exporter, you might rely on the status quo (which equals doing nothing) with your customer after the sale, but his needs will change over time. Check in with him. Silence isn't always golden and it can't hurt to get a status update more often than not to find out what your customer may or may not need.

Tip Every once in a while it can't hurt to ask yourself, "Do I want more business or better business from my customers?" More business can mean additional sales, but better business can be far more profitable. Check your income and balance sheet statements on a regular basis.

Use Cultural Diversity to Your Advantage with Your Customers

When you provide an exceptional export service to customers worldwide, you need to understand the diverse needs of those customers. The different perspectives and cultural norms of your customers force you to dig deep into cultural differences and offer a vibrant source of ideas and process improvement to meet customer expectations. It is only when exporters leave their comfort zones that they can then grow and become stronger both personally and professionally.

Rather than focus on cultural differences with your customers—what you don't have in common—look at what you do have in common. When you're in a new environment, ask questions about how you should behave. Seek help in understanding your customer's culture and the way things are done.

Develop an open culture that encourages feedback so that your employees, customers, and suppliers, wherever they may be located, will know their opinions and ideas matter and are valued. Culture permeates all relationships. It's not an afterthought. It's a first thought. Exporters who work on their cultural skills will be able to offer more value to customers, be better colleagues, and triumph in the export marketplace.

Face Bad News or Bad Times Head On with Your Customers

Have you ever had to share bad news with a customer? I have. The best way to share disheartening news is to deliver it in the same fashion you would want to receive it: in person or, if distance is a problem, via a telephone call. If it's by telephone, make sure you reach the person directly that needs to be told. Picking up the telephone to discuss the situation with your customer lets you reassure them that the situation can be resolved, and will be, and provides you with an opportunity to answer any questions or concerns they might have. The same holds true for an in-person visit. Just make sure you give your customer plenty of time to meet, receive the information, react to it, and discuss.

If you handle a matter correctly, the customer will not remember that bad news was shared. They will remember that you were honest and forthright and kept them apprised of the state of the situation, even when it did not go according to plan.

Recommend Others for Your Customers When You Can't Do the Job Yourself

Ever have your customer ask you to do something that is out of your realm of expertise and you know just the company to fill the bill? A competitor. You might balk at that thought, but if a competitor you are on good terms with offers a fairly better product or service export offering than you do, and your customer's success heavily depends on the quality of that product or service, then everyone is better off when you recommend the competitor. Nothing beats providing exceptional export service like a willingness to forgo short-term gains for long-term success for all.

Make that kind of behavior your trademark and you will find your unselfishness returned a hundred times over by way of becoming a trusted advisor to your customer and an honest, fair, and transparent company to your competitor. New export business will follow.

Create Meaningful and Compelling Product Offerings for Your Customer

Don't become too proficient. You may be good at what you do, but are you churning out the same product time and again with minimal changes? Your customers don't always want bigger and better or new and improved. They want breakthroughs.

To create meaningful and compelling product offerings for your customers, bring them into the conversation. Liberate them to speak up on what they want. It starts with asking for input. After all, you are seeking new approaches and variations on what you are currently exporting. There's no better way to breakthroughs than to listen to your customers, see under the surface of what your customers really want, and then deliver on it.

Be Thankful and Show Appreciation for Your Customers

One last bonus philosophy that I know most of you already do: Thank a customer for their business in person or via the telephone. Then follow up by expressing further sincere appreciation via e-mail. These are musts, absolutes, givens. Don't miss a beat here.

If I were to sum up in one sentence how I approach my clients during and after a sale, it would be this: I provide the service, I'm interested, I care, and I will do my best to help.

The Absence of Complaints

In the article "After the Sale Is Over," marketing professor Theodore Levitt says: "One of the surest signs of a bad or declining relationship is the absence of complaints from the customer. Nobody is ever that satisfied, especially not over an extended period of time. The customer is either not being candid or not being contacted. Probably both."[v] That said, treat customer complaints as a gift and an expectation that can now be met.

Delivering exceptional customer service is complex. That explains why there are very few businesses that make us look forward to every transaction we have with them. If you show some passion and enthusiasm for what you do, do what you do exceptionally well, and have fun, your customers will come back happy and with great gusto.

Summary

In the final analysis, you must have the courage and strength to do what you know is right for the benefit of your customers. Adhering to key values plays a big role in differentiating your firm from someone else's and can lead to a more effective management tool for a firm.

You must also constantly drive and evolve your business profitably and safely in today's world. As you evolve and mature as an exporter, your customers and the market itself evolve and mature. Delivering superior customer service for your exports is the essential ingredient to profiting from the power of your customers and reflects a moment of truth for any high-performance, successful organization. Great customer service is a collaborative effort among your employees, your suppliers, and your customers. If you are constantly asking your customers what they need and want, your employees can deliver the best. Do your best work and your exports will grow.

Notes

i. Tom Peters, *Re-Imagine! Business Excellence in a Disruptive Age* (New York: DK Publishing, 2003), 113.

ii. "Service to Our Customers," Sam Walton, Walmart China, http://www.wal-martchina.com/english/service/aim.htm.

iii. A book on the success of Zappos was written by Tony Hsieh. It is called *Delivering Happiness: A Path to Profits, Passion, and Purpose* (New York: Business Plus, 2010).

iv. Howard Schultz and Dori Jones Yang, *Pour Your Heart into It: How Starbucks Built a Company One Cup At a Time* (New York: Hyperion, 1997), 332.

v. Theodore Levitt, "After the Sale Is Over...," *Harvard Business Review*, September 1983, http://hbr.org/1983/09/after-the-sale-is-over.

Cross-Cultural Learning

The Importance of Communicating with Cultural Intelligence

Seventy percent of international ventures fail because of cultural differences.

—David Livermore, author, *Leading with Cultural Intelligence*[i]

What does it mean to be a global worker and a true "citizen of the world" today? It goes beyond merely acknowledging cultural differences. In reality, it means you are able to adapt your behavior to conform to new cultural contexts without losing your authentic self in the process.

—Andy Molinsky, author, *Global Dexterity*[ii]

Whether you realize it or not, thanks to the Internet, everyone is part of the global marketplace. Just look at the billion+ people who use Facebook worldwide. To thrive, all companies must develop a multicultural perspective, cultural intelligence, or cultural literacy. When exporting and using digital platforms like Facebook to support those efforts, you must try your best to understand people, no matter where they are from.

© Laurel J. Delaney 2016
L. J. Delaney, *Exporting*, DOI 10.1007/978-1-4842-2193-8_24

In this chapter, I'll discuss the elements of cross-cultural consciousness and how it can make or break your business success. I'll also offer a short list of online resources, books, and intercultural tips to help you minimize embarrassments and misunderstandings so that your global negotiations proceed comfortably and productively.

■ **Tip** Don't assume that a market is like America, even if it is an English-speaking country. Every country has its own cultural norms. Get culturally competent. It's a critical element to success in the export marketplace.

What is culture? It's how people learn, the way people do things, or how they share and interact with each other. Culture affects every part of daily life and makes up one's social heritage. From a business standpoint, culture consists of many components—language, social interactions, religion, education, and values, for example—that create diversity among peoples and influence our expectations of what is appropriate or inappropriate. For the aspiring exporter, recognizing cultural diversity is imperative. The greater your commitment to expanding your cultural consciousness, the more comfortably and effectively you will function within business and social environments beyond your own borders.

Soon Ang and Linn van Dyne define cultural intelligence—or literacy—as "a person's capacity for functioning effectively in situations characterized by cultural diversity."[iii] In another instance, van Dyne, professor of management at the Eli Broad Graduate School of Management at Michigan State University, says: "Knowledge of your Cultural Intelligence provides insights about your capabilities to cope with multi-cultural situations, engage in cross-cultural interactions appropriately, and perform effectively in culturally diverse work groups."[iv]

If you want to derive the greatest personal and professional profit from your travels, your goal should be no less than to enter a different culture and engage successfully in cross-cultural interactions. This goes back to the global mindset I talked about in Chapter 1: the ability to venture out in the world and adapt as you go. You must also have the propensity to learn and succeed in your endeavors. Don't just go to another country, take care of business, and come home. Confront and welcome the differences and let them affect and alter you. International travel is one of the most exciting, memorable, and precious experiences that any of us will ever have. On-the-ground exposure to other cultures and other ways of doing things helps develop skills in dealing and working with people from other cultures. And you will enjoy the experience much, much more if you can cross your own mental borders to experience cultural diversity in the process.

For the businessperson, selling a product or service overseas takes particular sensitivity to the values and concerns of overseas customers. International training, including language acquisition, is vital to building an optimal trade relationship in your target market. Things move very fast in the business world of the twenty-first century, so it's best to learn at least the most fundamental social norms and basic grammar now—not later. Don't wait for your product or service to take off—it will be too late!

Note   While many customers, including myself, appreciate the consistency in service, quality and cleanliness of McDonald's and Disneyland worldwide, local adaptation is not totally ruled out. McDonald's, for example, now serves beer and wine in Europe and adapted the menu to local tastes. Disneyland Paris allows alcoholic beverages to be served within the park, at sit-down restaurants. Both companies are paying attention to cultural differences in order to satisfy customers.

Are You Culturally Aware? Test Yourself!

Here are some questions to ask yourself to see how well you know your prospective target market:

1. *How do people typically dress there?* Casual or formal? Dark or light clothing? Are any body parts to be covered at all times when out in public or when making business calls? Are there different norms of dress for men and women?

2. *What do body mannerisms convey?* Are your customers' arms always folded when discussing serious issues? Do they wave their hands a lot while talking? Do they avoid your eyes while speaking to you? Do they grin while you are telling them bad news?

3. *Do your customers expect you to accept all hospitable gestures and participate in all group activities when visiting?* If they ask you to join them for a smoke and you decline, will that mean no business? If they smoke and you make a big fuss, will that hurt business? If they offer you an alcoholic beverage before noon and before you've even started business discussions, what should you do?

4. *What about religious or political issues?* Will your customers be flattered or offended if you partake in a religious ceremony when it is clear that you are not a practitioner of that particular faith? Should you go toe to toe with the head honcho in a political discussion or had you best just back off?

5. *What are the customs that are considered offensive?* Your host cleans his teeth during dinner. Would his country- men regard him as a vulgar clod? Should you do the same? Should you be shocked?

If you fumbled for answers to some of these questions, it's time to culti- vate some intercultural awareness. First of all, cultural ignorance sets you up for culture shock, which compounds the stress of international travel and deprives you of much of its pleasure. Second, culture is so subtle and perva- sive that there is no way of estimating how your ignorance might impact your business. You will feel paralyzed and inept because you won't dare to take any initiatives for fear of looking foolish and offending your customer. Why spend anxious hours wondering if something you said or did with a prospective overseas customer helped or hindered your efforts? The more you learn, the more freedom, mobility, and confidence you will have.

Get the Global Edge: Learn the Language!

Learning the language is arguably the best start you can make in your cultural training. Language acquisition gives a global marketer a definite edge in a new market by reducing the stress of cultural adjustment and increasing rapport with overseas associates. Language itself primes an individual's cultural values and attitudes, which can affect behavior. It also empowers you by increasing awareness of what is happening during negotiations and by earning immediate respect from your hosts.

You're probably asking yourself, "Must I learn a whole new foreign language before I can do international business?" Yes and no. Yes, it helps—the payoffs are incalculable. No, you don't have to. But I have found that my most gratify- ing and profitable business relationships have happened in those parts of the world where I've made an effort to study the language, learn the culture, read the national history, and visit in person as often as possible.

Resources for Cultivating Cultural Awareness

You don't need to go far off the beaten path to acquire the information you need to jump-start your cultural learning. Start with your bank. Many big inter- national banks, HSBC for example (https://globalconnections.hsbc. com/global/en/tools-data/country-guides), offer country guides right on their site. Universities also offer a rich, in-depth pool of resources covering cross-cultural country insights. A good example: Michigan State University's globalEDGE: http://globaledge.msu.edu/global-insights/by/coun- try. Then start searching for what you are looking for on the Internet. After that, visit a store that specializes in world travel equipment and incidentals (like http://www.WorldTraveler.com). They typically sell books, CDs, and digital recordings with which you can brief yourself on the economy, dress, cuisine, etiquette, and other vital statistics of just about any country in the world. Some specialize in lessons on what to do and what not to do when conducting business in specific foreign countries.

Travel bookstores (Magellan's, for example: http://www.magellans.com/country_guides/country-guides); Amazon; and bookstore chains like Barnes and Noble usually have a respectable selection of sophisticated country-by-country travel guides. You'll find more than enough to get you started.

I particularly recommend the following books:

- Roger E. Axtell's *Gestures: The Do's and Taboos of Body Language Around the World* (1977) is a simple, amusing, and informative survival guide to understanding cultures other than your own.

- Dr. David Livermore's *Leading with Cultural Intelligence: The New Secret to Success* (2009) provides solid academic research and years of experience on how to become more adept at managing across cultures. He's also written *The Cultural Intelligence Difference: Master the One Skill You Can't Do Without in Today's Global Economy* (2011), which is also worth a look.

- Axtell's *Do's and Taboos of Hosting International Visitors* (1990) is another good guide to everything from entertaining, to business protocol, to what overseas guests find peculiar about the American way.

- Terri Morrison and Wayne A. Conaway's *Kiss, Bow, or Shake Hands (The Bestselling Guide to Doing Business in More than 60 Countries)* (2006) discusses cultural overviews, behavior styles, negotiating techniques, protocol, and business practices in sixty countries. They also have books in the same series for Asia, Europe, and Latin America, and on sales and marketing.

- Jerome Dumetz and colleagues' *Cross-Cultural Management Textbook: Lessons from the World Leading Experts* (2012) helps people develop the behaviors and skills necessary to adapt to a culturally diverse world.

- Meyer's *The Culture Map: Breaking Through the Invisible Boundaries of Global Business* (2014) helps you navigate through cultural differences and decode cultures foreign to your own.

- Smit's *How to Overcome Cultural Differences in Business: Avoid the Mistakes that Everyone Else is Making When Doing Business Internationally* (2014) is a practical guide to aid you in bridging the multicultural differences that you face when doing business across borders.

- Lewis's *When Cultures Collide, 3rd Edition: Leading Across Cultures* (2005) discusses the need to consider cross-cultural differences in managing any company in today's global world.

- Molinsky's *Global Dexterity: How to Adapt Your Behavior Across Cultures Without Losing Yourself in the Process* (2013) discusses how to adapt your behavior to conform to new cultural contexts without losing your authentic self in the process.

A few blogs on cross-cultural understanding worth a look:

- The Culture Mastery (`http://theculturemastery.com/blog/`)

- The Culture Prophecy (`http://dfaintercultural.com/the-culture-prophecy/`)

- Cultural Detective Blog (`https://blog.culturaldetective.com`)

- Cross Culture (`http://www.crossculture.com/category/blog/`)

- David Livermore: Global Thinker and Author (`http://davidlivermore.com/blog/blog/`)

For more country-specific cultural information, you might also try the following online sites:

- National Geographic (`http://www.nationalgeographic.com/`)

- Living Abroad (`http://www.livingabroad.com`)

- Lonely Planet (`http://www.lonelyplanet.com/usa`)

- Fodor's Travel guides (Ireland's guide, for example, can be found here: (`http://www.fodors.com/world/europe/ireland`)

- Export.gov "Travel and Tourism" (`http://export.gov/industry/travel/`)

- Central Intelligence Agency's "World Factbook" (`https://www.cia.gov/library/publications/the-world-factbook/docs/profileguide.html`) offers information beyond a country's culture, including on geography, the people, government, economy, and transportation.

Tip I use *National Geographic* for quick cultural tips. Conduct a search for "cultural tips, Russia," for example, and you'll end up with a Russia guide (`http://travel.nationalgeographic.com/travel/countries/russia-guide/`). An alphabetical list of other guides can be found here: `http://travel.nationalgeographic.com/travel/countries/`. They are wonderful!

Cross-Cultural Training

If you truly value cultural literacy and want to learn more and leverage that knowledge as a competitive advantage for your firm, you might consider participating in a cross-cultural training program. A good program will address the very deep issues of the different ways in which people live their lives and how they see the world. These programs offer best thinking and best practices on conducting business in different countries, modifying your own behavior, and working confidently with cultural differences in a virtual context or face-to-face meetings.

Although such training can be helpful, some experts find training may have more impact after a person has some firsthand experience to reference. Say you just started exporting to China, for example, and your key manager runs into communication problems not tied to a language barrier. They have more to do with a stylistic or behavioral issue on the part of the manager in that she likes to confront every detail in a conversation as if she's trying to hit the ball out of the ballpark to score a home run, and this is too contentious for the Chinese communication style. After all, that's how she is accustomed to behaving at the home office in the United States, and with much success. The Chinese, on the other hand, like to minimize provocation and keep complaints or disagreements polite and discreet. That prods you to figure out how to keep the communications fluid and make a success out of your interaction with this market. Dealing with the reality that something isn't working prompts questions, and questions lead to solutions.

If you get stuck and have doubts about how to handle a particular situation in an overseas market, training might be your next step. Conduct a web search on "cross-cultural training" and several resources will come up, including web-based training available at your convenience. The US Department of State offers a list of companies that offer cross-cultural training and consulting programs (http://www.state.gov/m/fsi/tc/79756.htm). Before participating, be sure to get references from people who have used these services successfully.

■ **Note** Cross-cultural differences don't only apply to language. Culture impacts food choices (eating and well-being), design (viewed through a cultural filter formed by language), and religious beliefs (interpretation), for example. If you need help with any of these specific areas, conduct a web search using the words "cross-cultural _____" (fill in the area—design, for example), and you will discover a wealth of information to guide you in your work.

Quick Intercultural Tips

It's unlikely you'll be able to learn everything there is to know about any given overseas country, so I've constructed a list of quick tips to apply to interacting with all cultures. These tips are based on what a typical international traveler usually does wrong when trying to conduct global business. Keep these guidelines in mind and you will be a global chameleon:

- *Slow down!* The rest of the world does not do business at lightning speed. Practice patience. This can actually be enjoyable if you are an American, because you probably don't often get the chance!

- *Decide by consensus and take your time arriving at one.* Refrain from making unilateral decisions. The more opinions and comments you can get from all parties involved, the more satisfactory your final decision will be. It's always better if everyone feels like the decision was a consensus of the whole group, anyway.

- *Show sincerity.* Listen to what your customer is saying and be interested. Don't be superficial—a plastic cheerleader smile won't cut it. You are building a long-lasting relationship.

- *Embrace the environment and its people to make it your own.*

- *Take a passive approach rather than an overly aggressive one.* Go with the flow. Don't arrive with an ironclad action plan geared toward achieving results within a week.

- *Smile and communicate contagious enthusiasm.*

- *Develop a strong sense of self.* This allows interaction with another person or culture without fear of losing one's own identity.

- *Act ridiculously polite.* Be forever trying to win them over with your humble, courteous manner. Too often people take an adversarial approach to business deals, as if the other party is one to be gotten the better of.

- *Make on-the-spot attempts to learn the other party's culture.* Try to master some words and phrases of their language, ask about their history, observe their ways.

- *Refrain from desiring instant feedback and the expectation of immediacy caused by the focus on time.* Instead, demand richer, deeper interactions that fuel a lifelong relationship.

- *When in doubt, get over your embarrassment and ask questions.* Gather input to find solutions and to learn as much as you can. You have nothing to lose, and it shows them you care.

- *Compromise when you should.* Collaborate as needed. Be open to possibilities that may leave you feeling vulnerable, yet grow you as a human being and the relationship.

- *Wear a pin or accessory that symbolizes a global perspective, not a national one.* A symbol that represents world peace can only help.

- *When you catch yourself being driven by an ingrained ethnocentric attitude, pull it up out of your subconscious and take a good hard look at it.* Remember that no matter how ill at ease you are, you should welcome every encounter with the unknown and unfamiliar as an opportunity to cultivate your global mindset (review Chapter 1). And expect to be ill at ease, because we all believe that what we are accustomed to is the natural order of things! This is why we need to keep a sense of humor about our own and others' interpersonal missteps. Exercise tolerance and make good-faith efforts to bridge differences and find common ground.

Caution Not all exports will be successful. Understand how to deal with cultural differences concerning failure. What may seem like a failure to you and the end of a business relationship could be quite the opposite to a company in another market that perceives failure as a need to learn from it and start over. Resist walking away. There's a point where it can only get better. The way to find out is to keep plugging away.

Cultural differences and quirks make our life rich, diverse, exciting, and unnerving—and in the fast-changing world of international business, they will play an increasingly important part in all our lives. How you deal with the differences can make or break your business success. Your mastery of culture will enhance your competence in all areas of your international business—in coping with the simple logistics of living and getting around in another country, in establishing trust, in pacing negotiations, in knowing which gifts and gestures will please people of that nationality, and in knowing whether you've got a deal or not. There is no better way to understand the people who are going to buy or use your product twelve thousand miles away than by meeting them, literally or figuratively, on their own ground. Start getting ready for your cross-cultural encounter today.

A Real-Life Example of Learning Culture on the Fly

One of my most delightful and memorable encounters with another culture happened in my own hometown—in fact, practically in my own home. Some very dear Japanese friends, a gentleman and his two daughters, were staying in a guest suite next door to my apartment. We had spent several activity-packed days together, but on the last morning before my friends were to return to Japan, we found we didn't have enough time to go out for a proper leisurely breakfast. Naturally I hated the thought of just saying goodbye from the lobby and sending them off on their long, wearying flight overseas. So I got up early, boiled a huge kettle of rice and phoned them an hour before I knew they had to leave to see if I might help them with anything. My friend replied, "My daughters are complaining they are hungry." I said I would be right over. I grabbed a carton of eggs, some butter, a frying pan, a bunch of chopsticks, and my kettle of rice. The latter was my contingency plan—I knew that Asians eat rice at every meal, but I frankly had no idea if the Japanese ate fried or scrambled eggs, for breakfast or otherwise!

I walked in and announced that I was going to make a quick American breakfast of either an omelet or scrambled eggs. I don't know if the girls even heard me, though—their eyes fell on that kettle of fresh steaming rice and their faces immediately lit up as if they had never been offered anything so delicious in their lives! Before I could say another word, they asked if I had soy sauce. Thanking my lucky stars that that Asian staple has been a familiar American grocery item for decades, I ran back to my apartment and grabbed my bottle from the refrigerator. By the time I returned, the girls had begun cracking raw eggs into the rice pan. Then they set the pan on the stove and slowly stirred in the egg, carefully adding just the right amount of soy sauce. Once done, we all happily dug in with the chopsticks.

I had improvised the best I could, but I had no idea that I was offering my guests such a satisfying and familiar breakfast—or that I would find myself eating barely cooked eggs in rice with soy sauce! And to think that my friend asked if I had any relish to go along with it! Sometimes on cold winter mornings I make this dish for breakfast and fondly remember my friends from overseas who shared it with me.

The same thing will happen to you in the international marketplace. If you do your best to act with cultural sensitivity, value your own culture, learn about your associates' culture, and then let them meet you halfway, you can build a cross-cultural bridge and achieve world-class excellence together.

Summary

You don't want to show up to a meeting without preparing in advance. The same holds true for understanding other cultures. Don't assume that a market is like that in America. Even if you think it is (in Ireland, Australia, or the United Kingdom, for example), you don't want to export or travel to it without first learning everything you can about the culture. Whenever you feel you have underestimated the importance of cultural differences, come back to this chapter for a refresher. It will mean everything to your customers and might make or break your export business. Last, keep an open mind, be flexible, and place trust in your international business relationships, and encourage cooperation. Profitable exports will surely follow.

Now that you've mastered the basics in cross-cultural learning, you are ready to develop your moral compass, which intersects with intercultural intelligence. Read on.

Notes

i.   David Livermore, *Leading with Cultural Intelligence: The New Secret to Success* (New York: AMACOM, 2010), xiv.

ii. Andy Molinsky, *Global Dexterity: How to Adapt Your Behavior Across Cultures without Losing Yourself in the Process* (Harvard Business Review Press, 2013), http://www.amazon.com/Global-Dexterity-Behavior-Cultures-Yourself/dp/1422187276.

iii. Soon Ang and Linn van Dyne, *Handbook of Cultural Intelligence: Theory, Measurement, and Application* (Armonk, New York: M.E. Sharpe, 2008), 415.

iv. Linn Van Dyne, Linn van Dyne, [REPETITION OK HERE? –LP] "Cultural Intelligence (HQ)," http://www.linnvandyne.com/cq.html.

The Export Journey

Global Ethics

The Export World's Rules on Ethical Conduct

To build a truly great, global business, business leaders need to adopt a global standard of ethical practices.

—Bill George, author, Harvard Business School professor, and former CEO of Medtronic[i]

People with high levels of personal mastery . . . cannot afford to choose between reason and intuition, or head and heart, any more than they would choose to walk on one leg or see with one eye.

—Peter M. Senge, American scientist, author, founding chairperson of the Society for Organizational Learning, and senior lecturer at the Massachusetts Institute of Technology[ii]

Many people think of values as soft; to some they are usually unspoken. A South Seas island society uses the word mokita, which means, "the truth that everybody knows but nobody speaks."

—Thomas Donaldson, author and professor, Wharton School of the University of Pennsylvania in Philadelphia[iii]

While conducting business across borders, companies need to be mindful of ethics and laws, especially as they relate to exporting. You will have to contend with different cultures, different rules and regulations of each country you plan to do business with, different perspectives, and different end goals. There are so-called right and wrong behaviors, and there are also gray behaviors,

© Laurel J. Delaney 2016
L. J. Delaney, *Exporting*, DOI 10.1007/978-1-4842-2193-8_25

which can make things complex. In this chapter, I'll talk about the impact of unethical behavior such as bribes, unveil how sound ethics are our best competitive advantage in the digital global economy, and discuss why each of us must have a moral compass.

Unethical behavior can damage a business or take it down. Just look at Enron, WorldCom, Arthur Andersen and Bernard L. Madoff Investment Securities LLC. US firms are restricted from bribery, yet bribery abroad is rampant and is a serious issue facing all exporters.

What is a bribe? A bribe is anything of significant value—including money—given to someone who influences the individual to do something she wouldn't ordinarily do had she not received the special treatment for her own benefit. What constitutes bribery can vary from country to country, depending on local customs, values, and practices. But let me be perfectly clear about one point: If a US company offers a bribe, not only is it breaking the law; it is sending a signal that it can't compete legally without illegal help. And that behavior typically starts with a cavalier attitude about the law.

In the case of an export business, bribes are sometimes made to foreign officials, foreign political parties, or candidates for foreign political office for the purpose of obtaining or retaining business. This is illegal and the penalties can be fierce. According to the Foreign Corrupt Practices Act (FCPA), which affects every US company that does business outside the country, you can face large fines, prosecution and jail, and be barred from receiving US government contracts, for engaging in bribery.[iv]

Whether you are a broker, sales agent, supplier, or exporter, the temptation to accept or give bribes (to move goods through ports faster, to get unions to unload ships, or to have customs officials turn a blind eye to sketchy documentation, for example) or act unethically exists in the pursuit of business. When any of these things is done with the understanding that payoffs could come later, that's a bribe. In other words, when another party persuades you with the logic "Do it now and good things will follow—and probably under the table," they're tempting you with bribery.

Why the FCPA?

In 1977, Congress enacted the US Foreign Corrupt Practices Act (FCPA, or "the act") in "response to revelations of widespread bribery of foreign officials by U.S. companies. The Act was intended to halt those corrupt practices, create a level playing field for honest businesses, and restore public confidence in the integrity of the marketplace."[v]

Congress said this when drafting the FCPA: "The payment of bribes to influence the acts or decisions of foreign officials, foreign political parties or candidates for foreign political office is unethical. It is counter to the moral expectations and values of the American public. But not only is it unethical, it is bad business as well. It erodes public confidence in the integrity of the free market system. It short-circuits the marketplace by directing business to those companies too inefficient to compete in terms of price, quality or service, or too lazy to engage in honest salesmanship, or too intent upon unloading marginal products. In short, it rewards corruption instead of efficiency and puts pressure on ethical enterprises to lower their standards or risk losing business."[vi]

The bottom line: FCPA rules apply to all companies, irrespective of size, and its terms are not negotiable. As a small business exporter, even though you may lack the time, human resource capabilities, legal expertise, or financial resources to meet overseas regulatory requirements, you must still have an effective compliance program and measure in place. What's worse is that criminal penalties may impact a small business exporter at a far greater magnitude than they do a large business, because the fines imposed will make up a larger proportion of the small business exporter's earnings.

How Poor Ethics Plays Out

Here's how poor ethics can play out, and don't think for a second these scenarios do not apply to you as a small business exporter! In any company, you or one of your people could be tempted do one of these things to increase or expedite business:

- Make a call to get an export delivery sped up, and if it is done, in return you could offer a prestigious club membership to the organization controlling the port, trucking lines, or what have you

- Make improper payments through your intermediaries (wholesalers or sales agents, for example) to foreign government officials to win business in India, China, and Russia

- Fail to prevent a sales agent or importing wholesaler from taking the performance-based bonuses you gave them as gifts and secretly using them to make unauthorized payments to governmental officials in Korea

- Pay routine bribes, referred to as "flowers," to Argentinian officials in order to obtain lucrative sales contracts with government hospitals

- Make illicit payments to a US government veterinarian responsible for certifying your American company's beef products for export sales

- Accept improper payments made by employees at your UK subsidiary to food industry officials in the United Kingdom

Ethical Ground Rules

So how do you avoid or handle bribery temptations and disputes in the first place? It gets back to your company culture, vision, and shared values. Ask yourself this: *What's your gold standard for the way people should behave in pursuit of export business?*

Not only should you define this standar, but you should develop guidelines and procedures around it, implement a training program for all levels of worldwide business to quickly address red-flag temptations, get involved, and have a process in place to investigate and address any reports of misconduct. This is done to stay within the law.

■ **Tip** Explore the International Business Ethics Institute (http://business-ethics.org/) to help you develop a global business ethics and integrity program and try World Citizens Guide (http://www.worldcitizensguide.org/) to brush up on becoming a better global citizen.

Beyond developing your standard, offer an open two-way dialogue with your employees about your ethical policy, enforce it rigorously with practical conversations having to do with real-world situations, and seek feedback. As Angus Loten of Inc.com says, "Making employees feel secure enough to raise concerns is a key factor in creating an ethical workplace."[vii] Drive the message home until it sticks. Make sure everyone involved in the company, regardless of where they are located, applies the culture of integrity (trust, credibility, etc.) in discussing both their private and public lives so there are no murky areas. And there should be no exceptions to the policy—not even for star performers!

Who Should Be in Charge of a Gold Standard Code of Ethics?

In "How to Avoid Bribes in International Business," published by About.com, I write:

> Designate someone at the top . . . to be responsible for FCPA compliance and be accountable for the FCPA program. This should be an individual who stays at the pulse of all international activities and is not necessarily top legal counsel (small firms typically don't have their own in-house legal representation so it shouldn't be an issue) or the president. The designated person can work in tandem with the top legal inside or outside counsel and president, but he/she should also have the ability to act on his/her own, be capable of making sound moral judgments and demonstrate prudent ethical decisiveness.[viii]

The bottom line: Engage someone—maybe it's you—to take charge of writing guidelines and upholding strict ethical standards throughout the entire organization. You want to investigate any red flags and remediate where necessary. "Applying 'situation ethics' in developing countries is the fastest way to destroy a global organization. To sustain their success, companies must follow the same standards of business conduct in Shanghai, Mumbai, Kiev, and Riyadh as in Chicago," says author, Harvard Business School professor, and former CEO of Medtronic Bill George.[ix]

My suggestion is to use US federal law, including the FCPA, as a baseline for determining appropriate behavior and as a model for your own country's value structure, and apply those things to your dealings with all countries. And always, always, explicitly state your ethical guidelines so people know what to expect. Then be consistent with your actions.

Tip Including FCPA terms in every single one of your contracts allows you to steer clear of bribery trouble and to exemplify that you intend to do clean, transparent international business. This can be as simple as stating: "Export Company ABC will not tolerate corruption with either our foreign partners or our own sales staff." Also incorporate a statement in the agreement you have with agents or distributors that acknowledges that both parties (seller and buyer) recognize the existence of the FCPA and will honor its rules and regulations by not making any improper payments or performing other such conduct. Incorporate the ability to terminate the agreement should your partner ever be in violation of the FCPA. Consult with your attorney to ensure you've done everything right.

There are other ways in the export field to easily, and unintentionally, break the law.

Note When someone has broken the law, even if unknowingly, it can still be a matter of legal dispute whether that person knew or was aware of the matter.

The next sections detail a few areas to be aware of when it comes to getting into ethical trouble and that it is important for the person in charge of your ethics program to write into your guidelines.

Travel Act

The Travel Act involves traveling around or using the mail system to violate a law. TA "prohibits traveling between states or countries or using an interstate facility in aid of any crime, and carries a 5-year jail sentence for most offenses."[x] To avoid violating the Travel Act, don't pay bribes to officers or employees of companies you are conducting business with in other countries to obtain or retain business.

Money Laundering

Trade-based money laundering consists of concealing and disguising proceeds, usually via wire fraud, false or double-invoicing, or over- or underinvoicing goods that are exported regularly around the world. A good portion of money that has been laundered is moved out of the country through undervalued exports (to move money out) or overvalued exports (to move money in). Buyers and sellers agree on a price and so as long as the price is not unrealistic, the chances that customs officials will detect suspicious activity by bankers, brokers, or law enforcement officials are slim. Hence, the opportunity to earn, move, and store proceeds disguised as legitimate trade becomes a small business exporter's new alternative remittance system. To avoid money laundering, don't let financial complacency creep into your financial methods: follow the money trail from beginning to end, match up your exports to imports, and obey the law.

Mail and Wire Fraud

Mail and wire fraud happens when someone knowingly executes or attempts to execute a scheme via mail or wire communication to defraud another for the purpose of obtaining money or property. To illustrate how this works, let's say, for example, you export products to an importing wholesaler in Vietnam. Per the instructions of the wholesaler, you send money by wire to an off-the-books bank account in the market that the company controls. Out of that account, illegal commissions and kickbacks are paid to local or contiguous country officials but disguised as trade allowances, distribution costs, trade show expenses, refunds, or other seemingly legitimate expenses.

Tax Violations

Tax violations can be anything from taking illegal tax deductions for bribes to declaring false sales commissions. When exporting, failing to pay income taxes on the amounts you owe, especially as they pertain to foreign-earned income, can result in severe penalties (costly fines and imprisonment, for example) and other major sacrifices down the road, including reputational consequences. Many governments, that of the United States for one, are increasing taxes and stepping up tax enforcement for exports. The solution: Get the help you need from an international tax accountant, have open and frank conversations about *all* your money-making export activities with him, and honestly and willingly report and pay what you owe in taxes. This allows you to manage and anticipate potential tax risks on export activities.

Certification and Reporting Violations

Producing a false certification—whether it be an Electronic Export Information (EEI), an export license, a health certificate, a claim made to the Export-Import Bank for a direct loan or loan guarantee—may give rise to criminal liability for manufacturing a false statement. Don't do it. You should enforce a zero tolerance policy on any deviation from total truth, transparency, and accuracy. A case in point: In 2007, the Disciplinary Committee of the Royal College of Veterinary Surgeons (RCVS) concluded that an Oxfordshire-based veterinary surgeon should be removed from the RCVS Register on the basis of disgraceful professional conduct. According to the RCVS, "John Williams of the Avonvale Veterinary Practice in Ratley, near Banbury, admitted signing export health certificates for three horses in October 2006 to state that they had received negative test results for the contagious equine metritis organism, before these results were actually available. At the time, Mr Williams was working in his capacity as an Official Veterinarian (OV) for DEFRA."[xi] In a nutshell, never *ever* provide a false certification (forged documentation, for example), and *never* bribe people to provide one either.

■ **Tip** For more information on the Foreign Corrupt Practices Act, download the free 130-page guide *A Resource Guide to the U.S. Foreign Corrupt Practices Act* from `http://www.sec.gov/spotlight/fcpa/fcpa-resource-guide.pdf`. For more information on the actual act, download the ten-page report *Foreign Corrupt Practices and Domestic and Foreign Investment Improved Disclosure Acts of 1977* from `http://www.justice.gov/criminal/fraud/fcpa/history/1977/senaterpt-95-114.pdf`.

The Honest Export Business

So, what is an honest export business? It's one that uses its moral compass as a guide to be as truthful, accurate, and transparent as possible in its dealings and one that maintains a high level of standards in everything it does.

■ **Tip** To brush up on procedures concerning enforcement actions and learn how to fully comply, see the Security and Exchange Commission's *Enforcement Manual* at `http://www.sec.gov/divisions/enforce/enforcementmanual.pdf`. To learn the basics on what small legal departments need to be aware of to stay FCPA compliant, see the "Top Ten Basics of Foreign Corrupt Practices Act Compliance for the Small Legal Department" at `http://www.acc.com/legalresources/publications/topten/SLD-FCPA-Compliance.cfm`. To assess the level of some of the more corrupt countries in the developing world, see "These are the 18 most corrupt countries in the developed world" at `http://www.independent.co.uk/news/world/these-are-the-18-most-corrupt-countries-in-the-developed-world-a7066391.html`.

Rules and Regulations of Each Country

A subdivision of the US Department of Commerce's International Trade Administration, the Trade Compliance Center, in its issuance of policies on bribery (http://tcc.export.gov/Bribery/index.asp), is the US Government's key source of monitoring foreign compliance with trade agreements to see that US firms and workers get the maximum benefits from these agreements. The center also provides access to information to help US exporters understand and evaluate opportunities created by trade agreements that the United States has negotiated. Additionally, the WTO offers the *Trade Policy Reviews* (TPR; http://www.wto.org/english/tratop_e/tpr_e/tp_rep_e.htm), which are fully searchable market-access reports with information on foreign trade policies and regulations. To ensure you are current, spend some time reviewing these.

■ **Tip** Don't let your employees get conflicted between their values as individuals and the compromises they think they must make for your organization. Spell out what you expect and hold steady to it. Incorporate your ethical policy into your overall business strategy.

Learn More About Bribes and Corruption

The following key resources will help get you up to speed on bribery and corruption issues and help you create an ethics policy for your company:

1. *Top Ten Basics of Foreign Corrupt Practices Act Compliance for the Small Legal Department*: (http://www.acc.com/legalresources/publications/topten/SLD-FCPA-Compliance.cfm). This document provides ten points small legal departments need to be aware of to stay FCPA compliant.

2. *The United States Department of Justice's information on the Foreign Corrupt Practices Act*: (http://www.justice.gov/criminal/fraud/fcpa/). The Department of Justice offers several ways to contact the office to get information on the FCPA. The FCPA helps you to protect your business and reputation and to understand what the law and regulation requires of you. It can also help you identify the customers who are a higher risk.

3. *Trade Compliance Center*: (http://tcc.export.gov/Bribery/index.asp). Run by the US Department of Commerce's International Trade Administration, the Trade Compliance Center offers a "Bribery" page on its

Web site covering trade agreements between the United States and other countries and international conventions devoted to combating bribery and corruption.

4. *Documents related to the OECD's Bribery in International Business conference:* (http://www.oecd.org/daf/anti-bribery/oecdantibriberyconvention.htm). Held by the Organization of Economic Cooperation and Development, this conference provides cutting-edge measures for governments and businesses to combat corruption. Many of the statements and information provided at the conference are available for download at the OECD's Web site. As the OECD says, "Corruption knows no boundaries, or border …"[xii]

5. *The FCPA Blog:* (http://www.fcpablog.com). Pro business and pro compliance, The Foreign Corrupt Practices Act blog provides free and unrestricted coverage of all things related to the Foreign Corrupt Practices Act enforcement actions. It can help you understand how corruption happens, what it does to people and companies, and how anti-corruption laws and compliance programs work.

6. *Transparency International:* (http://www.transparency.org). Transparency International works together with governments, businesses, and citizens to stop the abuse of power, bribery, and secret deals.

▨ **Caution** If you run up against a problematic country with continual ethical dilemmas, pull out. Why jeopardize your company's stellar reputation?

Summary

Payoffs, bribes, or gifts should never ever be a means to accomplishing your business goals. Reputations are the lifeblood of organizations. Ethical deficiencies can put the entire reputation of a company at risk. One mistake can ruin a company overnight. To overcome the potential for ethical misconduct, promote a two-way conversation with your employees on the importance of keeping ethics in check. Draw a line in all ethical areas that no one can overstep, clearly defining the violations in each matter. Set a zero tolerance policy for behavior deviations that are not in sync with the company's culture. And keep your moral compass top of mind at all times to accommodate cultural differences that you may not understand. This will allow you to not sell yourself short—or out.

Global business ethics are an ongoing effort and need to be instilled in people. We most certainly must work together to protect our companies, our employees, and our constituency base.

In the next chapter, I address international travel. Before you pack your bags, learn the dos and don'ts of traveling abroad.

Notes

i. Bill George, "Ethics Must Be Global, Not Local," *Bloomberg Businessweek*, February 12, 2008, http://www. businessweek.com/stories/2008-02-12/ethics-must-be-global-not-localbusinessweek-business-news-stock-market-and-financial-advice.

ii. Peter Senge, *The Fifth Discipline* (New York: Doubleday, 2006), 157.

iii. Thomas Donaldson, "Values in Tension: Ethics Away From Home," Harvard Business Review, September-October 1996, accessed June 5, 2016, https://hbr.org/1996/09/values-in-tension-ethics-away-from-home.

iv. "Foreign Corrupt Practices Act," United States Department of Justice, accessed June 5, 2016, http://www.justice.gov/criminal/fraud/fcpa/.

v. The Criminal Division of the US Department of Justice and the Enforcement Division of the US Securities and Exchange Commission, *FCPA: A Resource Guide to the Foreign Corrupt Practices Act*, November 14, 2012, accessed June 5, 2016, http://www.sec.gov/spotlight/fcpa/fcpa-resource-guide.pdf.

vi. Committee on Banking, Housing, and Urban Affairs, United States Senate, *Foreign Corrupt Practices and Domestic and Foreign Investment Improved Disclosure Acts of 1977*, May 2, 1977, http://www.justice.gov/criminal/fraud/fcpa/history/1977/senaterpt-95-114.pdf.

vii. Angus Loten, "What Enron Didn't Teach Us," Inc.com, January 1, 2008, http://www.inc.com/articles/2008/01/ethics.html.

viii. "How to Avoid Bribes in International Business: Brush Up on the Foreign Corrupt Practices Act," Laurel Delaney, About.com: Import & Export, accessed November 5,2013,http://importexport.about.com/od/RegulationsOfForeignTrade/a/How-To-Avoid-Bribes-In-International-Business.htm.

ix. Bill George, "Ethics Must Be Global, Not Local," *Bloomberg Businessweek*, February 12, 2008, http://www.businessweek.com/stories/2008-02-12/ethics-must-be-global-not-localbusinessweek-business-news-stock-market-and-financial-advice.

x. "Travel Act Bribery Cases Made Simple," accessed November 5, 2013, http://www.fcpablog.com/blog/2011/12/19/travel-act-bribery-cases-made-simple.html.

xi. "Oxon Vet Struck Off For False Export Certification," RCVS, November 16, 2007, http://www.rcvs.org.uk/news-and-events/news/oxon-vet-struck-off-for-false-export-certification/.

xii. Roberto A. Ferdman, "How the World's Biggest Companies Bribe Foreign Governments – in 11 Charts," *The Washington Post*, December 3, 2014, accessed June 5, 2016.

International Business Travel and Security Tips

What does it mean to pre-board? Do you get on before you get on?

—the late George Carlin, comedian

Twenty years from now you will be more disappointed by the things you didn't do than by the ones you did do. So throw off the bowlines, sail away from the safe harbor. Catch the trade winds in your sails. Explore. Dream. Discover.

—Mark Twain, American author and humorist

As a woman I have no country. As a woman my country is the whole world.

—Virginia Woolf, English writer

As a fearless exporter, you must be prepared to boldly go where you have never gone before! At the beginning of your export venture, and to help save money, you might use e-mail, Skype, Google+, or Apple's FaceTime for conversations with your international customers. But at some point, a face-to-face meeting with them is absolutely essential to cement a quality business

© Laurel J. Delaney 2016
L. J. Delaney, *Exporting*, DOI 10.1007/978-1-4842-2193-8_26

relationship. The practical aspects of international business travel can make or break your trip. Use this chapter as a checklist of the details you'll want to attend to in order to have a safe, comfortable, and productive journey.

Sweating the Details Comes with the Global Territory

Before we get to the checklist, I want to share the following experience with you. This story proves the importance of having an open mind (it gets back to that global mindset I talked about in Chapter 1), remaining flexible, and being adaptable as you navigate through an uncharted export marketplace.

The first time I had to travel from my hotel in Tokyo to a customer's office a few miles away, I got a little more of an adventure than I bargained for. Clutching the phone in my four-by-four–foot hotel room, I listened as my customer gave me directions for getting from my hotel to his office via Japan's intricate subway system. I didn't have the heart to tell him I couldn't follow his rapid-fire Japanese English to save my life. Besides, my customer seemed to have such a flattering confidence in my ability to conduct myself like an old pro that I was unwilling to give him cause to change his opinion, and so I didn't ask him to repeat himself. In this situation, a normal person would have just jumped in a cab, given the driver the address, and felt assured of getting there cool, collected, and on time. But when I travel, I always keep two central objectives firmly in mind: (a) growing as a person and (b) saving money, and not necessarily in that order. So, I decided to take a chance on the subway. I figured the worst thing that could happen was that I might go a bit astray and have to flag down a cab after all. So I closed the conversation by saying brightly, "I understand, no problem! I'll see you at 3 p.m.!"

Then, I flew straight down to the concierge's desk, showed her my customer's address, and asked her to tell me in English how to get there via the subway system. She carefully mapped out the directions and patiently reviewed them with me, and once I thought I understood what she was explaining, I asked her to write it all down again in Japanese. That way, if I got lost and had to ask someone for help, I could just show him the piece of paper.

Well, it worked. I arrived at my customer's subway stop just in time—only to find that I was by no means done sweating the details. It was a hot and humid day. I got up to the street level, already rather worn and rumpled from the trip, and instantly felt beads of sweat begin to crawl down my neck. Before long, I could feel thick strands of my hair sticking to my damp face. Just exactly the sort of first impression every businessperson wants to make! I looked around for my customer, and lo and behold, there he was standing next to his sporty little motor scooter that had enough room, just barely, for another person. He greeted me with a firm handshake and a broad smile, gestured to his bike and asked, "Do you mind?"

"Of course not!" I said, smiling just as broadly, and hopped on, skirt, pumps, and all. What else was there to do?

Welcome to the world of international business travel. If there's one thing you can expect, it's the unexpected. The more prepared you are for the predictable demands, stresses, and pitfalls of travel beyond your borders, the more grounded and confident you'll feel when the unexpected happens.

The trip I just described took place in the 1990s, when traveling felt far safer. Since September 11, 2001, however, our world of domestic and international travel has changed. Terrorism and other criminal activities are a fact of life in our interconnected world. To combat threats, one must become knowledgeable of what's going on in the world, have a heightened awareness of her surroundings, and develop a personal-security competence sufficient to dissuade potential assailants. Crime can affect anyone, almost anywhere. The prevention starts with creating protective strategies to ensure that your international travel is safe, comfortable, and productive.

■ **Tip** Tap into powerful new apps that are available for international travelers and your travel experience can seem like a walk in the park (see "3 Must Have Apps for Global Travelers:" http:// importexport.about.com/od/GlobalResourceCenter/fl/3-Must-Have-Apps-for-Global-Travelers.htm)

Scouting Out the Territory Before You Leave

An excellent way to start planning your overseas trip is to surf the Internet, preferably well in advance of your departure date. The Internet is an incredibly useful tool for finding out everything from the weather to the local currency exchange rate in the country you are about to visit. Three particularly handy sites you'll want to check out are:

1. *Travel.State.Gov:* (https://travel.state.gov/content/ passports/en/alertswarnings.html). A service of the Bureau of Consular Affairs, Travel.State.Gov's Travel Alerts are issued by the US Department of State to publicize conditions that make a country dangerous or unstable. They are what are used by the State Department to recommend that Americans avoid or consider the risk of travel to a certain country. The site also provides tips on traveling abroad and information on passports and visas to help make your travel more enjoyable and profitable.

2. *Foreign & Commonwealth Office*: (http://www.fco.gov. uk/en/). Featured on the GOV.uk site, the FCO is an organization that sponsors an international network of embassies and consulates. Its site offsets the conservatism of Travel.State.Gov by giving you a balanced picture of what's really happening in a country. The FCO provides useful information for countries throughout the world (https://www.gov.uk/foreign-travel-advice). For example, you can find a country by clicking on its region on a map or by using an A–Z country name selection process.

3. *Smart Traveler Enrollment Program (STEP)*: (https://step. state.gov/step/). STEP is a free service to allow U.S. citizens and nationals traveling abroad to enroll their trip with the nearest U.S. Embassy or Consulate. It also then sends out travel and security updates about your destination.

Note When you are unsure of the real safety level of traveling to a foreign country, it helps enormously to contact officials who are on the ground in a country. Reach out to the US Commercial Service for information. A case in point: Recently, when a colleague of mine was debating whether to travel to Egypt, I e-mailed the commercial consular at the Foreign Commercial Service in Egypt for her and inquired about the safety conditions in the country. She responded within five hours with a helpful report. My colleague and I then compared the consular's report with the information on the Travel.State.Gov and the British Foreign & Commonwealth Office sites. Based on our careful examination of all the different alerts and updates, my colleague was able to make an intelligent decision as to whether she could travel safely to Egypt.

For help you can't get online, cover the following checklist:

1. *Go over all the logistics of your trip with your travel agent.* These include ticketing, hotels, arrival and departure times, ground transportation, baggage handling, currency adjustments, health precautions, and possible language barriers. Discuss whether you need to get any insurance coverage before you depart. If your US health care plan does not cover you overseas, consider buying supplemental insurance to cover medical costs and emergency evacuation. Ask for a map of the town center or urban area where you will be staying. If your agent doesn't have one, you can ask your hotel concierge upon arrival or check the local phone directory or tourist guide in your room if there is one.

2. *Share your itinerary.* It is always prudent to share your itinerary with family, friends, and co-workers. It is good for people to know where you are in case you have an emergency or they do. And don't forget to stay in touch throughout your trip.

3. *Learn the local culture.* Spend some time brushing up on local culture and customs. You never know when being up on news might be helpful in your conversations and travels.

4. *Call your bank's international department and ask for a short lesson, or perhaps a brochure, on your country of destination's currency and how the various bills and coins relate to one another.*

5. *Ask the US Department of State about passport, visa, and immunization requirements.* Allow at least eight weeks for processing the documents, especially if you are going to be traveling during a peak tourist season. Immunizations can cause some lingering pain and discomfort, so if several immunizations are required, allow time for them to be administered in stages rather than all at once.

6. *Check with the US Embassy (http://www.usembassy. gov/) on the holiday schedule and regular business hours for the country you are about to visit.* This will affect your access to stores, services, and public transportation.

7. *Find out about the usual climate of the country you are about to visit as well as the weather forecast for the time of your trip by consulting your travel agent or an international newspaper.* Take these things into consideration when packing.

8. *Contact your local Chamber of Commerce for a directory of your country's government offices throughout the world.* If the directory is pocketable, bring it along, or, if it is available online, bookmark it for later use. Many US government offices have more than one branch in each country. For example, the Department of State has five different office locations in Japan (refer to http://www.state.gov/p/eap/ci/ja/c3122.htm). You could end up visiting all of them online! This is because, in the United States, there is a separate directory of the key officers at foreign-service posts American business executives would most likely need to contact. The directory lists all embassies, missions, consulates general, and consulates. Each of their commercial officers will probably arrange appointments with local businesses and government officers and also identify potential importers, buyers, agents, distributors,

and cross-border partners for your business. It may also be worthwhile to pay a visit to administrative officers who are responsible for normal business operations and agricultural officers who promote the export of US agricultural products. You should contact these offices in advance to schedule a visit. Explain the purpose of your visit so they can set you up with the appropriate officer.

9. *Prepare for the time and weather change.* Take note of the time change and what time you will arrive. Once you know, try adjusting your sleep patterns slightly to accommodate your new arrival time. Determine what the weather will be upon arrival and dress accordingly.

10. *Install on your mobile phone your destination maps, local guides, and transportation apps.* These will come in handy when you hit the ground running in your new locale.

Tip   Get e-mails and telephone numbers of key officers at embassies, consulates, and foreign service posts located in the country you plan to visit in case you have any type of emergency, including a medical one. Should you suddenly get sick where you can't leave your bed, nothing is more comforting then knowing help is just a phone call or e-mail away.

---

11. *Finally, sit down with pen and paper and review your itinerary yourself.* Envision yourself going through each day of your trip. Whom will you meet? Where will you need to be each day and at what times? How will you get there? What will you need to wear? What will you need to bring to each appointment? How much money will you need for your daily expenses? Then, based on this activity schedule, list all the items you think are important enough to bring. If no one, such as a bell captain, taxi driver, or limo attendant, will be available to assist you upon arrival in a remote part of the world, will you be able to handle the amount of luggage you will have? This consideration will encourage you to pack what you need—and only what you need.

Packing Smart

I wish someone would have intervened and set me straight when I planned my first business trip overseas. Because I was going so far from home, my natural impulse was to bring everything I could possibly imagine needing, so naturally I ended up with much, much more stuff than I could possibly use. This excess baggage burdened me both physically and mentally throughout the trip.

I remember literally dragging my overstuffed garment bag, hard overnight case, and cumbersome attaché case (yes, we had attaché cases back then), dreading the thought of the next hotel move—the third within a week—when I would have to pack up and haul everything all over again. I came close to ditching possessions that proved useless, except I knew I'd need them when I got home. I vowed not to make the same mistake again.

Tip   Many airports not only conduct the full body scan before you head to your airline gate, but also can request to open your carry-on luggage to discuss suspicious items. Pack light. Pack neatly.

The next section contains some essentials for a one-week business trip, including wardrobe, accessories, and documents. Needed items will naturally vary according to the type of trip you are making and the activities to which you've committed yourself. If it seems highly unlikely that you'll be partaking in any given activity, for example, athletic recreation or formal evening outings, don't bother to pack garments appropriate for that activity "just in case." And don't make the opposite mistake of omitting essential items, such as business attire, on the presumption that you'll be able to buy whatever you need when you arrive. You are on a business trip, not a shopping spree—and you might find that you don't have time. Equip yourself so you arrive ready to conduct business.

Note   For creative and high-tech people, some of these packing considerations may not apply. Crisp and neat business casual, for example, is popular in the United States but not necessarily in other parts of the world. Wherever you plan to travel, do your research in advance, dress the part, and pack accordingly. The point is to be who you are and dress with style and authority.

One-Week Packing Checklist

Here are my suggestions on what you should pack for a weeklong business trip:

- *Your passport and visa, if required, plus additional photo identification in case these items are lost or stolen:* I always make a copy of my passport and place it in a different piece of luggage or even in my bra—depending on whether the country I am going to is a known trouble spot.

- *Three good suits:* For men, basic businesswear solids—in charcoal or navy blue—are generally preferred within the worldwide business culture. Women should also choose clearly coordinated suits (pants or slightly below-the-knee skirts) in these subdued shades, with more feminine tailoring. I don't recommend pinstripes for women, as many international businessmen think they look too masculine; rather you should go with a leaner, meaner power suit with slimmer sleeves and more flattering lines. Keep your shoes on the conservative side, too. Men should wear shoes with laces—loafers look too casual. Women should wear low-heeled pumps with a closed toe.

- *Eight shirts or blouses:* Men should stick to white or light-blue shirts, while women can add off-white and other pastel colors as well. Tapered cuts and button-down collars are acceptable for men; women can wear soft suit shells and blouses in richer textures like satin or silk. You should stay away from thin and see-through materials. The shells and blouses should complement or add some color under your suit. Avoid low necklines at all costs—they are distracting and simply not businesslike.

- *For women, a good supply of stockings:* International sizes and textures of stockings can vary greatly from what you're used to buying back home, and you may find them neither comfortable nor attractive. You won't want to waste valuable business time finding acceptable fit by trial and error.

- *One complete outfit of "play clothes" if you and your associates are booked for sightseeing or other outdoor recreation:* Such clothes consist of casual slacks (never jeans!), a short- or long-sleeved collared shirt, and good walking shoes. This attire will be suitable for all but extremely hot climates; if you happen to be going to one, tailored walking shorts and a thin short-sleeved cotton shirt with a collar along with good-quality sandals would be considered acceptable.

- *A super-compact umbrella and a classic lightweight rain or all-weather coat:* A good coat is suitable for damp, cool, or variable climates. (Burberry's coats are the most commonplace in international business circles.)

- *Business essentials:* These consist of a smart phone with international service, a tablet, a laptop, a computer adapter for any presentation that requires a projector connection (commonly needed for Apple computers), an international charger, a portable travel lock for hotel doors, plenty of business cards (put them in several different locations in case you lose a bag), courtesy gifts, sales and marketing information, and any other items that might be required in your specific situation.

- *Health-related items*: Such items include aspirin, cough drops, eye drops, flu remedies, stomach aides, antihistamines, tea bags, vitamin pills (if you usually take them), and any other medicine you need to maintain good health.

- *Incidentals (keep them to a minimum)*: These might be a portable electric converter, a USB flash drive, a stand-alone digital camera, a high-security money belt, and a bilingual dictionary (it can't hurt!).

Making Your Hotel Work for You

Good accommodations are worth shopping around for. You want your stay to be comfortable as well as efficient from a business standpoint. Here are some things to consider when choosing a hotel:

- *Location*: Map out your appointments and activities and find a hotel from which you can access them all without too much difficulty. You'll also want easy access to public transportation, shopping, restaurants, and entertainment. But be careful not to position yourself in a very "happening" area where it's crowded, overly expensive, and hard to get around. Make business your priority—that's why you're there—and plan accordingly.

- *Business travelers' rooms and suites*: The accommodations in the hotel room where you choose to stay should be as precisely worked on as the work you will do there, providing a peaceful refuge but also allowing you to keep in touch with associates, family, and world news. Reserve a room that offers at least enough table or desk space to spread out your papers and hold your digital equipment, electrical outlets that are placed conveniently and will accept your converter, and sufficient lighting to enable you to go over paperwork and attend to your appearance. Any reputable hotel will have a television with a variety of cable offerings so that you can relax and sample local mass culture. The newest and best hotels offer guest suites that include a separate room furnished with a large console table and mobile writing desk, with power outlets and a modem jack easily accessible in the console top, a movable task light, and an adjustable, ergonomically designed upholstered chair. Some even offer a kitchen area for those who want all the conveniences of home, so that they needn't interrupt their business by having to get food outside.

- *Business centers*: Absolutely essential for the savvy business traveler, many hotels offer business centers on the premises that are equipped with computers, fax machines, voicemail systems, and copiers, and are staffed by multilingual receptionists. Most have e-mail capabilities, video conferencing, and daily business papers available for reading and keeping abreast of what is going in the world. Many of the individual features can be rented by the hour, day, or month, or even indefinitely. These business center services are offered in addition to Wi-Fi capabilities in every room (whether complimentary or for a flat, per-day rate).

- *Miscellaneous conveniences*: The bigger hotels offer coffee shops, restaurants, and bars on-site. You may prefer to eat at outside restaurants, especially if you're going to a city known for its fine dining, but for impromptu business meetings, the hotel's facilities often have admirable appearances and can serve as convenient, comfortable sites.

Surviving the Flight

Every time I'm due to board a plane going overseas, I grab just about every magazine at the newsstand so I'll be occupied for as much of the trip as possible. When you're traveling internationally, it can be a lo-o-o-o-ng flight, and boredom can be the least of your worries. By setting up a few preliminary requirements, you can guarantee yourself a certain level of comfort and minimize your travel fatigue:

- *Expedited screening at the airport*: The Transportation Security Administration (TSA) protects our transportation systems to "ensure freedom of movement for people and commerce."[i] You can become eligible for expedited screening through TSA Pre√ (http://www.tsa.gov/tsa-precheck) by signing up through selective airlines (not all participate—be sure to check) or by applying directly to US Custom Border Patrol's (CBP) Global Entry Program (http://www.globalentry.gov/). Through the program, a passenger's "information will be embedded in the barcode of a passenger's boarding pass" to ensure rapid clearance for preapproved travelers.[ii] You can also save time by using your airline mobile app to check in and get a mobile boarding pass.

- *Window, middle, or aisle seat:* This is a choice you'll be making if, like most economical travelers, you're flying coach. A naive or youthful traveler will pick the window seat, so he can look out of it. This may prove disappointing if the weather clouds over and you are forced to squeeze past two sets of knees to get to the restroom. The window seat offers a nice solid surface to park your pillow against, but that's about it (don't forget to bring your special travel or bed pillow if it helps you sleep better). The middle seat usually ends up being occupied by a person who didn't give the issue any thought or by the significant other of a window or aisle seat holder. The aisle seat is for those who, like myself, have flown over the ocean too many times to want to look at it and who want the option of standing up and walking around at will. You'll be much less stiff and sore at the end of the trip if you book the aisle seat.

- *Economy or business class:* Economy class offers standard seating that reclines slightly; a fold-down table; an in-flight movie; snacks; complimentary nonalcoholic beverages; and in-flight, duty-free shopping. Business class provides special privileges like a nifty ticket holder; bag tags; priority baggage check-in and boarding; entrance to the airline's club; special extra-large seats (some being lie-flat seats) in a separate cabin; electronic headsets; meal service consisting of several courses of gourmet food; brand-name complimentary beverages; and a case of practical amenities containing mouthwash, lip balm, moisturizing lotion, socks, and facial tissues.

- First-class service offers all the same privileges as business class and then some, including: highest boarding priority, a complete seven-course meal that can be better than the fare at most four-star restaurants accompanied by the finest in brand name beverages, personalized service during the flight, sleeper seats that can be adjusted horizontally, and concierge service at the airport for personal business assistance. First class is the way to go when you have an ample budget. So, if you can afford it, book it. Once you do, you will find it's the most luxurious and pleasurable way to travel long distances. Second best is business class—not as expensive as first class but nearly as comfortable. Not all airlines make the distinction between first and business class any longer, so check. All airlines have restrictions on economy and discount fares, so be sure to inquire.

- *Reading material and music:* If you can't sleep on planes, you'll need something to occupy your mind (an old-fashioned printed book or a Kindle, Nook, or iPad)—this also discourages the determinedly friendly chatterbox next to you! Make your in-flight reading selection do double duty—choose an informative and entertaining e-book about the country you are about to visit to educate yourself and product- or company-specific reading to catch up on everything there is to know about your customer.

- A variety of music is always available for free on flights—the same holds true for movies and special programs—yet with apps such as Pandora or TuneIn Radio uploaded onto your digital device and a good set of earplugs, you can be off in your own little jazz, rock, or classical music world until you land at your destination.

- *Quiet section:* If you like a quieter seat on a plane, be sure to request a seat as far away as possible from the plane engine but near the exit area (these exist just below the wings, near or in the tail—ask the airline before you book your flight; the kitchen; or close the the lavatory areas (in the front, middle, and tail of the plane). Even the best noise-reduction headphones or earplugs can't eliminate the distraction of people constantly standing next to you in your seat, so it's important to stake out the quiet areas. It's too long a flight to be stuck in a situation you can't tolerate!

■ **Tip** To really tune out what's going on during your plane journey, use earplugs and eye masks for sleeping. Just remember that when you put them on, you'll miss any important announcements or suspicious behavior.

- *Refreshments:* Although we all like to relax and unwind on what seems like an endless journey, do be careful of excessive alcohol intake—it causes dehydration, acts as a depressant, and causes your body to retain water. Even if you don't consume alcohol, you may experience painful swollen feet from sitting for prolonged periods of time. That's why some airlines distribute packages of disposable slipper socks—because so many passengers end up wanting to remove their shoes. Keep yourself hydrated with natural refreshments, like water or juice. And again, get up and walk.

Managing Your Money

Most international travelers know that they should have enough of their own currency on hand to get from their home to their final destination and back again, plus enough extra to pay for a meal should there be a serious flight delay. In addition, check with your travel agent and bank as to where you can get the best rates of exchange on the currency you'll be using upon arrival. Convert enough money to last you a few days. Keep these usual expenses in mind when figuring out the amount of cash you will need to make it to your hotel:

1. Transportation costs from overseas airport to your hotel via airport shuttle or taxi.

2. Tips for baggage handlers at the airport and at your hotel.

3. Baggage transport fees from the airport to your hotel (paying for your bags to be transported for you eliminates the chore of handling it by yourself altogether and oftentimes requires payment in advance).

4. Gifts you purchase at the overseas airport shops, often because you ran out of time to shop before leaving home.

5. One night's stay at your hotel. You want to plan to have enough currency or traveler's checks to pay for staying one night at a hotel and to stash it somewhere other than your wallet. Most people pay their hotel bills by credit card, but if you lose your wallet you'll be glad you kept extra money somewhere else in case of emergency— especially on that critical first night when you arrive fatigued and jet-lagged and really need the rest.

There are many ways to pay for goods and services while traveling overseas: in cash; using the local currency; or by credit cards, traveler's checks, and debit cards. Before you leave home, call your credit card financial institution to ask if your credit cards are widely accepted in your country of destination and to let them know you will be traveling abroad so they won't think a charge is suspicious behavior and freeze your card. That's a surprise you don't need. At the same time, ask for the locations of international ATMs. Unless the machines are a part of your card's network, you can't use them!

And don't forget to activate the global features on your cell phone before you depart on your international trip! Roaming without an additional charge is not a default feature and can lead to extra costs. Consider buying a special data package and insert its SIM card into the phone. These are called prepaid international SIM cards. In some instances, you can order a SIM card ahead of time so you can get it before your trip or have it delivered to your hotel. Also, if you are on a tight budget, never make phone calls to your home or office from your hotel room. Having the hotel operator connect you while you stretch out on your bed is the height of comfort and convenience, but it's an expense the thrifty exporter will want to avoid. Instead, sign up with an international discount telephone service and use public telephones. It's less efficient, but it can save you a bundle—the call that costs US$10 from a pay phone can run you as much as US$50 from your room! Keep that in mind.

■ **Tip**   Many international hotels offer complimentary Wi-Fi service. Inquire. In lieu of a phone call, you can e-mail people at your home office from your laptop to let them know you arrived safe and sound or report on other important matters. Download some of the free communication services such as WhatsApp, the data-based app for messaging and calling, or in China, the messaging app WeChat. Skype or Apple's FaceTime can be alternative ways to contact people using your laptop.

Security Tips

International travel should be an enjoyable and enriching experience, but don't leave your street smarts at home! As a tourist, you are a prime target for crime. Criminals and con artists of all kinds know that you are likely to be carrying significant quantities of money and valuables and that you are likely to be naive, bewildered, and distracted. Don't be a victim. Here are some major precautions you should take when traveling, sightseeing, or conducting business overseas:

- *Protect your money.* Never keep all your money in one place while traveling internationally. When boarding your flight, hide your payment resources in a variety of places: in your carry-on bag, inside your breast pocket, in your money belt, in your bra, wherever it feels comfortable and least likely to be stolen while you are distracted or sleeping. After arrival, take your cash, checks, and credit cards with you when you leave your hotel room or lock them up in the hotel safe.

Tip Some savvy international business travelers carry a fake wallet along with their real wallet. The fake wallet serves as the detour for robbers. Load it with $30 or $40 (consisting of singles, a five, and a twenty), photos of strangers or someone else's baby, and expired credit cards. If an assailant targets you, don't resist. Turn over the fake wallet. This will avoid a situation going from bad to worse.

- *Pay attention to your belongings when taking pictures.* Never set your purse, tote, or briefcase down next to you to photograph some spectacular sight. While you're absorbed in getting that perfect shot, someone can snatch your stuff. I have seen this happen in my own hometown with international guests! We couldn't run fast enough to catch the culprit, and even if we could have, it would have been dangerous to try to apprehend the person without police assistance. Be careful. And it goes without saying: never set your smart phone down anywhere unattended or ask a stranger to use your smart phone to take a picture of you and your companions. Some people can run faster than a speeding bullet, and you don't want to take the chance of witnessing it as they dash off with your smart phone.

Tip Two fantastic pamphlets, *Managing Travel Risks* (http://www.chubb.com/businesses/csi/chubb2205.pdf) and *Managing Terrorism Risks* (http://www.chubb.com/businesses/csi/chubb2206.pdf), produced by the Chubb Group of Insurance Companies should be read by everyone who plans to travel to minimize a wide array of risks.

- *Be careful about talking with strangers.* Always be on guard when approached by strangers. They may be genuinely helpful and hospitable locals or they may be tourists like yourself needing a little assistance, but they may also be smooth professional thieves. Pickpockets often work in teams. One will get your attention and engage you in conversation while her counterpart proceeds to dig through your handbag, pocketbook, or briefcase. Keep your belongings close to you and minimize lengthy conversations when you are approached by a group, especially when they look and act suspicious.

- *Find out which locations are the most safe.* Always ask your local business associates or hotel concierge which neighborhoods or districts should be avoided, especially if you are traveling alone.

- *Be aware of scams.* Don't fall prey to con artists that offer you special deals. For example, people may approach you and offer to take your picture for a price, only you never receive the photo, or offer to drive you somewhere at a bargain fare, only you find out later that it cost you five times the normal cab rate. Anytime someone comes up to you with an aggressive sales pitch and you are uncertain of their truthfulness or decency, walk away from him fast. Keep a degree of healthy skepticism. Ask your host or local contacts about what is legitimate and acceptable behavior in the country you are visiting.

- *Carry your local contact information, US embassy or US Consulate and emergency phone numbers with you in English and the local language.*

- *Be cautious about what you drink.* The safest choice of beverages while traveling internationally is bottled water, where you recognize the brand and can open it yourself. Be extra careful of all beverages served in public places where you are unfamiliar with the people. In particular, be careful of your consumption of alcohol while traveling internationally. Alcoholic beverages can easily be tampered with while you're not looking. Further, watch how much you drink because you may not know your limits (especially when factoring in time zone and altitude changes).

- *Carry or wear personal high-value items in discreet places.* If you carry a shoulder bag or laptop computer, wear it on the side opposite to where all the traffic is. You want to avoid a bicyclist or motorcyclist grabbing and running off with your precious commodity. When traveling on a bus or train or in a taxi, wear a minimum of expensive jewelry and carry as few expensive tech items as possible. You don't want to stand out as an easy theft target. And speaking of taxis, only hire taxis from a regular cab service and never let a taxi driver encourage you to sit in the front seat alone or add strangers to your taxi ride— even if it will save you money. You don't know her motive. Don't take the chance.

- *Use a tracking software to locate your devices in case they're lost or stolen.*

Health Tips

Accidents and illness can happen anywhere and may be more likely to happen while traveling internationally. Whether you sprain an ankle, experience the sudden onset of a toothache, or suffer a bad case of Montezuma's revenge (better known as traveler's diarrhea), you want to know you can get adequate medical care fast.

In traveling, what constitutes a serious health risk? The most important determinant of a health risk is your destination. "All travelers should familiarize themselves with conditions at their destination that could affect their health (high altitude or pollution, types of medical facilities, required immunizations, availability of required pharmaceuticals, etc.)," advises the US Department of State.[iii] High-risk destinations include developing countries in Latin America, Africa, the Middle East, and Asia. Additional risk factors include known risks such as a recent outbreak of influenza (check the World Health Organization's Web site for any recent outbreaks of infectious diseases abroad: http://www.who.int/en/) or something as simple as thinking it was perfectly safe to drink hotel tap water in a developing country, for example.

What should you do if you are struck with an unexpected illness and need help? Contact your hotel concierge, the local American Embassy (http://www.usembassy.gov/), or, provided you are already a member, a company such as International SOS (https://www.internationalsos.com/en/) or the Ackerman Group through the Chubb Corporation (http://www.ackermangroup.com/index.php). Before you go, however, you might want to consider getting a health insurance policy (check the US Department of State's Medical Insurance providers at https://travel.state.gov/content/passports/en/go/health/insurance-providers.html) designed specifically to cover international travel.

International SOS is an international healthcare, medical assistance, and security services company that provides solutions that help people wherever they live or travel, 24/7. Once a member, you can contact ISOS's nearest assistance center regarding any emergency you encounter while traveling (http://internationalsos.com/en/emergencies.htm) by selecting the country you are in and simply clicking "Go." ISOS also offers a variety of membership plans—comprehensive, medical, security, project, or simply a membership that covers your next trip. Fees vary, so be sure to inquire. Members get pretravel information and advice, a fast response, emergency help, evacuation capabilities, and more. Optional medical and travel insurance is also available. According to ISOS, "Whether you are concerned about finding a qualified doctor, obtaining accurate security advice, or getting travel assistance for lost documents or airline tickets, ISOS can help in these and other worrisome situations."[iv]

The Ackerman Group is best known for a broad range of security and investigative-related issues, with the emphasis always being on prevention. It works in conjunction with the insurance giant Chubb Group of Insurance Companies to produce its kidnap/ransom policy geared more toward publicly traded companies. Chubb says, "Extortion, crime, and political instability are facts of life that corporate leaders must deal with when transacting business in an increasingly global, and unfortunately, hostile environment."[v]

While traveling, above all, trust your instincts, be alert at all times, keep moving toward your destination, and don't let yourself be deterred from going about your business.

What Women Want While Traveling for Business

Today, women make up nearly half of all business travelers—and that number will surely increase thanks to the number of women in the workforce and starting businesses. Up until now, I made a point not to distinguish between businessmen and businesswomen in regard to international travel because they are similar. But there are subtle differences.

I have a message for the travel industry, and hotels in particular. Women, more than men, want safe, super-clean rooms with high-end toiletries and hair dryers and complete access to what they may need along their journey: a curling iron, illuminated and magnified makeup mirror, a swimsuit, a bathrobe that fits, extra hangers, razors, a yoga mat, inexpensive nickel-free earrings (pierced or clips), socks, hose, Vaseline, hairspray, and Q-tips, for example. All of these items need to be available to women either on loan or for purchase. In addition, women like lighter fare when it comes to food, particularly when arriving late at night. Hotels that provide a holistic, good-for-you approach to food will win more women for their facility. And women want tech amenities that work, and when they don't work they want 24/7 support. These are the perks that women want when they travel for business.

What women in particular need to watch out for while traveling internationally is walking around alone after dark in foreign countries where they are unfamiliar with the area, particularly in developing countries. Don't take a chance. If an area is questionable, hire a driver assigned by your hotel concierge to take you to where you want to go. If it's late and you are hungry, order room service or order food recommended by the hotel to be delivered to your room.

■ **Tip** Stay away from rooms that are on the ground floor. You don't want to make it easy for someone to break in. Rather, choose a hotel room that is several floors up but not so high up that should you need to jump (in the case of a fire, for example), you won't survive.

Summary

Perhaps the most important things you can take with you on your international travels are patience, enough money, and a sense of humor. Operations that are relatively simple at home, like catching a bus across town, can seem overwhelming, complicated, and uncertain when you're off your native turf. You feel like you will never get to your destination, you're never sure if you're on the right bus, and you don't know if the bus is going in the right direction. When you ask people for help, they either don't speak your language or tell you things exactly backward. But if you keep your head up and persist, you'll get everywhere you need to go and accomplish what you came for. And afterward, you'll probably feel that the journey was far more valuable than most other things you've done in life thus far.

At some point, international business travel is essential to cement a quality business relationship—and the practical aspects of international business travel can make or break the success of your trip. To ensure you have a safe trip, do your homework before you leave home and keep a heightened awareness throughout your trip.

Between one-quarter and one-third of the world's businesses are owned by women—they are a new breed of globetrotters and a key driver of competitiveness. That's what I am going to discuss in the next chapter.

Notes

i. "About TSA," accessed June 10, 2016, http://www.tsa.gov/about-tsa.

ii. "TSA Preü FAQs," Transportation Security Administration, last modified October 25, 2013, accessed June 5, 2016, https://www.tsa.gov/tsa-precheck/faq.

iii. "Medical Care," United States Department of State, Bureau of Education and Cultural Affairs Exchange Programs, accessed June 5, 2016, https://exchanges.state.gov/us/medical-care.

iv. "Get a Quote: Worldwide Reach, Human Touch," International SOS, accessed June 10, 2016, http://buymembership.internationalsos.com/.

v. "Executive Protection Portfolio Kidnap/Ransom & Extortion Insurance," Chubb Group of Insurance Companies, accessed June 10, 2016, http://www.chubb.com/.

Women Business Owners: Engine of Global Growth

A New Breed of Globe-Trotters Take On the World

Women must try to do things as men have tried. When they fail, their failure must be but a challenge to others.

> —Amelia Earhart, the first woman to cross the Atlantic by plane and the first female pilot to make solo transatlantic and transpacific flights[i]

But for those as yet unknown women to distinguish themselves, we as a society need to create an environment where anything is possible for all women and girls. We celebrate achievement, but we make achievement possible with opportunity.

> —Donna Brazile, CNN contributor and a Democratic strategist[ii]

© Laurel J. Delaney 2016
L. J. Delaney, *Exporting*, DOI 10.1007/978-1-4842-2193-8_27

I want to start this chapter with the fact that women drive the world economy and then share a story that relates to businesswomen in the world marketplace. Forty years ago, Harvard Professor Theodore Levitt was conducting a case discussion in his marketing class about a person's rise in the workplace. The fact that the person in this particular case was a woman was disguised to the students, who were predominantly men. After a long brainstorming discussion, Professor Levitt finally told the class that the protagonist in the case was a woman: "Boys, you'd better wake up now, because there are going to be more and more women in management, and they're going to have an edge. You fellows are going to be so competitive with each other that the thought of collaboration [with women] is never going to cross your minds. Women will come in willing and able and ready, and you're going to lose."[iii]

Let's face it: "Women . . . really and truly do rule!" as put by my colleagues Tom Peters and Marti Barletta.[iv] If you pretend they are invisible, look again: for the first time in history a woman, Hillary Clinton, clinches nomination, presumptively, of a major party for president of the United States in 2016. Women are dynamic, cutting-edge players in the current age of entrepreneurship (or even politics), beating the odds, epitomizing bootstrap success, and becoming an engine of economic growth. They represent a growth market more than twice as big as China and India combined and control $20 trillion in global consumer spending, own or operate in the US between 25-33% of all private businesses, and earn an estimated $13 trillion.[v]

Women need to be recognized for who they are, what they do, and how significantly they impact the global economy. To maximize their complete business potential, women need help in expanding internationally. This notion is not just that it's good for business but that it's good for the global economy—and citizens of the world are finally waking up to it. "[Big businesses are] fundamentally seeing that entrepreneurs, women especially, are really the key to our global and sustainable future," says entrepreneur, investor, and media personality Ingrid Vanderveldt.[vi] Make no mistake, these globe-trotting women are not leaning in, as Sheryl Sandberg says in her book *Lean In: Women, Work, and the Will to Lead*;[vii] they are leaping in by choice. As Babson Professor Candida Brush says, "It is impossible to be an entrepreneur by leaning—you have to commit, take risks and take action."[viii] Surely, and I speak from experience, leaping in is a vital prerequisite to entering the export marketplace.

According to the OPEN Forum, American Express, there are more than 9.4 million women-owned businesses in the United States alone, generating nearly $1.5 trillion annually in revenues and employing more than 7.9 million people.[ix] It is no secret as to why there are more and more women starting businesses in America. In early 2003, I wrote an article called "Escape from Corporate America" for *Across the Board*, the magazine of the Conference Board.[x] In it, I talked about the reasons why women were abandoning corporate America to strike out on their own. Many of the inspiring women business owners mentioned in the article—Sara Blakely, who opened the body-shaper company Spanx (http://www.spanx.com) and Maxine Clark, who began Build-a-Bear Workshop (http://www.buildabear.com/), for example—have successfully expanded their businesses internationally. How? By having what is required to take on the world. It's not just good collaboration skills that have brought them this far. It's a slew of other great characteristics that women possess, such as being more risk averse (i.e., less likely to throw the dice on making a decision); being more sensitive to losses; being less prone to toot their own horn (putting the other person first); being more prone to emphasis; and having a tendency to take a long-term view on business matters.

In this chapter, one that is dear to my heart, I'll address the state of women business owners, their impact on the world economy, and the issues that confront women business owners who are actively exporting or planning to engage in global trade. I'll also address the special characteristics women bring to the international business table, how those characteristics can be used as a competitive tool in export business, and how women can succeed in exporting.

Women Take On the World

The timing has never been better for businesswomen to get out of their own backyards and transition from local, regional, or niche-market players into global players. According to the *Global Entrepreneurship Monitor's (GEM's) Special Report Women's Entrepreneurship: 2015,*[xi] in which entrepreneurial activity in 83 economies around the world is monitored, globally, women play a major role in driving the world economy, controlling about $20 trillion in annual consumer spending, a number expected to rise to nearly $28 trillion in the next five years. In GEM's 2012 report, it indicated there are more than 126 million women entrepreneurs worldwide. An estimated 98 million women are running established businesses—which are ripe for growth through exporting. In countries surveyed for the 2015 report—Suriname, Barbados, and Kuwait, for example, —women exhibit higher rates of entrepreneurial intention than men. The GEM report also indicates that economies with high female labor-force participation rates are more resilient and experience slowdowns of economic growth less often..

Between one-quarter and one-third of the world's businesses are now owned by women. According to the Global Entrepreneurship and Development Institute (GEDI) The Female Entrepreneurship Index (FEI), in 2015, the top ten countries for female entrepreneurs are as follows:[xii]

The top ten countries for female entrepreneurs

Rank	Country	Score
1	United States	82.9
2	Australia	74.8
3	United Kingdom	70.6
4	Denmark	69.7
5	Netherlands	69.3
6	France	68.8
7	Iceland	68.0
8	Sweden	66.7
9	Finland	66.4
10	Norway	66.3

Despite the fact that the global market presents a huge opportunity for women to advance their careers and impact the world of business, "in 2014, only 13 percent of the more than nine million US women-owned firms exported. But the women-owned businesses that did export had a lot to be proud of: average receipts for women-owned exporting firms were $14.5 million compared with $117,036 for women-owned nonexporting firms."[xiii]

The data doesn't stop there. Here's more from the latest available US Census Bureau's *Ownership Characteristics of Classifiable U.S. Exporting Firms: Survey of Business Owners Special Report* on the impact exporting has on women-owned firms:

- Women-owned, nonexporting firms employ on average 8 employees; the comparable number for women-owned exporting employer firms was 42.

- Women-owned, nonexporter's average productivity (i.e., receipts per employee) was $107,288; the comparable calculation for women-owned employer exporters was $389,757.[xiv]

It is evident that through export activities, women-owned firms grow more rapidly, hire more people, create more jobs, and are more productive. Just like sports, exporting can also be a major confidence builder for women, and confidence, even being overly confident, is what women need at all stages of business growth.

Tip   For a look at the best and worst countries for women's employment, based on benchmarked gender gaps in economic, political, and education- and health-based criteria, download the World Economic Forum's *2015 Global Gender Gap Report* (http://reports.weforum.org/global-gender-gap-report-2015/). The United States ranks number twenty-eight out of 145 countries, which collectively contain more than 90 percent of the world's population. The report is a collaborative effort by experts from Harvard University, the University of California, Berkeley, and the World Economic Forum.

Women-owned businesses offer a promising opportunity to increase American export activity. Yet, women owners of export-oriented small- and medium-sized businesses (SMEs) face unique challenges and opportunities, many of which begin at the start-up stage of a business. To help eliminate those challenges, government policy makers have tailored initiatives and programs in their respective countries to best serve women entrepreneurs. The Gem report outlines two of these programs—one that targets initiatives that provide women entrepreneurs with equal access to opportunities, as suppliers of goods and services worldwide, and the other program, designing educational and training programs for women entrepreneurs that go beyond the start-up stage and focus on growth (through exporting, for example).

Tip   For a bird's eye view on what challenges and opportunities women business owners face around the world, download the fone-hundred fifty-nine-page *Global Entrepreneurship Monitor 2015 Special Women's Report* at http://gemconsortium.org/report/49281 .

Issues Confronting Women Business Owners Who Currently Export or Plan to Export

In early 2012, the State Department's Bureau of International Information Programs asked me to write an article called "Women Entrepreneurs Energize Economies." In it, I talk about my experience in starting and running a global business. The key point I make not only applies to starting a business but also to exporting: "To gain self-confidence and overcome inhibiting social attitudes, women need to network continuously, support each other, look for role models, update their knowledge and skills as well as have a clear vision of what they wish to accomplish."[xv] My esteemed colleague Dr. Marsha Firestone, founder and president of the Women Presidents' Organization, adds to that, saying: "Social conventions often discourage women from pursuing entrepreneurial activities. Additionally, the lack of outside investments women-owned and led businesses receive puts them at an immediate revenue disadvantage compared to their male counterparts. Barriers aside, however, there has never been a better time to be a woman entrepreneur on a global scale."[xvi]

Based on my experience running a successful global business, serving as a consultant to countless global women business owners, and being President of Women Entrepreneurs GROW Global (WEGG), a nonprofit that educates women entrepreneurs and business owners on how to go global, my observations indicate that women entrepreneurs must condition themselves to be risk oriented, innovative, and proactive (RIP) in order to achieve any reasonable level of success in the export marketplace. Like everyone else, they must also achieve five things before venturing out beyond borders (much of which has already been covered in previous chapters): becoming ready mentally, particularly emotionally; being ready operationally; having run a successful local business; knowing how to use the latest technology; and having a business with export potential.

Also, in my view, a perceived lack of credibility is the number one barrier for women doing business globally. This perceived deficiency lack makes it difficult for women to access markets, market information, and establish relationships. If you don't already have an influential person in your life who can tout your capabilities, find one and cultivate the relationship.

Tip Women Entrepreneurs GROW Global's makes exporting affordable and accessible for women entrepreneurs and business owners worldwide. It meets its mission and vision by providing women-owned SMEs worldwide with tuition-free online education that walks them through the practical aspects of exporting and provides them with concrete strategies for global entrepreneurship. Check it out https://womenentrepreneursgrowglobal.org.

Lack of access to capital is also a serious problem for women business owners in the global marketplace, which causes an inability to scale their operations and garner greater market share. While male and female business owners alike face barriers to obtaining sufficient and affordable capital to start or acquire a venture, lack of access to credit and the ability to make use of it remains the number one obstacle to US women entrepreneurs starting and expanding their businesses. Fast Company says, "Today, women still struggle to access the capital they need to spur economic development. While women entrepreneurs are now understood to be an accelerator of global growth, their difficulty acessing capital is a pernicious global brake.."[xvii]

In spite of that, many women still finance their start-ups or businesses using credit cards, personal savings, second mortgages, or with the help of family and friends. That means that without special financing programs for women's ventures, only women who have savings or friends with savings can become entrepreneurs, let alone export. Much work has to be done in this area to resolve the problem so women entrepreneurs can be on equal footing with men.

■ **Tip** Check with the Small Business Administration and the Import-Export Bank of the United States to learn what special programs are available for women exporters who are in need of working capital. Also, some of the new crowd-funding sites such as Indiegogo, Kickstarter, and Fundable might have ways to finance an export activity. According to *Crowdfund Insider*, "The success rate for women-led crowdfunding projects was 65 percent as opposed to just 35 percent for men." They go on to say, "Analyzing crowdfunding campaigns collectively, about 42 percent are run by women."[xviii]

Training is another obstacle for women business owners who aspire to grow, especially into international markets. How does a woman get the appropriate training to trade outside her own local area? This book is a start. In addition, online resources such as Women Entrepreneurs GROW Global (https://womenentrepreneursGROWglobal.org), the "Office of Women's Business Ownership" page on the SBA Web site (https://www.sba.gov/starting-business/how-start-business/business-types/women-owned-businesses); US Export Assistance Centers (http://www.sba.gov/content/us-exports-assistance-centers); the Women's Business Development Center (https://www.wbdc.org/); the "Export NOW" page on the Women Impacting Public Policy site (http://www.wipp.org/?page=ExportNOW); and a page listing global business initiatives on the Women's Business Enterprise National Council (WBENC) site (http://www.wbenc.org/global-business-initiatives/) -- all offer research, webinars, workshops, podcasts, and videos on growing a business through exports. Women need to consult with their export dream team—their professional banker, logistics expert, international accountant, and lawyer—for advice on minimizing the challenges that come with exporting into new and unfamiliar markets.

Before the Internet, women had a difficult time getting access to markets and networking or finding like-minded individuals with whom they could end their isolation, share challenges, and gain access to strategic information. Now, however, there are hundreds of women-centric online community forums readily available and designed specifically for women business owners who desire to connect with women the world over, acquire knowledge, develop enriching relationships, and keep learning and growing. Dell has the Women's Entrepreneur Initiatives (http://www.dell.com/learn/us/en/uscorp1/women-powering-business?c=us&l=en&s=corp&cs=uscorp1); IBM has the

Women-Owned Businesses SME Toolkit (http://us.smetoolkit.org/us/ en/category/3201/Women-owned-Businesses); and PNC has the Women In Business (https://www.pnc.com/en/small-business/topics/women-in-business/women-in-business0.html).

Special Characteristics Women Bring to the International Business Arena

With women starting and growing businesses at a record rate, they are or will become a major force in the export marketplace. Even though the business world demands that we leave a lot of unworkable behaviors and attitudes behind, the emotional sensitivity and the capacity for human connectedness usually attributed to women can be very useful in overseas business negotiations. To win their colleagues' confidence and respect, the key element for women is to stick to a complex business agenda and never deviate. Based on my experience and observations, let's have a look at the interpersonal habits that women have traditionally been encouraged to cultivate and how absolutely indispensable they are in international business. Note: These are general impressions, not absolutes, and many characteristics will also apply to men.

- We tend to be more attentive and supportive toward others. We are socialized to give care and support to the people close to us, and we often extend this caretaking impulse to people outside our family circle. This trait can serve you well in an export business, too. You wouldn't want to upset or offend a foreign associate, and it's not possible to tell what will offend anyway. All you can do is be gentle, gracious, and respectful, and let your colleagues guide you. When they see that you are committed to their comfort and happiness, they're likely to forgive any minor blunders and keep negotiations moving forward.

- We study people, "read" their behavior, and make judgments. We're concerned about why people do and say what they do. We do this because we want to act effectively in the interpersonal world. We've developed an instinct for taking accurate readings in a hurry and acting accordingly. Trust that instinct. Where language and cultural barriers hinder communications, it might be all you have. Don't let anyone disparage your impressions because you can't produce empirical proof. They're based on a lifetime's experience, and that's all the proof you need.

- We typically have patience and a capacity for forgiveness. The international business arena belongs to people who can give others the benefit of the doubt and let misunderstandings slide. Frustration, discomfort, and embarrassing social gaffes are the rule rather than the exception when you're conducting a complex transaction in a strange environment. Women who export stand fast through good and bad times and ultimately can bring out the best in their foreign colleagues.

- We have been conditioned to follow etiquette and appropriate social behavior. Understanding foreign cultures, customs, and protocol is absolutely essential for anyone who wants to succeed overseas. You can't afford not to learn the local system. If you don't make yourself acceptable, you won't do business. When you're traveling the globe, you might find yourself beating drums, eating with your hands, even bathing with your associates! The next day you and those same people are in on a grueling round of negotiations and you realize that you're working together better than you dreamed possible. When you respect foreign ways, it's noticed—and appreciated.

- We generally have an intuitive knowledge of how to converse with interesting and thoughtful questions, and when we have in-person meetings, we pay close attention to a person's facial expressions and body language. We also know when to give the floor to someone else if we've been talking too much.

- We are raised to be charming and pleasant to be around. Our sincerity and willingness to offer a conciliatory smile can save the day when things get awkward or even outright nasty. Foreign associates appreciate charm, so smile graciously—but stay on track. And don't indulge in humor. You never know if foreign associates get the joke, or how they'll take it. Just because they're laughing doesn't mean they're amused. It means they're watching what you do and going along with it to keep from rocking the boat. Spare your associates the discomfort—everybody's more comfortable when you stick to business. You can still entertain by storytelling. I do this quite often. It's one of the oldest, purest ways to communicate and always puts people at ease.

- We take a collaborative approach in our relationships by listening and know how to build them to get business done. Women are ready, willing, and able to connect with people to develop win-win situations.

- We have the ability to be resilient, foster a sense of teamwork and connect with a global community. The more competitive a woman becomes in business, the greater the necessity to pull on resiliency. Fostering a sense of teamwork is an essential part of a successful and nurturing workplace. Connecting with a global community is fundamentally human, requiring women, who are naturals at this, to share, connect and come together the world over.

For a few more positive characteristics that women possess, read, "11 Reasons 2014 Will be a Breakout Year For Women Entrepreneurs" http://www.forbes.com/sites/geristengel/2014/01/08/11-reasons-2014-will-be-a-break-out-year-for-women-entrepreneurs/#61b24ca1ef1d

---

■ **Tip** I'll make your day. According to Pew Research, "When it comes to essential traits of a leader, both men and women saw women as being more compassionate, organized and honest than men, and saw men as being more ambitious and decisive (though for most traits, an even higher share said both genders possess them equally)!"[xix]

The lucrative and wide-open world of export business is the businesswoman's natural habitat. Our gentler qualities are powerful assets that can transform the way the world does business. "Nonsense!" you might say. "Foreign businessmen don't take women seriously!" It's certainly intimidating to head over to a country where, in some instances, women are forced to walk ten paces behind their husbands, but take heart. Many savvy international businesswomen have been pleasantly surprised by their reception in the business arena and have discovered the following perceptions about them to be significant reasons for their welcome:

1. *They're still a novelty.* Because businesswomen are unusual in some countries, they are highly visible. Think about it—there's something unremarkable about men doing business, domestically or overseas. So when a woman enters the business world, it automatically stands out. She gets attention—and deservedly so—for her confidence and professionalism as well as her gender. Use your status as a relative novelty to your advantage. Be confident, act confidently, and know your stuff. Then do what you came for.

2. *They're educated.* Even in countries where women are indisputably second-class citizens, educated women command respect.

3. *North American women are known for seeking top management positions and aspiring to break through what is commonly referred to as the "glass ceiling."* This perception gives them a particular advantage in international business. The thinking is that in struggling against the invisible barriers to advancement, these women have had to become superbly competent, creative, and resourceful—all of which adds up to an exceptionally fine businessperson.

America continues to stand for equality and for a strong work ethic. People expect Americans, men and women, to be smart, gutsy, and aggressive, and to mean business. An American businesswoman overseas tends to be viewed first as an American, then as a representative of her own or someone else's company, and lastly as a woman. So, an American global businesswoman can hope in most places to be understood and respected on her own terms—and the more women who export and make the global arena their own, the better the chance of shattering that glass ceiling for good!

My fellow women readers, if you still find yourself feeling intimidated, call on the old-fashioned "masculine" qualities of single-mindedness, confidence, and determination. First of all, remember that you must have a product they want or you wouldn't be there. Second, put your knowledge on the table. Look your associates in the eye and tell them what you know. No need to be an arrogant know-it-all; just state your case and stand your ground. Natural confidence commands respect. Finally, if you stay focused on doing the job you flew halfway around the world to do, nobody else can stop you.

A woman business owner who exports is a whole human being. She calls on both masculine and feminine traits and can be both gentle and powerful at the same time. She knows how to adapt her interpersonal instincts to fit smoothly into the professional environment and how to show authority and inspire confidence without intimidating and alienating others. A woman business owner who exports adds value to any business, whether it's her own or that of her home corporation—pushing limits, shaking things up, competing vigorously in the world marketplace, and making the world a better place in which to live.

Building a Global Empire via the Internet

When it comes to developing social or e-commerce platforms, women might have the edge. Why? Women use a universal language that everyone can understand—the language of conducting business with high integrity and honesty—and they are apt to carry a stronger emotional quotient than men, which can be invaluable for striving to make things perfect and accessible to the everyday Jane or Joe. According to the blog posting "Are Women Leaders Better than Men?" on the *Harvard Business Review Blog Network:* "Specifically, at all levels, women are rated higher [than men] in fully 12 of the 16 competencies that go into outstanding leadership."[xx] That entails everything from taking initiative, to displaying high integrity and honesty, to solving problems and analyzing issues. A women's attitude is: If my mom or grandma can figure this e-commerce platform out and like it, the whole world will too. And in most instances, they are likely to be right.

Here's one example of a woman taking advantage of social media to start her own multimillion-dollar business and reach customers: At a mere thirty-two years of age, the contrarian thinker, capitalist, and CEO of Nasty Gal (http://www.nastygal.com) Sophia Amoruso built her fashion retail empire in just seven years from zero to $300 million[xxi] by starting an eBay vintage store and then developing it into her own e-commerce site. She named the company after jazz legend Miles Davis's second wife, the funk and R&B singer Betty Davis, who produced an album of the same title.[xxii] Her company sells edgy, retro-inspired stylish clothes, shoes, and accessories at reasonable prices to a loyal customer base of young women worldwide.[xxiii]

What are her secrets to success? First and foremost, she went with her gut instincts on her business decisions. She has a good business model: She buys hip clothing dirt cheap and resells it on her site at a sizable profit margin (for example, she resold a Channel leather jack she found for $8 at a Salvation Army on her site for $1,000). She uses approachable clothing models that everyone can relate to and applies her own styling to the photos of them. She has developed an intense social media presence (via Instagram, Pinterest, and Facebook, for example) among her audience to keep them actively engaged. Her clothes allow her user base of independent young women to dream yet also make their dreams a reality through their purchases. She puts every penny of profit she makes right back into the business, carrying zero debt. And when asked by the *Wall Street Journal* what she thinks has set her apart from others, Amoruso's simple response was, "Nasty Gal really emerged from a conversation. I've probably spent more time than any other brand reading every last comment. To listen to people the way you're able to online is very powerful. I think other companies are just starting to figure that out."[xxiv]

Summary

The current rise of woman-owned businesses in our country has the potential to have a significant impact on American competitiveness. Women the world over should celebrate the unique qualities that make them born leaders in the global marketplace.

As my friend and esteemed colleague Karen Kerrigan, president and CEO of the Small Business & Entrepreneurship Council (SBE Council), says: "Women who become successful entrepreneurs need to be celebrated and held up as role models for other women. This is a powerful tool in helping to reshape the mindset of women in terms of visualizing what is possible."[xxv] Regardless of race, age, gender, religion, education, locale, or income status, everyone must have equal opportunity to participate in the export marketplace.

My final message to fellow women business owners: Exporting can serve as a lever to vault your business onto a level global playing field. Yes, there will be challenges and, yes, you will work hard because you are put to a different test than men. Enjoy and cultivate yourself, love what you do, and plot your own export course. Only good things will follow.

Notes

i. *Women Who Changed the World: Fifty Inspirational Women Who Shaped History* (London: Smith-Davies, 2006), 110.

ii. "Breaking the Ultimate Glass Ceiling, CNN.com, accessed June 10, 2016, http://www.cnn.com/2016/06/07/opinions/womens-voices-on-hillary-clinton-clinching-nomination-roundup/.

iii. "Ted Levitt Changed My Life," Harvard Business School: Working Knowledge; the Thinking that Leads, December 7, 2008, http://hbswk.hbs.edu/item/6054.html.

iv. Martha Barletta and Tom Peters, *Trends: Recognize, Analyze, Capitalize* (London: DK Publishing, 2005), 12.

v. Sylvia Ann Hewlett, Melinda Marshall, and Laura Sherbin, "How Women Drive Innovation and Growth," August 23, 2013, accessed June 11, 2016, https://hbr.org/2013/08/how-women-drive-innovation-and.

vi. Miles Kohrman, "Can Women Entrepreneurs Make Bureaucracy a Word of the Past?," *Fast Company*, accessed June 21, 2013, http://www.fastcompany.com/3012900/creative-conversations/can-women-entrepreneurs-make-bureaucracy-a-word-of-the-past.

vii. Sheryl Sandberg, *Lean In: Women, Work, and the Will to Lead* (New York: Knopf, 2013).

viii. Candida Brush, "'Leaning In' Is Not Enough: Women Entrepreneurs Need to 'Leap In,'" *Forbes,* accessed April 13, 2013, http://www.forbes.com/sites/babson/2013/04/13/leaning-in-is-not-enough-women-entrepreneurs-need-to-leap-in/.

ix. Julie Weeks, "Women-Owned Firms Springing Up All Over, OPEN Forum, American Express May 18, 2015, accessed June 10, 2016, https://www.americanexpress.com/us/small-business/openforum/articles/women-owned-firms-springing/.

x. Laurel Delaney, "Escape from Corporate America," *Across the Board: The Conference Board Magazine of Ideas and Opinion,* March/April 2003, 39–43.

xi. Donna J. Kelley, Candida G. Brush, Patricia G. Greene, Mike Herrington, Abdul Ali, Penny Kew, *GEM's Special Report Women's Entrepreneurship 2015 Women's Report,* 2015, accessed June 11, 2016, http://gemconsortium.org/report/49281.

xii. Female Entrepreneurship, Global Entrepreneurship Development Institute, 2015, accessed June 11, 2016, https://thegedi.org/research/womens-entrepreneurship-index/.

xiii. ExportNOW2, Women Impacting Public Policy, accessed June 11, 2016, http://www.wipp.org/?page=Export NOW2.

xiv. US Census Bureau, *Ownership Characteristics of Classifiable U.S. Exporting Firms: Survey of Business Owners Special Report,* June 2012, accessed June 11, 2016, http://www2.census.gov/econ/sbo/07/sbo_export_report.pdf.

xv. Laurel Delaney, "Women Entrepreneurs Energize Economies," IIP Digital, March 1, 2012, http://iip-digital.usembassy.gov/st/english/publication/2012/03/20120301135847jezrdna0.1726757.html#axzz2jyxqxZDU.

xvi. "How to Conquer the Global Economy," Marsha Firestone, PhD, Enterprising Women Magazine, 2013, 24-25.

xvii. Melanne Verveer, "The Other Gender Gap: How Women Entrepreneurs Are Getting Screwed Out Of Funding," May 7, 2014, accessed June 11, 2016, http://www. fastcompany.com/3030144/bottom-line/gender-inequality-isnt-just-about-pay-why-female-entrepreneurs-need-greater-acce.

xviii. Chris Tyrrell, "Crowdfunding is Changing the Female Entrepreneurial Landscape, Crowdfund Insider, July 15, 2015, accessed June 11, 2016, http://www.crowdfun-dinsider.com/2015/07/71191-crowdfunding-is-changing-the-female-entrepreneurial-land-scape/.

xix. D'vera Cohn and Gretchen Livingston, "Americans' Views of Women as Political Leaders Differ By Gender," Pew Research Center, May 19, 2016, accessed June 11, 2016, http://www.pewresearch.org/fact-tank/2016/05/19/americans-views-of-women-as-political-leaders-differ-by-gender/.

xx. "Are Women Better Leaders than Men?," blog entry by Jack Zenger and Joseph Folkman, *Harvard Business Review: HBR Blog Network*, last modified March 15, 2012, http://blogs. hbr.org/2012/03/a-study-in-leadership-women-do/.

xxi. https://womenentrepreneursgrowglobal. org/2016/06/04/nasty-gals-sophia-amoruso-puts-her-big-global-girl-shoes-on/.

xxii. "Betty Davis: A 'Nasty Gal' ahead of Her Time," Meredith Ochs, October 26, 2009, NPR Music, accessed June 11, 2016, http://www.npr.org/templates/story/story.php?storyId=114171958.

xxiii. "Shop by Currency," Nasty Gal, accessed June 11, 2016, http://www.nastygal.com/index.cfm/fuseaction/localization.home.

xxiv. John Ortved, "Sophia Amoruso Expands Nasty Gal," *Wall Street Journal*, last modified August 22, 2013, http:// online.wsj.com/article/SB10001424127887324354 70457863787008658966.html.

xxv. "International Women's Day Q&A with CIPE Board Chair Karen Kerrigan," blog entry by Karen Kerrigan, *CIPE Development Blog*, accessed June 11, 2016, http:// www.cipe.org/blog/2013/03/08/international-womens-day-qa-with-karen-kerrigan/.

New Frontiers in Emerging Markets

Brazil, Russia, India, China, and South Africa

Emerging markets offer an extensive and generous opportunity, and if you are going to be successful, you need to take advantage of what benefits doing business overseas can provide for your company.

—Ty Morse, CEO of Songwhale[i]

Many [companies] continue to focus on the BRICS (Brazil, Russia, India, China and South Africa) and a few other economies. But the emerging-market growth story extends to pockets all across the globe, and offers a premium to fast movers.

—Matt Reilly, Managing Director, Accenture's Management Consulting business across North America[ii]

Do you have a product or service that you could sell to nearly 3 billion people? That is a question millions of global citizens and companies alike are asking themselves, because the world is shifting its attention to BRICS

© Laurel J. Delaney 2016
L. J. Delaney, *Exporting*, DOI 10.1007/978-1-4842-2193-8_28

(Brazil, Russia, India, China, and South Africa) in the next phase of globalization to drive export revenue growth. The BRICS countries are a major force in the world economy where a rising middle class promises a long-term customer base. Even with recent market turbulence and a slight stall on exports, the potential of BRICS is too big for companies to limit their activities to developing countries.

BRICS, a term that Jim O'Neill, of investment bank Goldman Sachs coined, currently have "combined foreign currency reserves of $4.4 trillion and account for 43 percent of the world's population."[iii] The long-range impact of this multitrillion-dollar group of countries includes: the creation of jobs, the reduction of trade deficits, and an increase in prosperity throughout the world economy. Jonathan Lemco, senior investment strategist with Vanguard Investment Strategy Group says, "The quality of life for people in these countries, with some exceptions, has never been this good."[iv] It is only a matter of time before you will need a strategy that will land your product or service in BRICS, no matter how complex, remote, or tumultuous. And I'm not referring to sourcing or manufacturing there. I'm referring to a pure selling export strategy.

This chapter highlights the key growth drivers for BRICS, important market facts and products in demand in these countries, the implications for small businesses operating in them, a blueprint for export success to the countries, and other second-tier fast-growth countries to watch out for in the future. The key question to think about as you read through this section is this: do you have a product or service that BRICS want and can afford?

■ **Caution** The markets mentioned in this chapter are not easy to enter. It takes time, knowledge, money, and patience to make headway. It took companies like Intel, KFC, and GE years to make inroads in emerging markets. They invested millions of dollars over a protracted period of time before ever seeing a dime in profit. But they did this because of upside potential down the road. One example is Coca-Cola where future growth will be fueled by emerging markets, which are naturally showing higher rates of growth.[v]

What Drives Growth in BRICS?

The BRICS countries are the focus of many companies when they set their sight on targeting big, fast-growth markets for exports. After all, four of the five countries (all of them except South Africa) are the world's largest emerging economies, with China being the biggest in population.

What drives this unprecedented demand for imports by BRICS? Besides a having a hardworking group of people anxious to improve the quality of their lives, most of the BRICS countries have these characteristics in common:

1. A large land mass or extensive territories

2. A huge population. The total population for the five countries is 3.02 billion.[vi]

3. Massive infrastructure demands

4. Strategic economic policies in place to support rapid
growth

5. The specific goal of expanding trade and investment with
the world

The discussion of the BRICS countries and the reasons to export to them in
the following sections provides important market facts for and specific products and services in demand for each market.

Note Although the actual GDP growth rates of BRICS may appear to be modest, you must take
into consideration the general outlook for each economy, including its past and present conditions
and its future potential. The source for the data is the Central Intelligence Agency's *World Factbook*
unless otherwise noted.

Tip I have made a point to highlight the more Internet-savvy countries, the languages spoken,
and the preferred online payment methods when dealing with them. Take these factors into
consideration as you prepare to tweak or build your e-commerce site. Your goal should be to satisfy
consumers' needs in each of these markets.

Brazil

The following are general statistics about conditions in Brazil related to
exporting:[vii]

- *Languages*: Portuguese (official and most widely spoken
language); Spanish (less common)

- *Population*: 204,259,812—making it the sixth-largest country (July 2015 estimate)

- *Population growth rate*: 0.77 percent (2015 estimate)

- *Internet usage*: 108.2 million, representing a 53.4 percent
penetration rate (percentage of population as of 2014
estimate) Internet country code is .br

- *Preferred online payment method*: Debit and credit cards remain the most popular method of online payment[viii]

- *Gross domestic product*: US$3.192 trillion (2015 estimate)

- *GDP growth rate*: -3.8% (2015 estimate)

- *Inflation rate*: 9 percent (2015 estimate)

- *Per capita GDP*: US$15,600 (2015 estimate)

- *Imports*: US$174.2 billion (2015 estimate)

Why Brazil?

According to the Office of the United States Trade Representative, U.S. goods and services trade with Brazil totaled $95.4 billion in 2015 (latest data available for goods and services trade). U.S. goods exports to Brazil in 2015 were $59.5 billion, imports were $35.9 billion—making Brazil the United States' 12th largest goods trading market in 2015 and the 11th largest goods export market in 2015.[ix]

Brazil's primary trading partners are the United States, Argentina, Germany, Netherlands, Nigeria, and China.

A hot tip for exporting to Brazil: You need patience, persistence, and an understanding of the market to enter into Brazil. Brazilians are known to be enthusiastic, confident, innovative, and adaptable. They enjoy dealing with foreigners. Learn how to leverage this in your favor. Be open to developing relationships with Brazilians from the outset, and dedicate time to growing the relationship.

The best prospects for general exports to Brazil are: Footwear, coffee, machinery, electrical, and transport equipment (including airplane and helicopter parts); chemical products, oil, automotive parts, and electronics; pharmaceutical drugs for humans and veterinary medicine; and so forth. Specific to United States, the top export categories in 2012 include: Machinery, mineral fuel, aircraft, electrical machinery and optic and medical instruments. The leading agricultural categories include: wheat, dairy products, prepared foods, chocolate and cocoa products, and feeds and fodders. (Note: Brazil is preparing for the Olympics in 2016, which can be promising for US exports.) The top US exports of private services to Brazil are in the following areas: transporation, telecommunications, computer, travel, and information service sectors.

Russia

Russia's general conditions relative to the export process are:[x]

- *Languages*: Russian (official); many minority languages
- *Population*: 142,423,773—the tenth-largest country (July 2015 estimate)
- *Population growth rate*: −0.04 percent (2015 estimate)
- *Internet usage*: 84.4 million, representing a 59.3 percent penetration rate (percentage of population; 2014 estimate); Internet country code is .ru
- *Preferred online payment method*: e-wallets such as QIWI[xi]
- *Gross domestic product*: US$3.718 trillion (2015 estimate)
- *GDP growth rate*: -3.7 percent (2015 estimate)
- *Inflation rate*: 15.5 percent (2015 estimate)
- *Per capita GDP*: US$25,400 (2015 estimate)
- *Imports*: US$197.3 billion (2015 estimate)

Why Russia?

Russia is the world's eigth-largest economy by population and has undergone significant changes since the collapse of the Soviet Union. A combination of falling oil prices, international sanctions, and structural limitations pushed Russia into a deep recession in 2015, with the GDP falling by close to 4%. Yet Russia is still considered a high-income country, with a highly educated and trained workforce and sophisticated, discerning consumers. One should, however, proceed cautiously because conducting business there currently might be impeded. According to export.gov, "The recent events in Ukraine have changed the landscape of the bilateral trade and investment relationship between the United States and Russia."[xii]

A hot tip for exporting to Russia: Personal relations are vital to build trust with Russian businesspeople. Business discussions can often be slow and detailed, so patience is required, along with punctuality at meetings. Russians are tough negotiators (with interpreters who speak both Russian and English and provide information in both languages) and rely on fact-based information on hand at meetings. Plan on developing and maintaining long-term relationships when traveling to Russia.

The best export prospects to Russia are: Machinery; vehicles; pharmaceutical products; plastic; semifinished metal products; meat, fruits, and nuts; optical and medical instruments; and iron and steel. Note: Russia's biggest import trading partners for 2015 are Netherlands, China, Germany, and Italy.

Tip Just as there is Tmall (http://www.tmall.com) in China—the country's B-to-C shopping destination for brand-name goods letting companies sell directly to the public (review chapter 7)—there are Ozone Holdings (http://www.ozon.ru/) and Ulmart (http://www.ulmart.ru) in Russia, two of the country's largest e-commerce companies. Although e-commerce is in the early state of its development in Russia, it is very much alive and flourishing. The trick for small businesses in that country is to partner or collaborate with companies such as Ozone and Ulmart. That can only happen with the appointment of a good on-the-ground person to stay at the pulse of consumer action.

India

Here are the conditions for India that relate to exporting:[xiii]

- *Languages*: Hindi, Bengali, Telugu, Marathi, Tamil, Urdu, Gujarati, Kannada, Malayalam, Oriya, Punjabi, Assamese, Maithili, and others, including English (considered a subsidiary language but nonetheless an important language for national, political, and commercial communications)

- *Population*: 1,251,695,583—the second-largest country (July 2015 estimate)

- *Population growth rate*: 1.22 percent (2015 estimate)

- *Internet usage*: 237.3 million, reflecting a 19.2 percent penetration rate (percentage of population); Internet country code is .in

- *Preferred online payment method*: Direct debit accounted for more than a half of B-to-C e-commerce payment transactions in 2012[xiv]

- *Gross domestic product*: US$7.965 trillion (2015 estimate)

- *GDP growth rate*: 7.3 percent (2015 estimate)

- *Inflation rate*: 4.9 percent (2015 estimate)

- *Per capita GDP*: US$6,200 (2015 estimate)

- *Imports*: US$432.3 billion (2015 estimate)

Why India?

With a population of more than 1.2 billion, India is the second-most populous country in the world. Approximately 30 percent of the country's population resides in urban areas.

A hot tip for exporting to India: Indian society has a very strong belief system based on the family, and these beliefs extend to business, so get to know your business partner first before ever negotiating one ounce of business—do not rush the process. Adapting a laid-back approach with clear and direct communications is the best approach to dealing with Indian businesspeople.

The best export prospects are: crude oil, precious stones, machinery, fertilizer, iron, steel and chemicals. The hot industry sectors are: corrosion control; defense; architecture; civil aviation; education services; environment and water; health care and medical equipment; infrastructure/smart cities (roads, ports, and railroads); mining and mineral processing supply chain/logistics; power and renewables; and travel and tourism.[xv]

Note: As of 2015, India's best trading partners are China, the United Arab Emirates, Saudi Arabia, Switzerland, and the United States.

China

The following statistics are relative to China's exports:[xvi]

- *Languages*: Standard Chinese or Mandarin (Putonghua, based on the Beijing dialect); Yue (Cantonese); Wu (Shanghainese); Minbei (Fuzhou); Minnan (Hokkien-Taiwanese); Xiang; Gan; Hakka dialects; and other minority languages

- *Population*: 1,367,485,388—the world's largest country (July 2015 estimate)

- *Population growth rate*: 0.45 percent (2015 estimate)

- *Internet usage*: 626.6 million, representing a 46.0 percent penetration rate (percentage of population; estmate 2014); Internet country code is .cn

- *Preferred online payment method*: Cash on delivery (COD), credit cards (China UnionPay cards), and debit cards (China UnionPay cards), AliPay, WePay by TenCent and WeChat. Apple Pay and Samsung Pay will be new entrants – keep an eye out.[xvii]

- *Gross domestic product*: US$19.39 trillion (2015 estimate)

- *GDP growth rate*: 6.9 percent (2015 estimate)

- *Inflation rate*: 1.4 percent (2015 estimate)

- *Per capita GDP*: US$14,100 (2015 estimate)

- *Imports*: US$1.596 trillion (2015 estimate)

Why China?

China's sheer geographic size, population, and growth prospects offer unlimited possibilities. Building a large and profitable presence in China requires exporting top-quality products that are affordable to the masses. Small businesses that might not have the deep financial pockets that big companies do need to be extra careful on how they approach entering China. Be on heightened awareness at all times because one big China export misstep could cost you your business. As I write in an article for *The Wall Street Journal*, "You better put on your boxing gloves, for China can seem more like a sparring partner than a trading partner."[xviii] I say this because of having had first-hand knowledge of conducting business in China and it being a tough nut to crack. As a result of my experience with China, its popularity, and its growth prospects, I am providing more information on the country.

Here are some hot tips for exporting to China (which might apply to the other countries in BRICS as well):

- *Create desirability*. Get to know your customer in order to determine which of your products offers the greatest appeal for the Chinese consumer and fits best with the local culture.

- *Provide your product or service at your lowest price.*

- *Have a negotiating strategy*. The Chinese expect you to have a strategy, and if you don't, they will take advantage of you. Know where you want to end up and how you plan to get there.

- *Build strong relationshipsnegotiating strategy because they are the lifeblood of business in China*. It's not how much you know but whom you know in China. Look for a partner who already has a Chinese presence and a great reputation in your industry. Take care of the people who take the time to make introductions for you. Thank them, thank them again, and thank them one more time.

- *Set the right course and slow your pace*. Your success will be based not on how well you craft your strategy but on how well you execute the deliverables.

- *Be courteous.*

- *Invest a significant amount of time and money to build and monitor sales, marketing, and distribution.*

- *Prepare for a fierce competitor.* The Chinese are known to flex their muscle relative to the sheer population size of the market they are dealing with, insist that you partner or form a joint venture together, learn everything you do and improve on it, and then turn around and compete against you. Do you have a strategy in place to combat that?

- *Put people on the ground in China who are respected, know the market, the language, the industry, and the lay of the land.*

- *Train staff at the national HQ and locally in China to work with the country well in advance of developing business.* Training helps your staff connect, become knowledgeable on what needs to be accomplished, and develop confidence in their ability to get things done.

- *Take extra precaution in protecting your intellectual property.* Will it be sufficiently complicated for someone in China or other emerging markets to duplicate your product? Figure it out and then come up with a plan that acts like a Sun Tzu *Art of War* contingency plan. "The supreme art of war is to subdue the enemy without fighting," Tzu says.[xix]

Tip   A great primer on operating in China is *Doing Business in China for Dummies* (2007). Robert Collins, my friend and colleague and the CEO of the Shanghai-based company Doing China Business, coauthored the book with Carson Block. The book is not just for dummies, as it covers everything we all want to know about how business is done in China. It also includes a cheat sheet on common business blunders and discusses Chinese business values and even fun ways to spend your downtime in China. The chapter "Managing Risks" is particularly insightful for those who are concerned at the outset over managing legal (intellectual property, for example) and environmental issues, if any. Another good book is Jeffrey Towson's *The One Hour China Book: Two Peking University Professors Explain All of China Business in Six Short Stories* (2014). One hour with this and Collins' books will make you an instant expert on business in China.

The best export prospects for China are: electrical equipment and other machinery, oil and mineral fuels, optical and medical equipment, nuclear reactor, boiler and machinery components, metal ores, motor vehicles, and a range of professional services. Note: The biggest trading partners on China's imports for 2015 are Japan, South Korea, United States, Germany, Taiwan, and Australia.

South Africa

Here are the general statistics about South Africa:[xx]

- *Languages:* IsiZulu, IsiXhosa, Afrikaans, Sepedi, English (9.6 percent—widely spoken in business circles), Setswana, Sesotho, Xitsonga, siSwati, Tshivenda, and isiNdebele

- *Population:* 53,675,563—the twenty-sixth largest country (July 2015 estimate)

- *Population growth rate:* 1.33 percent (2015 estimate)

- *Internet usage:* 24.8 million, constituting a 46.9 percent penetration rate (percentage of population); country code is .za

- *Preferred online payment method:* Visa, PayPal through First National Bank (FNB), Ukash, M-Pesa, Cell Pay Point, Zapper and FlickPay.[xxi]

- *Gross domestic product:* US$723.5 billion (2015 estimate)

- *GDP growth rate:* 1.3 percent (2015 estimate)

- *Inflation rate:* 4.6 percent (2015 estimate)

- *Per capita GDP:* US$13,200 (2015 estimate)

- *Imports:* US$86.81 billion (2015 estimate)

Why South Africa?

The United States is a critical trading and technology partner for South Africa, and ranks annually as South Africa's third largest partner in two-way trade by value.

According to Export.gov, "The African Growth and Opportunity Act (AGOA), renewed for a final 10 year period with last minute eligibility for South Africa in 2016, provides duty-free access to the U.S. market for most sub-Saharan African countries, including South Africa. The United States and South Africa signed a new Trade and Investment Framework Agreement (TIFA) in 2012. The United States and SACU concluded a Trade, Investment and Development Cooperation Agreement (TIDCA) in 2008."[xxii] These agreements will eliminate tariffs and other trade barriers, which will enable trade to expand with South Africa.

A few hot tips for exporting to South Africa: Take it slow, start with trusting relationships (South Africans like sticking with known suppliers), and perform due diligence on the companies you are dealing with. South African companies are receptive to a range of partnering arrangements with U.S. companies that can range from licensing to joint ventures to acquisitions.

The best export prospects for commodities are: Machinery and equipment, electrical, chemicals, petroleum products, scientific instruments, and food-stuffs. Opportunities exist for a wide range of consumer products and services as well. Note: as of 2012, South Africa's biggest trading partners are China, Germany, United States, Saudi Arabia, India, and Nigeria.

Achieving Success Exporting to BRICS

Even the poorest markets in the world can generate revenue for small businesses provided they tailor their products and services to meet the needs of the consumers. If you target countries that have a healthy GDP, are Internet savvy, and have a population with a high percentage of people using the Internet, you will greatly improve your chance for success. Before entering a market, check with the World Bank Group's ranking of 189 economies to learn the ease of doing business in each country at http://www.doingbusiness.org/rankings and the full *Doing Business 2016* report at http://www.doingbusiness.org/~/media/GIAWB/Doing%20Business/Documents/Annual-Reports/English/DB16-Full-Report.pdf. A high ranking on the index means that the country's regulatory environment is more conducive to the starting and operation of a local firm but is not necessarily representative of the ease of exporting there. Nonetheless, it will give you a good idea of the complexity or ease of entering into any given market.

Here is a blueprint for success in operating in BRICS. Consider these my export imperatives or immutable rules. Take these lessons with you on your journey and then use your own insight and intelligence to make good decisions.

- *Develop a distinctive quality product at a very low price.* Many people in the emerging parts of the world are at the bottom of the pyramid living in poverty. They cannot afford many products, so price as low as you can while still making sure you will earn a profit, and use the pricing as a basis for entering other markets.

Tip Develop products for emerging markets, which can serve as invaluable breeding grounds for innovations that were originally developed for these markets. These products will pioneer new uses when introduced back to the developed countries (the United States, for example). Authors Vijay Govindarajan, Chris Trimble, and Indra K. Nooyi describe the developing world as a fertile research and development lab for companies in any market in their provocative book *Reverse Innovation: Create Far from Home, Win Everywhere* (2012).

- *Tap into markets that have a healthy GDP, are creditworthy, are Internet savvy, and whose population has a high percentage of people using the Internet (in China, for example).* You are seeking a tipping point where consumers and businesses are just getting a knack for e-commerce.

- *Determine your best BRICS market by comparing opportunities across borders within a particular industry based on a sector-specific methodology.* Check with *Top Markets: A Market Assessment Tool for U.S. Exporters* `http:// trade.gov/topmarkets/?utm_source=blog&utm_ medium=tradeology&utm_campaign=topmarkets`. Each report is available for download.

- *Access the Bureau of Economic Analysis (BEA) Data Tool to get a quick snapshot of statistics on trade and investment between the United States, BRICS and other countries by simply clicking on a world map:* `http://bea.gov/international/ factsheet/`.

■ **Tip** According to [the late] C. K. Prahalad, who created the "bottom of the pyramid" concept, "The dominant assumption is that the poor do not have money to spend and, therefore, are not a viable market. Certainly, the buying power for those earning less than $2 per day cannot be compared with the purchasing power of individuals in the developed nations. However, by virtue of their numbers, the poor represent a significant latent purchasing power that must be unlocked."[xxiii] For an in-depth look at bridging the Internet gap and creating new global opportunities in low- and middle-income countries, read Intel's "Women and the Web" at `http://www.intel.com/ content/www/us/en/technology-in-education/women-in-the-web.html`.

- *Prequalify potential business partners and maintain constant communications with them so you can rapidly respond to the whims of customers.*

- *Take a long-term view on goals and progress (five to ten years out) because that is where opportunity enters.* By then, you will have acquired new knowledge and developed sufficient expertise to act on it.

- *Be patient—overseas business, especially in emerging markets, sometimes seems like it takes forever to get done.*

▓ **Tip** Goldman Sachs has a complete 272-page e-book on the growth potential of BRICS and what the future holds *BRICS and Beyond* available for immediate download (http://www. goldmansachs.com/our-thinking/archive/archive-pdfs/brics-book/brics-full-book.pdf). PWC offers *The World in 2050: Will the Shift in Global Economic Power Continue?* also available for immediate download (http://www.pwc.com/gx/en/issues/the-economy/assets/world-in-2050-february-2015.pdf).

Useful Guides on Doing Business with BRICS

The US Commercial Service, part of the US Department of Commerce, has already taken initiatives to help you learn about, and take advantage of, the new and existing opportunities for your business in BRICS. The following reports offer rich, in-depth looks at different countries' political and economic environments and selling US products and services to those countries and discuss their trade regulations, investment climate, contracts, market research, trade events, and even market entry strategies. To understand the challenges and opportunities BRICS present, it is important to read these publications. The reports are the latest available.

- *Doing Business in Brazil: 2016 Country Commercial Guide for U.S. Companies:* http://www.export.gov/ccg/brazil090732.asp

- *Doing Business in Russia: 2016 Country Commercial Guide for U.S. Companies:* http://www.export.gov/ccg/russia090879.asp

- *Doing Business in India: 2016 Country Commercial Business Guide for U.S. Companies:* http://www.export.gov/ccg/india090814.asp

- *Doing Business in China: 2016 Country Commercial Business Guide for U.S. Companies:* http://www.export.gov/ccg/china090765.asp

- *Doing Business in South Africa: 2011 Country Commercial Business Guide for U.S. Companies:* http://www.export.gov/ccg/southafrica090960.asp

---

■ **Caution** As you drill down on the information, look for each country's credit rating to determine how fluid the market is. In other words, can capital flow in and out freely? Consult with your banker. Also look at "Global Online Payment Methods Report 2015—Second Half 2015" (http://www. researchandmarkets.com/research/zndp9d/global_online) to determine each country's preferred method of e-commerce payment. There is a fee.

Challenges of Operating in Emerging Markets

With any opportunity comes a host of challenges. When entering into BRICS, there is no single cookie-cutter approach because each market varies along with the individual companies. But this I can guarantee: You will face unpredictable market conditions; limited human resource capabilities; corruption; high-income inequality; weak infrastructure (poor transport systems that make shipping goods particularly problematic, for example); spotty retail systems (small local retailers and kiosks vs. small number of big chains); lack of credit card penetration (the vast majority of purchases, including online ones, being made in cash); electrical shortages; and weak fixed line telecommunications. The bottom line: In many instances, the countries are too underdeveloped to get into. Still, it is worth a try to beat your competitors from getting the first-mover advantage on new customers. Take your conquest of BRICS in steps or stages and you will fare best.

■ **Caution** Trade and technology regulations and standards vary from country to country, which makes life difficult for manufacturers and exporters. Always check with a variety of sources to determine whether the regulations and standards specific to a country can become obstacles to trade. The "Technical Barriers to Trade" section on the World Trade Organization site (http://www.wto.org/english/tratop_e/tbt_e/tbt_e.htm) is a good place to start.

Other Opportunities in New Frontier Markets

Frontier markets or next-generation emerging markets often have shakier economies with a much younger labor force, yet in the next five years, growth could become much faster for frontier markets than in the established emerging markets. For now, monitor the following markets closely for growth and development: Indonesia, Malaysia, Mexico, Columbia, Poland and Kenya (Africa's other growing economy). Some will grow so fast that they move into the emerging-market category.

Tip For addiitional emerging markets, read, "The Top 20 Emerging Markets: Global Emerging Markets `http://www.bloomberg.com/slideshow/2013-01-30/the-top-20-emerging-markets.html#slide1`

While these markets are still in their early stages of growth and development, they can be attractive export opportunities that offer long-term economic growth with strong profit-return potential, provided you actively manage this area. There is nevertheless great risk, volatility, and inefficiencies in frontier markets, so tread carefully.

Summary

A successful export business revolves around satisfying customer demand. If you want to succeed in BRICS and other second-tier fast-growth markets, you must make extraordinary efforts, understand the operating environment and consumer trends, have the financial capacity to sustain the journey, offer products that are in demand at low prices, take a risk, and get the right people on board to execute your strategy. Nothing feels more satisfying in the business world than claiming your place as a high-powered export player in BRICS, especially if you are improving billions of lives in the process. If you are up to the challenge and persist, you will reap the benefits for years to come.

After venturing into BRICS and other second-tier countries, what's next? The world is larger than you think for opportunity! In the next chapter, I will look at ten export markets that are possibly the most attractive for selling your products.

Notes

i. "5 Reasons Your Startup Isn't in Emerging Markets (And Why It Should Be)," Huffpost Business, June 1, 2016, accessed June 12, 2016, `http://www.huffingtonpost.com/young-entrepreneur-council/5-reasons-your-startup-is_b_10166316.html`.

ii. "How Smart Businesses Are Winning in Emerging Markets," Reuters, February 22, 2013, accessed June 12, 2016, `http://blogs.reuters.com/great-debate/2013/02/22/how-smart-businesses-are-winning-in-emerging-markets/`.

iii. "BRICS Nations Plan New Bank to Bypass World Bank, IMF," Mike Cohen and Ilya Arkhipov, Bloomberg, March 26, 2013, http://www.bloomberg.com/news/2013-03-25/brics-nations-plan-new-bank-to-bypass-world-bank-imf.html.

iv. "Beyond the BRICS: Emerging Markets Opportunity," Vanguard, March 23, 2016, accessed June 12, 2016, https://personal.vanguard.com/us/insights/article/beyond-brics-032016.

v. "Coca-Cola 'Still the Largest Brand' As Local Players Apply Pressure, FoodBev, June 9, 2016, accessed June 12, 2016, http://www.foodbev.com/news/coca-cola-still-the-largest-brand-as-local-players-apply-pressure/.

vi. "The World Factbook; Country Comparison: Population," Central Intelligence Agency, July 2015, https://www.cia.gov/library/publications/the-world-fact-book/rankorder/2119rank.html?countryname=Brazil&countrycode=br&regionCode=soa&rank=5#br.

vii. "The World Factbook; South America: Brazil," Central Intelligence Agency, last modified October 25, 2013, https://www.cia.gov/library/publications/the-world-factbook/geos/br.html.

viii. Patrick Bruha, "Payment Methods in Brazil," The Brazil Business, January 19, 2015, accessed June 12, 2016, http://thebrazilbusiness.com/article/payment-methods-in-brazil-1421683322.

ix. "Brazil," Office of the United States Trade Representative, accessed June 12, 2016, http://www.ustr.gov/countries-regions/americas/brazil.

x. "The World Factbook; Central Asia: Russia," Central Intelligence Agency, last modified June 7, 2016, accessed June 12, 2016, https://www.cia.gov/library/publications/the-world-factbook/geos/rs.html.

xi. Anna Kuzmina, "An Introduction to Online Payments in Russia," Internet Retailer, June 30, 2015, accessed June 12, 2016, https://www.internetretailer.com/commentary/2015/06/30/introduction-online-payments-russia.

xii.   "Doing Business in Russia: Market Overview," export.gov, last modified June 7, 2013, `http://export.gov/russia/doingbusinessinrussia/index.asp`.

xiii.   "The World Factbook; South Asia: India," Central Intelligence Agency, last modified October 31, 2013, `https://www.cia.gov/library/publications/the-world-factbook/geos/in.html`.

xiv.   "Global Online Payment Methods Report 2013–First Half 2013," *Wall Street Journal*, May 30, 2013, `http://online.wsj.com/article/PR-CO-20130530-906555.html`.

xv.   "India Country Commercial Guide," Export.gov, last updated October 13, 2015, accessed June 12, 2016, `http://www.export.gov/ccg/india090814.asp`.

xvi.   "The World Factbook; East & Southeast Asia: China," Central Intelligence Agency, last updated June 7, 2016, accessed June 12, 2016, `https://www.cia.gov/library/publications/the-world-factbook/geos/ch.html`.

xvii.   Oren Levy, "Where In the World Are the Mobile Payment Users?" ATM Marketplace, June 10, 2016, accessed June 12, 2016, `http://www.atmmarketplace.com/articles/where-in-the-world-are-the-mobile-payment-users/`.

xviii.   Laurel Delaney, "Trade Routes to China," The Wall Street Journal, June 12, 2000, `http://www.wsj.com/articles/SB960218205555337004`.

xix.   "The Art of War Quotes," Sun Tzu, goodreads, `http://www.goodreads.com/work/quotes/3200649---s-nz-b-ngf`.

xx.   "The World Factbook; Africa: South Africa," Central Intelligence Agency, last modified June 9, 2016, accessed June 12, 2016, `https://www.cia.gov/library/publications/the-world-factbook/geos/sf.html`.

xxi.   "Crossborder-Ecommerce | Payment Methods South Africa," The Paypers, accessed June 12, 2016, `http://www.thepaypers.com/payment-methods/southafrica/25`.

xxii. "South Africa Market Overview," Export.gov, last updated June 7, 2016, accessed June 12, 2016, http://apps.export.gov/article?id=South-Africa-Market-Overview.

xxiii. C. K. Prahalad, *Fortune at the Bottom of the Pyramid: Eradicating Poverty through Profits,* Revised and Updated 5th Anniversary Edition (Philadelphia: Wharton School Publishing, 2009), 35.

The Top Ten Export Business Markets

The best way to predict your future is to create it.

—Peter Drucker, management consultant, educator, and author

Knowing is not enough; we must apply. Willing is not enough; we must do.

—Johann Wolfgang von Goethe

By now, you've learned what it takes to find fulfillment and fortune beyond your national borders as an export business executive. Now it's time to get started, and there's no time like the present. So where are the hot export markets? I won't leave you guessing for long.

In this chapter, I discuss America's ten best export trading markets. It is likely that your domestic competitors could already be taking advantage of these markets, which may or may not influence your decision to export to them. Check with your state trade office to see what kind of exporting support it provides. It could be anything from helping companies land new overseas opportunities to determining if an overseas inquiry is a scam or even offering export financing ideas. In Illinois, where I am based, there is fantastic support

© Laurel J. Delaney 2016
L. J. Delaney, *Exporting*, DOI 10.1007/978-1-4842-2193-8_29

through the Illinois Department of Commerce and Economic Opportunity, the International Trade Association of Greater Chicago, the Export Assistance Center Illinois, the US Department of Commerce and Economic Opportunity, and the International Trade Centers.

The Illinois Department of Commerce and Economic Opportunity alone operates ten foreign trade offices in cities ranging from Mexico City to Shanghai. Both, as you will see, are top export markets for American companies. What does that mean for small businesses operating in Illinois? Free assistance to conduct business in those ten countries. Most people don't even know about this magical gem of a resource offered by Illinois or that their own state has international trade office support. So, again, reach out to your state before you get started to see what kind of support it offers.

Once armed with your state's best-kept secrets on export trade resources, it's up to you to take action and expand your business into the hot markets. Let's go!

America's Best Export Markets

Here's a look at the exporting facts related to America's top ten export trading partners this year to date through April 2016, according to the United States Census Bureau.[i] All numbers shown are in billions of dollars and reflect exports from the United States to a specific country. The data are for goods only.

■ **Note** Review the Trans-Pacific Partnership Agreement (http://trade.gov/fta/tpp/?utm_source=hero&utm_medium=tradegov&utm_campaign=tpp) and North American Free Trade Agreement (https://ustr.gov/trade-agreements/free-trade-agreements/north-american-free-trade-agreement-nafta) to see how these agreements might eliminate tariffs, lower service barriers, and increase competitiveness in some of these markets.

---

1. Canada

More than $176.7 billion worth of US goods were traded with Canada year to date April 2016, and the total exports from the United States year to date equal $87 billion (18.6 percent of export trade).[ii] Given its closeness in geographic proximity, the similarity in business cultures, and the North American Free Trade Agreement (NAFTA), Canada offers excellent business opportunities for qualified US firms, especially those operating in such key sectors as aerospace, energy, travel, tourism, automotive, and government procurement.

Tip   Looking for importers in Canada? You can contact the US Commercial Service in Canada (http://export.gov/canada/), or you can get an even-faster idea of companies importing goods into Canada by product, by city, and by country of origin through the Canadian Importers Database (https://www.ic.gc.ca/eic/site/cid-dic.nsf/eng/home) on the Industry Canada site. The information is based on 2014 data collected by the Canada Border Services Agency (CBSA).

---

2. Mexico

The total exports from the United States to Mexico so far this year are $75 billion (16.1 percent of export trade). Mexico was the second-largest goods export market for the United States in 2016. This is in part based on the North American Free Trade Agreement (NAFTA), which has fueled international trade activity between the United States, Canada, and Mexico due to the elimination of duties and other trade restrictions. In 2016, according to the latest data available, $170.5 billion worth of US goods alone were traded with Mexico.[iii]

According to the Office of the United States Trade Representative, the top export categories for Mexico in 2015 were machinery, electrical machinery, mineral fuel and oil, vehicles, and plastic. Mexico ranks as the third largest US agricultural export market, reaching $18 billion for that year. The leading export categories are corn, coarse grains, pork and pork products, beef and beef products, soybeans, and dairy products. U.S. exports of services to Mexico were an estimated $30.8 billion in 2015. Travel, intellectual property (computer software), and financial services, as well as the travel industry, accounted for most of US services exports to Mexico.

Tip   All small business owners worry about getting paid on exports. When doing business in Mexico, it's no different. Keep your payment options open. The fifteen-page PDF report (2012) *Mexico: Financing Options for your Mexican Buyer* (http://www.buyusainfo.net/docs/x_5718905. pdf) will help you minimize risks associated with each payment option and ensure you get paid.

---

3. China

The total exports from the United States to China year to date 2016 are $33.9 billion (7.3 percent of export trade). Trading with China—the more than 1.3 billion-person Goliath—strengthens our economy and at the same time creates jobs for American workers. As reported by export.gov, "China is currently our largest goods trading partner with $598 billion in total (two way) goods trade during 2015. Goods exports totaled $116 billion; goods imports totaled $482 billion."[iv] Opportunities abound for businesses of all sizes in China. You don't have to look far. The following Web sites, organizations, and programs provide valuable information for doing business with China:

- *Commercial Service China*: (http://www.export.gov/ china/). Every year, this site analyzes the best opportunities for exports from the United States to China—from education and training to automotive components markets and travel and tourism.

- *AccessAmerica*: (http://export.gov/china/services/ accessamerica/index.asp). This program promotes the services of US-based firms to customers and investors in China, giving access and exposure to Chinese clients seeking US expertise in trade finance, branding, legal, insurance, and other needs.

- *E-to-China.com*: (http://www.e-to-china.com). Have a look at the only Web site authorized by the General Administration of Customs of P. R. China (GACC) to provide comprehensive Chinese customs information in English.

- *The National Bureaus of Statistics of China*: (http:// www.stats.gov.cn/english/). This organization is the authoritative source of trade statistics collected by the Chinese government.

- *The Sinocism China Newsletter*: (https://sinocism.com). This free email newsletter helps readers better understand China with commentary and curated links to the important English and Chinese news of the day.

- *A Pocket Guide to Doing Business in China*: (http://www. mckinsey.com/business-functions/strategy- and-corporate-finance/our-insights/a-pocket- guide-to-doing-business-in-china). McKinsey & Company provides trends shaping the world's second-largest economy to explain what companies must do to operate effectively.

▨ **Caution** China continues to be a challenging environment for intellectual property protection. To safely market your products and services abroad, visit `http://www.STOPfakes.gov`. Also review the Inernational AntiCounterfeiting Coalition site, where several big companies such as Tiffany & Co., Gucci, and Michael Kors withdrew their participation due to the organization admitting Chinese e-commerce company Alibaba Group Ltd.—a company that doesn't combat fakes online—as a member in April 2016: `http://www.iacc.org`.

---

4. Japan

The total exports from the United States to Japan at this point in 2016 equal $19.7 billion (4.2 percent of export trade). Japan is the world's third largest economy, after the United States and China. Japan is the fourth largest export market for U.S. goods and services, exporting over $66.5 billion (8 billion yen) worth of goods to Japan in 2015.[v] The top export categories for Japan are: civilian aircraft engines, equipment, and parts; medicinal equipment; pharmaceutical preparations; meat and poultry; and corn, to name just a few.

Due to Japan's "silver" market, where in 2014, twenty-six percent of the country's population is sixty-five years old or older,[vi] home care products, nursing homes, and hospital products are very much in demand.

▨ **Tip** For a comprehensive look on what it's like to do business in Japan, visit Japan Commercial Country Guide at `http://www.export.gov/ccg/japan090820.asp`. For additional support and help with your exports to Japan, try the Japan External Trade Organization (JETRO) Web site at `http://www.jetro.go.jp/usa/`. JETRO helps American companies enter and expand in the Japanese market.

---

5. United Kingdom

Exports from the United States to the United Kingdom total $18.4 billion (3.9 percent of export trade) as of this point in 2016. According to the CIA's 2015 *World Factbook*, the United Kingdom is a major international trading power, holding the position of the third largest economy in Europe after Germany and France.[vii] According to export.gov, the United Kingdom has few trade barriers and is the entry market into the European Union for more than forty-three thousand US exporters.[viii] However, with the recent news that the UK has removed itself from the European Union, referred to as Brexit, Britain must seek new trade accords with countries around the world. Watch closely for how Brexit pans out in the future and whether trade between the US and the UK is impacted, if at all.

Major export categories for US companies to the United Kingdom include aerospace products; building products and sustainable construction; cyber security; medical equipment; pet products; low-carbon energy and smart grids; and travel & tourism.

■ **Tip** For a comprehensive look at conducting business in the United Kingdom, access *Doing Business in the United Kingdom: 2016 Country Commercial Guide for U.S. Companies* from http://export.gov/unitedkingdom/doingbusinessintheuk/eg_gb_026650.asp. For more on Brexit, visit http://importexport.about.com/od/TradePoliciesAndAgreements/fl/Stunned-UK-Votes-to-Remove-Itself-from-European-Union-EU.htm.

---

6. Germany

The total exports going from the United States to Germany so far in 2016 are $16.3 billion (3.5 percent of export trade). Germany is considered the largest market in the European Union for American exporters. It is the largest European trading partner of the United States and is the fifth largest market for U.S. exports for 2015. Further, Germany is the largest consumer market in the European Union, with a population of 81.3 million in 2015. U.S. exports to Germany in 2015 were $49.9 billion.[ix]

The primary US export and import commoditites to Germany (the latest available data is from 2013) are: apparel, chemical goods, electrical equipment, beverages, machinery, and cars and car parts.

■ **Tip** The PDF report *Doing Business in Germany: 2015 Country Commercial Guide for U.S. Companies* (http://www.export.gov/germany/build/groups/public/@eg_de/documents/webcontent/eg_de_087922.pdf/) offers a look at how to sell US products and services to Germany; the leading business sectors for US export and investment; and trade regulations, customs, and standards. If you are interested in moving to Germany, try Expatica (http://www.expatica.com/), an online portal of news and information for the international community. Women should try the Berlin International Women's Club (http://www.biwc.de/).

---

7. Netherlands

The total exports from the United States to the Netherlands at this point in the year are $13.3 billion (2.8 percent of export trade). The Netherlands is a smart choice to export to because it is considered Europe's largest port of entry, making the country a gateway to Europe. The Netherlands is an ideal European starting point for new-to-export companies looking for their first European distributor. The United States is the largest foreign investor in the Netherlands, and its largest bilateral trade surplus is with the country.[x]

The Netherlands offers excellent business opportunities for qualified US firms, especially those operating in such key sectors as agriculture (seafood products, food preparations, tree nuts, vegetable oils, and planting seeds) and commercial clean technology; computer and communications equipment; cyber security services; energy; healthcare technology/medical devices; biotechnology; renewable energy; marine supplies and pleasure boats; seaport security equipment and systems; automotive parts and accessories; aerospace; aircraft parts and associated equipment; airport security equipment; and systems and software.

Tip For a comprehensive look at what it's like to do business in the Netherlands, access the *Doing Business in the Netherlands: 2016 Country Commercial Guide for U.S. Companies* at `http://www.export.gov/ccg/netherlands090862.asp`.

---

8. South Korea

The total exports from the United States to South Korea to this point in the year are $12.7 billion (2.7 percent of export trade). The United States is the third largest exporter worldwide to Korea. US firms are in a stronger competitive situation to sell more made-in-the-USA goods, services, and agricultural products to Korean customers following the United States-Korea Free Trade Agreement (KORUS FTA).[xi]

The leading sectors for exports from the United States to Korea include: aerospace, agricultural products, cosmetics, defense, ecommerce, education services, energy (new and renewable), entertainment and media, environmental, medical equipment and devices, semiconductors, and travel and tourism.

Tip For more information on how to do business with Korea, access *Doing Business in Korea: 2016 Country Commercial Guide for U.S. Companies* from `http://www.export.gov/ccg/korea090824.asp`.

---

9. Belgium

The total exports being delivered to Belgium year to date from the United States are $11.1 billion (2.4 percent of export trade). Belgium is strategically situated in Europe, and home to many European Union institutions, such as NATO, making it an extremely attractive place to do business. It also enjoys the highest per capita income in Europe. With its major ports (Antwerp is the second largest port in Europe) and excellent logistical infrastructure, a significant portion of bilateral trade either originates in, or is destined for, other countries in Europe.[xii] The best prospects for US exports include: aerospace and defense, agricultural products, civil nuclear energy, ecommerce and mcommerce, medical devices, renewal fuels and biomass wood pellets, safety and security, and travel and tourism.

■ **Tip** To access the latest (2015) report *Doing Business in Belgium: 2015 Country Commercial Guide for U.S. Companies*, visit `http://www.export.gov/ccg/belgium090679.asp`.

---

10. Hong Kong

The total exports being delivered to Hong Kong from the United States are $10.8 billion (2.4 percent of export trade). Some reasons the country is good for US exporters are that Hong Kong offers a great base from which to enter China; it has a fairly reliable financial and legal infrastructure; and it has experienced local trilingual (English, Mandarin, and Cantonese) executives and consultants that can be hired, making it easier to establish and conduct business there. More important, "Hong Kong is a free port that does not levy any customs tariff and has limited excise duties."[xiii] The best prospects for US exports include: electronic components; medical equipment and pharmaceuticals; environmental technologies and services; aviation and airport equipment; transportation infrastructure; environmental technologies; safety and security equipment; financial services; education and training services; travel and tourism services; retail; and consumer goods, such as packaged food, wine, cosmetics, and toiletries.[xiv]

■ **Tip** To access the latest (2016) report *Doing Business in Hong Kong and Macau: 2016 Country Commercial Guide for U.S. Companies*, visit `http://export.gov/ccg/hongkongmacau090680.asp`. For more details on import/export policies in Hong Kong, visit `http://www.gov.hk/en/business/global/importexport/index.htm`.

Summary

Before you take on America's ten best export-trading markets, check with your state trade office to see what kind of exporting support it provides and find out if any trade agreements are in effect. You will want to enter these exciting markets in a practical, effective, and cost-conscious fashion. And don't be discouraged if you don't see your products or services listed in the hot prospect lists. By the time this book goes to press, the markets will have changed, offering new and different opportunities that might present a better fit for your capabilities. If you want to get your products and services into these markets, you must anticipate having to work hard. But you can also anticipate transforming your business into a profitable export enterprise where you own, and are proud of, the result.

To succeed as an exporter, you must apply fortitude and practice—by starting to do—what you have learned. But before getting started, you should take into consideration what others have done in the export marketplace to overcome challenges and become successful. To gain some inspiration from some star exporters, turn to the next chapter.

Notes

i. "U.S. Top Trading Partners—April 2016," United States Census Bureau, accessed June 13, 2016, https://www.census.gov/foreign-trade/statistics/highlights/toppartners.html.

   The source for the listing is provided by the US Census Bureau News, Foreign Trade, U.S. Top Trading Partners.

ii. Ibid.

iii. Ibid.

iv. "The People's Republic of China," export.gov, accessed June 14, 2016, https://ustr.gov/countries-regions/china-mongolia-taiwan/peoples-republic-china.

v. "Doing Business in Japan," export.gov, last modified December 15, 2015, accessed June 14, 2016, http://export.gov/japan/doingbusinessinjapan/index.asp.

vi. "Fear of Dying Alone: The State of Japan's Aging Population," The Wall Street Journal, accessed June 14, 2016, http://blogs.wsj.com/japanrealtime/2015/06/16/fear-of-dying-alone-the-state-of-japans-aging-population/.

vii. "The World Factbook; Europe: United Kingdom," Central Intelligence Agency, last modified October 29, 2013, https://www.cia.gov/library/publications/the-world-factbook/geos/uk.html.

viii. "United Kingdom Market Overview," export.gov, last modified April 17, 2016, http://apps.export.gov/article?id=United-Kingdom-Market-Overview.

ix. "Welcome to the U.S. Commercial Service Germany," export.gov, last modified May 17, 2016, accessed June 14, 2016, http://www.export.gov/germany/.

x. *Netherlands Country Commercial Guide*, US Commercial Service, last modified April 17, 2016, accessed June 14, 2016, http://apps.export.gov/article?id=Netherlands-Market-Overview.

xi. "New Opportunities for the U.S. Exporters Under the U.S.-Korea Free Trade Agreement," Office of the United States Trade Representative, accessed June 14, 2016, http://www.ustr.gov/trade-agreements/free-trade-agreements/korus-fta.

xii. "Belgium Market Overview," export.gov, last modified April 17, 2016, accessed June 14, 2016, http://apps.export.gov/article?id=Belgium-Market-Overview.

xiii. "Doing Business in Hong Kong," export.gov, last modified September 7, 2015, http://export.gov/hongkong/doingbusinessinhongkong/index.asp.

xiv. Ibid.

Export Mastery

Export Success

Real-Life Accounts of Successful Export Businesses

We've come a long way in our journey, and now it's time to learn from other small business owners on how they overcame challenges and became successful exporters. In this chapter, you'll find personal experiences supported by sound advice about what it takes to run a successful exporting business.

Success Stories and Key Lessons

World Blazer: Run Your international Division like it is a Start-up (Even if it isn't)

Here's a deep dive into World Blazer Consulting LLC (http://www.world-blazer.com) founder Alison Larson's way of thinking, and a look at insights from her 26 years of international business experience in the apparel industry. Larson served as vice president, Global Business Development for Carter's, the No. 1 children's wear brand in the USA, where she was instrumental in taking Carter's from a label with little international recognition to a brand exceeding 20 percent international growth per year.

Prior to Carter's, Alison worked as managing director, international for OshKosh B'Gosh, where, for 15 years, she helped build the brand from its international infancy to a premier children's brand selling apparel, accessories, and other related product categories in top retail locations around the world.

© Laurel J. Delaney 2016

L. J. Delaney, *Exporting*, DOI 10.1007/978-1-4842-2193-8_30

I interviewed Larson to find out what it takes to be successful developing an international brand.

Laurel Delaney: To put things in perspective, give us an idea of what annual sales for OshKosh were at the time you started, and what percent was international? What countries were you selling to?

Alison Larson: In 1990, OshKosh company sales were approximately $323M (wholesale and retail). International was about $22M (wholesale and licensed) or 6 percent of company sales. At the time, OshKosh was doing a small amount of export and licensed business in Europe, Asia/Pacific, the Caribbean, Mexico, Canada, and the Middle East. The business had been managed by the US sales team until about a year before I joined. When I came on board, there was only the general manager of international and a customer service rep out of Wisconsin.

Delaney: What were some of the first initiatives you took to develop an international presence for OshKosh?

Larson: One of the first things we did was create brand development manuals so we could ensure that we established a high-quality, consistent brand image for OshKosh around the world. We developed an international retail concept for freestanding stores and shops and a corresponding do-it-yourself manual so our international partners could implement the concept locally under our specifications. Along with that, we developed a merchandising manual and video that showed our partners exactly how to present and merchandise our products at retail. We also created an international marketing manual that outlined specific guidelines for implementing our advertising layouts, images, and message around the world. The ads were adapted slightly for international markets and were updated every season. We also put together approval procedures in marketing, product development, retail, and quality control in order to make sure that we protected our brand image and were consistent in all markets.

Delaney: What was the single greatest challenge you faced in getting the OshKosh brand accepted, recognized, and established on a global scale? What was your greatest success while building the OshKosh brand globally?

Larson: In the early nineties, the US was behind many of the major markets in terms of fashion trends and quality standards. Our US designers would often go to Europe for design inspiration, so the trends that we incorporated were typically a year behind Europe. Therefore, international buyers, especially those in Europe, would complain that our designs were out of trend. We also were offering poly/cotton tops when many of the international markets wanted 100 percent cotton. As a result, we found that certain aspects of the Oshkosh line had to be adapted in order to meet the high standards of the European and often Asian consumer.

I believe that our greatest success in building the OshKosh brand globally was being able to position it at a more premium level as compared to our business in the United States. The international consumer was looking for brands that were more upscale and could be sold in higher-end department stores. In the US, we were selling to a few mid-level department stores, but much of our business was being done in outlet centers. This meant that we had to upgrade everything we did: product, store design, marketing materials, etc. As a result, our brand image around the world was higher than that in the US, and our stores and shops internationally looked better than any of the stores we had in the United States.

Delaney: Can you share a failure and how you turned it into a powerful learning lesson going forward?

Larson: At the very beginning of my career, OshKosh wanted to explode its European business and decided to enter into a joint venture (JV) with a company in France. In Europe, OshKosh's bib overall was very well-known, as both Princes William and Harry of the UK were photographed often wearing the overalls when they were children. At the time, OshKosh was exporting a modest amount of product throughout Europe but recognized that adaptations to the product, marketing, and retail concept would have to be made in order to better satisfy the needs and requirements of the European consumer. The JV company opened subsidiaries in Germany, the UK, and France and serviced the rest of Europe through the Paris headquarters. To make a long story short, OshKosh ended up having to buy out the JV partner a couple of years later and formed a wholly owned subsidiary.

The venture was a disaster from the beginning. The organization that was established was for a company with an international business the size of Levi's, not for a medium-sized company like OshKosh with a small international business. Also, the general manager of Europe was not experienced enough to run such a complicated business. Moreover, we adapted the product so much for Europe that it lost much of its midwestern American heritage and became a very upscale European brand. The product costs and corresponding retail prices were so high that the company had difficulties selling everything but the bib overall and couldn't make enough profit to cover the high overhead of the company.

Unfortunately, millions of dollars later, when the decision was finally made to close down the company, many people lost their jobs, including my boss at the time. I was very fortunate, as I had been able to spend a great deal of time in Europe, working in the offices and the stores and at trade shows. The European experience I gained and the lessons I learned were invaluable and shaped my career for years to come.

Delaney: Did you have a companywide commitment to grow the international business for Carter's?

Larson: In the beginning, there was not a real companywide commitment to grow the international business at Carter's. The CEO at that time really wanted to focus on the US business. It was very difficult because we had the lowest priority in the company when it came to resources and visibility. If the company was short product, it came from international orders. If there were delays, international was shipped last. There was a very small budget allocated to international development. We had a skeleton staff and had to develop most of our materials ourselves. Our partners suffered the most because, although they were investing heavily in beautiful stores, their voices were never heard. Compared to the size of the US business, their businesses were too small to matter.

The great thing was that it forced us to be very resourceful and creative and focus on building a strong foundation for the Carter's brand and great relationships with our international partners. We were left alone by corporate and could develop what we felt the business really needed.

When the next CEO took over, things began to change. The company realized that international would be an important growth vehicle for the company and therefore decided to give our division more visibility, more priority, and more resources.

Delaney: Based on your global business experience, what are some critical errors that companies make when going global?

Larson: A common mistake that companies make is going with the first company that approaches them. There usually is little to no research done, no strategy developed, and no other partners considered. They quickly launch in a foreign market and then eventually pull out when the business fails to make money and becomes a big distraction to the team. They then spend the next year or two cleaning up the market and trying to rebuild their reputation.

Another common error I see is companies going global before they are ready. When things are difficult in their home market and they need to increase sales, they look to international for growth. This is a bad approach, as problems typically get magnified when entering a new market. A company that is financially strong with a solid business in its home market almost always has a much greater chance of success in international expansion than a company that is struggling at home.

Delaney: When developing an international strategy and conducting competitive assessments on a brand, how much focus should be placed on competitors who appear to be successful?

Larson: I believe that a thorough competitive analysis is one of the most important parts of the market assessment process and the company's ultimate success in the country. It is critical that a company look at competitors in their industry and specific category in order to succeed internationally. And, while I feel that it is important to look at brands or companies that have been successful in that particular country, it is probably equally if not more important to look at those that have been unsuccessful. After all, why repeat the same mistakes that others have made before you if you don't have to?

Delaney: Many companies talk about the importance of forming partnerships to grow their business internationally. What's the best way to decipher a good partner from a bad partner?

Larson: In my opinion, the partner that you choose will be the most important determinant of whether you will be successful in a foreign market. This is not a process that should be rushed through, yet the majority of companies that I come across enter international markets by accident, not by design. They often go with the first company that approaches them without doing significant research on the market or the partner. Choosing the wrong partner can damage your company or brand's reputation, cost you significant amounts of money, and set you back years in a market.

In the vetting process, I typically use the following criteria in evaluating a company. First, you should look at the quality of the other brands they carry. The best brands get the best partners, but there are also good companies that carry lesser known but quality brands as well. The company's reputation in the market is also very important. If possible, one should check a company's references by calling one or two of the brands that the company represents.

Good partners must be strong financially so they can invest in the business. Make sure that you always do a credit check on the company before signing a contract to make sure that they are financially sound. Having a strong distribution network is key in getting your brand placed with the right retailers. Many companies will list a bunch of retailers that they will sell your product to, but often they have no idea whether the retailer will even take your brand, especially if they are not already doing business with them.

A product and cultural fit with your company is critical when selecting a good partner. The company's brands and product lines should be complementary to yours and not compete directly. When determining cultural fit, you want to make sure that your two companies have the same values and vision for the future of your brand or product. You also need to establish mutual trust. If you do not fully trust the company or seem to have a lot of disagreements during the negotiating process, chances are this company is a bad cultural fit. And lastly, make sure that the business plan the company submits to you is realistic and well thought out. Aggressive business plans with big numbers look great on paper but often do not get executed.

Delaney: Is there such a thing as an inability to adapt a product for an international market?

Larson: Yes. For smaller brands, localizing can be particularly difficult, if not impossible, due to an inability to reach production minimums. Often, a brand must wait until it has developed a significant volume in its core business before it can realistically begin to adapt any of its products for international markets. With that said, design, spec, and other product adaptations can put a lot of pressure on the supply chain, so it is critical that there is enough need and demand for the new product. Minimums need to be met and product costs, margins, and pricing must make financial and commercial sense.

I also see brands that refuse to adapt their product for international markets due to ego or the desire to keep the authenticity of the brand. Sometimes, when a brand is very strong in its home market, it assumes that the product will work around the world without any tweaks. The problem is that fashion can be especially difficult to cross borders because consumers' preferences vary considerably in terms of design, color, silhouettes, and fit.

While I do believe that localizing products for certain international markets may be necessary, the decision to do so should not be taken lightly. Not every trend works for every brand, and not every style works in every country. The most successful brands are those that can tweak their offering without the consumer ever really knowing that changes have been made because the product looks and feels like the original.

Key Lessons

Larson offers a plethora of insights. Make sure your brand and company have a strong foundation before you go global. Adapt your strategy to each new market. Do your homework, take a long view, and legally protect your brand at all costs. Choose your overseas partner with the same care and attention as you would selecting a personal partner, because it can make or break your success.

Philip Pittsford, Chairman of the National District Export Council: Learn the Rules of the Export Road

What is the key to success in cracking open an international market? What are the challenges? Have trade agreements fueled export opportunity for businesses? These are among some of the questions I asked Philip Pittsford, chairman of the National District Export Council (http://districtexportcouncil. org). Pittsford served as Vice President of International Sales for Corr-Jensen for one year, and prior to that he spent 15 years as International Sales Manager at NOW Health Group, where he oversaw operational issues, including a network of in-country distributors active in more than 60 countries. Pittsford has won numerous awards for exporting excellence, namely the President's E-Award for Export Excellence, and the Illinois Governor's Export Awards.

Laurel Delaney: What is the key to success in cracking open international markets?

Philip Pittsford: Commitment. Determination. Focus. Patience. There must be a true commitment in pursuit of international markets. This commitment should include being open to making changes to your products so that they comply with local and/or regional requirements in your targeted market(s). Have a determination to follow through on the commitment to ensure that your products can be legally imported and sold into the market. Focus on providing the documents needed for market entry and/or compliance. A great deal of international commerce succeeds or fails on the documents available. Whether they are related to product registration, a specific certification, or customs entry, much of the difficulty in exporting is due to having the proper documentation. Paper drives a lot of international commerce, and the fact that a company is willing and able to produce the required documents or pursue a license needed to enter a market is what separates it from the rest. In the case of nutritional supplements, these documents will pertain to registrations, product specifications, and certain product licenses for the import and/or export of the item. For industrial goods, they could include specific product certifications. Without these licenses or certifications, your product will not enter the market. These behind-the-border obstacles can keep you from entering the market. Patience comes into play because gathering the necessary documents takes time, and submitting for review for a license or registration in a foreign market also takes time.

Delaney: On the opposite side of the spectrum, what is the single greatest international growth expansion challenge for companies and how is it overcome?

Pittsford: The biggest challenge is getting the full commitment of the owner and senior management to what is needed to fully take advantage of the opportunities that international markets offer. Oftentimes there need to be changes in formulations and label text, for example. Not all small- to medium-sized businesses (SMEs) are in a position to offer these product adaptations.

Delaney: Have trade agreements fueled new overseas market entries for companies?

Pittsford: The Trans-Pacific Partnership (TPP) offers great promise for many SMEs in that it will bring down many of the behind-the-border obstacles that can keep companies from gaining access to new markets. TPP addresses product standards and it offers a unique opportunity for the US to contribute the establishment of many of the standards that will be used for years to come. This would do away with much of the additional testing and applications that many companies must go through as they are trying to enter new markets. These add significantly to the cost of doing business overseas, adding to the price at which companies must sell their products in order to be profitable. TPP also brings down tariffs. Imagine having an additional duty of 20%, 30%, or 60% added to the cost of your products upon clearing customs in a foreign market. In many cases, your product just went from being competitive to becoming more expensive and possibly no longer competitive. TPP will be good for American manufacturers and exporters in opening up a large and growing market for American companies. There are currently about 350 million middle-class consumers, and it is believed that this number will exceed 3 billion by the year 2030.

Delaney: What action should a business owner take when international sales stall as a result of a strong dollar or competitive pressure?

Pittsford: In the industries in which I have been working, raw materials are sourced from all over the world, and as a result exchange rates have an impact on costs, whether they go up or down. However, with few exceptions, the impact is not enough to lead to a change in prices. The cost of labor and packaging can far outweigh the cost of the actual product itself. A strong dollar has had the biggest impact on product prices at retail. I refrain from offering discounts based on the strength of the dollar, based on the above reasons. In the past I have worked to offer smaller package sizes—in this way you are offering a less expensive product to meet certain market conditions without having to lower your prices.

Delaney: Is there a lesson you have learned the hard way on international sales expansion?

Pittsford: Take a hard look in the mirror and ask yourself if you are ready to go international. Export sales should not be approached as a last desperate act to save your company, nor should international markets be considered as the dumping ground for excess inventory or sub-standard product. Consumers overseas are sophisticated and they read labels. If you are successful in your home market, your business is solid, and you have excess capacity, you should consider exports with the understanding that it is a long-term commitment. Do not just jump in. Take a hard look at what will be required for you to enter targeted markets and choose your targets carefully. Most exporters are "accidental" in that they were approached by a foreign buyer and took the order. This can work for a while, but it is not the way to build an export business.

Delaney: Any major trend you see around the corner that will impact how all of us will conduct business globally?

Pittsford: The Internet has already changed the face of retail in terms of how, when, and where consumers shop and what they expect as customers. Companies today must have an online presence at all levels. They also need to have a web strategy so that they have some control of over pricing. We can suggest retail prices, but we cannot dictate what companies charge their customers. As a result, you should carefully consider your pricing when looking at a multi-channel strategy. A well-planned and executed strategy should allow you to pursue both online and brick and mortar sales. Be sure that your web site is mobile friendly, as a lot of consumers now buy from their mobile devices.

Key Lessons

The takeaway from Pittsford's advice is to be open to making changes to your products. Make sure export documentation is prepared accurately and that your product can be legally sold in a market you are about to enter. Look into active trade agreements such as the Trans-Pacific Partnership Agreement to see how you might benefit from it. Above all else, be patient. In the case of exporting, it is truly a virtue.

Paulson Manufacturing: Listen to Your Customers and Take the Long View

Think that the face shields for firefighters' helmets, the riot shields for police helmets, and the body shields worn by police are difficult to export? Not for Roy Paulson, president of California-based Paulson Manufacturing (http://www.paulsonmfg.com) and director of Paulson International in Germany, who makes these trademarked products and exports them all across the planet. Paulson Manufacturing's total sales for 2017 are projected to be $20 million, with international sales at 25 percent.

Paulson's business is very similar to that of the millions of small businesses in the United States that are eager to export. I spoke with him to find out how he's become successful and what tips he can offer newcomers to the export industry.

Laurel Delaney: What's the secret sauce to your international success?

Roy Paulson: What's set us apart is that we have concentrated on developing our exports and rechanneling the innovations from all the international contacts into products for our domestic markets. We build our products in California, prioritize the use of domestic materials and, hence, we are able to successfully sell all around the world.

Delaney: Are you globally competitive on everything you manufacture?

Paulson: It is selected product items that sell the best internationally. We find that the most innovative products sell the best internationally, and it is very important to listen to what the customer wants. Don't shove what you have down their throats; your business will not grow and you will be resented.

Delaney: How do you gauge what new product or new market to take on next?

Paulson: The feedback from our international sales team is very important to developing our international product line and business plans. We consider the feedback precious, good or bad news—does not matter—we take it all in and use it to our advantage. In the end it is to the advantage and benefit of our customers.

Delaney: Where can a small business owner get blindsided in his export activities?

Paulson: It is very important to make sure that everyone is making money in the entire supply chain. Otherwise, the business will be short term. This is the responsibility of the US exporter.

Delaney: What about the product side of pricing at a profit?

Paulson: Price rarely comes up, unless there is a large Request for Quotation (RFQ) or a competitive situation. My position is to not sell on price, but rather to sell on innovation.

Delaney: Where are you putting your energy these days to squeeze out or fuel growth for your business?

Paulson: We have placed tremendous efforts on developing new markets. We now have ten distributors in India. We are taking the long view, as we all know that it takes time to develop these advanced export markets. By taking this point of view and avoiding getting distracted with short-term, one-time sales, we are building for the future.

Delaney: What factors have been challenging for you at Paulson Manufacturing?

Paulson: While we have continued to grow our sales, the value of the US dollar has created a significant headwind. Along with the value of the dollar, the drop in the price of oil created a loss of sales in many areas of the world.

Delaney: What's the work-around, or how do you navigate through such trying times?

Paulson: We have lowered prices, increased inventories for faster delivery, and hired additional salespeople to visit our customers on a regular basis.

Delaney: What's helped you sleep at night? In other words, tell me what export solutions you have put into play that have worked.

Paulson: In general, we are making a physical visit to every customer four times per year. These efforts have kept the exports sales growing, and we are continuously looking for more customers and new markets to counter the next headwind that may blow in at any time.

Delaney: What other advice can you provide relative to what you've learned on the road to exporting success?

Paulson: I have two more critical points: First, visiting customers in their own country is one of the keys to exporting success. These visits must be on a regular basis and within the time frame expected of the customer. We have the tendency to rush in and out. This will not work in export development. When you visit your customers, take your time and stay a while. You will get more business simply because of your attitude.

Second, I have traveled the world, selling our products and developing relationships with my customers, and discovered the key to achieving export sales is relationship selling. There is a simple formula I use related to developing exports. In domestic sales, for example, we cherish and defend a transactional selling method where the prioritization is on price, quality, and delivery. Domestic sales are typically 75 percent transactional and only 25 percent relational. With export sales, relational selling is 75 percent of the equation with 25 percent being transactional. This is the key to developing export sales and achieving long-term export success.

Key Lessons

The takeaway from Paulson's advice is to listen to your customers and take the long view to build for the future. Make sure the entire supply chain is making money. Don't sell on price; sell on innovation. Visit your customers in person and on a regular schedule that the customer expects to keep exports growing. Continuously look for new customers and new markets to counter the next headwind that may blow in at any time. When you sell, develop the relationship and then focus on the transaction.

Roberts & Company: Get Things in Writing

Taking companies global helped Barbara Roberts[i] increase her revenue. Before it was sold to Getty Images, FPG (Freelance Photographers Guild) International, the company that Roberts was formerly the president of, was already one of the largest stock photography companies. The company sold the rights to use its photographs in local advertising and editorial products internationally. It did this by finding a local stock photography company and contracting with it to allow the company exclusive licenses of FPG's photographs in its country.

The other company that Roberts served as president of, Acoustiguide, is the supplier of audio tours, equipment, and staff for museums and historical sites around the world. At the time she was president, Acoustiguide supplied these audio tours through direct sales, joint ventures in a specific country, and wholly owned subsidiaries.

With both of these companies, international business grew to account for between 30 and 40 percent of revenues. I talked with Roberts (Roberts & Company [http://www.brobertsco.com]) to find out what she learned when she took these products global.

Laurel Delaney: What did you learn from your exporting experience that you can share?

Barbara Roberts: First, you cannot go international without having a lot of things in writing. In both of these companies, the product that we were selling was intellectual property. Accordingly, legal work and documents were a critical part of our process and success or failure. For successfully selling this type of product, putting all details, expectations, rules, and obligations in a contract was necessary for success. This was of course important doing business in the US, but if there are language barriers in verbal discussions, it is even more critical to have very detailed written documents that can be translated into any necessary language.

Second, you will be more successful in international sales if you have the right local partner or employee. In my experience, people who found me often worked out better than people I actively sourced. Potential international partners who had found me typically had done research on me and our company and had carefully thought through how we fit into their strategy and market. They had a much better understanding of how we fit than we ever could have understood as an outsider. The process to come to an agreement often went faster and more smoothly. You also need to be easy to find, so the development of a strong web presence and attending and speaking at international conferences in one's industry are good starting steps to developing an international business. You want to be known and easy to find.

Third, when going global, you may find that collecting money is easier than firing [overseas] staff. Many business people are hesitant to go global because of the fear of collecting money. In my experience, if one sets up the right legal structure, this is not a common problem. A bigger learning point for me was the fact that many countries have much more stringent rules and financial penalties for firing people or closing unsuccessful operations than we experience in the US. If you hire local people or start a local operation, it is critical to learn up front what the local rules and financial penalties are for firing someone or closing an operation.

Lastly and most important, you should see going international as an exciting learning adventure. One cannot be successful internationally without a willingness to suspend judgment and be open to accepting that everyone carries a cultural bias. Licensing photographs internationally and developing audio content to explain local cultural institutions particularly demanded the willingness to always assume one could get something very wrong. For instance, simple things like the number of golf balls in a photo or the color of the scarf someone wore could instantly make a photograph that earned thousands of dollars in the American market worthless in another country. One had to learn different numbers mean bad luck in different countries and the color red in particular has very different connotations worldwide.

However, I do want to comment on the fact of increased personal risk for business people who internationally travel. I experienced a kidnapping attempt in Venezuela and do recommend that if one does international business travel that you are thoughtful and deliberate about your personal security.

Key Lessons

What you should take away from Roberts's advice is to get things in writing. You also need to hire the right people, make yourself easy to be found on the web, set up the right legal structure, and enjoy the adventurous ride!

Marlin Steel: Translate Your Web Site to be Foreign Friendly

"We were once a company nearly felled by cheap steel from China. We're now a thriving business that exports to thirty-six countries," says Drew Greenblatt, president of Marlin Steel (http://www.marlinsteel.com), about his company's explosion into exporting. Exports constitute about one-fifth of the company's sales. Marlin Steel exports steel products to Argentina, Australia, Austria, Belarus, Belgium, Brazil, Canada, China, Columbia, Costa Rica, the Czech Republic, Denmark, Estonia, Finland, France, Germany, Guinea, Hungary, Iraq, Ireland, Israel, Italy, Japan, Mexico, the Netherlands, New Zealand, Norway, the Philippines, Poland, Puerto Rico, Saint Thomas, Singapore, Sweden, Switzerland, Taiwan, the United Kingdom, and Uruguay.

I asked Greenblatt his thoughts on why exporting is a valuable business decision for American companies.

Laurel Delaney: Why should American small business owners look to export?

Drew Greenblatt: Free trade agreements get some bad publicity—that they'll cost American jobs—but export businesses create a lot of jobs. About 95 percent of the world's potential clients live outside the United States. That market is becoming wealthier and will require services and products. There's a growing world of customers beyond our borders. And the waves of activity that occur in your niche in America may have nothing to do with the same niche in Japan or Canada or Germany. Your local economy could be in the doldrums, while your prospects halfway around the world could be good. Export jobs typically also pay better—20 percent more on average.

Delaney: What's been challenging or troublesome for you since we last connected?

Greenblatt: Since 2014, exports to Europe have taken a beating due to the strength of the U.S. dollar, which is up 25 percent and makes our products way too pricey in that market right now. However, to make up for that sales shortfall, sales in Canada and Mexico, markets close in proximity to the United States, have been strong and showing an appreciable savings on freight. Further, companies in these markets are seeking high-quality products.

Delaney: What's been an "aha" or awakening for you on export growth avenues?

Greenblatt: American-based companies that we do business with are referring new potential export business to Marlin Steel. For example, Toyota, Ford, and General Motors, due to operating on a global scale, refer new business to Marlin Steel on an as-needed basis. They begin to serve as an evangelist for Marlin Steel. We no longer have to sell ourselves.

Delaney: Have you changed any of your payment methods as a result of tightening your belt?

Greenblatt: In addition to Exim bank, we now pursue the path of cash in advance where it works so we don't rely so heavily on financing organizations. We extend credit where we can but prefer the cash in advance payment method.

Delaney: What tips can you provide to help a small business get started with exporting?

Greenblatt: After receiving initial expressions of interest from overseas and a major order from Asia several years ago, Marlin Steel expanded its export business plan with help from the Baltimore Export Assistance Center. The US Department of Commerce International Trade Administration runs similar centers around the country. It helps connect businesses with trade promotion events, trade missions, and other programs.

Our state of Maryland is very helpful in opening doors to trade for our organization. For example, Maryland Economic Development Corporation (MEDCO; http://www.medco-corp.com) pays fifty percent of overseas expenses for pre-qualifying export companies ($10,000, for example, to translate a web site) and the Baltimore Development Corporation (BDC) in Baltimore, Maryland (http://baltimoredevelopment.com) helps businesses grow.

That said, we've done several things to grow in the international marketplace. We translated our Web site to be friendlier to foreign customers. We now have versions in Japanese, German, Spanish, and Korean. You have to make it easier for those customers to find you.

We've also tapped several government programs that have been helpful. One of those is, as mentioned earlier, the Export-Import Bank of the United States' guarantee of receivables. When we shipped wire forms to an electronics maker in Singapore, the Export-Import Bank provided the guarantee for a small insurance premium. I'd never heard of the electronics company and neither had my banker, but we were both able to sleep at night because the transaction was covered. The government kept 0.5 percent of the deal for the coverage; I got the other 99.5 percent. Not to be overlooked, my employees got some overtime out of the contract and a local producer received my steel order. Many manufacturers are probably not aware of the program. It could help lessen some of their anxiety about exporting.

Another helpful program is the Gold Key Matching Service by the US Commercial Service of the Department of Commerce. For a nominal fee, the service prequalifies prospective companies to meet with overseas and provides a translator and a driver (important in places where you can't read the street signs). The service covers about seventy nations that constitute most export markets for US business. I used the service when I visited Korea on a trade mission with the governor of Maryland in 2011 and I intend to do another trip to Spain and Germany in 2016 through the help of the Gold Key Program.

Delaney: What other insights are we overlooking or missing that might help small businesses get started with exporting?

Greenblatt: Nurture and cultivate your key accounts, for you never know where your re-orders might come from, and the only way to find out is to stay on top of your game. Learn about other projects from customers or key people in your supply chain. Expand the relationship, visit customers, and get your customers to serve as evangelists for your business so you never have to do the selling yourself.

Delaney: What did you learn the hard way?

Greenblatt: The paperwork thicket can still be frustrating. While we need only a few minutes to fill out the requisite forms when we ship to Canada or Mexico, it takes twenty minutes per form when shipping to a non-NAFTA country. A few years ago, we took a photograph of two Marlin Steel employees standing beside the cartons that held our files to respond to regulations; the stack was three feet taller than they were.

There are cultural issues to recognize as well. The exchange of a business card with Japanese and other Asian prospects requires more formality and procedure, for example, than that same act between American businesspeople.

Although some folks have gotten cynical and don't always give it its due, "Made in the USA" remains a coveted brand worldwide. American businesses are missing opportunities by not taking more advantage of that.

Key Lessons

The most important lesson here is to nurture and cultivate your key accounts (you never know where your re-orders might come from, and the only way to find out is to stay on top of your game); translate your web site to be friendlier to foreign customers; learn about other projects from customers or key people in your supply chain; expand the relationship; visit customers; and get your customers to serve as evangelists for your business so you never have to do the selling yourself. Also, take advantage of governmental programs for export assistance, allow time to prepare shipping documentation, be sensitive to cultural differences, and be proud of and promote the "Made in the USA" brand.

Summary

Operating in the export marketplace is an exciting learning adventure and an avenue to a brighter and more prosperous future. By following the advice of the small business exporters I communicated with, your chances for success will increase dramatically.

Now it's time to discover my personal basic truths for achieving export success and to keep our conversation going. I will put you in the MOOD (massive open online dialog)! Turn the page to learn more and get involved.

Note

i. https://www8.gsb.columbia.edu/entrepreneur-ship/sites/entrepreneurship/files/barbara%20roberts%202014%20entrepren%20residence.pdf.

Essential Keys to Export Success

And the only way to do great work is to love what you do. If you haven't found it yet, keep looking. Don't settle. As with all matters of the heart, you'll know when you find it.

—The late Steve Jobs, founder of Apple[i]

Getting to the future first is not just about outrunning competitors bent on reaching the same prize. It is also about having one's own view of what the prize is. There can be as many prizes as runners; imagination is the only limiting factor.

—Management consultants Gary Hamel and the late C. K. Prahalad[ii]

The ability to learn faster than your competitors may be the only sustainable competitive advantage.

—Arie De Geus, Head of Planning, Royal Dutch/Shell[iii]

In this chapter, I introduce you to a group I established at LinkedIn and provide my sixteen basic truths to achieving export success. Each one represents the culmination of the learnings and insights in this book. There are many more, but I have found that by paying attention to these sixteen, you are pretty close to export nirvana.

© Laurel J. Delaney 2016

L. J. Delaney, *Exporting*, DOI 10.1007/978-1-4842-2193-8_31

1. Develop a global mindset. Set aside time to think about and determine whether you are cut out for exporting. Look back at Chapter 1.

2. If you love what you do, once you decide to export, pick one core capability (a product or service)—it's the answer that wells up within you that matters the most—stay fully committed to it, and show some heart (care) at every step of the way. Refer to Chapters 1, 2, and 11.

3. Put in the homework up front (learn the market and distribution network for a particular country, for example) and use your export dream team throughout the journey. Get a company-wide commitment before you begin to take full advantage of opportunities international markets offer. Review Chapters 3, 12, 17, and 30.

4. Generate cash flow and always watch your profit margins. The single more important consideration in an export business or any business is cash flow. It is the difference between success or failure of an enterprise. Be creative. Conserve cash at all costs. Ask for advance payment or delay a payment whenever you can. We touched on this in Chapters 2, 20, 21, 23, and 30.

5. Target a market and adapt to it on an as-needed basis; that includes modifying products and services to customers' needs. See the discussion in Chapters 12, 13, and 14.

6. Find customers and nurture them to death. Customers are the lifeblood of a business. Without them, there is no business. "The value of your company is based upon the value of your present and future customer relationships," says best-selling author of *The Customer Revolution* Patricia B. Seybold.[iv] Look back at Chapter 16.

7. Stop treading warily around technology, and dive right in. Embrace computers, digital devices, and social media as early as possible in your export activities, because you are going to have to get out there online and sell yourself and your business to get ahead. Refer to Chapters 2, 6, 9, and 14.

8. Learn how to work effectively with others and treat your customers, employees, and anyone else who matters like royalty. Be reliable. This is discussed in Chapters 4 and 24.

9. Develop and follow an export plan, even if it is scribbled on the back of a napkin, because that will help make your export dream a reality. You can adjust your plan as you

go along, so the details don't have to be perfect, but to truly shape your export universe you must set aside time to do some focused thinking on how you will get there. After all, what you are doing is planning your actions for the most advantageous time for your export business. What will that look like? Take another look at Chapter 2.

10. Leverage trade agreements to access new markets, reduce costs, increase flow of goods, create competitive pricing opportunities, and maximize your bottom line. We discussed this in Chapters 2, 3, 25, 29, and 30.

11. Keep your finger on the pulse, not just in terms of competition but of industry trends in general, where sudden, massive changes or improvements can disrupt or create a whole new market space at the bat of an eye. And don't play in your competitor's sandbox. Build your own. That's what Steve Jobs did at Apple, and it worked. Refer to Chapters 23, 25, and 30.

12. Define and create a superior online presence that resonates with the world. Online interactions support offline networking. The bulk of your customers will do most of their buying online. See Chapters 5, 6, 7, and 8.

13. Get paid on export transactions—no ifs, ands, or buts— and make a profit—always. Re-read No. 4 and go back to the discussion in Chapter 20.

14. Plan for success, give it all you've got, and don't forget to give to others your help when they need it or ask for it. Take a long view because it takes time to develop advanced export markets. This was part of the discussion in Chapter 30.

15. Stick to what you know. It makes it easier to go forward when you are knowledgeable about something. Learn to see everyday problems not as obstacles, but as possible business opportunities—and encourage your customers, employees, and suppliers to work together to set up ventures or create new products to solve them. See Chapters 6, 27, and 30.

16. Stay fresh, take risks, and do something—anything—that gets you one step closer to your exporting goal. You never want to be crippled by fear of failure. Success rarely comes to those who play it safe. We discussed this in both Chapter 1 and 30.

If you aspire to act on these key points, you are guaranteed to succeed with your export business. They will allow you to get to the top and stay there.

Summary

Success in exporting largely boils down to you. You must want to export and then take the initiative to do so. At this point, based on the knowledge you have acquired, you should be at the 99.9-percent-ready-to-export state. Now go make the world your business.

And One More Thing . . .

I want to leave you with an invitation to join the Export Guide Group (MOOD), a massive open online dialog that I established on LinkedIn. It's where you will find me and everyone else, like you, who has read this book and has a relentless desire to keep learning and growing. There, we connect and answer questions, process new ideas, and exchange best practices in exporting. I liken this practice to a radical export revolution. Come join the conversation: `http://tinyurl.com/kpgbdwf`. See you there!

■ **Note**   Should you get stuck, feel free to e-mail me at ldelaney@globetrade.com. I may not be able to get to and answer every question you pose, but I most certainly will try.

Notes

i.   Steve Jobs, "'You've Got to Find What You Love,' Jobs Says," Stanford commencement address, June 2005, `http://news.stanford.edu/news/2005/june15/jobs-061505.html`.

ii.   Gary Hamel and C. K. Prahalad, *Competing for the Future* (Boston: Harvard Business Review Press, 1996), 27.

iii. As quoted in Peter M. Senge, *The Fifth Discipline: The Art & Practice of the Learning Organization* (New York: Doubleday Currency, 1990), 4.

iv.   Patricia B. Seybold, with Ronni T. Marshak and Jeffrey M. Lewis, *The Customer Revolution* (New York, Crown Business, 2001), 77.

Index

© Laurel J. Delaney 2016
L. Delaney, *Exporting*, DOI 10.1007/978-1-4842-2193-8

Get the eBook for only $5!

Why limit yourself?

Now you can take the weightless companion with you wherever you go and access your content on your PC, phone, tablet, or reader.

Since you've purchased this print book, we're happy to offer you the eBook in all 3 formats for just $5.

Convenient and fully searchable, the PDF version enables you to easily find and copy code—or perform examples by quickly toggling between instructions and applications. The MOBI format is ideal for your Kindle, while the ePUB can be utilized on a variety of mobile devices.

To learn more, go to www.apress.com/companion or contact support@apress.com.

Apress®
THE EXPERT'S VOICE™

CPSIA information can be obtained
at www.ICGtesting.com
Printed in the USA
LVOW04s0740260417
532192LV00002BA/22/P

9 781484 221921